Philip E. Muehlenbeck is Professorial Lecturer in History at George Washington University and the author of *Czechoslovakia in Africa, 1945–1968* (2015) and *Betting on the Africans: John F. Kennedy's Courting of African Nationalist Leaders* (2012). He is also the editor of *Religion and the Cold War: A Global Perspective* (2012); *Race, Ethnicity, and the Cold War: A Global Perspective* (2012); and *Gender, Sexuality, and the Cold War: A Global Perspective* (2017).

Natalia Telepneva is a British Academy Postdoctoral Fellow at the University of Warwick, where she is working on Soviet ideas on development and modernization in Africa. Her research is focused on Soviet policy in Africa during the Cold War. She is currently preparing for publication a manuscript that investigates Warsaw Pact support for the anti-colonial movements in the Portuguese colonies and the internationalization of the Angolan Civil War in 1974–5.

'This remarkable book is a good medicine for those who still believe that the Cold War was a zero-sum struggle with clear rules of subordination. In the Soviet bloc, the post-Stalin Thaw, Khrushchev's idealism and decolonization created entirely new horizons for the autonomy of Eastern Europe. The book's contributors conclude that for Warsaw Pact countries and individuals, the Third World became much more than an area of geopolitical struggle. In the 1950s to 1970s, it was the place where Soviet satellites became autonomous actors, pursuing their own political interests and profit. It was even more so for the thousands of people from Eastern Europe – journalists and spies, doctors and teachers – who worked and travelled in Africa, Asia and Latin America. They came as "agents of communism" yet encountered a fascinating variety of humanity and cultures, that ultimately challenged their views and identities. The book will be a valuable addition to courses on the Cold War and the international history of the twentieth century.'

Vladislav Zubok, Professor of International History, London School of Economics

'From the moment Prague started selling arms to Nasser in 1956, the Soviet Union encouraged its satellites to become involved in the Third World. The degree to which they responded, and the nature of their response, depended on domestic considerations. That is the essence of the discussions addressed in this remarkable collection of essays, which brings an important new perspective to an understudied aspect of Soviet foreign policy. If Czechoslovakia and Bulgaria used the Third World to show their ideological purity, Poland, Romania, Hungary and the GDR had national interests to pursue.'

Geoffrey Swain, Emeritus Professor, University of Glasgow

WARSAW PACT INTERVENTION IN THE THIRD WORLD

Aid and Influence in the Cold War

Edited by
PHILIP E. MUEHLENBECK
AND
NATALIA TELEPNEVA

BLOOMSBURY ACADEMIC
LONDON • NEW YORK • OXFORD • NEW DELHI • SYDNEY

BLOOMSBURY ACADEMIC
Bloomsbury Publishing Plc
50 Bedford Square, London, WC1B 3DP, UK
1385 Broadway, New York, NY 10018, USA

BLOOMSBURY, BLOOMSBURY ACADEMIC and the Diana logo
are trademarks of Bloomsbury Publishing Plc

First published in Great Britain by I.B. Tauris 2018
This edition published by Bloomsbury Academic 2020

Copyright Editorial Selection © 2018 Philip E. Muehlenbeck and Natalia Telepneva

Copyright Individual Chapters © 2018 Jordan Baev, Csaba Békés, Iris Borowy,
Lorena De Vita, Elena Dragomir, Przemyslaw Gasztold, Jan Koura,
Philip E. Muehlenbeck, George Roberts, Marek W. Rutkowski, Natalia Telepneva,
Dániel Vékony, Robert Anthony Waters Jr and Larry L. Watss

Philip E. Muehlenbeck and Natalia Telepneva have asserted their right under the
Copyright, Designs and Patents Act, 1988, to be identified as Editors of this work.

All rights reserved. No part of this publication may be reproduced or
transmitted in any form or by any means, electronic or mechanical,
including photocopying, recording, or any information storage or retrieval
system, without prior permission in writing from the publishers.

Bloomsbury Publishing Plc does not have any control over, or responsibility for,
any third-party websites referred to or in this book. All internet addresses given
in this book were correct at the time of going to press. The author and publisher
regret any inconvenience caused if addresses have changed or sites have
ceased to exist, but can accept no responsibility for any such changes.

A catalogue record for this book is available from the British Library.

A catalog record for this book is available from the Library of Congress.

ISBN: HB: 978-1-7883-1055-0
PB: 978-0-7556-0012-0
ePDF: 978-1-8386-0985-6
eBook: 978-1-8386-0984-9

Typeset in Garamond Three by OKS Prepress Services, Chennai, India

To find out more about our authors and books visit
www.bloomsbury.com and sign up for our newsletters.

CONTENTS

List of Tables ix
Preface x
Notes on Contributors xii

Introduction 1
    Philip E. Muehlenbeck and Natalia Telepneva

    Part I The Re-Discovery of the Third World 5
    Part II 'Intermediaries': Spies, Journalists, Doctors,
       Teachers and Diplomats in the Third World 10
    Part III Money and Influence: Diplomacy, Trade and Aid 15

PART I   The Re-Discovery of the Third World

1. **Ulbricht, Nasser and Khrushchev: The GDR's Search for Diplomatic Recognition and the Suez Crisis, 1956** 25
   Lorena De Vita

   Chasing Sovereignty, German-Style 28
   Ulbricht's Frustration 32
   The Suez Crisis – an East German Opportunity? 38
   Conclusion 43

2. Reassuring Comrades and Courting the Non-Aligned: Poland, the 1957 Goodwill Tour in Asia and the Post-October Diplomacy   51
Marek W. Rutkowski

    Engaging Asia   54
    Reassuring Allies and Shaping the Bloc: Cyrankiewicz in the Far East   58
    Counting on Non-Alignment? Cyrankiewicz in South East Asia   62
    Conclusion   67

3. 'They are as Businesslike on that side of the Iron Curtain as they are on this': Czechoslovakia and British Guiana   74
Jan Koura and Robert Anthony Waters Jr

    Stalinism and the Early Thaw, 1948–58   75
    Latin American Communism Ascendant, 1959–63   79
    Czechoslovak Decline; Guianese Disaster, 1964–6   85
    Conclusion   88

4. The Third World as Strategic Option: Romanian Relations with Developing States   95
Larry L. Watts

    Small-State Theory and Third World Activism   97
    The Six Day War and its Aftermath   101
    Before and After the October War   107
    The Third World in Romanian Strategy   111

PART II 'Intermediaries': Spies, Journalists, Doctors, Teachers and Diplomats in the Third World

5. Cold War on the Cheap: Soviet and Czechoslovak Intelligence in the Congo, 1960–3   125
Natalia Telepneva

    The KGB–StB Mission in Léopoldville, 1960   128
    Arms for Gizenga, 1961   133
    Czechoslovak Plans for the Congo, 1962–4   137
    Conclusion   142

6. **Press, Propaganda and the German Democratic Republic's Search for Recognition in Tanzania, 1964–72** 148
   George Roberts

   The Inter-German Cold War Comes to Tanzania 149
   The ADN and the *Nationalist* 154
   Tanzanian Politics, Cold War Interventions and the GDR 158
   Exploiting West German Policy in Southern Africa 162
   Conclusion 166

7. **Medicine, Economics and Foreign Policy: East German Medical Academics in the Global South during the 1950s and 1960s** 173
   Iris Borowy

   Official Policy and Personal Motivation 175
   Medical Research 180
   Trade in Pharmaceutical Products 183
   Conclusion 189

8. **Lost Illusions: The Limits of Communist Poland's Involvement in Cold War Africa** 197
   Przemysław Gasztold

   Gomułka's Phase: Economic Opportunities vs. Ideological Principles 200
   Gierek's Phase: Support for Anti-Colonial Movements and the Development of Economic Ties 208
   Conclusion 212

PART III Money and Influence: Diplomacy, Aid and Trade

9. **Romania Blocks Mongolia's Accession to the Warsaw Treaty Organization: The Roots of Romania's Involvement in the Sino–Soviet Dispute** 223
   Elena Dragomir

   Introduction 224
   Mongolia's Request for Admission 228
   Secret Romanian–Soviet Talks 234
   Conclusion 241

10. Czechoslovak Assistance to Kenya and Uganda,
    1962–8   249
    Philip E. Muehlenbeck

    Czechoslovak Relations with Kenya Prior to Independence   250
    Czechoslovak Relations with Uganda Prior to Independence   253
    Foreign Military Aid to Kenya and Uganda   257
    Unfulfilled Expectations   261
    Conclusion   264

11. Unfulfilled Promised Lands: Missed Potentials in
    Relations between Hungary and the Countries of
    the Middle East, 1955–75   271
    Csaba Békés and Dániel Vékony

    Diplomatic Relations Before the 1956 Revolution   274
    The 1956 Revolution in the Mirror of Middle Eastern
       Relations   276
    Relations After the End of Diplomatic Isolation   277
    Relations with Israel   279
    Economic Relations: When the East becomes 'West'   282
    'Special Goods'   285
    Conclusion   288

12. Bulgarian Military and Humanitarian Aid to Third
    World Countries: 1955–75   298
    Jordan Baev

    The Middle East   300
    Asia   310
    Africa   311
    Latin America   314
    Conclusion   320

Conclusion   326
    Philip E. Muehlenbeck and Natalia Telepneva

Select Bibliography   332
Index   338

LIST OF TABLES

Table A.1. Hungary's foreign trade with some Middle Eastern countries (million convertible Forints) 292

Table A.2. Hungary's overall foreign trade (million convertible Forints) 292

PREFACE

Since the end of the Cold War and the subsequent opening of government archives in Eastern and Central Europe, scholars have been able to obtain important documents from the other side of the Iron Curtain. These have reshaped our understanding of the foreign policies of Soviet bloc countries as well as the internal dynamics of the relationships between Moscow and its 'junior allies'.[1] In an article in *Diplomatic History* at the turn of the century, Tony Smith developed the idea of 'pericentrism', in which he argued that junior allies on the periphery of the Cold War often pulled the super powers into new areas of conflict.[2]

Yet, the level of coordination between the Soviet Union and its Warsaw Pact junior allies in the developing world, as well as the degree of autonomy that each Eastern European state had in pursuing its own policies independent of Moscow, is an understudied topic in Cold War studies. We embarked on this project with the presumption that the relative level of autonomy enjoyed by Moscow's junior allies had varied over time, location and between Eastern European capitals. Since it would be nearly impossible for a lone scholar to have the requisite linguistic abilities and funding to tackle this topic individually, we have assembled a group of historians working in the archives of each of the former Soviet bloc states in an attempt to answer these questions collectively.

This volume is not comprehensive, of course, nor could such a collection of essays ever hope to be so. Nonetheless, by broadening the study of the Cold War in the Third World to include closer examinations of the roles played by the junior members of the Warsaw Pact, this volume – with its multidisciplinary approach and emphasis on multi-archival research (primary-source research for this project having been conducted in 12 different countries) – aspires to serve as inspiration for further research on the role that Moscow's junior allies played in the Cold War in the Third World.

We would like to thank the following individuals for offering peer-review comments on prospective chapters for this volume: Peter Busch, Ben Cowan, Craig Daigle, Elena Dragomir, Kristen Ghodsee, William Glenn Gray, Corina Mavrodin, Katalin Miklossy, Lise Namikas, Eric Pullin, Przemysław Gasztold, Massimiliano Trentin and Michal Zourek. Special thanks also go to Csaba Békés and Rob Waters for their valuable input on the Introduction. Finally, we would like to thank Tom Stottor, our acquisitions editor at I.B.Tauris, and Ian McDonald, our copy editor. This volume is a much better final product because of their involvement.

Notes

1. The term 'junior allies' was first used in relation to the smaller states in the Warsaw Pact by Zbigniew K. Brzezinski in *The Soviet Bloc: Unity and Conflict* (Cambridge, MA, 1967).
2. Tony Smith, 'New Bottles for New Wine: A Pericentric Framework for the Study of the Cold War', *Diplomatic History* 24 (4) (2000), pp. 567–91.

NOTES ON CONTRIBUTORS

Jordan Baev is Professor of International History and Senior Research Fellow of Security Studies at Rakovski National Defence College, and a visiting professor at Sofia University. Since 1998, he has been a vice president of the Bulgarian Association of Military History and coordinator of the Bulgarian Cold War Research Group. He has held several research fellowships at, amongst others, the Woodrow Wilson International Center for Scholars, the US Institute of Peace in Washington, DC and the Nobel Institute in Oslo. Over the last 20 years, he has been invited as a representative of Bulgaria onto many international research projects, managed by academic institutions in the USA, Switzerland, Germany, Poland, Great Britain, China, the Netherlands, Greece, Brazil and other countries. Baev has written roughly 300 publications, published in 14 languages in 22 countries in Europe, Asia, and North and South America – amongst them, ten monographs and 12 documentary volumes on diplomatic, political, military and intelligence history; international terrorism; peacekeeping; and civil–military relations.

Csaba Békés is Research Chair at the Centre for Social Sciences, Institute of Political Studies, Hungarian Academy of Sciences and founding director of the Cold War History Research Center. He is also Professor of History at Corvinus University of Budapest, and a recurring visiting professor at Columbia University. His main field of research is Cold War history, the history of East–West relations, Hungarian foreign policy after World War II, the history of the Soviet Bloc and the role of the East/Central European states in the Cold War. He is the author or editor of 25 books, including *The 1956 Hungarian Revolution: A History in Documents* (co-editor, 2002), and a contributor to the three-volume *Cambridge History of the Cold War* (2010). He is a member of the editorial boards of the *Journal of Cold War Studies* and *Cold War History*. His latest book (as co-editor) was published in 2015: *Soviet Occupation of Romania, Hungary, and Austria 1944/45–1948/49*. His book *Hungary, the Soviet Bloc and World Politics, 1944–1991* is forthcoming.

Iris Borowy is Professor of History at the University of Shanghai. She was educated at the universities of Tübingen, Germany and Maryland at College Park, USA. In 1989, she received an MA in Contemporary History, Economics and American Studies, followed by a PhD (1997) and a habilitation (2007) from the University of Rostock, Germany. She has worked at the University of Rostock and various universities and institutes in Germany, France, Brazil, Norway and Britain. Her research has addressed the history of international health and its relationship with the economic and environmental policies of international organizations. In recent years, her research focus has shifted towards development concepts and the evolution of the idea of sustainability. Her publications include *Coming to Terms with World Health: The League of Nations Health Organisation* (2009) and *Defining Sustainable Development for Our Common Future: A History of the World Commission on Environment and Development (Brundtland Commission)* (2014). Her most recent book, a volume co-edited with Matthias Schmelzer, is *History of the Future of Economic Growth: Historical Roots of Current Debates on Sustainable Growth* (2017).

Lorena De Vita is Assistant Professor in the History of International Relations at Utrecht University (Netherlands). She is currently finalizing a monograph on the overlap between German–German Cold War rivalry and the Arab–Israeli conflict during the 1950s and 1960s. De Vita obtained a BSc in Political Science and International Relations from the University of Roma Tre in 2008, an MSc from the London School of Economics in 2010 and a PhD from Aberystwyth University in 2016. During the course of her PhD, De Vita held a DAAD Research Fellowship at the Friedrich-Schiller-University, Jena, and a Joseph Wulf Fellowship at the Memorial House of the Wannsee Conference, Berlin. Her research has been published in *International Affairs* and *Cold War History*.

Elena Dragomir defended her doctoral dissertation, entitled 'Cold War Perceptions: Romania's policy change towards the USSR, 1960–1964', in 2014 at the University of Helsinki. She has published on Cold War Romania's foreign policy, with a focus on Romanian–Soviet relations and Romania's opposition within the Eastern European bloc. Her publications include 'The formation of the Soviet bloc's Council for Mutual Economic Assistance: Romania's involvement', in *Journal of Cold War Studies* (Winter 2012); 'Romania's participation in the agricultural conference in Moscow, 2–3 February 1960', in *Cold War History*; and 'Hotel Intercontinental in Bucharest: competitive advantage for the socialist tourist industry in Romania', in Katalin Miklóssy and Melanie Ilic (eds), *Competition in Socialist Society* (2014).

Przemysław Gasztold is PhD Research Fellow at the Historic Research Office of the Institute of National Remembrance in Warsaw. He received his PhD from the Warsaw University Faculty of Journalism and Political Science in 2016. He is currently conducting research on factions within the Polish United Workers' Party; relations between communist Poland, the Middle East and African countries; and the ties between the Soviet bloc and international terrorism during the Cold War. He has published *Koncesjonowany nacjonalizm. Zjednoczenie Patriotyczne 'Grunwald' 1980– 1990* [Licensed Nationalism. Grunwald Patriotic Union 1980–1990] (Warsaw, 2012) and is the co-author (with M. Trentin and J. Adamec) of *Syria During the Cold War: The East European Connection* (2014). His recent book, *Przemysław Gasztold, Zabójcze układy. Służby PRL i międzynarodowy terroryzm* [Deadly Conspiracies. Polish Communist Services and International Terrorism], was published in 2017.

Jan Koura is Lecturer at Charles University's Institute of Global History in Prague and head of the Cold War Research Group at the Institute of the Study of Strategic Regions (Charles University). He has been a Fulbright-Masaryk Scholar at George Washington University and has received fellowships in several European countries. He is the author of a book, *Zápas o východní Středomoří. Zahraniční politika Spojených států amerických vůči Řecku a Turecku v letech 1945–1953* [The Struggle for the Eastern Mediterranean: The foreign policy of the USA in Greece and Turkey, 1945–1953] (Prague, 2013); co-author (with Robert Anthony Waters Jr) of a Cold War International History Project e-Dossier,

'Cheddi Jagan and Guyanese Overtures to the East'; and author of numerous articles and book chapters on the Cold War.

Philip E. Muehlenbeck is Professorial Lecturer in History at George Washington University and the author of *Czechoslovakia in Africa, 1945–1968* (2015) and *Betting on the Africans: John F. Kennedy's Courting of African Nationalist Leaders* (2012). He is also the editor of *Religion and the Cold War: A Global Perspective* (2012); *Race, Ethnicity, and the Cold War: A Global Perspective* (2012); and *Gender, Sexuality, and the Cold War: A Global Perspective* (2017).

George Roberts is Junior Research Fellow at Trinity College, University of Cambridge. He gained his PhD from the University of Warwick, and is currently working on a monograph manuscript on politics, African liberation and the Cold War in Dar es Salaam. George's work has previously been published in the *Journal of Eastern African Studies* and *Cold War History*.

Marek W. Rutkowski is Lecturer in Global Studies at Monash University Malaysia. He completed his PhD dissertation at the National University of Singapore in 2017 on the subject of the International Control Commission (ICC) in Vietnam. His research focuses on the intersection of the Global Cold War and decolonization in Asia with an emphasis on non-alignment, development and the role played by Eastern European actors.

Natalia Telepneva is a British Academy Postdoctoral Fellow at the University of Warwick, where she is working on Soviet ideas on development and modernization in Africa. Her research is focused on Soviet policy in Africa during the Cold War. She is currently preparing for publication a manuscript that investigates Warsaw Pact support for the anti-colonial movements in the Portuguese colonies and the internationalization of the Angolan Civil War in 1974–5.

Dániel Vékony is Senior Lecturer at the International Business School, Budapest, Hungary and has a PhD from Corvinus University of Budapest. He is also a former research coordinator and a research associate of the Cold War History Research Center, Budapest. His main field of research is the Islamic presence in Western and Central Europe.

He has also conducted research on Hungarian foreign policy in the Middle East.

Robert Anthony Waters Jr is Associate Professor of History at Ohio Northern University, and was formerly a civil-rights lawyer. He is the author of *The A to Z of United States-Africa Relations* (2010) and co-editor of *American Labor's Global Ambassadors: The International History of the AFL-CIO during the Cold War* (2013); co-author (with Jan Koura) of a Cold War International History Project e-Dossier, 'Cheddi Jagan and Guyanese Overtures to the East'; and author or co-author of articles about the USA, the Caribbean and Africa.

Larry L. Watts is Senior Consultant of the Roundtable on Ethnic Relations and Associate Researcher at the Romanian Academy of Sciences. A former RAND consultant, he was security-sector reform advisor to various Romanian authorities during 1991–2008. Between 1990–8, he was also senior consultant to the Carnegie-sponsored Project on Ethnic Relations working to prevent violent ethnic conflict. His work has appeared in *European Security*, *Armed Forces & Society* and *Studies in Intelligence*. He is the author of *With Friends Like These: The Soviet Bloc's Clandestine War Against Romania* (2010); and *Extorting Peace: Romania And The End Of The Cold War, 1978–1989* (2013). He recently authored the Cold War International History Project working paper, 'Mediating the Vietnam War' (2016), and a chapter in B. De Graaf and J. Nyce (eds), *Handbook of European Intelligence Cultures* (2016); and the book *Fighting Along Interior Lines: Romanian Security Policy in the Cold War* (2018).

INTRODUCTION

Philip E. Muehlenbeck and Natalia Telepneva

'The Middle East: The Trojan Horse' blared the headline of a 7 November 1955 story in *Time* magazine, the most popular news weekly in the USA, with a circulation of more than 5 million copies per week. *Time*'s anonymous authors editorialized, 'In the port of Alexandria last week, at piers sealed off from prying eyes, Egyptian longshoremen carefully uncrated a Trojan horse. It came from Czechoslovakia, but bore Moscow's greeting card'.[1] The delivery came as part of an arms deal in which Prague sold Egypt a massive amount of weaponry – including various types of military aircraft, armoured personnel carriers, tanks, artillery guns, rocket launchers and anti-tank guns – for the price of US$45.7 million. Egypt was to pay 25 per cent by the end of March 1956, while the Soviet Union underwrote the rest by offering Egypt a 30-year loan at 2-per cent interest.[2] The news sent shock waves around the world when Egypt's radical nationalist leader, Gamal Abdel Nasser, announced the deal on 27 September 1955.[3] Western officials and observers, as *Time*'s article shows, considered the arms deal a 'Trojan Horse' that brought the Soviet Union into Egypt via Czechoslovakia.[4]

This belief extended to all the Soviet Union's relations with its Eastern and Central European allies. When, on 14 May 1955, the leaders of the Soviet Union, Bulgaria, the German Democratic Republic (GDR), Czechoslovakia, Hungary, Poland, Romania and Albania signed the Treaty of Friendship, Cooperation and Mutual Assistance – formally inaugurating what became known as the 'Warsaw Pact' – most Western observers believed that the alliance represented nothing more than a 'cardboard castle', a superficial entity that masked Soviet domination of its satellites.[5] Were the countries in Eastern and Central Europe actually the proverbial Trojan Horse for Soviet policy in the Third World? Based on newly declassified documents from those countries the authors in this volume deal with this question as they investigate how non-Soviet Warsaw Pact (NSWP) countries – the GDR, Czechoslovakia, Bulgaria, Hungary, Romania and Poland – responded to decolonization and the rise of the Third World.[6]

The term 'Third World' was first coined by the non-communist European Left in the 1940s. It was meant to represent a 'third force' or 'third way' in world politics, as distinct from Western-style capitalism and Soviet communism. By the 1970s, the 'Third World' came to be defined as countries in Africa, Asia and Latin America that were bound together by common history, had experienced various forms of foreign domination and faced similar economic conditions. The 'Third World' became a political project that sought to rebalance the power disparity in international economic relations for countries outside of the Organisation for Economic Co-operation and Development (OECD) and the Council for Mutual Economic Assistance (CMEA) – the economic substructures established to support the economies of the 'First' and 'Second' worlds respectively.[7] While Soviet bloc officials did not like the term 'Third World', and used it only in inverted commas, it is adopted throughout this volume in a way that was commonly understood from the mid-1950s to the mid-1970s.

The conversation about the nature of the Soviet Union's relationship with its Eastern and Central European allies started soon after the establishment of the Warsaw Pact in 1955. In *The Soviet Bloc: Unity and Conflict*, Zbigniew Brzezinski was the first to suggest the emancipation of NSWP countries from 'satellites' into 'junior allies', which challenged the view of the Warsaw Pact as an impenetrable monolith.[8] However, he still argued that the Warsaw Pact was a forum for the articulation of support for Soviet foreign-policy initiatives. He thus barely touched upon (with the exception of China) the implications of this emancipation for the foreign policy of NSWP states in the Third World. Brzezinski's and other studies were written at a time when primary source materials were unavailable, leaving much room for speculation. An emerging consensus (which was shared by US

Government intelligence at the time) was that Bulgaria, Czechoslovakia, East Germany, Hungary, Poland and to a lesser extent Romania were little more than surrogates of Soviet foreign policy who took instructions from Moscow and had little autonomy in the direction of their foreign-policy initiatives. This viewpoint can be summed up in a quote by Andrzej Korbonski, one of the scholars of this genre, who in 1987 wrote, 'I assume that the Kremlin is able to control the Third World policy [of its Eastern European allies] to a fairly substantial degree'.[9] As a result, several dozen books published in the 1970s and 1980s focused on Soviet bloc activities in the developing world, but the NSWP countries made only rare appearances.[10] The NSWP states' general absence from this historiography can be illustrated by the fact that shockingly (given the title of the book) only one out of ten chapters in *The Soviet Union, Eastern Europe, and the Third World*, edited by Roger Kanet, actually discusses the role of Moscow's junior allies.[11]

The end of the Cold War and the subsequent opening of archives in Eastern and Central Europe has reshaped our understanding of the Warsaw Pact and the foreign policies of the NSWP countries. One development has been the recovery of the agency of the so-called 'junior members in the international system' that, in the words of Tony Smith, 'took actions that tried to block, moderate, and end the epic contest [and] also took actions that played a key role in expanding, intensifying, and prolonging the struggle between East and West'.[12] Hope Harrison's *Driving the Soviets Up the Wall* provides a striking example, from inside the Soviet bloc, of how East German leader Walter Ulbricht managed to convince the reluctant Soviets to construct what became the key symbol of the Cold War – the Berlin Wall.[13] Another development, partly sparked by the publication of Arne Westad's *The Global Cold War*, has concerned the greater importance attributed to the Third World in the history of the Cold War.[14] A growing body of scholarship has dealt with the ways that 'junior members in the international system' such as Cuba, North Korea, Vietnam and China, to name a few key examples, shaped the way that the Cold War unfolded, evolved and ended.[15] In a parallel development, historians of transnationalism have focused on the roles played by international organizations, non-governmental organizations (NGOs), multinational corporations and experts on both sides of the Iron Curtain in the construction of the post-1945 world order. Historians of transnationalism have expanded the definition of internationalism beyond the study of liberal intellectuals to include ideas, people and institutions in the socialist world. An emerging body of scholarship has offered fresh perspectives on the ways that the socialist experiment opened up opportunities for experts and workers to build socialism abroad, including in the Third World.[16]

Historians of Eastern and Central Europe have thus begun to write the history of the region into international, transnational and global history. Many have started to explore the motivations and actions of individual NSWP countries in exchanges between the North and South or as agents who deployed new openings to the Third World in the 1950s in pursuit of self-interest.[17] Recent years, especially, have seen an outpouring of works that analyse the policies of East Germany in the Third World in the context of its competition with West Germany.[18] From these works, we know now that the Warsaw Pact was characterized by substantial debates on policy in the Third World, and that Moscow was often unwilling – or unable – to control the policies of the NSWP states there. As Laurien Crump has shown in *The Warsaw Pact Reconsidered*, the establishment of the Pact inadvertently provided the NSWP countries with opportunities to emancipate themselves from the Soviet grip and to influence bloc policy on such issues as the Sino–Soviet split and the Vietnam War.[19]

However, the scholarship that deals with the engagement of state-socialist East–Central Europe still suffers from a number of limitations. Firstly, the field is dominated by studies on the GDR and its competition with the Federal Republic of Germany (FRG). Other NSWP countries, in particular Czechoslovakia and Bulgaria, receive – with only a few exceptions – little attention. Secondly, international historians have only just started to consider the economic conditions of the NSWP countries in their engagement with the Third World, especially in the light of recent debate about the place of the Soviet bloc in the world economy in view of the publication of Oscar Sanchez-Sibony's *Red Globalization*.[20] Finally, there is still a significant disconnect between diplomatic histories of nation states in East–Central Europe and the emerging scholarship on transnational exchanges and postwar socialist internationalism. Drawing on newly declassified archival resources now available in Moscow, Prague, Sofia, Berlin, Budapest, Warsaw and Bucharest, this volume aims to fill some of these gaps. While contributors differ in their interpretations of motivations for individual countries amongst the NSWP members and their relations with Moscow, the majority point to a revisionist reinterpretation of the place of NSWP countries in the Warsaw Pact and their policies in the Third World, thus contributing to what James Hershberg terms a 're-active de-bipolarization' of the Cold War.[21]

This volume is arranged around key themes in rough chronological order. Part I highlights how the political leadership in the Warsaw Pact countries sought to 're-discover' the Third World, as a wave of decolonization and revolutionary movements swept across Asia, Africa and Latin America in the 1950s. Part II investigates the roles that various groups of elites – journalists, scientists, diplomats, teachers and spies – played in Warsaw Pact engagement with the Third World. Part III aims to provide an overview of the diplomatic and commercial engagement of individual NSWP countries with various regions in the Third World. Chronologically, the volume extends from Nikita Khrushchev's seminal speech at the Twentieth Congress of the CPSU in February 1956 and goes up to the signature of the 1975 Helsinki Declaration – the highpoint of European detente in the 1970s. The 1956–75 period is significant because the transformation of the Warsaw Pact coincided with decolonization and the emergence of the Third World as a political project, with the dissolution of the Portuguese Empire in Africa in 1975 marking the end of formal European colonialism. The year 1975 coincided with peak optimism about the prospects of socialism in the Third World – at just the point at which a long era of economic and psychological stagnation (*zastoi*) settled in to dominate domestic life in the Soviet bloc until reform and the opening up of the mid-1980s.[22] The period covered in this volume thus provides a rich laboratory from which to explore the policy of NSWP states at this key historical juncture.

Part I The Re-Discovery of the Third World

The 're-discovery' of the Third World in the Eastern bloc became possible due to leadership changes in the Soviet Union after the death of Joseph Stalin in March 1953 and his replacement by Nikita Sergeevich Khrushchev as the new first secretary of the Central Committee of the Communist Party of the Soviet Union (CC CPSU). The Soviet Union had a long history of support for socialist revolution abroad, dating back to the foundation of the Third Communist International (the Comintern) in 1919. However, preoccupied with reconstruction and the emergence of the Cold War in Europe, Stalin was not particularly interested in developing contacts with non-communist leaders in Africa, Asia and Latin America after the end of World War II. The rapid decolonization and social revolutions that swept through the Third World in the late 1950s offered new opportunities for Stalin's successors. A pragmatic party apparatchik who had risen through the ranks as a Party boss in Soviet Ukraine and Moscow, Khrushchev saw in decolonization an opportunity to 'extend a helping hand' to the newly independent nations and thus to gain allies amongst Third World leaders.[23] Khrushchev's pragmatism fitted well with his belief, held by many Bolsheviks of his generation, that the Third World was the new frontier for the expansion of socialist revolution and that it was the duty of the Soviet Union to help.[24] He also believed that it was possible to reconcile an improvement of relations with the West with an activist strategy in the Third World. On a 1955 tour of Asia, Khrushchev appealed to the West to 'verify in practice whose system is better' and 'compete without war'.[25]

Khrushchev also wanted to move away from the model of Soviet dominance, strictly controlling the USSR's satellites, to a more equitable relationship based on the principle of 'proletarian internationalism' and 'socialist friendship'. This approach started with China: whereas Stalin had treated China as a 'junior ally' in a socialist empire, Khrushchev greatly expanded transfers of economic, military and technical assistance to Beijing, and sought to redefine the relationship on a more equal footing.[26] Khrushchev envisioned that with the establishment of the Warsaw Pact in May 1955, the NSWP countries could play more independent roles in foreign policy in order to become credible allies to the Soviet Union on the world stage. In a January 1956 meeting of Eastern European communist parties in Moscow, he proposed that Eastern European countries should take action in foreign policy and then Moscow would provide support in what Csaba Békés coined the 'active foreign policy doctrine'.[27] Khrushchev's proposals found a positive reception amongst the NSWP countries, with the GDR, Czechoslovakia, Hungary and Romania all engaged in active discussion of policy options.[28] Soviet policies in Eastern and Central Europe dovetailed with domestic changes in the Soviet Union known as the 'Thaw', as thousands of political prisoners were amnestied and released from the Stalinist labour camps and Soviet intellectuals were to a certain extent allowed to challenge the rigid Stalinist orthodoxy in the arts. The Soviets opened foreign tourism to the USSR and cultural exchange with a wider range of actors in the West and the Third World. However, there were limits to the 'Thaw', as Soviet East European allies soon discovered.

Khrushchev's denunciation of Stalin's crimes at the CPSU Twentieth Congress in February 1956 sent shockwaves throughout the Soviet bloc. In Hungary and Poland, it led to protests and strengthened those reformists in the leadership of the communist parties who sought to redefine their relationship with the Soviet bloc. In October 1956, the Polish leader, Władysław Gomułka, managed to negotiate a new relationship with the Soviet leadership and thus avoided intervention. In Hungary, a series of anti-Soviet protests turned increasingly violent. With the newly appointed reformist chairman of the Council of Ministers, Imre Nagy, unable to calm street protests that threatened the disintegration of the communist regime in Hungary, on 31 October, the CC CPSU Politburo approved an invasion. On 4 November, Soviet tanks rolled into Budapest crushing the revolution. Nagy was replaced by János Kádár and executed in a secret trial in June 1958.[29] While intervention in Hungary indicated the limits of 'national roads to socialism' available to the NSWP states and established a number of 'red lines' that the Soviets were unwilling to cross, the doctrine of 'active foreign policy' remained in place. In fact, in the 1960s, the Warsaw Pact developed various ways to coordinate political, economic and cultural policies in the Third World in a variety of bilateral and multilateral forums, as contacts between newly independent countries and liberation movements in Asia, Africa and Latin America and NSWP countries expanded exponentially in the late 1950s and 1960s.[30]

The period covered in Part I coincided with momentous change around the world. The foundation of the People's Republic of China (PRC) in October 1949 and the withdrawal of French troops from Indochina in 1954 heralded the end of European colonialism in Asia and revived the prospects of socialist revolution. In Africa, the rapid disintegration of the British, French and Belgian empires led to the emergence of a string of new independent states that entered the United Nations and other international organizations by the mid-1960s.

The victory of the Cuban Revolution in 1959 heralded a new era in the constellation of forces in Latin America. In the first Afro–Asian conference in Bandung, Indonesia in April 1955, the delegates from 29 mainly newly independent states called for unity on the basis of self-determination, mutual economic assistance and neutrality, thus laying the foundations of the Non-Alignment and other Third Worldist projects that aimed to supersede Cold War divides.[31] While delegates at Bandung envisioned that the ideology of non-alignment would contribute to world peace, the rising importance of the Third World actually led to the intensification of the Cold War. The period between 1956 and 1963, in particular, coincided with an unprecedented number of crises – Suez, the Taiwan Straits, Berlin, U-2, Laos, Congo and Cuba.[32] The contributors to this volume tackle how the leadership of the NSWP countries responded to the changes in the international environment, the first diplomatic initiatives that they took and the challenges that they encountered.

One of the first NSWP countries to benefit from the leadership change in the Soviet Union was the GDR. In 1955, the Soviets officially recognized the GDR and established formal diplomatic relations with the FRG. From the work of Hope Harrison and others, we already know how skilfully Walter Ulbricht, the first secretary of the Socialist Unity Party (SED), managed to leverage the GDR's key location in order to pursue the survival of East German socialism in its competition with the FRG. Similarly, Lorena De Vita looks at the origins of competition between East and West Germany in the Third World as she explores the GDR's response to the 1956 Suez Crisis. The Suez Crisis started in August 1956 when the Egyptian leader Gamal Abdel Nasser proclaimed the nationalization of the Suez Canal Company in response to Western refusal to fund the construction of the Aswan Dam. In October, Israel, Britain and France invaded Egypt in order to retake control. De Vita describes an extraordinary public campaign – the first of its kind – that the East German leadership launched in support of Egypt, highlighting the FRG's links with Israel in an attempt to break out of its own diplomatic isolation. She shows that the SED leadership was willing to go to great lengths – up to the point of sending East German volunteers to fight in Egypt – in order to achieve diplomatic recognition from Cairo, with the Soviets providing a moderating influence.

While Khrushchev's commitment to socialist East Germany allowed Ulbricht to secure (measured) Soviet support for its foreign-policy initiatives, it was Poland that underwent a particularly significant transformation after the events of 1956. Recent research has focused particularly on the Polish leader, Władysław Gomułka, whose ability to negotiate a new relationship with the Soviets in October 1956 allowed for a large degree of independence within the Soviet bloc. While most research on Polish diplomatic history after 1956 focuses on Warsaw's relationship with the West, the Soviet Union and Asia, Marek Rutkowski analyses how various foreign and domestic policy concerns connected during Prime Minister Józef Cyrankiewicz's trip to Asia in 1957. Rutkowski shows how Cyrankiewicz tried to establish close relations with Asian countries as a way to strengthen Poland's position within the Soviet bloc, and also finds circumstantial evidence that, in India, Cyrankiewicz sought support for the Rapacki Plan, one of the most well-known of Poland's postwar diplomatic initiatives. Rutkowski's account reveals the Polish leadership engaged in a careful balancing act, eager to solidify its new-found autonomy and yet unwilling to upset a balance with Moscow.

While the diplomatic initiatives of the GDR and Poland have been previously tackled by international historians, Jan Koura and Robert Anthony Waters Jr, provide insight into a topic that has been almost completely ignored by historians – the role of the Soviet bloc in Latin America. A known 'brand' in the region, Czechoslovakia was well poised to take advantage of Khrushchev's opening up to the Third World. Not unlike the GDR's Walter Ulbricht and Bulgaria's Todor Zhivkov, the first secretary of the Czechoslovak Communist Party (CCP), Antonín Novotný, staked his political survival after 1956 on a close alliance with the Soviet Union. Koura and Waters reveal that Prague remained highly enthusiastic about the revolutionary potential in Latin America up until 1966, as they analyse how Czechoslovakia tried to forge a new and active role in the region, which included the multiplication of business ties, expansion of trade and the transfer of arms. When Prague decided to supply weapons to Cuba, this accorded it a greater status and respect from the Soviets. The story of Czechoslovak relations with Cheddi and Janet Jagan, the leaders of the left-leaning People's Progressive Party of British Guiana, shows not only how much Czechoslovak policy developed based on these assessments but also the increasingly important role that Prague played in the region at that time. The chapter illuminates the fact that Czechoslovakia went far beyond what the 'businesslike' Soviets (in the words of Janet Jagan) were willing to do in the case of British Guiana.

Larry Watts focuses on the diplomacy of Romania in the Third World. Arguing that Romanian behaviour in the Warsaw Pact represented 'not so much autonomy as mutiny', Watts contends that Bucharest saw in the Third World an ally in its endeavour to obstruct Soviet unilateralism. This was particularly the case during the 1967 Six Day War, when Bucharest not only failed to break off relations with Israel but also refused to allow its territory to be used to transport military supplies to Soviet allies in the region. Unsurprisingly, the Soviet Union and its loyalist allies saw Romania's policies in the Middle East as a direct challenge. Moscow tried to isolate Bucharest in international forums, but stopped short of undertaking drastic action. Romania pursued policies that countered Soviet interests, not only in the Middle East but also in Africa and Latin America. Watts argues that the Third World became the 'central pillar' of Romania's soft power, rather than simply an attempt to counter Soviet hegemony.

The authors in Part I advance our understanding of how NSWP countries used the opening accorded by de-Stalinization and Khrushchev's 'active foreign policy' doctrine to forge new forms of engagement with countries in Africa, Asia and Latin America. New activist engagement in the Third World was crucial to the NSWP states asserting their agency in foreign affairs, with Moscow sometimes having to curb the enthusiasm of its allies in the diplomatic arena. If chapters in Part I deal with high-level diplomatic initiatives, the contributors to Part II look at those men and women across the Soviet bloc who became actively involved in international initiatives as the NSWP countries turned their attention to the Third World.

Part II 'Intermediaries': Spies, Journalists, Doctors, Teachers and Diplomats in the Third World

The mid- to late 1950s was a period of opening up towards the outside world, with students, scientists, musicians and artists from Africa, Asia and Latin America for the first time pouring in across the Iron Curtain. Some would stay for long periods in order to receive education in a wide range of arts and sciences or for military training. Others would come to participate in an ever-expanding range of events – conferences, seminars, festivals or simply tours – all organized in order to showcase the achievements of socialism and deepen contacts with Third World elites. In July 1957, the CC CPSU sponsored the World Youth Festival in Moscow, which for the first time brought young people from Africa, Asia and Latin America in contact with thousands of Soviet citizens, heralding the dawn of a new era. Similar events, albeit of modest proportions, would become common across the Eastern bloc. Newspapers, magazines, radio programmes and TV broadcasts filled up with reports about the lives of peoples in Asia, Africa and Latin America. When two Czechoslovak adventurers, Jiri Hanselka and Miroslav Zikmund, travelled across Africa, Asia, Latin America and Oceania in a silver Tatra 87, their regular radio show attracted enormous audiences and their travelogues a huge readership across the Soviet bloc, making them the best-selling writers in twentieth-century Eastern Europe. The 1950s thus saw a multiplication of exchanges between Eastern and Central Europeans and foreigners.[33]

Travelling and working abroad was still closely regulated by communist party officials, and thus remained a marker of privilege bestowed upon a narrow elite. The men and women who travelled or worked abroad – journalists, teachers, medical professionals, economic advisors, scientists, artists, writers, ballet dancers, opera singers, diplomats and spies – were all carefully selected and vetted for their particular mission, which was to serve the cause of socialism. At the same time, the motivations of those men and women who went abroad in various capacities differed. While postings in the West generally remained the preferred option for elites across the Soviet bloc, the opening up to the Third World provided opportunities for personal career advancement. For some, working abroad accorded opportunities for earning extra cash and gaining access to Western consumer goods. Others were attracted by a sense of adventure and a desire to see and experience foreign cultures. However, for many men and women across the Eastern bloc, Third World revolutions and national liberation movements seemed to validate the socialist experiment. Many were genuinely convinced about the superiority of socialism over capitalism and believed it was their 'internationalist duty' to help the emerging nations throw off the shackles of colonial and neocolonial exploitation and help to advance the cause of socialist-style modernization in the Third World.[34] While engagement with anti-colonial and anti-imperialist campaigns had its precedents in interwar Soviet Union and East–Central Europe, the purges of European communist parties and the Comintern during the Great Terror of 1936–8, the trauma and loss of the Great War and Stalinization in Eastern and Central Europe after World War II meant that Soviet bloc countries were lacking in cadres with knowledge or contacts in the Third World.

The men and women who travelled or lived abroad fulfilled multiple roles, sometimes under double identities. One group that was at the forefront of Eastern bloc propaganda efforts in the Third World comprised the journalists who staffed the press agencies of the Soviet bloc – the Soviet TASS and APN, Cuba's Prensa Latina, Czechoslovakia's Četeka, and the GDR's Allgemeine Deutsche Nachrichtendienst (ADN). The journalists usually lived away from the embassies, so they had greater room for manoeuvre and thus better opportunities to launch personal relations with the heads of local media services. Unsurprisingly, press agencies were often used as a cover for Eastern bloc intelligence agencies, with journalists – but also diplomats, and representatives of Soviet cultural organizations abroad – actually being officers of the Soviet KGB, the Czechoslovak StB or the GDR's Ministerium für Staatssicherheit (Stasi). University campuses and hospitals also offered opportunities for informal engagement and exchange. The four chapters in Part II provide examples as to the roles that these elites – journalists, spies, teachers and medical professionals – played in conducting NSWP policy in the Third World.

Soviet and Czechoslovak intelligence officers are at the centre of Natalia Telepneva's chapter on the Congo Crisis, 1960–4. The Congo, formally a Belgian colony, became embroiled in a crisis that saw an army mutiny, a general strike, the secession of the resource-rich Katanga province and Belgian intervention all follow in quick succession after the country became independent in June 1960. Telepneva follows a small group of Czechoslovak and Soviet intelligence officers who worked together for the first time in sub-Saharan Africa in order to support the Congo's first prime minister, Patrice Lumumba, in a country that quickly turned into a Cold War hotspot. By 1961, the Soviets realized that they were neither willing nor capable of seriously resisting Western action in the Congo. In this context, intelligence became the key way to protect their allies in the country – a Cold War 'on the cheap'. Soviet and Czechoslovak intelligence officers tried, despite all the odds, to recruit informants and agents and maintain contacts with the pro-Lumumbist opposition, whilst at the same time facing pressures from Moscow and Prague. While these efforts ultimately failed, covert operations became an established foreign-policy practice in Africa where Western power and influence greatly outweighed that of the Soviet bloc.

George Roberts analyses how East German journalists and diplomats tried to work towards full diplomatic recognition of the GDR in Tanzania. In 1964, a chain of events in East Africa created a situation in which, after a protracted diplomatic struggle, Dar es Salaam became the first sub-Saharan capital to house representatives of both German states. Roberts analyses how the GDR employed *Öffentlichkeitarbeit* (publicity work) in order to achieve full diplomatic status in the late 1960s – a complicated set of measures that included a campaign to discredit the FRG as a successor to imperial Germany. In particular, he focuses on a group of ADN journalists in Dar es Salaam and their relationships with local elites. The GDR's propaganda efforts, argues Roberts, produced mostly negative results, aggravated by the Warsaw Pact invasion of Czechoslovakia, which was met with opprobrium in Dar es Salaam. In the end, Tanzania's decision to open full relations with the GDR in December 1972 had 'nothing to do' with East Germany's policies in Africa. Roberts portrays the GDR as a 'scavenger state', whose policies were constantly contingent on local dynamics.

If Telepneva and Roberts deal with such 'usual suspects' in intra-governmental exchanges as diplomats and spies, Iris Borowy focuses on the backgrounds, motivations and actions of East German medical academics in Asia, Africa and Latin America. The GDR leadership wanted medical academics to spearhead medical-research cooperation in the Third World and promote the East German pharmaceutical industry abroad, yet such cooperation was often inadequate due to a lack of expertise and political will, with the exception of a few cases such as the GDR's cooperation with Brazil. Trade in drugs with Third World countries was never substantial, yet it represented an important marker of prestige and foreign-currency earning. Borowy looks closely at a number of famous East German academics, such as Hans Knöll and

Richard Kirsch, who were particularly involved in such missions – with mixed results. Perhaps the most surprising conclusion of Borowy's chapter is that the GDR's medical professionals actively encouraged and cajoled East German authorities to develop various forms of cooperation with the Global South. Borowy's chapter is an important reminder that going beyond an emphasis on diplomatic relations (or even beyond the State) enriches our understanding of twentieth-century international history and complicates the Cold War narrative.

While East German medical academics were generally eager mediators in exchanges between NSWP countries and Third World elites, Polish officials and teachers appear to have been more reluctant agents of socialist internationalism, as is evident from Przemysław Gasztold's survey of Polish policy in Africa. Gasztold argues that Warsaw was lukewarm towards developing an activist policy in Africa, which reflected Gomułka's autonomy in foreign policy and the fact that Poland's initiatives on the continent were mainly motivated by economic profit. Neither Polish officials in Warsaw nor teachers and academics working in Africa hid their scepticism about socialist transformation in Africa, and they often openly expressed unorthodox economic views. One striking example involved the case of Jan Drewnowski, a prominent Polish economist teaching at the University of Ghana, who was only sent home after President Kwame Nkrumah complained that his teaching exposed a preference for Western economic thought. While Poland's commitment to support national-liberation movements somewhat increased under Gomułka's successor, Edward Gierek, Polish support was mainly limited to the provision of scholarships for African students.

Part II highlights the fact that if we are to understand the policies of NSWP countries in the Third World, it is imperative to take into account the context of the Cold War, and the concerns of national governments and local elites, and to place them alongside the personal experiences, motivations and actions of individuals on the ground. Its four chapters each deal in some way with the agency of those men and women who tried to navigate a complex web of local politics, pressures from national governments and Cold War geopolitics. They were very much at the forefront of NSWP countries' policy in the Third World, acting as important intermediaries.

Part III Money and Influence: Diplomacy, Trade and Aid

Economic performance was a crucial component of competition between capitalism and socialism, between the 'First' and 'Second' worlds, during the Cold War. Swayed by evidence of rapid interwar industrialization in the USSR, many Third World leaders in the 1950s and 1960s were enthusiastic about Soviet-style industrialization based on economic planning. It was primarily economic competition that Khrushchev referred to when he challenged the West to a 'peaceful competition' between the two systems. The late 1950s was a period of high optimism for the Soviets, who believed that, with assistance from the Eastern bloc, Third World countries could successfully replicate the 'Soviet model of development', which implied collectivization of agriculture, nationalization of enterprises and high levels of investment in infrastructure and industrial development. Meanwhile, US economists – most famously Walt Rostow at MIT's Center for International Studies – offered their own models of development based on investments in agriculture and infrastructure. Economic development thus became a crucial weapon in the Cold War.[35]

Meanwhile, the economic relationship inside the Warsaw Pact was also under revision in the 1950s. If Stalin had sought to extract capital and resources from his satellites in order to achieve economic autarky, Khrushchev looked towards its more technologically advanced allies in Eastern and Central Europe as a source of expertise; advanced industrial practices; and, most crucially, as a source of access to Western technology in order to 'catch up with and surpass' the West in terms of living standards.[36] Khrushchev wanted to revive the USSR-led Council for Mutual Economic Assistance (CMEA) on the basis of specialization and supranational integration. In 1961, the Commission for Technical Assistance (CTA) was established in order to coordinate the provision of developmental assistance to the Third World based on the principle of economic specialization and the 'division of labour'. This goal produced significant debates and many disagreements, and intra-bloc rivalry rather than cooperation in the Third World was commonplace. By the late 1960s, the Soviets and their allies in Eastern and Central Europe believed that they could no longer afford to export the 'socialist model of development' at any cost. The disillusionment with early Soviet development efforts in the Third World and the onset of European detente in the late 1960s led to a more pragmatic approach and an emphasis on East–West cooperation in developmental assistance.[37]

The trademark of the 1970s in Second–Third World economic exchanges was economic rationality. Khrushchev's successor, Leonid Brezhnev, wanted the Warsaw Pact to further Soviet foreign-policy interests yet also to improve economic growth and increase consumption and political stability. After 1967, the Soviet Union made clear that the NSWP countries could not rely solely on Moscow as the only supplier of strategic raw materials, and encouraged them to look to the Third World for alternatives. Such pressures increased in the 1970s. With NSWP countries increasingly reliant on the import of strategic raw materials from resource-rich countries of the Global South, mutual economic advantage became the catchphrase.[38] At the same time, the 1970s saw the postwar breakdown of the international economic order when the Organization of the Petroleum Exporting Countries (OPEC) showed its collective might as it hiked up the price of oil in the wake of the 1973 war between Israel and Egypt. The oil-rich yet conflict-ridden countries of the Middle East thus became major recipients of Soviet bloc arms exports. The Soviet Union benefited significantly, receiving around $19 billion in hard currency from arms sales, and earned around $23 billion on bilateral or soft-currency arms sales between 1974 and 1984.[39] The NSWP also hoped that trade with Third World countries could rebalance their budgets, which increasingly relied on the import of consumer goods and technology from the West. However, trade with the Third World could not be rebalanced, as is evidenced by the $57 billion in debt that the Soviet bloc had accumulated by 1979.[40]

The authors in Part III explore the interplay of diplomacy, aid and trade in the foreign policies of the NSWP countries in the Third World. These chapters investigate how concerns over domestic economic performance and Soviet proposals for economic specialization of the Warsaw Pact countries factored in the policies of the NSWP countries in the Third World. They investigate how these states responded to those changes, as they tried to exploit new commercial-relations opportunities in the Third World at a time of growing indebtedness, transformation and crises in the Eastern bloc and the world economy.

Amongst the NSWP countries, Romania was the key critic of Soviet proposals for economic specialization within the Warsaw Pact framework. Research has focused on how the Romanian leadership managed to thwart these initiatives and turned to the Third World as a source of economic profit.[41] Elena Dragomir adds to this growing body of scholarship in her chapter, which analyses Romania's strategy in the little-discussed episode of Bucharest blocking Mongolia's admission to the Warsaw Pact in July 1963. Unhappy about Soviet proposals on CMEA specialization, which would have relegated Romania to the role of raw-material provider within the Eastern bloc, Bucharest skillfully exploited Sino–Soviet disagreements as leverage in order to block Mongolia's membership.

Economic considerations are the focal point of Philip Muehlenbeck's chapter, which examines Czechoslovak policy in East Africa in the 1960s. A leading exporter of small arms to the Third World, Czechoslovakia had used military assistance in order to gain influence in the developing world. However, facing a stagnant economic situation by the mid-1960s, Prague became increasingly unwilling to provide military assistance as a gift, and instead sought customers for its arms. In Kenya and Uganda, Czechoslovakia established personal contacts with Oginga Odinga and Milton Obote respectively, and proceeded to sell arms and provide military training as both leaders wanted to reduce British influence in their countries. Czechoslovak involvement in Kenya was so extensive that Prague financed Odinga's 'shadow government'. If Kenya eventually moved for closer cooperation with Britain, Uganda established a strong military relationship with Prague, with Czechoslovakia surpassing the UK and Israel as its main supplier of arms between 1964 and 1968. While the Soviet intervention of 1968 significantly curbed Czechoslovak influence in Africa, in the 1960s Prague not only acted without diktat from Moscow, but often drove communist policy on the continent.

Domestic economic concerns also occupy a central position in Csaba Békés's and Dániel Vékony's account of Hungarian policy in the Middle East. After 1956, the cornerstone of János Kádár's domestic policy was raising living standards for his subjects under a mixed economy commonly known as 'goulash socialism'. Khrushchev's concept of 'active foreign policy' thus corresponded with Kádár's aims as it offered commercial opportunities, especially in the cash-rich Middle East. Since the Soviet arms industry owned a comparative advantage in the region, Hungary continuously pushed for specialization and eventually developed military industry and its own market share in the Middle East – an initiative that proved much more successful, while ordinary trade with the countries of the region did not fulfil the high hopes of the Hungarian leadership in the long run. Originally it was assumed that trade with the Middle East, including arms shipments, could considerably contribute to solving the problem of Hungary's constant balance-of-payments deficit vis-à-vis its non-Soviet bloc partners, but this goal never materialized. By the late 1980s, Hungary gave up on the 'promised lands' of the Middle East and re-established full diplomatic relations with Israel.

While Dragomir, Muehlenbeck, Békés and Vékony all in various ways emphasize the key role of domestic economic considerations in analysing motivations for NSWP engagement with the Third World, in his survey of Bulgaria's relations with the Third World Jordan Baev underlines the primacy of political considerations. The central reason Bulgaria provided assistance to a mind-boggling number of actors in the Middle East, Africa and Latin America was primarily driven by political concerns, as Todor Zhivkov was eager to back up Soviet ambitions in the region. Baev argues that the benefits of commercial exchange with Third World countries were relatively small, but Bulgaria managed to leverage its loyalty in order to obtain economic benefits from the Soviet Union. The Bulgarian leadership thus pursued an active foreign policy in the Third World in order to increase the country's prestige within the Warsaw Pact in the name of class solidarity.

This volume contributes to key debates about the agency of the NSWP countries in the Soviet bloc and the Cold War, and the place of Eastern and Central Europe in postwar developments. Firstly, the volume reinstates the concept that the engagement of NSWP countries with a variety of actors in Africa, Asia and Latin America was not driven by Soviet concerns and directives, contributing to the 'decentralization' of the Cold War narrative. Recent studies have contributed to our understanding as to how de-Stalinization reshaped relations between the states of socialist Eastern and Central Europe, the Soviet Union and the West. The investigation of NSWP policies in the Third World adds a missing dimension to this body of work that investigates 1956 as the crucial moment in the emancipation of state-socialist Eastern and Central Europe in the postwar period. Secondly, the volume re-emphasizes the roles of elites in international politics. While it deals mainly with intra-state relations, an emphasis on specific individuals and groups – such as diplomats, teachers or medical professionals – brings international historians into conversation with scholars of transnationalism who look beyond the State in order to investigate expert groups, NGOs and transnational 'epistemic communities' that often transcended Cold War divides.[42] *The Warsaw Pact in the Third World* thus makes a significant contribution towards the emerging scholarship of both alliance politics and the Cold War in the Global South. The volume draws on a rich body of archival material from Eastern and Central Europe that either has been recently declassified or has been largely ignored in the English-language literature, often for linguistic reasons. It also draws on the regional expertise of its contributors, providing a view on international politics from a regional perspective.

Notes

1. 'The Middle East: The Trojan Horse', *Time*, 7 November 1955.
2. Philip E. Muehlenbeck, *Czechoslovakia in Africa, 1945–1968* (New York, 2016), pp. 91–5.
3. On official US reaction to the deal, see Impact of the Egyptian–Czechoslovak Arms Deal, August 27–November 16, 1955 (Documents 226–415), *Foreign Relations of the United States, 1955–1957, Arab-Israeli Dispute, 1955, Volume XIV* (Washington, DC, 1985).
4. On Nasser's reasons for the deal, see Guy Laron, 'Cutting the Gordian Knot: The Post-WWII Egyptian Quest for Arms and the 1955 Czechoslovak Arms Deal', *Cold War International History Project*, Working Paper No. 55 (2007).
5. The term 'cardboard castle' belongs to a NATO official. See Vojtech Mastny and Malcolm Byrne (eds), *A Cardboard Castle?: An inside History of the Warsaw Pact, 1955–1991* (Budapest, 2005).
6. This list does not include Albania for three reasons. First, as the smallest and poorest member of the Warsaw Pact, it was the least involved politically and economically with the Third World. Secondly, Albania ceased to be an active member of the Warsaw Pact by the early 1960s and formally withdrew from the alliance in 1968. Finally, and most importantly, we were unable to find a contributor who uses Albanian archival material to study Tirana's relations with the developing world. For an exceptional new study, see: Elidor Mëhilli, *From Stalin to Mao: Albania and the Socialist World* (Ithaca, 2017).
7. On evolution of the term, see: B. R. Tomlinson, 'What was the Third World?' *Journal of Contemporary History*, 38 (2) (April 2003), pp. 307–21.
8. Zbigniew K. Brzezinski in *The Soviet Bloc: Unity and Conflict* (Cambridge, MA, 1967).

9. Andrzej Korbonski, 'Eastern Europe and the Third World; or, "Limited Regret Strategy" Revisited', in Andrzej Korbonski and Francis Fukuyama (eds), *The Soviet Union and the Third World: The Last Three Decades* (Ithaca, NY, 1987).
10. Prominent examples of this genre include Roger E. Kanet (ed.), *The Soviet Union and the Developing Nations* (Baltimore, MD, 1974); Roger Kanet (ed.), *The Soviet Union, Eastern Europe, and the Third World* (New York, 1987); Michael Radu (ed.), *Eastern Europe and the Third World: East vs. South* (New York, 1981); Korbonski and Fukuyama, *The Last Three Decades*; and Alvin Z. Rubinstein, *Moscow's Third World Strategy* (Princeton, NJ, 1988).
11. Kanet, *The Soviet Union, Eastern Europe, and the Third World*.
12. Tony Smith 'New Bottles for New Wine: A Pericentric Framework for the Study of the Cold War', *Diplomatic History* 24 (4) (2000), p. 568.
13. Hope M. Harrison, *Driving the Soviets up the Wall: Soviet-East German Relations, 1953–1961* (Princeton, NJ, 2003).
14. Odd Arne Westad, *The Global Cold War: Third World Interventions and the Making of Our Times* (New York, 2013).
15. Some of the most recent examples of this approach are Tanya Harmer, *Allende's Chile and the Inter-American Cold War* (Chapel Hill, NC, 2011); Lien-Hang T. Nguyen, *Hanoi's War: An International History of the War for Peace in Vietnam* (Chapel Hill, NC, 2012); Piero Gleijeses, *Visions of Freedom: Havana, Washington, Pretoria, and the Struggle for Southern Africa, 1976–1991* (Chapel Hill, NC, 2013); and Jeremy Friedman, *Shadow Cold War: The Sino-Soviet Competition for the Third World* (Chapel Hill, NC, 2015). For a historiographical discussion, see David C. Engerman, 'The Second World's Third World', *Kritika: Explorations in Russian and Eurasian History* 12 (1) (Winter 2011).
16. For an overview of the field, see Ana Antic, Johanna Conterio and Dora Vargha (eds), 'Agents of Internationalism', a special issue of *Contemporary European History*, 25, 2 (2016).
17. Some recent studies include James G. Hershberg, 'Peace Probes and the Bombing Pause: Hungarian and Polish Diplomacy during the Vietnam War, December 1965–January 1966', *Journal of Cold War Studies*, 5 (2) (Spring 2003), pp. 32–67; Zoltán Szoke, 'Delusion or Reality? Secret Hungarian Diplomacy during the Vietnam War', *Journal of Cold War Studies* 12 (4) (2010), pp. 119–80; Margaret K. Gnoinska, 'Poland and the Cold War in East and Southeast Asia, 1949–1965', PhD dissertation, George Washington University, Washington, DC, 2010; and Muehlenbeck, *Czechoslovakia in Africa*.
18. Some examples include William Glenn Gray, *Germany's Cold War: The Global Campaign to Isolate East Germany, 1949–1969* (Chapel Hill, NC, 2003); Gareth Winrow, *The Foreign Policy of the GDR in Africa* (Cambridge, 2009); Klaus Storkmann, *Geheime Solidarität: Militärbeziehungen und Militärhilfen der DDR in die 'Dritte Welt'* [Secret Solidarity: GDR Military Relations and Military Aid to the 'Third World'] (Berlin, 2012); Young-sun Hong, *Cold War Germany, the Third World, and the Global Humanitarian Regime* (New York, 2015); Jeffrey Herf, *Undeclared Wars Against Israel: East Germany and the West German Far Left*

1967–1989 (New York, 2016); Massimiliano Trentin, '"Tough negotiations". The two Germanys in Syria and Iraq, 1963–74', *Cold War History* 8 (3) (2008), pp. 353–80.
19. See, for example, Laurien Crump, *The Warsaw Pact Reconsidered: International Relations in Eastern Europe, 1955–1969* (New York, 2015).
20. Oscar Sanchez-Sibony, *Red Globalization: The Political Economy of the Soviet Cold War from Stalin to Khrushchev* (New York, 2014).
21. James G. Hershberg, 'The Crisis Years, 1958–1963', in Odd Arne Westad (ed.), *Reviewing the Cold War: Approaches, Interpretations, Theory* (London, 2000), p. 304.
22. On reflections about 1975 as a period of optimism for Soviet policy in the Third World, see Nikolai Leonov, *Likholetie* [Time of Troubles] (Moscow, 1997), pp. 135–45.
23. Georgiy Mirskiy, 'Na znamenatel'nom Rubezhe' [At the Threshold], *Vostok*, 6 (1996), p. 131.
24. See Sergey Khrushchev, *Nikita Khrushchev: Creation of a Superpower* (University Park, PA, 2000), p. 436.
25. Quoted in Alexander Fursenko and Timothy Naftali, *Khrushchev's Cold War: The Inside Story of an American Adversary* (New York, 2006), p. 57.
26. Westad, *The Global Cold War*, pp. 39–67.
27. For discussion of 'active foreign policy' doctrine, see Csaba Békés: 'The Warsaw Pact and the Helsinki process, 1965–1970', in Wilfried Loth and Georges-Henri Soutou (eds) *The Making of Détente: Eastern and Western Europe in the Cold War, 1965–75* (London and New York, 2007), p. 201.
28. On Hungary, see Csaba Békés, 'Hungarian Foreign Policy in the Bipolar World, 1945–1991', *Foreign Policy Review* 3 (2004), p. 78. On the GDR's discussions, see Lorena da Vita's chapter in this volume. On Czechoslovakia, see 'Party meeting with chiefs of foreign missions', 1958, National Archives of the Czech Republic, Records of the Communist Party of Czechoslovakia [hereafter NA-UV KSČ], Inv. 4, Ka. 8.
29. Csaba Bekes, 'East Central Europe, 1953–1956', in Melvyn P. Leffler and Odd Arne Westad, *The Cambridge History of the Cold War* (Cambridge, 2012) pp. 334–52.
30. Some of these forums included meetings between respective deputy foreign ministers, representatives of the International Departments, press agencies, solidarity committees and other 'public organizations', cultural bodies and academic institutes. On coordination, see Csaba Békés, 'Cold War, Détente and the Soviet Bloc', pp. 247–59; James Hershberg, Sergey Radchenko, Péter Vámos and David Wolff. 'The Interkit Story: A Window into the Final Decades of the Sino-Soviet Relationship', *The Cold War International History Project Working Paper Series* (February 2011).
31. On the Bandung Conference and its consequences, see Westad, *The Global Cold War*, pp. 100–9.
32. For a further discussion of this period, see James G. Hershberg, 'The Crisis Years, 1958–1963,' pp. 303–26.

33. On cultural exchange between the Second and Third Worlds, and especially on its effect on the public, see Tobias Rupprecht, *Soviet Internationalism after Stalin: Interaction and Exchange between the USSR and Latin America during the Cold War* (Cambridge, 2015); James Mark and Péter Apor, 'Socialism Goes Global: Decolonization and the Making of a New Culture of Internationalism in Socialist Hungary, 1956–1989', *Journal of Modern History* 87 (December 2015), pp. 852–89.
34. For discussion, see Vladislav Zubok, *Zhivago's Children: The Last Russian Intelligentsia* (Cambridge, 2011), pp. 88–121.
35. David Engerman, 'The Romance of Economic Development and New Histories of the Cold War', *Diplomatic History* 28 (1) (January 2004), pp. 23–54. On the 'Soviet Model of Development' and its application in West Africa, see Alessandro Iandolo, 'The Rise and Fall of the "Soviet Model of Development" in West Africa, 1957–64', *Cold War History* 12 (4) (November 2012).
36. Austin Jersild, 'The Soviet State as Imperial Scavenger: "Catch Up and Surpass" in the Transnational Socialist Bloc, 1950–1960', *American Historical Review* 116 (1) (February 2011), pp. 109–32.
37. Sara Lorenzini, 'Comecon and the South in the Years of Détente: A Study on East-South Economic Relations', *European Review of History: Revue Européenne d'Histoire* 21 (2) (2014), pp. 186–8.
38. Ibid., p. 188.
39. David Painter, 'Oil and geopolitics: the oil crises of the 1970s and the Cold War', *Historical Social Research* 39 (4) (2014), pp. 186–208.
40. Engerman, 'Romance of Economic Development', p. 49.
41. On the link between Romania's economy and its foreign policy see, among others, Elena Dragomir, 'Romania's Participation in the Agricultural Conference in Moscow, 2–3 February 1960', *Cold War History* 13, no. 3 (2013), pp. 331–51; Mioara Anton Romanian and Iesirea Din Cerc, *Politica Externa a Regimului Gheorghiu-Dej* (Bucharest, 2007); Dan Cătănuş, *Tot mai departe de Moscova: Politica externă a României 1956–1965* [Further from Moscow. Romania's foreign policy, 1956–1964] (Bucharest, 2011); Liviu Taranu, *Romania in Consiliul de Ajutor Economic Reciproc, 1949–1965* [Romania in the Council of Help and Mutual Assistance] (Bucharest, 2007); Corina Mavrodin, 'A Maverick in the Making: Romania's de-Satellization process and the Global Cold War, 1953–1963', PhD dissertation, London School of Economics and Political Science, 2017.
42. Erez Manela, 'A Pox on Your Narrative: Writing Disease Control into Cold War History', *Diplomatic History* 34 (2) (2010), pp. 299–323; Dora Vargha, 'Between east and west: Polio Vaccination Across the Iron Curtain in Cold War Hungary', *Bulletin of the History of Medicine*, 88 2 (2014), pp. 319–43.

PART I

THE RE-DISCOVERY OF THE THIRD WORLD

CHAPTER 1

ULBRICHT, NASSER AND KHRUSHCHEV: THE GDR'S SEARCH FOR DIPLOMATIC RECOGNITION AND THE SUEZ CRISIS, 1956

Lorena De Vita

On 7 October 1949, following the official proclamation of the foundation of the German Democratic Republic (GDR) in the eastern part of Germany, Soviet leader Joseph Stalin congratulated the East German leadership, praising the significance of this political development for the 'history of Europe'.[1] Two days later, the newly unanimously elected East German president, Wilhelm Pieck, addressed the East German Volkskammer (literally 'People's Chamber', i.e., the GDR's Parliament) promising that he would look on his task as that of a 'trustee for the interests of the *whole* of the German people', and that he would work to forge a 'great, rich and luminous' future for the country.[2] Four-and-a-half months earlier, celebrating the foundation of the Federal Republic of Germany (FRG) in the West, Chancellor Konrad Adenauer had made a similar point. A fierce competition, between East and West Germany, had officially begun. From a West German perspective, this struggle concerned which state should be considered *the* legitimate representative of the German people. On the other hand, East Berlin's less ambitious goal was to demonstrate that the GDR, too, was a legitimate German state, capable of being recognized internationally. The competition sharply intensified in 1955. In March 1954, the Soviets had announced the normalization of their relations with the GDR, proclaiming East Germany's 'full sovereignty in its internal and external affairs'.[3] They reiterated the message in September 1955, during the visit of an East German delegation to the USSR. While in Moscow, Prime Minister Otto Grotewohl signed a document declaring that relations between the Soviet Union and the GDR would be 'based on complete equality of rights, mutual respect of sovereignty, and non-interference in domestic affairs' – a move which evidently undermined the West German claim of being the sole representative for the whole of Germany (*Alleinvertretungsanspruch*).[4] In response to this, and in order to prevent other countries from establishing relations with the GDR, in December 1955 the West German Government released a statement declaring that from then onwards Bonn would interpret any recognition of the GDR as an 'unfriendly act' – a stance later known as the 'Hallstein Doctrine'.[5] East German efforts at gaining recognition from so-called Third World countries, and the relentless West German campaign to ensure that this would not happen, characterized German–German competition on the global stage throughout the 1950s and 1960s.

The year 1955 also saw a series of momentous developments in the Middle East. These included the establishment of a Western-sponsored military alliance, the Baghdad Pact, signed between Turkey and Iraq in February, and later joined by Pakistan, Iran and Great Britain. Amongst those who viewed this development as a serious threat to the stability of the Middle East was Gamal Abdel Nasser. By 1955, Nasser had affirmed himself as a leading political figure in Egypt as well as in the Arab and non-aligned world. At home, he had emerged victorious from the internal rivalries amongst the Free Officers who had ousted the Egyptian monarchy following the 1952 revolution, becoming the leading political figure in Egypt. Nasser's references to the problems of the Egyptian people as problems of the Arab peoples, and his emphatic support for the Palestinian cause, allowed him to attract the admiration of not only much of the Egyptian population but also of large sections of the public opinion within the Arab world.[6] In 1955, Nasser's anti-Israeli rhetoric harshened to an unprecedented level, especially following a very heavy attack waged by the Israeli Defense Forces in February–March in order to curb *fedayeen* infiltrations into Israeli territory from Gaza, which at that time was under Egyptian military control. The attacks re-ignited the humiliation suffered by Egypt and the Arab coalition on occasion of the 1948–9 war against Israel, in which Nasser himself had fought and which was still very much alive as a burning defeat in the collective memory of the Arab peoples.[7] In April 1955, the Egyptian leader established himself as one of the dominant personalities at the Bandung Conference, a meeting of 29 heads of state and government from Asian and African countries, which took place in Indonesia and aimed to assist the potential emergence, within the Cold War, of a non-aligned bloc of Third World states.[8] US Secretary of State John Foster Dulles remarked that under the current international political climate claiming neutrality was an 'immoral' policy.[9] Nasser's presence at Bandung, however, and his contribution to the eventual creation of the Non-Aligned Movement (NAM), allowed him to project his political allure onto the international stage.[10]

In the mid-1950s, the Arab Middle East became the main testing ground for East German experiments in dealing with Third World countries and with the new leaders that emerged from them. The importance of the Middle East for understanding East German foreign relations with Third World countries has mainly to do with chronology. Indeed, the area was the first in which the GDR managed to gain some kind of international network, having already signed a series of trade deals with the countries of the region by the first half of the 1950s. However, this also meant that for the first time when dealing with Middle Eastern countries, East German representatives confronted issues that would arise again and again over the following decades when dealing with nations in other areas of the non-aligned world. In the mid-1950s, projecting the GDR's appeal beyond the socialist bloc in an attempt to gain international recognition proved to be a challenging exercise. It was, however, one that East German leader Walter Ulbricht knew could be crucial for the survival of the GDR.

Egypt was the very first Third World country to sign an economic deal with the East German Government, in 1953. From then on, relations between the two countries assumed ever greater importance for the East German leadership.[11] So much so that in 1956, while the cohesion of the Soviet bloc was threatened by uprisings in Poland and Hungary, and the precarious stability of the East German state itself was at risk, Ulbricht became preoccupied with the necessity of reaching out to the Arab Middle East. This was also thanks to Nasser's understanding – before that of any other Third World leader – of how fruitful it could be to use one Germany to gain concessions from the other. Learning to deal with Nasser led Ulbricht to clash with his comrades at home, reviving old rivalries amongst East German communists, as well as with his Soviet masters in Moscow. Indeed, Ulbricht would learn a great deal from the frustration experienced in 1956. First, from his frustration with Nasser, who seemed not to be keeping his word, he would come to appreciate how much there was still to do to render the GDR at least economically if not politically attractive vis-à-vis Third World leaders. Second, he learned from his experience with the Soviets, who theoretically should have supported East German endeavours in the Third World but in fact were deeply concerned by the implications that Ulbricht's dynamism abroad might have for the socialist bloc. Ulbricht would come to appreciate the contradictions typical of the relationship between the GDR and its superpower. The picture that emerges from this analysis of the run-up to, and immediate aftermath of, the Suez Crisis is one of a constant pushing and pulling between East Berlin and Moscow in the summer of 1956 – the former eager to reach out to the countries of the Levant; the latter convinced that such initiatives would quickly backfire.

Chasing Sovereignty, German-Style

Nasser's charismatic political persona appealed to many, in Egypt and beyond. However, this in turn unleashed a series of political jealousies that would characterize intra-Arab politics for more than a decade to come.[12] And, in the West, the Eisenhower administration and the Eden government looked on the Egyptian President's political dynamism at both national and international level with increasing dislike. In an attempt to curb his political allure, in quick succession and with little advance notice the USA, the United Kingdom and the World Bank withdrew their offer to finance Nasser's most valued project, the building of a high dam at Aswan. Discussions about the project had begun shortly after the Free Officers ousted the monarchy, in 1952, although the planning of a high dam on the Nile dated back to the 1930s.[13] For Nasser, the dam was crucial. Its construction would have allowed Egyptian agricultural output to multiply, providing more food for the country's fast-growing population and supporting Egypt's rural and urban electrification plans. Amongst the first to explore how to engineer and finance the dam were West German firms.[14] However, in mid-1956 the news of the Soviet readiness to finance the works for the construction of the dam in Egypt led the USA to withdraw its offers of credit to Egypt – in the expectation that the project would put such a burden on the Soviet Union and its satellite states as to prove unfeasible for the Soviet bloc economy. In turn, this would guarantee facile Western propaganda victories in the Warsaw Pact countries while at the same time working as a warning to other Third World nations that might be toying with giving in to Soviet support offers.[15] Secretary of State Dulles communicated the US decision to withdraw the funding of the high dam project on 19 July 1956. The British followed suit on 20 July, and so did the World Bank on 23 July. The sudden Anglo-American withdrawal of funds for the high dam marked one of the heaviest blows to Nasser's domestic political project. Three days later, Nasser announced the nationalization of the Suez Canal and, two months on, the Egyptian leader broke the news that his country had finalized a groundbreaking arms deal with Czechoslovakia.[16] The new arms-procurement agreement between Cairo and Prague nullified the efforts of the US–British–French Near East Arms Coordinating Committee, which had attempted to control the flow of weapons to the region following the first Arab–Israeli war, and threatened to tilt the military balance in Egypt's favour. The deal further signalled that the Western position in the region was potentially at risk, and that the Soviets could and would militarily and economically penetrate the Middle East if given the chance to do so.

The West German secret services (Bundesnachrichtendienst, BND) suspected that the Czech–Egyptian arms deal could contain a secret clause binding Cairo to diplomatically recognize East Berlin.[17] This suspicion was heightened by the fact that the GDR had, in the meantime, managed to conclude trade agreements with Lebanon (1953) and Syria (1955), and a payments agreement with Sudan (1955); establish a permanent trade mission in Egypt (1954); and sign a long-term trade agreement and lay the foundations for the establishment of respective consulates in Cairo and East Berlin (November 1955).[18] East German propaganda emphatically claimed that these developments showed that the Hallstein Doctrine, and West German threats to third countries, made 'obviously little impression abroad'.[19] It was, however, an overstatement to claim, as East German propaganda did, that by the end of 1956 Egyptian leader Gamal Abdel Nasser would recognize the existence of two German states.[20] Nonetheless, the treaties that East German representatives signed in the Middle East between 1953 and 1955 did represent a remarkable success for the GDR in international affairs.[21] In order to capitalize on this success, and to discuss the upcoming goals linked to the GDR's engagement abroad, a conference of East German diplomats was organized in early 1956. The meeting took place on 1 and 2 February in East Berlin.

This was not the first meeting of its kind, given that East German representatives stationed in other socialist countries had first begun sharing their experiences within structured talks in March 1950.[22] However, the 1956 diplomats' gathering was substantially different at least in one respect: the emphasis placed by the highest echelons of the East German state on the importance of worldwide recognition of the GDR, with special attention paid to Third World countries. The topics discussed, focusing on the East German necessity to reach out to non-socialist countries and to win the diplomatic recognition for the GDR from as many Third World nations as possible, were in line with Khrushchev's commitment to seize the 'post-colonial momentum' to win clients in the non-aligned world.[23] Opening the meeting in East Berlin, Walter Ulbricht stressed one key point. Its recent attainment of sovereignty represented a crucial achievement for the East German regime. This achievement, however, also represented a point of departure. Elaborating on this, Ulbricht highlighted the two main goals of East German foreign policy for the foreseeable future. First, he underlined the importance of attaining international recognition from as great a number of states as possible (but leaving to the conference participants the task of identifying which states these might be). If outright recognition was not possible, Ulbricht emphasized, the diplomats' task would become one of 'at least pav[ing] the way' towards the construction of 'normal relations' with those countries that, for whatever reason, were not yet ready to recognize the GDR. Second, and closely related to the first point, Ulbricht stressed how crucial it would be to establish and develop solid economic ties with interested countries – and especially those hesitant, for the time being, to exchange diplomatic representatives with East Berlin.[24]

The tasks envisioned by East German Prime Minister Otto Grotewohl were equally ambitious. Exuding optimism about the GDR's allure on the international stage, Grotewohl stressed that East Berlin had a crucial task ahead: by 1960 the East German state needed to achieve such an enviable level of economic and political stability as to make it clear 'for each worker in the world' that only the socialist camp presented the working people with a viable, bright future. And, as Grotewohl underlined, this conviction about the role that the GDR could play in showcasing the attractiveness of the Soviet bloc was not just his, but was related to a 'change in [Moscow's] assessment of the GDR'. Grotewohl's speech ended with an appeal to the GDR to continue 'keeping the initiative, keeping abreast of the offensive' so as to not give 'the enemy' (i.e., West Germany) the opportunity to put East Berlin on the defensive.[25] His and Ulbricht's powerful speeches, however, were met with disillusionment by some of the attendees. For example, Sepp (Max Joseph) Schwab, ambassador to Hungary (and soon to become deputy foreign minister), lamented the 'lack of courage' that, in his view, characterized the GDR's foreign policy, as well as its 'inability to exploit the possibilities at hand'. Werner Eggerath, ambassador to Romania, claimed that, when stationed abroad, he knew only very little of East Berlin's 'general political line and its application to certain specific points', and not much more. Johannes König, the GDR's ambassador to Moscow, was even more indignant. He lamented the lack of 'authority' of the East German Foreign Ministry (Ministerium fur Auswärtige Angelegenheiten, MfAA) in comparison with that of other countries of the socialist bloc. He deemed that the other ministries – 'and not just the Ministries!' – crucially underestimated the importance of the MfAA and of the diplomats stationed abroad. He claimed that his, and his colleagues', job was further complicated by their fundamental lack of information about what went on in (East) Berlin between the GDR leadership and the representatives of the countries in which the East German diplomats were stationed. And the lack of awareness that the diplomats had about the FRG was, in his view, literally, 'a disgrace' (*eine Schande*) that put the East German diplomats stationed abroad in the position of not being able to answer even the friendlier queries on the topic.[26]

Further aspects worried the East German representatives. Ambassador König, for example, told his colleagues of a meeting he had recently had in Moscow with the Egyptian Ambassador to the Soviet Union. He had done his best to convey to his Egyptian colleague the East German enthusiasm about the prospect of eventually substituting completely for the FRG in its economic exchanges with Cairo. However, he recounted, his fervour was met with pragmatic disillusionment from the Egyptian side: 'If we break with the West Germans, can you [really] take upon yourselves the [economic] obligations that the West Germans have towards us?' For König, this meant one key thing: 'Our own economic strength plays a decisive role in our relations with these countries [and especially regarding] the question of the recognition of the GDR'.[27] Given the advantageous position in which the West German economy found itself, it is not hard to discern the cause of the anxiety of much of the East German diplomatic establishment. The discrepancy between the optimistic, grandiose outlook of Ulbricht and Grotewohl and the disillusioned reports and comments of the ambassadors stationed abroad is relevant for understanding the key juncture of 1955–6 for East German foreign relations. The first meeting of East German ambassadors to focus so explicitly on the Third World emphasized some of the idiosyncrasies of East German foreign policy, stretched between over-eager policy makers at home and disenchanted diplomats abroad. The meeting showed just how much the foreign political 'offensive' envisaged by Grotewohl gravitated around the importance of attaining recognition. This was a quest that, as some of the ambassadors realized, had to be supported by sustained economic growth and by the expansion of East German trade networks in the non-aligned world. Nasser's sudden nationalization of the Suez Canal, in the summer of 1956, had the potential to fit very nicely within East Germany's plans for boosting its credentials with Third World countries.

Ulbricht's Frustration

Egypt occupied a special place on the list of the GDR's foreign-policy priorities, for several reasons. In 1953, it had been the first non-communist, non-European country to be willing to negotiate economic agreements with the GDR. At the time, this was absolutely wonderful news for the East German regime. Indeed, the GDR establishment had been thrilled enough by Cairo's interest in dealing with it to commit itself to provide a series of items and raw materials that it could not possibly deliver, given its dire economic situation.[28] From the East German perspective, the Egyptian eagerness was too good a chance to miss – and it mattered little that Cairo was interested in dealing with East Berlin mainly in retaliation against West Germany's contacts with Israel, rather than because of East German allure per se. Indeed, East German–Egyptian economic relations developed after West Germany agreed, in September 1952, to pay a substantial amount of reparations to the State of Israel. The Egyptian establishment (alongside the governments of Syria, Iraq, Lebanon, Yemen and Jordan) interpreted this move as one of support for Israeli military strength, and implemented a series of measures to communicate their discontent to Bonn. The invitation of an East German trade delegation in March 1953 was part and parcel of Egypt's strategy on this front. The uprisings that would spread throughout East German territory a mere three months after the signing of the trade agreement between Cairo and East Berlin showed just how precarious the economic, and political, conditions of the country were at that time.[29] After the initial agreement, signed in 1953, commercial relations between the two countries flourished. In 1954, the GDR was granted the possibility – for the first time – of participating in the trade fair in Cairo. This was a great opportunity, which allowed the GDR to show off its (albeit limited) industrial prowess in front of a wide audience, and hence establish further commercial contacts with other countries in the region.[30]

In late October 1955, Cairo welcomed with open arms an East German delegation headed by Trade Minister Heinrich Rau. This was noteworthy, given that in his earlier visit to Delhi Rau had been given the cold shoulder by the Indian Government. In Cairo, however, things went much better. This was all the more important given Nasser's burgeoning reputation as a non-aligned leader. Striking a deal with him might very possibly mean that many other countries in the region – and, possibly, also beyond – would soon follow suit and agree to establish more meaningful relations with the GDR. In Cairo, the two parties agreed to a series of economic deals, as well as to exchange trade missions – a decision which seriously alarmed the West German foreign-policy establishment.[31] Indeed, Egypt was crucial for West Germany too, as it had been the first country in the Middle East to establish diplomatic relations with it. Weeks of open and covert

West German–Egyptian bickering followed, and the mutual recriminations reached a peak as Bonn decided to recall its ambassador, Walter Becker, from Cairo. At this point in the face-off, however, Nasser 'blinked'.[32] He granted an interview to one of the main West German newspapers, the *Frankfurter Allgemeine Zeitung*, in which he stated that Egypt had no intention of recognizing the GDR, nor of establishing consular relations with East Berlin. The West Germans, relieved, sent Ambassador Becker back to Cairo. Unsurprisingly, Ulbricht was furious – and he vented his rage at the man who had been so close to scoring a huge tactical victory for the GDR in Egypt, Trade Minister Rau.[33]

The West Germans' successful aborting of the opening of an Egyptian trade mission in East Berlin following the 1955 talks revived old animosities amongst East German comrades. Ulbricht accused Rau of having sent back false information from Cairo, in an attempt to mask the flaws of the agreement that he had drawn up.[34] According to a report of the head of the Near East Department within Bonn's Foreign Ministry, Rau responded that he could not possibly be faulted for Nasser's inability to withstand the pressure being exerted from West Germany.[35] The altercation between Ulbricht and Rau, sparked by Nasser's reversed decision on the Egyptian mission in the GDR, was perhaps not surprising in the light of the deep-rooted personal rivalries that existed amongst the SED (Sozialistische Einheitspartei Deutschlands – Socialist Unity Party of Germany) cadres. Mutual wariness pitted the old communists, like Ulbricht, who had escaped Nazi persecution by taking shelter and living a relatively comfortable life in the Soviet Union against those, like Rau, who had spent their exile in concentration camps.[36] On being stripped of his German citizenship (in 1937), and having relocated to Moscow, Ulbricht had worked to forge an internal resistance movement in Germany by keeping ties with the German communists who had stayed behind, or, after Hitler's attack on the Soviet Union in 1941, by attempting to 'convert' German prisoners of war 'into anti-Fascists' while hammering Soviet indoctrination and propaganda leitmotifs into them.[37] However, and to his bitter disappointment, indigenous resistance to Hitler's government and policies never reached the critical mass that would have been necessary to defeat the Nazis from within – a blow that would affect both his postwar stance towards (or, in Carola Stern's words, his 'complex ... hatred' of)[38] the (East) German people, and, inversely, his sense of obligation towards the Soviet Union, the liberators, whose stance in international affairs he would soon seek to emulate. Heinrich Rau's exile years had been more eventful than that. After spending two years in various German prisons between 1933 and 1935, Rau then left for Prague – to reach Moscow and finally Spain, where he joined the struggle in the Spanish Civil War.[39] There, he alternated the fighting with 'the old daily grind: learning, grumbling, still more learning', in other words the reading, with his comrades, of key texts of the Marxist–Leninist doctrine.[40] Having been wounded in the fighting, Rau left for France, where he was arrested, in 1939, and handed over to the Gestapo, in 1942. He spent the years between 1943 and 1945 in the Mauthausen concentration camp, the last to be liberated by the Allies. In July 1945, Rau was already back in Berlin, ready to take on the task of building a new, socialist Germany from scratch.[41] Figures like Rau 'who suffered [...] and yet did not give up' served as powerful role models for many of the younger SED cadres, which augmented Ulbricht's aversion towards old communists like Rau.[42] Furthermore, Rau had been one of the (few) politburo members who had openly attacked Ulbricht's incompetence in economic matters during the delicate months of the 1953 uprising. On that occasion, he had even come to suggest that the GDR deserved a new leader, and that Ulbricht should be replaced. He was one of the very few to have survived the purge of SED ranks in the early 1950s, possibly also thanks to the fact that the Soviets held him in high regard – indeed, they themselves had toyed with the idea of replacing Ulbricht at the time, and Rau was one of the candidates they had had in mind when sketching the future of a post-Ulbricht GDR.[43] This option, however, never materialized, and in 1953 Ulbricht successfully managed to quash any internal opposition. However, this also meant that in 1955 Rau did not have to face Ulbricht's fury alone. Soviet Ambassador to the GDR Georgy Pushkin tried to mediate between the two – in fact, he took Rau's side. During a meeting in East Berlin, Pushkin confirmed that all that Rau had claimed about the Egyptian readiness to open a trade mission in East Berlin stemmed from Nasser's own words. And although 'of course one cannot call Nasser a liar in public', the East Germans should wait for the opportune moment to remind the Egyptian leader of the promises he had made to the GDR.[44] More broadly, Pushkin exhorted Ulbricht to slow down the quest for international recognition, in the Middle East and elsewhere. He emphasized how dangerous the

GDR's policy of using the springboard of economic relations to jump to diplomatic recognition could be.[45] This attitude, from the Soviets' perspective, was not helpful. Instead, Pushkin highlighted, this would only result in ensuing 'Western countermeasures', without bringing any geopolitical advantage to the Soviet bloc. The dispute between Ulbricht and Rau thus ended up as a quarrel between Ulbricht and his Soviet masters. These, in 1955, did not approve of his 'overeager' foreign-policy ambitions.[46]

Nevertheless, the Soviets did prove willing to support the GDR's economic – rather than politico-diplomatic – ventures in the region, as long as the East German comrades refrained from using commercial and economic arrangements to tie the selected country to establishing diplomatic relations. The message was reiterated during a meeting of the Socialist Council for Mutual Economic Assistance (COMECON) in the summer of 1956.[47] The council officially approved of the idea that the GDR intensify its contacts with the Levant, with the aim of signing economic and cultural, though not diplomatic, agreements. In order to ensure that the GDR would be in a position to intensify its economic exchange with the Middle East, the COMECON agreed that Poland and the Soviet Union should increase their exports of, respectively, glance coal and coke, and ore, to East Berlin. This was not necessarily good news for the East Germans, who did not trust the Poles to live up to their commercial promises. Indeed, the East Germans had long been complaining about the fact that Polish deliveries fell far short of respecting their economic obligations towards the GDR.[48] Nonetheless, COMECON support was better than nothing. In late June 1956, a meeting of the East German Council of Ministers decided to begin a *kulturpolitisch* offensive, consisting mostly of cultural, educational and propaganda initiatives in the Middle East, which would accompany the GDR's economic offensive in the region.[49] After the blow suffered in Egypt, the GDR was determined to intensify its efforts to break through in the Levant. The Soviets, however, as Pushkin's words should have made clear, were not ready to see the GDR succeed in the Middle East in the way that Ulbricht was yearning for.

Therefore, when the East Germans again attempted to forge political ties with two more countries in the region – this time, Lebanon and Libya – Moscow again intervened to cool down the East German enthusiasm.[50] Ulbricht, in an allegedly 'very harsh' exchange, pointed to the fact that establishing political, not just economic, contacts with the Arab countries was crucial to strengthen the legitimacy of the GDR.[51] In order to back up his arguments about the Middle East, Ulbricht referred to the shaky political situation in Poland. In Poznań, a protest for fairer work conditions and political freedoms that started on 28 June 1956 had soon turned into a full-fledged uprising. A change of leadership in the local communist party had followed and, in the summer of 1956, Ulbricht understandably worried that the GDR may be the next Soviet satellite to vacillate under the weight of growing popular discontent and internal cracks amongst politburo members. In his view, the events in Poland showed that the GDR desperately needed to augment its international credibility, which would also reinforce the stability of its domestic political scene. Establishing political ties with the countries of the Arab Middle East could be a way to secure this aim.[52] For the time being, however, the Soviets were not to be persuaded. The option of consular or diplomatic relations with the countries of the Levant had to be suspended, Ulbricht's frustration notwithstanding.

The East German leadership, however, was not to be discouraged by continual Soviet rebukes of the SED's foreign policy, and persisted with its cultural and economic exchanges with the countries of the region. During a visit to the GDR in early August 1956, held as part of the cultural policy offensive announced by the Council of Ministers earlier that year, the governor of Egypt's Liberation (*Tahrir*) Province expressed his wish to establish an Egyptian trade mission in East Berlin before long – a news item emphatically celebrated in the GDR's Party press.[53] The previous week, East German President Wilhelm Pieck had sent a message to Nasser to congratulate him on the fourth anniversary of Egypt's Revolution Day, celebrating the Free Officers' seizure of power from the monarchy that had begun on the evening of 22 July 1952, guided by Nasser and others. The West Germans derided Pieck's note, claiming that Nasser had in fact announced that from 1956 onwards the celebrations of Revolution Day would shift to 18 June, marking the first anniversary of the last British troops' departure from the Canal Zone.[54] Pieck's telegraph, West German commentators emphasized, betrayed the East German lack of eye for detail when dealing with their Egyptian partners.[55] However, the Egyptian leader did not seem to mind, and telegraphed his wishes of 'glory and happiness' back to Wilhelm Pieck.

And, three days later, Nasser surprised the world by announcing the nationalization of the Suez Canal. Interestingly for the East Germans, Nasser's nationalization speech singled out the West German Holocaust compensation payments to Israel as just another example of how the Western powers constantly chose to side with Israel, and against the Arab world.[56] Indeed, the Egyptian leader fiercely denounced US hesitancy to financially support Egypt, especially because, he claimed, Washington was so openly subsidizing Israel – amongst other ways, via Bonn's compensations to the Jewish State. Though softening the blow by claiming that the reparations agreement had been signed by West Germany 'under American pressure', Nasser specifically mentioned Bonn's reparations to Israel in his speech on Egypt's 'battle against imperialism and the methods and tactics of imperialism'.[57] The fact that West Germany, and the reparations to Israel, featured in Nasser's nationalization speech gave credence to a series of claims that East German propaganda had been making since the West German–Israeli deal was signed: that this agreement was, in fact, just another Western machination aimed at the subjugation of the Arab peoples.[58] It was now time to exploit the situation.

The Suez Crisis – an East German Opportunity?

The Western powers swiftly organized an international conference, to be held in London, to discuss the consequences of Nasser's move. Omitting to mention the fact that the East Germans had not only not been invited to the London Conference but had also been turned away at the UK border after trying to gatecrash the international diplomatic summit,[59] Deputy Foreign Minister Schwab commented that Bonn's participation in the conference essentially confirmed that West Germany's foreign policy rested on 'the interests of the big monopolies'.[60] Bonn was seen as privileging the imperialist powers rather than the struggle for liberation of the oppressed peoples of the Levant, and it worked actively against their striving for emancipation from colonial rule.[61] During the conference, newly appointed Soviet Foreign Minister Dmitry Shepilov did point out that it could not 'be considered normal that just one German state was invited' to participate at the conference, but the question of East German participation was quickly brushed aside.[62] After all, Moscow had much more important business to conduct in

London than protecting East Berlin's wounded ambitions: the Soviet Presidium had sent Shepilov to the conference to show that the Soviet Union was an important player in the Middle East and that it was able, more than any Western power, to come up with policy solutions that respected and safeguarded the interests of Third World countries.[63] East German propaganda insisted on an anti-West German line. In Schwab's words,

> [The FRG] supports the claims of auctioneers of the nationalized Suez Canal Company [... and] this shows Bonn's real attitude, which for years now has expressed itself through the material support for Israel in the battle against the freedom of the Arab peoples.[64]

In the wake of the first London conference on Suez, the news spread that Nasser had proposed an alternative gathering, to be held in Egypt, to discuss the future use of the Suez Canal. This time East German diplomats worked hard to ensure that Moscow would guarantee that the GDR, too, was invited to the negotiations. East German participation at the Cairo conference would have implied that the GDR – and not only the FRG – was being internationally recognized as a legal successor of the German Reich that had signed 1888 the Convention of Constantinople, which defined the legal status of the Canal, declaring that 'it shall always be free and open' to ships of all countries, and this would have strengthened East Germany's broader claims to sovereignty and international recognition. The Soviets did eventually come round to promising their support for the East German request that East Berlin's representatives would, this time, be allowed to take part in the international debate on the Suez Canal and its future.[65] However, the unexpected Anglo–French–Israeli attack on Egypt (code-named 'Operation Musketeer'), prevented the East Germans from enjoying the fruits of the invitation that they had worked so hard to secure.

The British–French–Israeli aggression against Egypt seemed to justify the oft-repeated East German protests about the subversive potential of the West German reparation payments to the Jewish State, as the East German Prime Minister was soon to point out.[66] On 2 November 1956, Otto Grotewohl addressed the Volkskammer with a statement about the Suez events. The message was later translated into

English and circulated amongst the relevant Middle Eastern countries:[67] 'The aggression against Egypt reveals all the brutality of imperialist colonial policy', announced Grotewohl, adding by way of further condemnation, 'It shows that there is no equality of rights between the colonial powers and the countries marching forward on the way to national independence.' Grotewohl asserted East Berlin's 'sympathy' for the Egyptian 'struggle for national independence and self-determination', displaying the GDR's support for the country's postcolonial subjects. His declaration, however, placed specific emphasis on the difference between East and West German policies:

> The Government of the German Federal Republic [...] approves of and actively supports the British and French colonial policy. It grants the aggressive circles of Israel more than three thousand million German marks of so-called reparation payments which are used by Israel in her fight against the national independence movement of the peoples of the Near East. During the London Suez Conference the Federal Government supported the viewpoint of the colonial powers and turned against the justified demands of Egypt. The colonial attitude of the Federal Government does not contribute to strengthen the international reputation of the German people. Therefor the Government of the GDR calls on the Government of the German Federal Republic to immediately stop assisting Israel.[68]

Grotewohl made two important points. First, his words associated Bonn with the aggressors, the former colonial powers. Second, he identified it, through the *Wiedergutmachung* (compensation/reparation) payments agreed to by the FRG, as the enabler of Israel's military aggression against Egypt. Arab representatives had been worrying about the impact that West German restitutions would have on strengthening Israel since the early 1950s. In 1956, Grotewohl's message attempted to pin the blame for the Suez War on Bonn. The East German press reinforced Grotewohl's statements: 'It is without a doubt that these deliveries substantially contributed to Israel's military potential'.[69]

The request to West Germany for a U-turn on the matter of reparations was repeated by the GDR Foreign Ministry in the aftermath of the crisis. After a UN ceasefire came into force, on 7 November, a statement was issued by the East German Foreign Minister Lothar Bolz. The minister highlighted the fact that the Suez War would not have been possible without the transfer of goods and money from the Federal Republic to the Jewish State. Thus, the statement concluded that Bonn should now pay reparations to Cairo, to repair the damage inflicted upon Egypt by the Israeli invasion:

> The Government of the German Democratic Republic turns to the Government of the Federal Republic of Germany with the request to transfer to the Republic of Egypt the so-called reparations to Israel, which allowed the armament of the Israeli aggressor, in order to compensate for the damages inflicted upon the Republic of Egypt by the Israeli troops.[70]

After the Suez War, both the intensity and frequency of East German attacks against the West German presence in the Middle East, and against West German–Israeli ties, increased. Directives for the establishment of an East German general consulate in Cairo were dispatched on the same day that the French and British troops completed their removal from the area.[71] The attacks against Israel, and against *Wiedergutmachung*, became an integral part of this policy change, and a tactical device of prime importance to advancing East German recognition claims in the Middle East. The personnel of the East German trade mission in Egypt, reporting to Berlin on 17 December 1956, articulated a series of policy recommendations for the MfAA. The top three were: first, to support 'Egypt's neutrality policy'; second, to 'exploit Egypt's neutrality policy in order to attain political recognition of the GDR'; third, to defeat the 'West German strong influence {in Egypt}, for example through further political declarations of the GDR about the relationship between West Germany and Israel'.[72]

A West German analysis emphasized that the Suez Crisis had witnessed the 'first, big [propaganda] campaign' against West Germany in the Middle East – a campaign that had at its core an emphasis on the ties between the Federal Republic and Israel.[73] Indeed, the GDR leadership's stance regarding Nasser's nationalization of the Suez Canal featured, to no small degree, the FRG and its support for the Jewish State – a theme that Nasser himself had emphasized in his nationalization speech. Trade Minister Rau defined Nasser's move as 'the exercise of a legitimate right of the Egyptian people that built this Canal'.[74] Yet it was not through words alone that the GDR hoped to ingratiate itself with the Egyptians. Indeed, the SED cadres' public stance on the Suez Crisis was propped up by a spree of solidarity gestures that East German politicians, at national and local levels, directed to their Egyptian counterparts during the crisis. These included telegrams of solidarity, shipments of medicaments, food and clothing, as well as more substantial contributions. Between August and September 1956, East German and Egyptian journalists exchanged materials, information and visits.[75] And, in December 1956, the governor of the Egyptian Tahrir Province, Mohammed Hassanein, telegraphed his thanks to the East German press association for having defended the 'cause of justice, freedom and independence' when reporting on Egypt and the Suez Canal question.[76] The East German Peace Council (*Friedensrat*) claimed to have organized and hosted about 250 meetings in six weeks in the GDR in order to sensitize the population to the events that were taking place in the Middle East, inviting speakers from Egypt, Iraq, Syria and other countries.[77] The East German youth organization Freie Deutsche Jugend (FDJ) received hundreds of spontaneous applications on the part of volunteers eager to depart for Egypt.[78]

In 1956, East German cadres repeatedly showcased their readiness to send pilots in order to guarantee the continued flow of goods via the Suez Canal following its nationalization, as well as volunteers from the ranks of the National People's Army, the riot police, border police and military instructors and engineers.[79] In early November 1956, Foreign Minister Lothar Bolz went to Moscow to again insist on East German diplomatic recognition in the Middle East. The aim of his visit was to assess, with the help of the Soviets, whether 'the support of Egypt via material help and eventually also the dispatch of volunteers on the part of the GDR' could lead to a 'faster diplomatic recognition' on the part of Egypt, and whether this would be in line with the policies of the Soviet bloc.[80] Soviet Deputy Foreign Minister Valerian Zorin maintained that there was no need to send East German volunteers to fight.[81] Despite this, the SED's Central Committee resolved to make the most of the 'British-French aggression', which, 'undoubtedly' offered advantageous possibilities to intensify economic and political relations between the GDR and the Arab states.[82] Three years later, Grotewohl was officially invited to visit Egypt, and six years after that Ulbricht received an official invitation to visit Cairo. That was his first ever chance to visit a country outside of the Soviet bloc, and he had worked long and hard to make it happen.[83]

Conclusion

Few periods in the history of the Soviet Bloc and the Middle East are as momentous as the months of 1955 and 1956. The formation of the Baghdad Pact and the announcement of the Czechoslovak–Egyptian arms deal revealed that neither superpower was willing to simply allow the other to penetrate the Middle East without putting up a serious fight – while at the same time doing everything possible to avoid direct military confrontation. In 1956, Nasser's unilateral announcement of the nationalization of the Suez Canal clearly indicated that Third World powers were now a force to be reckoned with. The ensuing Anglo–French military intervention in support of Israel exposed the cracks within the Western alliance – just as the coincident crushings of the Polish and Hungarian uprisings did for the Warsaw Pact countries. All these developments contributed to shaping Ulbricht's perception, in 1955–6, that if the GDR wanted to consolidate its sovereign status and international allure it had to do so by reaching out to the countries of North Africa and the Middle East. In turn, the East German experience with Egypt over the same period proved to be crucial for improving the SED's understanding of what could and couldn't work, when dealing with Third World countries. Sustained propaganda campaigns on their own were certainly not enough to win the hearts and minds, and pockets, of the non-aligned world. However, lacking anything else, it was crucial to persist with key messages that connected the East German struggle against West Germany to whatever struggle the country in question was fighting in its own region. When translating this principle into practice with Egypt, the German–German struggle was likened to Cairo's fight against imperialism, and to Egypt's enmity vis-à-vis Israel. From a material point of view, although not yet strong enough to be considered a serious strategic partner by many Third World leaders, from the second half of the 1950s onward the East German economy would strengthen and East Berlin's leverage vis-à-vis the Soviet Union and other Soviet bloc countries would strenghten. In order to succeed in gaining recognition from Third World leaders, the GDR needed to become better at understanding when to strike and when to wait. Paradoxically, in the mid-1950s time was on East Germany's side.

Ulbricht's policy towards the Arab Middle East, in the mid-1950s, combined his own ambitious geopolitical agenda with his domestic priorities. According to the former, the GDR should consolidate its role internationally and attract Third World countries to Khrushchev's Soviet bloc, acting as a beacon of the socialist world. The latter pushed him to secure his own post at a time in which his leadership position, and the East German domestic political situation as a whole, was in flux. East German manoeuvres in the Middle East in 1955 and 1956 also reflected the frustration arising from the constant juxtaposition of great expectations and bitter disappointments. This frustration explains the disillusionment within the East German diplomatic establishment, and the bickering between East German ambassadors and the SED leadership between 1955 and 1956. The same resentment – on top of old political rivalries – explains the competition and recriminations amongst the various East German offices in charge of framing and implementing foreign policy, such as Ulbricht's Politburo and Rau's Ministry for Trade. It was this disgruntlement that the Soviets attempted to redress by simultaneously encouraging and constraining Ulbricht's ambitions. This entailed simultaneous support for East German economic expansion into the Arab Middle East and a curb on East German attempts to gain a political and diplomatic presence in the area.

In his contested memoirs, Khrushchev claimed that 'we [the Soviets] wanted our comrades in the GDR to be genuinely independent – to be able to build their own diplomatic, cultural, and economic relations with socialist and capitalist countries alike, according to their own interests and needs'.[84] In fact, in 1956 Moscow deemed it necessary to restrain East Berlin's ambitions in the Middle East – and to do so more than once. First, when the Soviet ambassador to the GDR, Georgy Pushkin, 'felt compelled' to take Rau's side against Ulbricht after Nasser decided not to follow through with his promise to open an Egyptian trade mission in the GDR in 1956.[85] On that occasion, Pushkin pointed out that Nasser's decision might in fact benefit the Soviet bloc, if not the GDR, by appeasing the West. Then, when Soviet Deputy Foreign Minister Valerian Zorin had to reiterate to Ulbricht that 1956 was certainly not the time to go seeking international recognition in the Middle East, in the midst of one of the most difficult times for the

Soviet bloc. Uprisings in Poland and Hungary, creeping unrest in East Germany and the Soviet Union itself, and the emerging challenge to the Soviet leadership posed by Mao Zedong's China were some of the main issues that rendered Ulbricht impatient to reach out to the Third World, and Khrushchev anxious not to let Ulbricht strike. True, Moscow in 1956 did prop up the GDR's efforts in the region, by encouraging it, via COMECON, to foster its commercial relations with the countries of the region. Yet, this meant that the East German ambition to establish diplomatic relations with countries outside the Soviet bloc had, for the time being, to be curtailed. Contrary to Khrushchev's remembrances, in 1956 he did not simply want East Berlin to be 'genuinely independent' – especially not if this might entail the risk of Western countermeasures or precipitate events in the Middle East, thereby sucking the Soviet Union into conflicts that Moscow was not interested in fighting.

Notes

1. Quoted in Wilfried Loth, *Die Sowjetunion und die deutsche Frage: Studien zur sowjetischen Deutschlandpolitik* [The Soviet Union and the German Question: Studies on Soviet Policy on Germany] (Göttingen, 2007), p. 95.
2. Emphasis added. *Dokumente zur Außenpolitik der DDR* [Documents on the Foreign Policy of the German Democratic Republic] (hereafter, DADDR), vol. I, Wilhelm Pieck's speech, following his election as President of the German Democratic Republic, 11 October 1949.
3. Referenced in Hope M. Harrison, *Driving the Soviets up the Wall: Soviet-East German Relations, 1953–1961* (Princeton, 2003), p. 67.
4. See Volker Gransow and Konrad H. Jarausch (eds), *Uniting Germany: Documents and Debates 1944–1993* (Oxford, 1994), p. 13.
5. Bulletin of the Press and Information Office of the Federal Government (Bonn), 'Jede Anerkennung der "DDR" ein unfreundlicher Akt' [Every Recognition of the "GDR" an unfriendly act], 13 December 1955, p. 1.
6. Laurie A. Brand, *Official Stories: Politics and National Narratives in Egypt and Algeria* (Stanford, CA, 2014), pp. 27–43.
7. Benny Morris, *Israel's Border Wars, 1949–1956: Arab Infiltration, Israeli Retaliation, and the Countdown to the Suez War* (Oxford, 1993).
8. The Non-Aligned Movement was formally founded in 1961, but the 1955 Bandung Conference was a major stepping stone in this process. See, for example, Nataša Mišković, Harald Fischer-Tiné and Nada Boškovska (eds), *The Non-Aligned Movement and the Cold War: Delhi – Bandung – Belgrade* (London, 2014).

9. Robert B. Rakove, *Kennedy, Johnson and the Nonaligned World* (New York, 2013), pp. 10–11.
10. See, for example, the Chinese comments on Nasser's participation to the conference in: Report from the Chinese Foreign Ministry, 'Comments on the Asian-African Countries from the Participating Countries after the Conference', 10 May 1955, History and Public Policy Program Digital Archive, PRC FMA 207-00059-01, available at http://digitalarchive.wilsoncenter.org/document/114686.pdf?v=7da7212d322f913e70a1a651bb9d9f92 (accessed September 2017).
11. On German–German rivalry in the Middle East see, for example, Wolfgang G. Schwanitz, *Deutschland und der Mittlere Osten im Kalten Krieg* [Germany and the Middle East during the Cold War] (Leipzig, 2006); Katja Engler, *Die deutsche Frage im Nahen Osten. Politische Beziehungen der Bundesrepublik Deutschland zum Irak und zu Jordanien 1951–1965* [The German Question in the Middle East. Political Relations of the Federal Republic of Germany with Iraq and Jordan, 1951–1965] (Berlin, 2007); Massimiliano Trentin, '"Tough negotiations". The two Germanys in Syria and Iraq, 1963–1974', *Cold War History* 8 (3) (2008), pp. 353–80.
12. Malcolm Kerr, *The Arab Cold War: Gamal 'Abd Al-Nasir and His Rivals, 1958–1970* (London, 1971).
13. Diane B. Kunz, *The Economic Diplomacy of the Suez Crisis* (Chapel Hill, NC, 1991), p. 40.
14. Ibid., See also Sven Olaf Berggötz, *Nahostpolitik in der Ära Adenauer: Möglichkeiten und Grenzen, 1949–1963* [Middle East Policy in the Adenauer Era: Possibilities and Limitations, 1949–1963] (Düsseldorf, 1998), pp. 335ff.
15. Laurent Rucker, 'The Soviet Union and the Suez Crisis', in David Tal (ed.), *The 1956 War: Collusion and Rivalry in the Middle East* (New York, 2001), p. 67; R. Stephens, *Nasser: A Political Biography* (London, 1971), pp. 170ff.
16. Guy Laron, 'Cutting the Gordian Knot: The Post-WWII Egyptian Quest for Arms and the 1955 Czechoslovak Arms Deal', Cold War International History Project, Working Paper No. 55, 2007.
17. William Glenn Gray, *Germany's Cold War: The Global Campaign to Isolate East Germany, 1949–1969* (Chapel Hill, NC, 2003), p. 257, fn. 141.
18. The Egyptians, however, did not open their GDR consulate until three years later.
19. 'Minister Rau im Außenministerium Indiens' [Minister Rau in India's Foreign Ministry], *Neues Deutschland*, 5 November 1955, p. 1.
20. 'Vom ganzem Herzen Glück ... ' ['Heartfelt congratulations ...'], *Freies Volk*, 1 August 1956.
21. As highlighted, for example, in Steffen Wippel, *Die Außenwirtschaftsbeziehungen der DDR zum Nahen Osten* [The External economic relations of the GDR with the Near East] (Berlin, 1996), p. 17.
22. Ingrid Muth, *Die DDR-Aussenpolitik, 1949–1972: Inhalte, Strukturen, Mechanismen* [GDR Foreign Policy, 1949–1972: Contents, Structures, Mechanisms] (Berlin, 2000), p. 103.

23. Georgy Mirsky, Soviet expert, quoted by Vladislav M. Zubok, *A Failed Empire? The Soviet Union and the Cold War from Stalin to Gorbachev* (Chapel Hill, NC, 2009), p. 139.
24. SAPMO-BArch DY 30/11348, Proceedings of the SED Ambassador's conference held in [East] Berlin on 1 and 2 February 1956.
25. Ibid.
26. Ibid., Muth, *DDR-Aussenpolitik*.
27. SAPMO-BArch DY 30/11348, Proceedings of the SED Ambassador's conference held in [East] Berlin on 1 and 2 February 1956.
28. Hermann Wentker, *Außenpolitik in engen Grenzen. Die DDR im internationalen System 1949–1989* [Foreign Policy within Narrow Confines. The GDR in the International System 1949–1989] (Munich, 2007).
29. Christian Ostermann, 'The United States, the East German Uprising of 1953, and the Limits of Rollback', Cold War International History Project, Working Paper No. 11 (Washington, DC, 2003).
30. See, for example, Katherine Pence, 'Showcasing Cold War Germany in Cairo: 1954 and 1957. Industrial Exhibitions and the Competition for Arab Partners', *Journal of Contemporary History* 47 (1) (2012), pp. 69–95.
31. See, for an early example, PA AA B11 381, West German Embassy in Cairo to Federal Foreign Ministry in Bonn. 'Establishment of diplomatic relations between Egypt and the Soviet Occupation Zone', Mirbach, 7 January 1955.
32. Gray, *Germany's Cold War*, pp. 53ff.
33. BAK B 206/614, Intelligence Report: Disagreements between Ulbricht and Rau, 29 December 1955.
34. PA AA B12 238, Memo: 'Controversies in the so-called GDR about the question of international recognition', Voigt, 7 January 1956.
35. Ibid.
36. Catherine Epstein, *The Last Revolutionaries: German Communists and Their Century* (Cambridge, MA, 2003), p. 125.
37. Wolfgang Leonhard, *Child of the Revolution* (London, 1979), esp. p. 150.
38. Carola Stern, *Ulbricht: Eine politische Biographie* [Ulbricht: A political biography] (Cologne, 1964), p. 96.
39. 'Wer war wer in der DDR?' [Who was who in the GDR?], 'Heinrich Rau'. Available at https://www.bundesstiftung-aufarbeitung.de/wer-war-wer-in-der-ddr-%2363%3B-1424.html?ID=2766 (accessed September 2017).
40. Quoted and translated in Epstein, *Last Revolutionaries*, p. 64.
41. Ibid.
42. Ibid., p. 229; Peter Grieder, *East German Leadership 1946–1973: Conflict and Crises* (Manchester, 1999), fn. 239, p. 154.
43. Joanna Granville, 'Ulbricht in October 1956: Survival of the *Spitzbart* during Destalinization', *Journal of Contemporary History* 41 (3) (2006), pp. 477–502; Harrison, *Driving the Soviets Up the Wall*, pp. 49ff.
44. PA AA B12 238, Memo: 'Controversies in the so-called GDR about the question of international recognition', Voigt, 7 January 1956.

45. BAK B 206/614, BND Intelligence Report: Disagreements between Ulbricht and Rau, 29 December 1955.
46. PA AA B12 238, Memo: 'Controversies in the so-called GDR about the question of international recognition', Voigt, 7 January 1956.
47. BAK B 206/619, BND Intelligence Report. Statements of the new acting Foreign Minister of the 'GDR' Sepp Schwab, 7 July 1956.
48. Sheldon R. Anderson, *A Cold War in the Soviet Bloc: Polish-East German Relations, 1945–1962* (Boulder, CO, 2001), esp. pp. 114–58.
49. BAK B 206/618, Intelligence Report. News from the Foreign Ministry of the 'GDR', 29 June 1956.
50. Wentker, *Außenpolitik*, p. 172.
51. BAK B206 620/184, Intelligence Report. Reason for the visit of the governmental delegation of the 'GDR' to Moscow and earlier clashes about the all-Germany policy of the SED, n.d.
52. Ibid.
53. The province was an army-run 'major public-sector venture of the Nasser era', as explained in Walter Armbrust, 'The Iconic Stage: Martyrologies and Performance Frames in the January 25th Revolution', in Reem Abou-El-Fadl (ed.), *Revolutionary Egypt: Connecting Domestic and International Struggles* (London, 2015), p. 94. For the reaction of the SED mouthpiece to the words of the governor, see 'Freude über Solidarität der DDR' [Delight at solidarity with the GDR], *Neues Deutschland* (Berlin), 2 August 1956, p. 1.
54. 'Nasser-Telegramm ohne Bedeutung' [Nasser telegram meaningless], *Der Tag*, 1 August 1956.
55. Ibid.
56. These payments were agreed upon in 1952. On West German–Israeli relations, see Yeshayahu A. Jelinek, *Deutschland und Israel, 1945–1965. Ein neurotisches Verhältnis* [Germany and Israel, 1945–1965. A neurotic relationship] (Munich, 2004); and on the East German attempts to exploit this situation in the Arab world during the 1970s and 1980s, see Jeffrey Herf, *Undeclared Wars Against Israel: East Germany and the West German Far Left, 1967–1989* (New York, 2016).
57. *Documents on International Affairs* 1956, 'Speech by President Nasser at Alexandria announcing the nationalization of the Suez Canal Company, 26 July 1956' (London, 1956), pp. 99–100.
58. See, for example, Gerda Weinberger, 'Die Politik des westdeutschen Imperialismus während des Suezkonflikts' [The Politics of West German imperialism during the Suez conflict'], in Heinz Tillmann (ed.) *Westdeutscher Neokolonialismus* [West German Neocolonialism] (Berlin, 1963), pp. 165–221.
59. 'German Reds Barred: Their Decision to Attend Suez Talks Rejected by Britain', *New York Times*, 14 August 1956, p. 3.
60. 'Bonn – Feind der Araber' ['Bonn – enemy of the Arabs'], *Neues Deutschland* (Berlin), 9 August 1956, p. 2.
61. Ibid.

62. 'Suez-Delegation. Was ist normal?' ['Suez delegation – what is normal?'], *Der Spiegel*, 34/1956, 22 August 1956, p. 9.
63. Rucker, 'The Soviet Union and the Suez Crisis'.
64. Ibid.
65. PA AA: MfAA A 9351/25, Excerpt from a file note from comrade Roßmeisl on a conversation in the 3. European Department of the Soviet Ministry of Foreign Affairs on 21 September 1956.
66. 'Die Aggressoren Einhalt gebieten!' ['Stop the aggressors!'], *Neues Deutschland* (Berlin), 1 November 1956, p. 1.
67. On the same day, the USSR Ambassador to Israel had been recalled and Soviet Foreign Minister Shepilov had stressed Soviet readiness to send Egypt military assistance. 'UdSSR fordert Zügelung der Aggressoren' [The Soviet Union calls for the curbing of the aggressors], *Neues Deutschland* (Berlin), 6 November 1956, p. 1.
68. PA AA: MfAA A 9351/16, The Ministry of Foreign Affairs to the Kingdom of Saudi Arabia. See also 'DDR verurteilt Aggression in Nahost' [The GDR condemns the aggression in the Middle East], *Neues Deutschland* (Berlin), 7 November 1956, p. 1.
69. 'West Deutschland und der Nahe Osten' [West Germany and the Middle East], *Die Wirtschaft* (Berlin), 20 December 1956, p. 9.
70. PA AA: MfAA A 9286/12, Statement by the Ministry of Foreign Affairs on the withdrawal of British and French troops from Egypt, n.d.
71. PA AA: MfAA A 9826/61, Schwab (East Berlin) to Scholz (Cairo), Directive on a proposal to the Egyptian government on the establishment of a GDR general consulate in Cairo, 23 November 1956.
72. PA AA: MfAA A 9286/3, GDR Trade Mission (Cairo) to MfAA (East Berlin) Preliminary assessment for the analysis of Egypt's foreign policy line. Stude, 17 December 1956.
73. Deutsches Orient Institut, *Die Angriffe der SBZ gegen die Nahostpolitik der Bundesregierung* [The Attacks of the Soviet Occupation Zone (the German Democratic Republic) against the Near East Policy of the Federal Government] (Hamburg, 1964), pp. 7 and 101.
74. *Neues Deutschland* reported the message of the Egyptian president almost in its entirety: 'Präsident Gamal Abdel Nasser erklärt in Alexandria: "Wir nehmen uns, was uns gehört"' [President Gamal Abdel Nasser states in Alexandria: 'We are taking what is ours'], *Neues Deutschland* (Berlin), 29 July 1956, p. 5. Rau's comment was also reported in *Neues Deutschland*: 'Enge Beziehungen Ägypten-DDR' [Close Egypt-GDR relations], 9 August 1956, p. 2.
75. Following an agreement signed in Cairo between Egyptian and GDR radio and press representatives on 6 August 1956: Deutsches Orient Institut, *Die Angriffe der SBZ*, pp. 7 and 101.
76. 'Dank an DDR-Journalisten' [A thank-you to GDR journalists], *National-Zeitung*, 23 August 1956.

77. BAL-SAPMO DY 30/J 2/2J/311, Memorandum. The events in the Middle East and the population of the GDR. Willmann, 13 December 1956.
78. BAK B 206/628, Volunteers for Egypt, 3 December 1956.
79. A series of reports was published by the East German news agency Allgemeiner Deutscher Nachrichtendienst (General German News Service, ADN) between 25 October 1956 and 21 January 1957. See also BAL-SAPMO NY 4090/216, Prime Minister Otto Grotewohl gives a statement on the Suez question before Egyptian journalists, n.d.; BAK B 206/626, BND Intelligence Report. Money collection for Egypt is supposed to finance deployment of volunteers from the NVA, the People's Police and other fighting groups, 13 November 1956; BAK B 206/1960, *Information*, 'Fachkräfte für Ägypten' [Specialists for Egypt], No. 16, September 1956; and BAK B 206/1960, *Information* No. 18, 'Ausbilder für Ägypten' [Instructors for Egypt], October 1956.
80. BAK B 206/626, BND Intelligence Report. 'Pushkin stopped "GDR" help for Hungary', 16 November 1956.
81. BAK B 206/627, BND Intelligence Report. Dr Bolz reports on talks with the Soviet Deputy Foreign Minister, Sorin, in Moscow, n.d.
82. BAK B 206/627, BND Intelligence Report. Discussion at the end of the 29th party plenum of the Central Committee of the SED, 29 November 1956.
83. Although full diplomatic recognition did not materialize until 1969.
84. Nikita S. Khrushchev, *Khrushchev Remembers: The Last Testament*, translated and edited by Strobe Talbott (London, 1974), p. 502.
85. PA AA B12 238, Memo: 'Controversies in the so-called GDR about the question of international recognition', Voigt, 7 January 1956.

CHAPTER 2

REASSURING COMRADES AND COURTING THE NON-ALIGNED: POLAND, THE 1957 GOODWILL TOUR IN ASIA AND THE POST-OCTOBER DIPLOMACY

Marek W. Rutkowski

The *New York Times* correspondent Harrison E. Salisbury sat in the office of Polish Prime Minister Józef Cyrankiewicz on 12 October 1957. It was just a week after the launch of the first artificial satellite, Sputnik 1, by the Soviet Union, but Cyrankiewicz was far from euphoric. Some people in Warsaw got up early in the morning to see Sputnik crossing the sky, but he did not. 'I already believed that the satellite existed', he told the American, adding that it was a '"common success" for world science' and expressing doubt in its 'political potentiality'. The Pole believed that not all scientific achievements must necessarily tip the balance of power. Indeed, he went a step further:

> He said he thought it would be better for the world to talk about coexistence and cooperation and not balance of power. He cited a statement by Prime Minister Jawaharlal Nehru of India regarding the enormous gap between man's achievements in technique and in human relations. In human relations, M. Cyrankiewicz said, many people still behave like the cavemen. There must be an equilibrium.[1]

Cyrankiewicz was a complex figure. An Auschwitz Death Camp survivor known for his love of fast cars, alcohol and women, he was at the same time probably the most intelligent member of the entire Polish leadership, had a sense of humour and was able to engage intellectuals.[2] The *New York Times* wrote in early 1957 that he was 'alone among the Polish leaders in displaying anything resembling a Westerner's conception of politicking'.[3] This ability certainly included opportunism, for Cyrankiewicz was able to forgo his socialist past in order to further an alliance with communists after World War II. Officially a head of government since 1947, he retained the position until 1970 (apart from a short interval from 1952 to 1954). However, in the wake of a forced merger between the communist Polish Workers' Party and the Polish Socialist Party in 1948, Cyrankiewicz served as a token socialist in the highest leadership and did not wield much real power.[4] Nikita Khrushchev remarked in his memoirs that Cyrankiewicz's premiership 'was the result of an agreement, the product of certain political combinations, and apparently Comrade Cyrankiewicz, being an intelligent person, understood all this'.[5]

Even though after 1956, the Premier assumed a more prominent role, forging a partnership with Władysław Gomułka, Cyrankiewicz could hardly formulate foreign policy on his own. His conversation with Salisbury was a reflection of new trends in Polish diplomacy, made possible by the reforms of the Polish October. The mention of Jawaharlal Nehru does not seem coincidental. Up to 1956, Polish relations with Asia were rather limited, but in early 1957 Cyrankiewicz became the 'face' of an extended tour across the continent, encompassing seven countries. An analysis by Radio Free Europe noted at the time that the Premier was 'believed to be strongly in favor of building up a fund of good will with China and India which might be useful to Poland if ever their good offices with the Soviet Union are required'.[6] Indeed, besides economic and cultural aims, the objectives of the trip seem to have been twofold. On the one hand, socialist allies of Asia had to be briefed about changes in Poland and reassured. On the other hand, more intriguingly, there seems to have been an interest in engaging non-aligned Asian countries,[7] primarily India, as allies of Polish foreign-policy initiatives.

There seems to be a consensus amongst Polish historians that Poland lacked an independent foreign policy from the tightening of the Stalinist grip in 1947 until the de-Stalinization of the Polish October, which brought to power Władysław Gomułka, advocating 'a Polish road to socialism' in 1956. Historian Włodzimierz Borodziej asserts that 'from 1948 to 1955, there is not a single issue with regard to which one can speak of a specifically original Polish [...] idea in comparison to the foreign policy of the USSR or of any independent Polish initiative'.[8] Fellow historian Jacek Tebinka calls 1956 a turning point in the history of Polish diplomacy. Władysław Gomułka, until recently imprisoned after demotion for 'rightist-nationalist deviation', was elected first secretary of the Polish United Workers' Party at the Eighth Plenum in October 1956, signalling the victory of a reformist faction within the Party over a dogmatic one. The new leadership held its ground in the face of the sudden arrival of Khrushchev in Warsaw, and refused to allow Moscow to continue to prescribe personnel arrangements. It was Khrushchev who had to back down and call off an intimidating advance of the Soviet Army towards Warsaw. Initially, Moscow was not sure how to deal with Poland and the possibility of intervention was not entirely dismissed, but the outbreak of the uprising in Hungary a week later and the Chinese opposition to open confrontation changed the situation and secured the position of the new Polish leadership.[9]

As historian Anita Prażmowska asserts, 'Gomułka claimed for Poland a degree of independence within the Soviet bloc, which no other state, with the exception of Yugoslavia, was able to do.' A devout communist, he never questioned the Soviet bloc as such, but, operating within a narrow room for manoeuvre acceptable to the Kremlin, was able to be flexible, particularly in dealing with internal issues.[10] In foreign policy, as well, a degree of independence increased considerably. On the one hand, Poland was able to rebuild its bilateral relations with the Soviet Union on a much more equal basis. On the other, previously non-existent room for independent international initiatives was now available.

Historians have written extensively on Polish–Soviet relations in this period.[11] The new leadership proved assertive – first, in demanding the expulsion of the Soviet-appointed minister of defence, Konstantin Rokossovsky, and later in the negotiation of the Agreement on the Legal Status of Soviet Troops Temporarily Stationed in Poland. The Poles were also able to successfully demand compensation for removal of Polish property after World War II, and to strongly push for the repatriation of Poles, including prisoners, still in the Soviet Union.

On the international plane, on 2 October 1957, Foreign Minister Adam Rapacki presented a plan for the neutralization of Central Europe – perhaps the most significant multilateral initiative by the Polish Government in the entire Cold War. The Rapacki Plan was essentially a Polish offer to agree to a ban on the production and stockpiling of nuclear arms, in exchange for a similar agreement on the part of both German states. Accepted by Czechoslovakia and East Germany, thus creating a potential zone of four countries, the proposal was ultimately rejected by the West. For years it was unclear whether the plan was truly a Polish initiative. In the light of recent archival research conducted by historians in Warsaw, however, its Polish authorship can be proven beyond reasonable doubt. Jacek Tebinka asserts that 'there is no doubt that the idea emerged in Warsaw' as an attempt to frustrate plans for arming West Germany with atomic weapons.[12] Piotr Wandycz convincingly argues that even though Polish diplomacy took Soviet concepts as a starting point, the developed plan reflected Polish national interests and the extent of consultations with communist comrades was limited.[13] Piotr Długołęcki, in turn, links the origins of the plan with early Polish considerations dating as far back as the end of 1955. He acknowledges that elements of the proposal were adopted by the Soviets, but asserts that the Poles insisted on presenting it as their independent initiative, which the Kremlin accepted.[14]

These two matters – relations within the Soviet bloc, on the one hand, and Polish ideas of disarmament, on the other – would dominate Prime Minister Cyrankiewicz's visit to Asian countries in the spring of 1957. Hitherto neglected by scholars, this trip offers an excellent opportunity to analyse Polish post-October diplomacy and assess its scope of opportunities and limitations. The visit would coincide with a new engagement with Asia and the non-aligned world, which was already in the offing after a series of disorganized attempts to deal with the region in previous years.

Engaging Asia

When journalist Ryszard Kapuściński was sent to India in 1956 on his first overseas assignment, he knew virtually nothing about the subcontinent. No book about India appeared in Poland until 1956, and Kapuściński had to resort to searching second-hand bookshops for pre-war publications.[15] Indeed, this could be said of the Far East in general, with the possible exception of China. Poland followed Soviet suit in its relations with Asia; before Stalin's death, the interactions were rather minimal.[16] Initial efforts to reopen a Polish mission in Thailand and establish one in Indonesia did not bear fruit.[17] With the exception of Beijing, Pyongyang and Ulan Bator,[18] Poland opened no embassies in any Far Eastern country until 1954 and limited its attention to the region to periodical proclamations of support for national-liberation movements[19] and occasional trade agreements.[20] The first real engagement with Asia came through the country's nomination to play a role on two control bodies established in July 1953 in Korea: the Neutral Nations Supervisory Commission and the Neutral Nations Repatriation Commission. This was followed by a similar assignment to three International Commissions for Supervision and Control in Indochina established by the 1954 Geneva Conference. In both cases, however, the selection seems to have been a result of a membership in the Soviet bloc and happened without any active seeking on Warsaw's part.[21] Poland exchanged ambassadors with India in 1954, with Burma in 1955 and *chargé d'affaires* with Indonesia the same year. With the exception of India, however, relations were not highly developed and Poland had difficulties in expanding trade. In terms of cooperation with 'socialist countries of Asia', exchanges with North Korea were limited and with Mongolia virtually non-existent. Only trade with China and North Vietnam (the Democratic Republic of Vietnam; DRV) was expanding, though the latter required the extending of credits.[22]

Department V, a permanent unit to deal with Asia and the Middle East, was established within the Polish Ministry of Foreign Affairs only in June 1954.[23] Even then, until mid-1956 most of the top positions within this department were filled on an acting basis.[24] A proposal to review the work of Department V from August 1956 offers an early glimpse into the Polish understanding of the political situation unfolding in Asia and Africa at the time of decolonization and its importance for the communist bloc. According to this analysis, the national-liberation struggle carried out by colonial countries after World War II brought about changes in the international balance of power. The document went on in detail:

The victory of the Chinese revolution was an event of great historical significance, which contributed to a serious deepening of a universal crisis of capitalism. People's Republic of China, Democratic People's Republic of Korea, Democratic Republic of Vietnam strengthened the socialist camp. A number of liberated countries of Asia and Africa like India, Indonesia, Burma and Egypt [by] carrying out a struggle to consolidate their independence, to free [themselves] from the yoke of foreign capital, [and by] carrying out the neutralist policy, are frustrating imperialist preparations for war. An international zone of peace was established encompassing countries of different socio-political systems.[25]

This analysis closely followed the new approach taken by Nikita Khrushchev in dealing with the Third World. Contrary to the indifferent years of Stalin, Asia now became the place where the Soviets could compete with the West. As historian Robert J. McMahon explains, '[t]he capaciousness of the "peace zone" category enabled the Soviets to embrace even capitalist-leaning Third World states as worthy partners – so long as their policies and interests dovetailed with those of the Soviet Union'.[26] The most visible demonstration of this new trend was a long tour undertaken by Khrushchev and Soviet Premier Nikolai Bulganin across India towards the end of 1955. This 'mission of friendship' was soon followed by a flow of aid, starting a competition between Santa Claus and Ded Moroz for the hearts and minds of the Third World, as historian David Engerman aptly terms it.[27]

The Polish leadership did not seem to go nearly as far as Moscow, but the practical point brought up by the ministry document was the need for increased engagement with Asia and Africa, which required reforms of Department V. It seems clear that the earlier approach towards Asia was rather disorganized, with a lack of qualified personnel specialized in that part of the world. Now it was suggested that the ministry take a more systemic route, including proper training and detailed study of the decolonizing world.[28] By November 1956, personnel arrangements within Department V were reviewed and hitherto temporary appointments were made permanent, including those of department director and heads of divisions. The majority of the personnel, however, still consisted of fresh graduates – 'youth just out of school', as Department Director Edward Słuczański described them.[29]

Initial initiatives in Asia nonetheless still seem to have been rather random and disorganized. In May 1956, for instance, the State Commission for Economic Planning came up with the idea of extending paid technical aid to 'some economically backward countries', particularly in the areas of hydrology and water-resource management. Polish diplomats in Asia and the Middle East were tasked with discussing this possibility with potential host governments, but the response was not encouraging and the matter appears to have been dropped.[30] A few months later, in September 1956, the Polish Institute of International Affairs prepared what appears to have been a comprehensive memorandum regarding the prospects of developing economic relations with 'countries economically undeveloped'. The document urged an expansion of economic ties and emphasized possible benefits for the Polish national economy. The Ministry of Foreign Trade concurred, noting, however, the need for fostering cultural relations, acquiring background knowledge and studying foreign languages as prerequisites for success in this area. The ministry frankly admitted having 'only scant information about [the] economic situation of backward countries and their developmental capabilities'.[31] Talking points prepared for a visit of Chinese Premier Zhou Enlai to Warsaw in January 1957 described Polish policy towards Asia as 'active'. However, besides mentioning opening diplomatic posts in Rangoon and Jakarta in 1955 and fostering cultural and trade relations 'as much as possible' there was little substance to support this claim in the document itself.[32] This was to change, however, with the Asian trip of Prime Minister Cyrankiewicz.

The Foreign Ministry was aware that consequences of the Polish October could be difficult to understand in full for Polish diplomats posted in Asia, who had not experienced the events first-hand at home. In order to familiarize them with the new situation, a meeting was organized in Hanoi on 4 April 1957. Ambassadors in India and Burma, the *chargé d'affaires* in North Vietnam and representatives of the Polish delegations to the International Control Commissions in Indochina gathered in the capital of North Vietnam[33] to listen to a detailed briefing by Deputy Foreign Minister Marian Naszkowski. Prepared for internal use, this fascinating document offers a glimpse into the Polish Foreign Ministry's understanding of the opportunities and challenges that it was facing. According to Naszkowski's presentation, the leadership was satisfied with relations within the Soviet bloc and boasted of the 'introduction of new principles in relations between socialist countries' based on 'Leninist principles of equality' as a result of the Polish October. In terms of the international situation, Warsaw believed that 'October [had] created new possibilities for [its] foreign policy' by demonstrating that Poland was not a Soviet satellite. While the Poles pledged to 'defend the unity of our camp', the document indicated that Warsaw opposed 'automatic emulation of initiatives' within the bloc and was happy with the room for manoeuvre achieved. Speaking specifically about Asia, Naszkowski noted that a setback in relations had resulted from the Soviet intervention in Hungary, but also recognized a 'convergence of interests in fundamental matters between countries of this area and our camp'. 'This convergence', he noted, 'is seen most of all in aspiration for [the] preservation of peace [. . .] matters of disarmament and [the] uplifting of [the] economy in these countries'.[34]

Prime Minister Cyrankiewicz started his Asian tour on 18 March in Burma, and the above mentioned briefing for it was arranged during his time in North Vietnam. The principles shared with ambassadors were to guide his whole trip, though emphasis was tailored to each hosting country specifically. In relations with socialist allies, the aim was to explain the events of October and promote new relations within the bloc. In relations with non-aligned countries, the focus was on the convergence of views on peace and disarmament, which could form a basis for cooperation.

Reassuring Allies and Shaping the Bloc: Cyrankiewicz in the Far East

Józef Cyrankiewicz was supposed to visit Asia in November 1956, reciprocating earlier visits by Indian Premier Jawaharlal Nehru and Prime Minister U Nu of Burma. Plans for a joint India–Burma trip were far advanced, including flight arrangements worked out with Air India, and even shortly after the Polish October the visit seemed set to progress as scheduled.[35] However, a last-minute postponement was occasioned by ongoing Polish–Soviet negotiations in Moscow. In these changed circumstances, the trip was moved to spring 1957 and turned into a long tour encompassing seven Asian countries and ending in the Soviet capital. Cambodia was added as a third neutralist country and the fraternal socialist states – North Vietnam, North Korea, China and Mongolia – joined the itinerary as well.

Cyrankiewicz was very pleased with his warm reception in North Vietnam. 'The Vietnamese avoided all possible controversies. They exploited us to the limit in terms of [seeking] information about our internal matters. They showed huge interest in these matters. They themselves didn't speak much', the Prime Minister reported.[36] His relief should not be surprising. Hanoi was initially apprehensive about changes in Poland, and its leadership never fully subscribed to Khrushchevian de-Stalinization.[37] Even though the visit went well, disagreements surfaced during the drafting of a joint communiqué. Only after a long discussion were the Poles able to secure an explicit statement of approval for changes in Poland, although any direct mention of the Eighth Plenum was omitted.[38]

Discussions in North Korea (the Democratic People's Republic of Korea; DPRK) and Mongolia seem to have been shorter and more general, primarily focused on possible economic cooperation and the situations in these countries. In both cases, the Poles encountered attempts at formulating communiqués in the 'old spirit', indicating subservience to Moscow and issuing strong anti-imperialist statements. On both counts, the Poles were successful in softening the approach and pointed out to the need for 'using a language, also in matters regarding relations within [the] socialist camp, matching the spirit of our times'.[39]

It seems clear that Poland took it upon itself to influence its Asian allies in their approach to relations within the bloc and on democratization. 'A process of socialist renewal is a central aspect of the internal situation in the socialist countries of Asia', a document prepared shortly after the visit explained. 'This process [however] progresses differently in different countries' the narrative followed. The document used very delicate wording, but it was pointed out that the 'process of renewal' in North Korea and North Vietnam was carried out 'cautiously and slowly' and through a top-down approach. The analysis concluded that the realities in these two countries and in Mongolia might cause difficulties in understanding Polish policies after October 1956. It was, therefore, assumed that the role of the Polish foreign service would be to inform its allies about the changes and achievements, and 'even sometimes to work on [their] understanding of the Polish

October'. Poland was also eager to gather all available information about similar processes taking place in Asian socialist countries.[40]

There was no need to explain the Polish situation in Beijing since Zhou Enlai had been comprehensively briefed in January 1957 in Warsaw.[41] Cyrankiewicz, however, made a point of thanking Mao Zedong for 'his interest in Poland and help in the difficult situation', referring to Chinese support for the Polish October. 'Thanks to that', he continued, 'we can better build socialism after the 8th Plenum'.[42] It was noted in diplomatic corps in Beijing that Cyrankiewicz's visit was much better received than that of a recent Czechoslovak delegation, with Chairman Mao himself present during the signing of a joint communiqué and at a reception. Also, Mao's acceptance of an invitation to visit Poland was viewed as sensational, and contributed to a belief that Beijing completely supported the new Polish leadership.[43] Indeed, China was singled out in Polish documents as the only Asian ally who 'understands [the] intentions and paths of Polish post-October policies'. This understanding was attributed to the Chinese' own process of democratization, 'carried out on a large scale and in consistent manner'. 'The Party and the leadership of the PRC decided not to constrain this creative ferment as long as it is within the limits of not threatening basic principles of the [political] system', the Polish Foreign Ministry commented approvingly.[44]

This seeming convergence of Polish–Chinese interests did not go unnoticed in the Western world. The *Washington Post* wrote that

> [Cyrankiewicz's] eight days in China were a landmark in Poland's efforts to wriggle loose from sole dependence on the Kremlin. For the Chinese comrades enunciated Mao Tse-tung's new theology of letting 'all flowers bloom' within the Communist society, of persuading and explaining rather than persecuting, of tolerating internal dissent so long as it isn't enmity.[45]

Indeed, the short-lived Hundred Flowers Campaign in China coincided with the Polish October. Cyrankiewicz told Mao in this context that 'the example of China [...] activity and works of Comrade Mao are of great importance to us'.[46] Consequently, the Chinese ambassador in Poland, Wang Bingnan, told his counterpart in Beijing, Stanisław Kiryluk, that the Polish Prime Minister's visit had brought both countries even closer together in their evaluation of political problems.[47] The mayor of Beijing, Peng Zhen, went a step farther in June 1957 telling a Polish diplomat that only parties in Poland and Yugoslavia could 'understand and accept changes happening in China', while others chose reserved silence.[48] It is also significant that Party Vice Chairman Liu Shaoqi, in conversation with Cyrankiewicz, found it fitting to compare the plight of Gomułka during the Stalinist period to the experiences of Mao in the 1930s, when the Party was following the Soviet model.[49] There was, however, little in the course of the visit to China that could be considered explicitly opposed to the Soviet Union.

The Poles were happy to exchange experiences and find commonalities; they appreciated Chinese support, but there is little evidence that any closer cooperation was contemplated. On the other hand, the Soviets must have been very sensitive on the matter for Khrushchev accused Cyrankiewicz in May 1957 of spreading anti-Soviet propaganda during his Asian tour. The information reportedly came from Kliment Voroshilov, chairman of the Presidium of the Supreme Soviet, who visited Vietnam and China shortly after the Poles left. Cyrankiewicz rejected the accusation in front of Khrushchev, asserting that the trip had not only been beneficial to Poland but also to the Soviet Union. He assured him that the talks were focused primarily on bilateral relations and did not touch upon the Soviet 'period of deviations'.[50] This was, however, not completely true. Cyrankiewicz would later recall that he said merely 'one hundredth of what [Khrushchev] did during the 20th Congress', which was closer to the truth.[51] There was not much in his talks in China that could be considered anti-Soviet, but he did talk about unequal treatment within the socialist bloc. The Prime Minister told Chairman Mao that the Polish defence industry was too inflated due to a lack of division of labour in the bloc. 'There was no division of labour, only division of duties, sometimes even without asking respective countries', he complained. Admitting that the situation was now improving, Cyrankiewicz said that the problem was still lacking a 'positive concept [of resolution]'. Predominantly, however, the talks concerned bilateral relations and experiences of dealing with errors and deviations, as well as economic difficulties in both countries.[52]

Khrushchev seems to have calmed down after his momentary outburst, and the matter was quickly resolved. Interestingly, it was Władysław Gomułka who was reportedly disturbed by the issue for a further six months. He told Khrushchev and Mao in November 1957 in Moscow that 'the matter needed to be resolved because the accusation was too serious'. Gomułka's mind was presumably put at rest when Mao reassured him that the Polish Premier had made only pro-Soviet comments throughout his stay in China.[53] It is clear that the Poles attempted to shape policies within the socialist bloc – without, however, offending the Soviets.

Counting on Non-Alignment? Cyrankiewicz in South East Asia

The part of the tour including India, Burma and Cambodia seems to have been even more intriguing than the visits to fraternal countries. The trip was ostensibly a goodwill tour, aimed at the participants learning about each other and fostering economic and cultural relations, which up to that point existed primarily in a nascent state. Fittingly, Cyrankiewicz was accompanied by the Minister of Culture and the Minister of Light Industry as well as deputy ministers of foreign trade and higher education. Relevant agreements in these fields were signed. However, circumstantial evidence suggests that the actual aims of the trip may have well been far beyond these rather limited achievements.

Some light can be shed by the recollections of Karol Kuryluk, minister of culture at the time, who joined Cyrankiewicz on the tour. Kuryluk had been a pre-war leftist newspaper editor, initially believing in the promise of a socialist state but quickly growing disgruntled with Stalinist Poland. He was briefly vindicated following the October reforms and given the portfolio of Minister of Culture, only to be sidelined two years later and sent to an unimportant diplomatic post in Austria.[54] His daughter, Ewa Kuryluk, remembers her father's impressions of the Asian tour. Kuryluk recalled the whole trip with distaste and remembered hiding under the airplane's wing to avoid being photographed with the official party at hosting airports. He believed that neither guests nor hosts were interested in the success of the whole trip. More importantly, however, Kuryluk believed that the actual aim of the tour was to secure support for an enlarged version of the Rapacki Plan, at the time under preparation, in which endeavour the delegation spectacularly failed.[55]

On the surface, it is difficult to find direct confirmation of Kuryluk's narrative in official documents. None mention the plan directly. The records in the Polish archives are incomplete and lack detailed minutes of conversations in India. Even a memo on drafting a joint communiqué in New Delhi, though preserved, misses one crucial page.[56] There is, however, an entire set of briefing documents prepared before the trip that offers an invaluable insight into the minds of the Polish leadership. One finds there an unusually strong emphasis on disarmament and collective security. The matter took up nearly four pages, and was ranked first in a list of 13 different political issues to be discussed.

The document stated that Poland believed in a universal collective security arrangement as its ultimate goal.[57] It was pointed out that India supported collective security measures through its opposition to military blocs, which could be a basis for discussions. Standing on the ground of universal security, the Poles would welcome a regional security arrangement as a step towards that goal. The document explicitly supported a security treaty for Europe with the participation of the USA, and suggested the possibility of a similar arrangement for Asia. Going beyond the level of ideas, the paper stated directly, 'While discussing problems of security, it is possible to touch upon the issue of a zone of limited and controlled armament in Europe', which would be an important contribution to detente and possibly a first step towards 'broader arrangements'. Finally, in the most unequivocal manner, the document stated that the 'Indian attitude towards collective security makes it possible to discuss these matters generally and form quite firm statements against armament [...] in the joint communiqué, as well as *to garner their {Indian} political support* for initiatives regarding the zone of limited armament in Europe'.[58]

It seems beyond reasonable doubt that the initiative mentioned in the last paragraph was in fact the Rapacki Plan for the denuclearization of Central Europe, even though nuclear weapons were not mentioned. It is striking to find nearly identical wording in Rapacki's speech at the United Nations on 2 October 1957 when the plan was proposed:

> Until a system of collective security is created in Europe, we will support even partial solutions directed towards the same ultimate objective. We will support them whether they are part of a larger

plan or the subject of separate agreements. Accordingly, we have felt and we still feel that it would be useful to set up limited and controlled armaments zones in Europe.[59]

It is also clear that Cyrankiewicz and his entourage were tasked not merely with discussing the matter but also with securing support for the initiative. There is, however, no indication that the Poles attempted to put together any wider international arrangement with their Asian partners. Karol Kuryluk must have overstated the matter. In any case, as it turned out, even their limited goal proved to be hard to achieve.

It is difficult to be completely sure whether Cyrankiewicz shared all the points with his Indian interlocutors. Clearly, however, the Premier tried to bring them up in his speeches. 'Mr. Cyrankiewicz made it clear that his country stood for disarmament and collective security so that the catastrophe of war could be averted', wrote the *Times of India*, reporting on the civic reception held in New Delhi on 25 March 1957.[60] A day later, Cyrankiewicz gave a speech to the Indian Council of World Affairs, a leading political think tank, declaring,

> We are determinedly opposed to all military blocs. We understand and appreciate India's attitude to this question. We, too, wish the elimination of all blocs, all bases on foreign soil and military pacts.[61]

It is clear that the Prime Minister tried to strike all the right notes. 'The main hall of Sapru House was packed to capacity and the audience repeatedly cheered the Polish Prime Minister as he discussed the common features between the foreign policies of Poland and India', an Indian journalist noted.[62] Cyrankiewicz followed his briefing papers by asserting that Polish membership in the Warsaw Pact was necessary due to 'German militarism', and expressed hope that in the future this would no longer be the case. The Polish position was that the German question could only be solved through collective security, in which neutralization could be the first step.

Commentaries in the Indian press were generally positive and the trip was considered a success in Poland, partly due to the seemingly effective stating of the Polish position vis-à-vis Bonn. This was particularly important for the Polish leadership in the wake of a visit to India by

Heinrich von Brentano, foreign minister of West Germany.[63] Cyrankiewicz himself also seemed satisfied. He recalled years later that 'Nehru displayed a full understanding of European problems' and 'of the aspirations of the Polish people about the integrity of the western frontiers of Poland', which he reportedly saw 'as an integral condition of peace in Europe and the world'.[64]

The Polish Prime Minister might have had fond memories of meeting Nehru. However, his positive narrative does not seem to find confirmation in documents. In terms of the collective security or the Rapacki Plan, there seems to be very little that Cyrankiewicz actually achieved after ten days in the subcontinent, quite in line with the recollections of Karol Kuryluk. Problems also occurred during the drafting of the joint communiqué. The Poles hoped for a strong condemnation of imperialism and military blocs, but to no avail. The secretary-general of the Indian Ministry of External Affairs, N. R. Pillai, pointed to a lack of uniform understanding of imperialism and differences between internal proclamations, often undertaken by Nehru, and international communiqués.[65] The Poles, however, believed that India became less forceful in foreign policy due to the poor international reception to its initially moderate position on the Soviet intervention in Hungary and a general worsening of the international situation.[66]

As it transpired, the Indians were, in turn, disgruntled by what they perceived as a forceful Polish attitude. Secretary-General Pillai confidentially told British High Commissioner Malcolm MacDonald that '[t]he Poles had been very difficult on certain matters in Delhi', apparently hoping to trade their recognition of Kashmir and Goa as belonging to India (rather than, respectively, to Pakistan and Portugal) for India's support of the Polish position on 'European questions such as their relations with East and West Germany'. Pillai found Polish pressure to insert these matters into the joint communiqué 'rather objectionable' and asserted that India had firmly resisted. Unfortunately, Pillai did not specify if these instances included views on collective security arrangements. He also criticized Cyrankiewicz for infusing into his speeches 'partisan propaganda', which as a guest he should not have done. More importantly, Pillai's overall opinion was that even though Poland acquired a level of internal freedom after October 1956, Cyrankiewicz 'supported Russian policy without any qualification whatever' in international affairs.⁶⁷ This might have been the biggest obstacle in convincing India to support the Polish position.

Although most attention was clearly paid to India, there is evidence that Poland also hoped to discuss the collective security matter, or at least to ensure condemnation of military blocs, in Burma and Cambodia, two other non-aligned destinations. Cyrankiewicz was more impressed by a warm reception in Phnom Penh, although in both countries he saw a dangerous struggle between neutralist and pro-American policies. Cambodia was willing to accept a Polish draft of a joint communiqué, but asked for the removal of a specific mention of military blocs.⁶⁸ The leadership in Rangoon was less forthcoming, though in both countries the joint communiqués were more in line with Polish aims, with a clear condemnation of imperialism, than the one signed in New Delhi.⁶⁹ There is also evidence that the matter was mentioned in North Vietnam, though it did not figure prominently in discussions. More importantly, however, it was not discussed in Moscow, where Cyrankiewicz talked to Khrushchev on the way back.⁷⁰ Contrary to Indian belief, Poland does not seem to have been acting on Moscow's instigation.

It is difficult to fault New Delhi for not seeing genuine Polish initiative behind the facade of socialist brotherhood. Even officials like Karol Kuryluk, remaining outside of the decision-making circles, thought that the whole concept was a Soviet ploy. The entire communist bloc embraced and started courting non-alignment following Khrushchev's lead. Moreover, the concept of universal collective security arrangements that Poland supported was originally a Soviet idea advocated during the 1954 Berlin Conference and later at the Geneva Summit in 1955.⁷¹ But, as indicated earlier, the Rapacki Plan was a Polish idea aimed at serving Polish national interests. It is intriguing that Cyrankiewicz chose to omit any mention of the matter in conversation with Khrushchev in April 1957 in Moscow en route home. He otherwise briefed the Soviet leader on other issues discussed in all the countries visited. It is possible that the omission was caused by the lack of tangible results. More probably, however, the Poles believed that after the events of October 1956 they were allowed to conduct a more active foreign policy and independently seek allies for their policies.

As Marian Naszkowski told Polish diplomats gathered in Hanoi, Poland was against the emulation of initiatives within the bloc after the Polish October. Even though the Rapacki Plan needed the final green light from Moscow, it was a pet project of Polish diplomacy and the latter saw fit to seek support amongst the non-aligned countries. The similarities between the Polish approach and the non-aligned position on disarmament and military blocs made a possible alliance conceivable and, given India's prominent role at the UN, highly desirable. Indeed, after the lack of success in New Delhi, the efforts did not cease. In December 1957, after the plan was officially announced, Adam Rapacki personally cabled the ambassador to India, Juliusz Katz-Suchy, regarding the matter. Referring to the upcoming NATO Council meeting in Paris, he wanted to engage India in order to frustrate possible NATO attempts at arming West Germany with nuclear weapons. Rapacki went to great lengths to compare the Polish approach to NATO with the Indian attitude towards the Southeast Asia Treaty Organization (SEATO), and implied that arming the former with atomic weapons may likewise result in arming the latter.[72] It does not seem that this attempt was successful, for Katz-Suchy cabled Warsaw that coverage of the Rapacki Plan had been disappointingly limited in parliamentary debates in New Delhi.[73] The Indian attitude towards the plan seems to have remained lukewarm throughout. Nevertheless, the very fact that Poland chose to directly approach Asian non-aligned states in order to further its foreign-policy goals testifies to a level of independence acquired after the Polish October.

Conclusion

It is striking to see how different the Polish approach was to joint communiqués in fraternal and non-aligned countries during Cyrankiewicz's visit to Asia. In North Vietnam, North Korea and Mongolia, the Poles did their best to mitigate the tone and limit the emphasis on imperialism. In India, Burma and Cambodia, they did the exact opposite, hoping for stronger condemnation of military blocs and imperialist policies. The trip clearly shows that Poland after October 1956 had a degree of autonomy and could be flexible in foreign policy, tailoring its approach to different audiences.

Poland's relations with Asia were merely in their nascent stage in 1956. In line with the new Soviet focus on the Third World after Stalin's demise, there was a need for stronger engagement and more information. This was to be accomplished, at least partially, by the Prime Minister's trip. The Polish October, however, created a new reality in which the visit would take place. On the one hand, the experience of reformulating relations with the Soviets prompted Warsaw to take up the role of a broker of new relations with fraternal parties in the Third World, in which Warsaw believed that China could be its partner. The 'old spirit' of subservience to Moscow had to be replaced by 'Leninist principles of equality', and inflexible condemnation of the West in joint communiqués by specific issues of mutual relations. On the other hand, its new-found room for manoeuvre in foreign policy enabled Poland to stop emulating initiatives and come up with ideas of its own. The Rapacki Plan for the denuclearization of Central Europe was the most significant example of Poland's autonomy. Not only did the Poles prepare the project on their own, they started seeking allies on their own outside of the realm of the Soviet bloc. Support could plausibly be available in non-aligned Asia, and India was specifically approached as an important voice at the UN, where it had for years advocated disarmament and opposed military blocs.

On neither count did the Poles openly oppose Soviet policies, even though Khrushchev lost his temper – accusing Cyrankiewicz of anti-Soviet activities in Asia. The Premier may have spoken too freely, but Warsaw knew just how far it could go. Poland's policies still needed the final green light from Moscow, and none of them would contradict the general line from the Kremlin. Yet, even though Warsaw was not able to assume a position similar to Yugoslavia and its autonomy in foreign affairs was conditional, the opportunities were now much greater and the Poles would seize them in order to further their national interests.

Notes

1. Harrison E. Salisbury, 'Polish Premier Urges Step By Powers to Solve Issues', *New York Times*, 13 October 1957, p. 1.
2. Piotr Lipiński, *Cyrankiewicz: Wieczny Premier* [Cyrankiewicz: Everlasting Prime Minister] (Wołowiec, 2016).
3. 'Durable Polish Premier: Jozef Cyrankiewicz', *New York Times*, 21 February 1957, p. 12.
4. Lipiński, *Cyrankiewicz*.
5. Nikita Khrushchev, *Memoirs*, edited by Sergei Khrushchev, Vol. 3, *Statesman* (University Park, PA, 2007), p. 609.

6. RFE News and Information Service, 'The Communist Leadership in Eastern Europe II: Poland', 14 May 1959, p. 18, Open Society Archives. Available at osaarchivum.org/files/holdings/300/8/3/pdf/40-3-96.pdf (accessed October 2017).
7. For the sake of simplicity, the terms 'non-aligned' and 'neutralist' are used interchangeably throughout this chapter following a pattern adopted by H. W. Brands. See H. W. Brands, *The Specter of Neutralism* (New York, 1989), p. 10.
8. Włodzimierz Borodziej, '1956 As a Turning Point in Poland's Foreign Policy', in Jan Rowiński (ed.), *The Polish October 1956 in World Politics* (Warsaw, 2007), p. 328.
9. Jacek Tebinka, '1956 – Rok przełomu' [1956 – A Groundbreaking Year], in Wojciech Materski and Waldemar Michowicz (eds), *Historia Dyplomacji Polskiej*, Vol. VI 1944/1945–1989 (Warsaw, 2010), pp. 444–67.
10. Anita J. Prażmowska, 'Władysław Gomułka', in Steven Casey and Jonathan Wright (eds), *Mental Maps in the Early Cold War Era 1945–68* (Basingstoke, 2011), pp. 121–8.
11. See, for example, Andrzej Skrzypek, *Mechanizmy Autonomii: Stosunki Polsko-Radzieckie 1956–1965* [Mechanics of Autonomy: Polish-Soviet Relations 1956–1965] (Pułtusk–Warsaw, 2005).
12. Jacek Tebinka, 'Dyplomacja popaździernikowa (1957–1960)' [Post-October Diplomacy (1957–1960)], in Materski and Michowicz, *Historia Dyplomacji Polskiej*, p. 468.
13. Piotr Wandycz, 'Adam Rapacki and the Search for European Security', in Gordon A. Craig and Francis L. Loewenheim (eds), *The Diplomats, 1939–1979* (Princeton, NJ, 1994), p. 296.
14. Piotr Długołęcki, 'Nieznany kontekst planu Rapackiego' [The unknown context of the Rapacki Plan], *Sprawy Międzynarodowe* [International Affairs], No. 1 (2011), pp. 116–20.
15. Ryszard Kapuściński, *Travels with Herodotus* (New York, 2007).
16. An important exception was a Chinese-Polish shipping company - Chipolbrok. See, Janusz Wróbel, Chipolbrok. Z dziejów polsko-chińskiego sojuszu morskiego 1950–1957 [The Chipolbrok. Aspects of the history of the Polish-Chinese maritime alliance, 1950–1957] (Łódź, 2016).
17. Józef Łaptos and Andrzej Mania, 'Dyplomacja Polska wobec Zimnowojennego Podziału Świata (marzec 1947 – grudzień 1955)' [Polish Diplomacy and the Cold War World (March 1947 – December 1955)], in Materski and Michowicz, *Historia Dyplomacji Polskiej*, pp. 425–31.
18. The ambassador was residing in Moscow and was concurrently accredited to Mongolia.
19. Eugeniusz Gajda, *Polska Polityka Zagraniczna 1944–1974. Podstawowe Problemy* [Polish Foreign Policy 1944–1974. Fundamental Issues] (Warsaw, 1974), pp. 113, 124.
20. Łaptos and Mania, 'Dyplomacja Polska', pp. 425–31.
21. For a study on the Polish role in Korea and Vietnam and Polish-Chinese relations, see Margaret K. Gnoinska, 'Poland and the Cold War in East and Southeast Asia,

1949–1965', PhD dissertation, George Washington University, Washington, DC, 2009. For a study on the work of the International Control Commission in Vietnam, see Marek W. Rutkowski, '"Getting in the Ring with the Big Powers": India, Canada, Poland and the International Control Commission in Vietnam (1954–1964)', PhD dissertation, National University of Singapore, 2017.
22. Notatka dotycząca stosunków PRL z krajami Azji [Memo on Poland's relations with the countries of Asia], undated (before 28 June 1957), Archiwum Ministerstwa Spraw Zagranicznych [Archive of the Polish Ministry of Foreign Affairs; hereafter, AMSZ], Zespół [Group; hereafter, Z.] 12, Wiązka [Bundle; hereafter, W.] 28, Teczka [File; hereafter, T.] 678.
23. Zarządzenie Ministra Spraw Zagranicznych w sprawie ustanowienia Departamentu V [Directive of the Minister of Foreign Affairs concerning establishment of Department V], 9 June 1954, AMSZ, Z. 23, W.1, T. 1.
24. Przemysław Ogrodziński to Adam Rapacki, 26 May 1956, AMSZ, Z. 23, W.1, T. 1.
25. Projekt uchwały w sprawie pracy Dep. V [Draft resolution on the works of Dept. V], undated (before 8 August 1956), AMSZ, Z. 23, W. 1, T. 2.
26. Robert J. McMahon, *The Limits of Empire: The United States and Southeast Asia Since World War II* (New York, 1999), p. 73.
27. Ded Moroz (Grandfather Frost) is a Russian equivalent of Santa Claus. David C. Engerman, 'Learning from the East: Soviet Experts and India in the Era of Competitive Coexistence', *Comparative Studies of South Asia, Africa and the Middle East*, 33:2 (2013), p. 228.
28. Projekt uchwały w sprawie pracy Dep. V [Draft resolution on the works of Dept. V], undated (before 8 August 1956), AMSZ, Z. 23, W. 1, T. 2.
29. Edward Słuczański to Marian Naszkowski, Notatka w sprawie reorganizacji Departamentu V [Memo regarding reorganization of Department V], 6 November 1957, AMSZ, Z. 12, W. 28, T. 672.
30. Edward Słuczański to Przemysław Ogrodziński, Notatka służbowa [Official memo], 22 September 1956, AMSZ, Z. 12, W. 28, T. 668. All other documents related to this initiative can be found in this file.
31. M. Dichter (Ministry of Foreign Trade) to Adam Rapacki, 18 September 1956, AMSZ, Z. 12 W. 28, T. 667.
32. Tezy do rozmów z Premierem Czou-En-laiem [Talking points for conversations with Premier Zhou Enlai], undated (before 11 January 1957), in Krzysztof Ruchniewicz and Tadeusz Szumowski (eds), *Polskie Dokumenty Dyplomatyczne* [Documents on Polish Foreign Policy], Volume: 1957 (Warsaw, 2006), p. 15.
33. It is unclear why the chargé d'affaires in Indonesia did not participate despite the fact that his name appears in early correspondence regarding the briefing.
34. Notatka z odprawy szefów placówek w Azji Południowo Wschodniej odbytej w Hanoi dnia 4 kwietnia 1957 [Memo about a briefing for the heads of posts in South East Asia, which took place in Hanoi on 4 April 1957], AMSZ, Z. 12, W. 28, T. 673.
35. Bronisław Musielak (New Delhi) to Edward Bartol (Warsaw), 7 September 1956, AMSZ, Zespół Depesz [Collection of Dispatches; hereafter, ZD] 6/77,

W. 50, T. 640; Edward Bartol (Warsaw) (?) to Jerzy Grudziński (New Delhi), 22 October 1956, AMSZ, ZD 6/77, W. 50, T. 641.
36. Józef Cyrankiewicz (Beijing) to Gomułka-Rapacki (Warsaw), 10 April 1957, in Ruchniewicz and Szumowski, *Polskie Dokumenty Dyplomatyczne*, pp. 221–2.
37. For an analysis on de-Stalinization in Vietnam, see Peter Zinoman, 'Nhân Văn – Giai Phâm and Vietnamese "Reform Communism" in the 1950s. A Revisionist Interpretation', *Journal of Cold War Studies*, 13:1 (Winter 2011), pp. 60–100.
38. Notatka z rozmów przeprowadzonych w dniach 4 i 5 kwietnia 1957 w sprawie wspólnej deklaracji polsko-wietnamskiej [Memo regarding discussions conducted on 4 and 5 April 1957 regarding Polish–Vietnamese joint communiqué], undated, AMSZ, Z. 12, W. 28, T. 675.
39. Notatka dotycząca rozmów w K.R.L.D. przeprowadzonych dnia 16.IV.1957 w sprawie wspólnego komunikatu [Memo regarding discussions in DPRK on 16 April 1957 regarding joint communiqué], undated; Notatka z rozmów z dnia 18 kwietnia 1957 w sprawie wspólnego komunikatu z Mongolską Republiką Ludową [Memo regarding discussions on 18 April 1957 regarding joint communiqué with Mongolian People's Republic], undated, AMSZ, Z. 12, W. 28, T. 675.
40. Notatka dotycząca stosunków PRL z krajami Azji [Memo on Poland's relations with the countries of Asia], undated (before 28 June 1957), AMSZ, Z. 12, W. 28, T. 678.
41. Notatka z przeprowadzonych rozmów w dniach 11 i 12.I.1957 miedzy delegacjami Ch.R.L. i Polski [Memo regarding discussions conducted on 11 and 12 January 1957 between Chinese and Polish delegations], 16 January 1957, in Ruchniewicz and Szumowski, *Polskie Dokumenty Dyplomatyczne*, pp. 28–55.
42. Protokół z rozmowy odbytej przez Przewodniczacego Polskiej Delegacji Rządowej w Chinach, Premiera PRL J. Cyrankiewicza z Przewodniczącym ChRL Mao Tse-tungiem w dniu 8.4.1957 w siedzibie Mao Tse-tunga [Minutes of the discussion between head of Polish government delegation in China, Polish Premier J. Cyrankiewicz and Chairman of PRC Mao Zedong conducted on 8 April 1957 at the headquarters of Mao Zedong], 12 April 1957, in ibid., p. 233.
43. Stanisław Kiryluk (Beijing) to Przemysław Ogrodziński (Warsaw), 16 April 1957, in ibid., pp. 245–6.
44. Notatka dotycząca stosunków PRL z krajami Azji [Memo on Poland's relations with the countries of Asia], undated (before 28 June 1957), AMSZ, Z. 12, W. 28, T. 678.
45. Delia and Ferdinand Kuhn, 'Poles Try to Control Own Foreign Affairs', *Washington Post*, 27 May 1957, p. A6.
46. Protokół z rozmowy odbytej przez Przewodniczacego Polskiej Delegacji Rządowej w Chinach, p. 238.
47. Stanisław Kiryluk (Beijing) to Edward Słuczański (Warsaw), 28 April 1957, AMSZ, ZD 6/77 W. 55, T. 734.
48. Stanisław Kiryluk (Beijing) to Marian Naszkowski (Warsaw), 14 June 1957, AMSZ, ZD 6/77 W. 55, T. 734.

49. Notatka z rozmowy tow. Premiera J. Cyrankiewicza z tow. Liu Szao-tsi odbytej w Kantonie dnia 6.IV.1957 [Memo regarding conversation between Comrade Premier J. Cyrankiewicz and Comrade Liu Shaoqi conducted in Canton on 6 April 1957], undated, AMSZ, Z. 12, W. 28, T. 675.
50. Notatka z rozmów przeprowadzonych w dniu 24 i 25 maja br. między delegacją partyjno-rządową PRL i delegacją partyjno-rządową ZSRR [Memo regarding discussions conducted on 24 and 25 May 1957 between Polish party-government delegation and Soviet party-government delegation], undated, in Ruchniewicz and Szumowski, *Polskie Dokumenty Dyplomatyczne*, pp. 393–5.
51. Mieczysław F. Rakowski, *Dzienniki Polityczne 1969–1971* [Political Diaries 1969–1971] (Warsaw, 2001), p. 158.
52. Protokół z rozmowy odbytej przez Przewodniczacego Polskiej Delegacji Rządowej w Chinach, pp. 235–6.
53. Rakowski, *Dzienniki Polityczne*, p. 158.
54. For more background about Karol Kuryluk, see the autobiographical novels of his daughter: Ewa Kuryluk, *Goldi* (Warsaw, 2004) and Ewa Kuryluk, *Frascati* (Warsaw, 2009).
55. Conversation with Ewa Kuryluk, Warsaw, 11 May 2015. The author would like to thank Ewa Kuryluk, an internationally accomplished artist and author, for taking her time to share recollections and materials related to her father's time in government.
56. There is no evidence to suggest that this was intentional, though such a possibility cannot be completely dismissed.
57. 'Collective security arrangement' meant a form of guarantee system in Polish documents of the period. Even though the term has since then acquired a meaning closer to 'military alliance', it was seen as an alternative to such an arrangement at the time.
58. Tezy do rozmów i wspólnej deklaracji w Indiach [Talking points for the discussions and joint communiqué in India], undated, AMSZ, Z. 12, W. 9, T. 221 (emphasis added).
59. United Nations, General Assembly, Twelfth Session, *Official Records*, 697th Plenary Meeting, agenda item 9 (2 October 1957) (New York, 1958), p. 237.
60. 'Peace Policy Determined By Past Experience', *Times of India*, 26 March 1957, p. 7.
61. Jozef Cyrankiewicz, 'Poland and Her Neighbours', *Foreign Affairs Reports*, Vol. VI, No. 4 (April 1957), p. 33.
62. 'Membership of Warsaw Pact: Poland's Policy Defended', *Times of India*, 27 March 1957, p. 1.
63. Józef Cyrankiewicz (New Delhi) to Gomułka-Rapacki (Warsaw), 30 March 1957, in Ruchniewicz and Szumowski, *Polskie Dokumenty Dyplomatyczne*, p. 181. On the reaction in the Polish press: Eric Berthoud (Warsaw) to Foreign Office, London, 9 April 1957, British National Archives, FO 371 128823.

64. Oral History Interview with Mr Josef Cyrankiewicz (transcript), conducted by Shri B. R. Nanda, 23 October 1971, Nehru Memorial Museum and Library [hereafter, NMML], India.
65. Notatka z rozmów nad ustaleniem tekstu wspólnego oświadczenia polsko-hinduskiego odbytych w New Delhi w dniach 26 i 27 marca 1957 [Memo regarding discussions over formulating of Polish–Indian joint communiqué conducted in New Delhi on 26 and 27 March 1957], 27 April 1957, AMSZ, Z. 12, W. 28, T. 675.
66. Józef Cyrankiewicz (New Delhi) to Gomułka-Rapacki (Warsaw), 29 March 1957, in Ruchniewicz and Szumowski, *Polskie Dokumenty Dyplomatyczne*, pp. 177–8.
67. From UK High Commissioner in India to Commonwealth Relations Office, 3 April 1957, British National Archives, FO 371 128823.
68. Józef Cyrankiewicz (New Delhi) to Gomułka-Rapacki (Warsaw), 26 March 1957, in Ruchniewicz and Szumowski, *Polskie Dokumenty Dyplomatyczne*, p. 167.
69. Józef Cyrankiewicz (New Delhi) to Gomułka-Rapacki (Warsaw), 29 March 1957, in ibid., p. 178.
70. Notatka z rozmowy na Kremlu w dniu 19.IV.1957 [Memo regarding a conversation at the Kremlin on 19 April 1957], undated, in ibid., pp. 250–60.
71. Geoffrey Roberts, 'A Chance for Peace? The Soviet Campaign to End the Cold War, 1953–1955', *Cold War International History Project* (CWIHP) Working Paper 57 (October 2008).
72. Adam Rapacki (Warsaw) to Juliusz Katz-Suchy (New Delhi), 6 December 1957, AMSZ, ZD 6/77, W. 55, T. 724.
73. Juliusz Katz-Suchy (New Delhi) to Marian Naszkowski (Warsaw), 25 December 1957, AMSZ, ZD 6/77, W. 55, T. 723.

CHAPTER 3

'THEY ARE AS BUSINESSLIKE ON THAT SIDE OF THE IRON CURTAIN AS THEY ARE ON THIS': CZECHOSLOVAKIA AND BRITISH GUIANA

Jan Koura and Robert Anthony Waters Jr[1]

The ideological struggle at the heart of the Cold War created many odd international alliances. The symbiosis of interest between the Soviet bloc and radical Third World regimes rested on the shared belief that freedom from the West's colonial and neo-colonial embrace would lead to true freedom and economic development while undercutting the imperial base of Western economies, thus speeding up the West's inevitable transition to scientific socialism. The quiet relationship between Czechoslovakia and British Guiana – Great Britain's only South American colony – was one of the Cold War's many such unlikely pairings. The Czechoslovaks acted as the Soviet bloc's bridge into Latin America.

This chapter uses a series of Czechoslovak foreign-policy documents to show the evolution of Prague's policy in Latin America from 1948 to 1966. Two of these documents, which the Czechoslovaks called 'conceptions', assessed the state of their Latin America policy and offered guidance on how to continue strengthening Eastern bloc ties while undermining US regional hegemony. Joseph Stalin pursued a 'hands off' policy towards Latin America. That changed with First Secretary Nikita Khrushchev, who had high hopes for socialist transformation in the region following the victorious Cuban Revolution in 1959. By 1964, though, general malaise in the Soviet bloc came accompanied by the conclusion that revolution in Latin America was a distant prospect. The Czechoslovak 'conception' illustrated the change in attitudes over the intervening period. Czechoslovakia's relationship with British Guiana and its primary leaders, Cheddi and Janet Jagan, provides an excellent but little-known test case that illustrates this jagged path from ignorance to optimism to resignation.[2]

Stalinism and the Early Thaw, 1948–58

Amongst Soviet satellites, Czechoslovakia was well positioned to move quickly from foreign-policy stagnation to activism in Latin America. Czechoslovakia was a highly industrialized country, which had a brief postwar and more lengthy pre-war history of diplomatic and business relations with Latin America. The country also had a small pool of experienced diplomats who had survived Stalinist purges. In essence, Czechoslovakia was a known 'brand' in Latin America, which opened the door for the rest of the Soviet bloc. Initially, Czechoslovak trade missions began to mend economic ties with the region. Restoring business relations opened the door to rebuilding political and cultural ties, although a Czechoslovak conception document later admitted that the Communist Party and the government had done a poor job of coordinating their efforts. Trade with Latin America was small – less than 2 per cent of the national total – but it continuously grew and offered a crucial opening to create a Latin American future in which anti-imperialist movements would step up their struggle for economic and political independence. Czechoslovakia made progress despite US pressure on Latin American countries not to open relations.[3]

By the end of 1958, Czechoslovak policy makers believed that Latin America's 'colonial and dependent nations' had reached a new historical stage of development, evidenced by popular rebellions overthrowing dictatorships in Colombia, Venezuela and Cuba. The struggle against US imperialism had also begun, exemplified by Venezuela's 'tumultuous demonstrations'. In May 1958, demonstrators attacked the motorcade of US Vice President Richard Nixon and his wife, nearly killing them both.

The Czechoslovaks believed that they were in the best position to provide a 'counterweight against imperialism in Latin America'. Working with the other Soviet bloc countries, they could 'show Latin American countries the true path out of economic difficulties and help them end their dependence on the United States'. In the light of these developments, the Central Committee of the Czechoslovak Communist Party formally and completely revised its Latin American policy in June 1959, creating its first 'conception' of relations with the region. By this time, it had diplomatic relations with Mexico and every South American nation except Venezuela, Chile and Peru; the Soviet Union, by contrast, had relations with only Mexico, Uruguay and Argentina.[4]

The new conception stated that Czechoslovakia would help its allies, 'especially the Soviet Union', by following a 'far more active policy' in Latin America: expanding trade, cooperation and political relations across the region. The Czechoslovaks vowed to use trade relations as a wedge to increase political cooperation. They also planned to intensify cultural contacts by providing academic scholarships to students from the region. Unfortunately for them, communist heavy-handedness, everyday racism and bitterly cold winters often caused the scholarships to backfire, turning Latin America students into ardent anti-communists.[5]

Fidel Castro's revolution accelerated Czechoslovakia's plans. The Czechoslovak Communist Party (CCP) had been in occasional contact with Cuban communists since the early 1950s, but their first contact with Castro only came in December 1958 when his forces, working through a Costa Rican import-company front, asked Czechoslovakia for weapons. The Czechoslovaks quickly and enthusiastically contacted the Soviets, who showed remarkable speed in granting permission on 27 December 1958, with the strict instruction that the Czechoslovaks must maintain the utmost secrecy and deniability. Five days later, Cuban President Fulgencio Batista fled the country and Fidel Castro led the victorious rebels into Havana. Czechoslovakia now had a friend in a Latin American presidential palace.[6]

The story of Czechoslovakia's involvement with British Guiana's Cheddi and Janet Jagan illustrated the ups and downs of policy in Latin America. Dr Cheddi Jagan was an American-trained dentist who was the son of East Indian sugar workers in British Guiana. First elected to the Legislative Council of British Guiana in 1947, in 1950 Jagan became leader of the newly founded People's Progressive Party (PPP). He was elected British Guiana's chief minister in 1953, and premier in 1957 and 1961. His wife and closest adviser, Janet Jagan (née Rosenberg), was born and raised in Chicago. She was the PPP's general-secretary, edited the party newspaper, was elected to the Legislative Assembly and served as a cabinet minister. She had been a member of the Young Communist League as a college student in the USA, and had a reputation as a Stalinist. The British and the Americans considered her to be the only competent leader in the PPP.[7]

British Guiana's relationship with the Soviet bloc appears to have begun in 1947, when Cheddi Jagan was seen entering the Soviet Embassy in Washington, DC. Thereafter, his dealings with the communists shifted to the headquarters of the British Communist Party and the Soviet bloc's London embassies. He first visited the Czechoslovak Embassy in 1949 and secretly met with the vice consul whenever he was in London during the next four years. Telegrams from the embassy to Prague inevitably referred to him as a 'progressive statesman' who was fighting for his nation's independence and to uplift his people from poverty.[8]

Cheddi Jagan formally introduced himself and British Guiana to the CCP's leadership during a 1951 visit to the Eastern bloc. He told the party's leaders that he led a communist-dominated political party, which needed anti-colonial assistance. The Czechoslovaks cabled Moscow to find out what they should do, and the Soviets replied that they had no interest in opening ties with British Guiana. Less than two years later, the Jagans and the PPP won an overwhelming victory in British Guiana's April 1953 national election.[9]

Once in office, the Jagans set themselves in opposition to the British authorities. They constantly criticized the British Governor despite the relatively few limits that he put on them, claiming theirs was a 'government that was in office but not in power'. They repeatedly went out of their way to antagonize the British and extend the party's tentacles across the colony through the creation of numerous party-backed intermediate institutions, from labour unions to peace councils and youth groups. Cheddi Jagan approached the Czechoslovak Embassy in London to make a secret request for a loan of US$5 million with which he could begin the industrial development of his country. He also suggested that they open a business office. Before the Czechoslovaks could respond, the British Government removed the Jagans and the PPP from power in October 1953. Cheddi Jagan rushed to London to plead his case to parliament. While there, he stopped by the Czechoslovak Embassy and asked for a printing press, printed propaganda, 16-mm movie projectors, loudspeakers and newsprint. Unexpectedly, in the light of Stalin's recent death and the ensuing confusion in foreign policy across the Soviet bloc, the Czechoslovaks were interested in helping. Before they could fill the order, however, the British jailed Cheddi Jagan and much of the party's leadership. Upon his release, Jagan quickly wrote a short and critical history of the intervention, *Forbidden Freedom*, published in 1954.[10]

Jagan's story captivated the Soviets. In 1955, they published a Russian-language edition of *Forbidden Freedom* that was translated by a Soviet intelligence officer, Ovidy Gorchakov. Possibly that same year, the Information Bureau of the Communist and Workers' Parties (Cominform) began to include the PPP on its 'Communist Parties Leaders List', identifying it as the 'Communist Party of British Guyana', with General-Secretary Janet Jagan listed as party leader. Of note, the list did not include any 'bourgeois' nationalist parties, and several backsliding communist parties were also omitted. A second list, handwritten and dated 28 March 1955, likewise listed the PPP as the Communist Party of British Guyana with Janet Jagan as leader.[11]

The PPP was initially a multiracial party in a country evenly divided between East Indians and other ethnic groups, the second-most numerous of which were Africans. The shock of its overthrow soon split the party. In 1955, the moderate PPP members who favoured British-style Fabian socialism split from those like the Jagans who supported Soviet-style scientific socialism. The British kept the PPP on the sidelines until the 1957 election, which the party won. The victorious Jagans and their colleagues began to govern more moderately, toning down their rhetoric to gain British confidence and thereby win independence. Following the election, the ideological split turned racial. Jagan's faction became an overwhelmingly East Indian party, while his leading opponents coalesced around a party dominated by members of African descent. In each succeeding election, the racial split grew more pronounced and violent.[12]

Latin American Communism Ascendant, 1959–63

Nikita Khrushchev liked to brag that 'Stalin had not penetrated the Western Hemisphere whereas he had'. It was through Czechoslovakia's link to Cuba that he did so. Castro's regime gave the Czechoslovaks the best intelligence contacts amongst the Soviet bloc nations, although their own *post hoc* analysis admitted that these contacts were not very good. Cuba used its connection to ask the Czechoslovaks to sell it guns, and in late 1959, Nikita Khrushchev personally overruled the Soviet Ministry of Foreign Affairs – which was frightened that if discovered, it would infuriate the Americans – and allowed the sale to go through. At the end of March, Castro's rapid turn to the East prompted Khrushchev to grant the Czechoslovaks even greater leeway in their trade with Cuba. They opened a very favourable line of credit and agreed to provide as much military assistance as the Cubans wanted. Defence Minister Raúl Castro visited Czechoslovakia in June 1960 (the Cubans naively believed that the Americans would find it less objectionable than a visit to the Soviet Union itself) and the KGB smuggled him to Moscow, where he negotiated further arms shipments and the Soviets agreed to send Spanish-speaking Soviet military advisors.[13]

The remarkable success of Soviet and Czechoslovak foreign policy prompted the KGB to call a 26 June 1961 meeting with Czechoslovakia's secret police, the *Státní bezpečnost* (StB), to discuss accelerating their support for anti-imperial forces in the Third World. The Soviets had transformed the January 1961 assassination of the Congo's prime minister, Patrice Lumumba, into a worldwide indictment of imperialism. In the Congo itself, Lumumba's supporters had taken control of half the country and were recognized by a dozen communist countries and their sympathizers. Ghana, Guinea and Mali were moving away from the Western camp and towards the Soviet bloc. In April, Fidel Castro defeated the US colossus at the Bay of Pigs, and at the start of June, Khrushchev himself had humbled President John Kennedy at the Vienna Summit Conference. With so many victories and the prospect for many more, the StB and the KGB had a great deal to talk about. The meeting lasted four days. Its length suggested that they actually discussed issues, rather than the KGB giving orders and the StB stenographically recording them. No doubt Czechoslovakia's successes in Cuba and Africa had caused the Soviets to view it with a new respect.[14]

Nonetheless, despite the meeting's length and the euphoria that the KGB and StB agents must have felt, the expanded Latin America programme was rather slim and unoriginal. Their new goals were to uncover and exploit opportunities to fight imperialism in the Third World; 'intensify activities for the consolidation and defence of the Cuban Revolution'; take 'active measures' to elevate 'progressive' figures into leadership of Third World liberation movements; expand anti-American movements in Latin America by working together through exiles and opposition movements; and work to subvert the Organization of American States, which they identified as the US enforcement arm for the Monroe Doctrine.[15]

Perhaps as a result of this confident new offensive, Czechoslovakia's relationship with Cuba grew rocky by the end of 1961. Czechoslovak intelligence pushed too hard to recruit agents within the Cuban Government and the Soviets warned them to ease up. There is evidence that the Soviets' motives stemmed as much from jealousy over the Czechoslovaks' successes as from concern that they would alienate the Cubans. Nonetheless, by March 1962 the Czechoslovaks had trained 178 Cuban military specialists ranging from fighter pilots to tank commanders.[16]

One month after the Cuban Missile Crisis, the Czechoslovaks again revised their policy, issuing a new conception in November 1962. The document explained that the reason for revision was to take advantage of the 'favourable conditions' created by the 'boom in the national liberation movement and the anti-imperialist struggle in Latin America' that had begun in 1961. Despite the very recent embarrassment caused by the missile crisis, the conception was very optimistic. Its analysts concluded that Czechoslovakia had made significant progress across the region, but agreed that lack of policy coordination continued to bedevil its efforts along with a surprising (for Marxists) failure to 'deeply analyse economic and political developments in Latin America'. In particular, they had failed to see the revolutionary potential offered by the Cuban Revolution and the ripple effect that it caused across the continent. The CCP's analysts did, however, credit themselves with having helped to lay the ideological groundwork for Castro's victory.[17]

Learning from their mistakes, for the first time, they argued that the region was not an undifferentiated mass. Henceforth, they would treat Latin America as consisting of countries with different economic, cultural and political conditions, and would analyse each country as being at different stages in its 'anti-imperialist, national-liberation struggle'. They analysed national trends and made projections for their future development. Along with the usual calls for increased economic and diplomatic penetration, the new conception emphasized the need to use propaganda to resist US President John Kennedy's 'reinforced anti-communism', which it said was exemplified by his Alliance for Progress and its focus on 'bourgeois' economic development. Prague proposed to counteract Kennedy by promoting the 'advantage' that socialism had given the people of Czechoslovakia, especially 'the growth of living standards and economic growth'. The report also noted that trade with Latin America would benefit Czechoslovakia and its 'growing need' for food and raw materials.[18]

Just as Castro's revolution had changed the Czechoslovaks' conception of their relations with the region, it had also transformed the Jagans' belief in the imminence of the Latin American revolution. In consequence, the Jagans dropped the mask of moderation. The PPP boldly supported Castro, and its rhetoric turned back to favouring the East. Likewise, the Guianese opened trade negotiations with the Soviet bloc. The government pushed hard to buy factories in order to start the rapid industrialization of the country. Covertly, Czechoslovak intelligence began to work with the PPP.

The PPP started to cooperate covertly with Czechoslovak intelligence at the end of 1960, during preparation for important national elections that it believed would determine who would rule the new nation of Guyana after independence. The PPP sent the leader of its Progressive Youth Organization, Moses Bhagwan, to Prague to meet with Czechoslovak officials. The Czechoslovaks must have believed that the meeting was important because Bhagwan met with Antonín Novotný, the eponymous son of the Czechoslovak Communist Party's General-Secretary. Bhagwan carried a letter of introduction from the PPP stating that he was 'empowered to interact with communist parties to ask for assistance with the upcoming election'. He explained the long-term significance of the election and said that he would be touring the communist world in search of 'material assistance'. Novotný told him that he would consult with the CCP's Central Committee. Strangely enough, after so many years of the Jagans meeting with officials at the London embassy and party leaders taking junkets to international meetings and festivals in the Eastern bloc, the Central Committee concluded that its contacts with the PPP had been too minimal to assess 'the character of the party'. They asked the Soviet Union what they should do. The Czech archives do not provide the answer.[19]

Whether or not anyone provided them with electoral assistance, the PPP won British Guiana's August 1961 election. Anxious for independence but worried that Britain or the USA would again remove the PPP from power, Cheddi Jagan proclaimed British Guiana's neutrality in the Cold War as he worked behind the scenes to move towards the Soviet bloc. He and Janet quickly set to work trying to acquire the money and expertise needed for rapid industrialization. The colony's economic relations with both East and West were hampered by Guianese failure to understand economic planning, Guianese grandiosity, US anti-communism and Soviet bloc parsimony. For Cheddi Jagan and his government, 'planning' meant bringing in Leftist economic development experts ranging from communists to Crippsian Labourites and asking them to create plans that would solve all the colony's economic difficulties. Then, without providing technical specifications or detail beyond the big picture overview, the Guianese would present the proposal to whatever country or international agency they thought might give assistance. It never went well. Most famously, with much fanfare, Jagan met with President Kennedy in October 1961 in search of US$40 million in aid. He returned to British Guiana with a tentative promise from Kennedy's foreign assistance advisers for US$5 million in infrastructure spending – and only if he provided the USA with extensive technical details about the projects. Furious and humiliated, Jagan turned to the Soviet Union and its satellites for help.[20]

Two months later, undeterred by her husband's US failure but exhibiting greater caution than the voluble and enthusiastic Cheddi could ever muster, Janet Jagan toured the Soviet Union, Poland and Czechoslovakia. Her purpose was ostensibly to discuss the possibilities of opening trade relations and attend international peace conferences. Along with the trade proposals, she carried a list created by famed French communist economist Charles Bettelheim – the man who had created Cuba's plan for crash industrialization. It truly was a wish list:

seven single-spaced pages requesting factories, technicians and scholarships to train Guianese technicians. The plan was remarkable for its unblinkered naiveté. Working from Bettelheim's crash-industrialization plan, Mrs Jagan asked the Soviets for US$275 million in assistance over 12 years in the form of prefabricated factory kits that the Soviets would build on land donated by the Guianese Government. Moscow was not impressed. Instead of assurances of assistance, Jagan listened to 'an exhaustive explanation of the USSR position in the matter of economic cooperation'. The upshot, the Soviets told her, was that '[t]he actual colonial status of British Guiana makes it impossible to establish direct economic contacts'. Jagan left the Soviet Union for Poland to speak to the All-Polish Peace Committee and ask for aid, and from there to Czechoslovakia for a meeting of the Czechoslovak Committee of Peace Defenders and to talk to the government about aid.[21]

After these meetings, Jagan flew to London for a quick visit on her way back to the Caribbean. She ruefully told the Colonial Office's Richard 'Peter' Piper that she had learned: 'they are as businesslike on that side of the Iron Curtain as they are on this'.[22]

From London, Jagan went to Cuba to meet with Fidel Castro. According to an StB report based on Cuban sources, she asked Castro if he thought Czechoslovakia would sell weapons to her government. With a flourish, he handed her a Czechoslovak pistol. He told her that she could be confident that they would. Whether or not she subsequently asked Czechoslovakia for weapons is unclear, but a few Czechoslovak machine guns had reportedly made their way into the PPP's hands by April 1964.[23]

During a stop in Trinidad, Jagan received the news that an antigovernment general strike had broken out in Georgetown, the Afro-Guianese-dominated capital. The strikers quickly turned violent. Looting turned to arson, and rioters burned several dozen stores in the city's business district. The British used the conflict as an excuse to postpone independence. Claiming that they needed more time to restore interracial peace, they began to lay the groundwork for removing the PPP from power. In response, the Jagans redoubled their efforts to cement British Guiana's relationship with the Soviet bloc.

While Janet Jagan's first trip to the Soviet Union was somewhat disappointing, she apparently had some successes. The Soviet Communist Party sent the PPP US$38,000 in 1962 and US$40,000 in 1963. She also made progress during her meetings with the fraternal socialist states, which apparently had no qualms about providing development assistance to colonies. Over the course of the next three years, Czechoslovaks, East Germans, Hungarians and even a Soviet mission went to British Guiana to discuss building factories on credit; Poles tried to sell a fleet of fishing trawlers; and everyone looked into buying Guianese agricultural commodities or lumber. The closest relationship, though, was with Czechoslovakia – with the Soviets in the background. The Czechoslovaks took the lead in sending trade and economic-development experts to the colony, and the Guianese Government sent leading PPP members to Prague to appeal for assistance.[24]

Cheddi Jagan wanted more than just trade, though. He repeatedly asked the Czechoslovaks if they could send an intelligence officer to British Guiana for a meeting. The Czechoslovaks trod lightly. They sent trade officials who were posted to their embassies in Brazil and Mexico, but not did not tell the Guianese that these men were StB agents who had been sent to analyse the situation. The last to visit, Jaroslav Mercl, was a high-ranking StB officer with much experience in the USA and Canada. After meeting with the Jagans and other top officials, Mercl reported to Prague: 'There are good conditions in this country for work against our main enemy' – i.e., the USA.[25]

Mercl's meeting was arranged through the cooperation of Rudolf David, an Afro-Guianese who was studying film in Czechoslovakia. The StB said that David was a 'close friend' of Cheddi Jagan, who had personally selected him to study in Czechoslovakia. Janet Jagan met with David during her stay in Czechoslovakia, the StB reported, and she told him that he would be appointed minister of education when he returned home. Although the StB did not register David as a spy, their records show that he had 'promised us every help'. They gave him the absurdly transparent code name, 'Black'.[26]

In March 1963, as British Guiana suffered a violent 80-day anti-government general strike that was backed by US labour unions, the Guianese pressured the Soviet bloc for aid. The KGB asked the StB if they had secret code connections in Georgetown that they could use. The StB said they did not, but added that they would arrange such a capability if they could establish a trade mission in the colony. Later that year, the British vetoed the request, killing the possibility of establishing an intelligence outpost. In June, Cuban intelligence sent two agents to British Guiana under cover as trade representatives, fulfilling the Soviets' need for a conduit.[27]

Czechoslovak Decline; Guianese Disaster, 1964–6

By the beginning of 1964, revolutionary fervour in Latin America had begun to decline. Economic problems also had begun to bedevil the Soviet bloc. In response, the Soviets and Czechoslovaks met on 4 January to assess whether or not they needed to create a new conception of Czechoslovakia's Latin American relations.

Their analysts concluded that Fidel Castro was their biggest problem. He believed that the Soviets had betrayed him during the Cuban Missile Crisis when they removed the missiles without consulting him. He felt humiliated, treated as if he were a Soviet pawn instead of the leader of a revolutionary state who had fought his way to power. His response was repeated sharp criticism of the Soviets and the other 'fraternal parties' for lacking 'revolutionary determination'. The attacks became so harsh and his efforts to launch revolutions in Latin America so overt that the Soviets and Czechoslovaks concluded that he had shifted to an 'erroneous' and 'adventurist' anti-imperialist line. Castro had also become much less enamoured with the way the Soviets managed socialism. They provided Cuba with shoddy goods, poor technical assistance and frequently sloth-like movement when it came to providing commodities and services that the Cuban economy required. Compared to recently departed US businesses, many Cuban Government officials grumbled, Soviet economic managers did a lousy job but were as interested in the bottom line as the Americans had been. Castro even began to praise the Chinese communists, infuriating the Soviets. In an unsuccessful effort to keep him in the fold, the Soviets agreed to let Castro use Czechoslovakia as a trans-shipment point for returning Latin Americans to their home countries after they had received guerilla training in Cuba, since most Latin American nations would bar people from entering after having visited Cuba. 'Operation Manuel', as it was known, returned 1,179 revolutionaries to their home countries between December 1962 and 1969.[28]

Across the hemisphere, reported the Czechoslovak analysts, problems were mounting for Czechoslovak foreign policy beyond the problem of

Fidel. The US Alliance for Progress had proven to be a 'strong weapon of anti-communism', strengthening right wing governments. The Chinese were also making progress with revolutionary movements around the hemisphere, dividing Latin America's anti-imperialist front. The Czechoslovaks themselves had suffered a precipitous drop in trade with the region. Nonetheless, the analysts wrote, they should continue their policy unchanged.[29]

British Guiana was also turning into a foreign policy setback. Following the 80-day general strike, on 31 October 1963, the British called a new Guianese election for one year hence and amended the Guianese constitution to favour the PPP's opponents. Desperate, Jagan's supporters launched a union-recognition strike in the sugar industry on 17 February 1964, with the goal of taking over the colony's biggest workforce. Controlling the sugar workers would help in the electoral campaign and give the PPP powerful leverage over the economy if they lost the election. The strike lasted 161 days and led to the deaths of 176 people, but the PPP's union failed to win recognition.[30]

Four days after the strike began, Czechoslovak Ambassador to Cuba Vladimír Pavlíček sent the foreign ministry a 'Special report about government, political parties and trade unions in British Guiana'. The Ambassador wrote that the PPP 'is with great effort trying to remain in power in order to liberate the masses from the horrors of colonialism and capitalism'. Its goal was 'to transform British Guiana from a capitalist state into a socialist state in which the major means of production and trade will be in the hands of the working class'. The government faced a 'corrupt' trade-union movement in league with the opposition and funded by US dollars. The report was purely informational, and Pavlíček offered no suggestions as to how the foreign ministry should handle the situation. Another report from Cuba – sent on 27 June, apparently by an StB agent and complete with comments from the Soviet 'friends' – claimed that the British were creating a 'special armed unit' to help 'limit the power of Jagan's government'. The unit would be ready to respond if the PPP began using 'guerrilla tactics'. The report also cited differences within the Guianese opposition party's leadership, which the 'friends' called 'valuable information'.[31]

As the situation worsened, Jagan sent a representative to Prague to ask for help. George David, Rudy David's brother and a man whom British intelligence characterized as 'a well-known Guianese

Communist' and PPP fundraiser, met with the CCP Central Committee. He explained that the election was coming and, although the PPP had handily won all three prior polls, the recent British-imposed constitutional amendments favoured the opposition. David asked if the Czechoslovaks could help the PPP campaign by providing two motorbikes, six loudspeakers for street agitation, 12 short films about Czechoslovakia and a collection of communist propaganda. The Central Committee approved each of these requests. Perhaps emboldened by his success, David then asked the Czechoslovaks for weapons: hand grenades, pistols, ammunition and small explosives. The Central Committee decided not to provide them. The method he had suggested – hiding them in a delivery of Czechoslovak beer – was too 'risky and unrealistic'. Due to Czechoslovakia's sclerotic bureaucracy, only the motorcycles made it to British Guiana before the election, which the PPP lost on 7 December 1964.[32]

Out of office but hopeful that he would win the next election, Cheddi Jagan travelled to Czechoslovakia in 1965 looking for assistance. A CCP International Department report called the PPP 'a progressive, radical party whose leading cadres tend to support socialism. Its leadership was seeking assistance from socialist countries to fight against imperialism.' The CCP said it was eager to help. Czechoslovakia would provide political backing, it told Jagan, and, if necessary, 'possibly adequate material assistance'. The nebulousness of the fiscal commitment suggests the impact of Czechoslovakia's growing economic difficulties. Jagan asked if they could give him movie projectors and tape recorders. The Czechoslovaks agreed to help, using the unspent funds that they had appropriated to pay for George David's pre-election request.[33]

On 26 May 1966, British Guiana received its independence as Guyana, under the leadership of Jagan's opponent, Forbes Burnham. Four days later, the Czechoslovak Ministry of Foreign Affairs noted that, while in office, the PPP had 'relentlessly struggled to elevate the workers' class consciousness and cohesion' so that the Guyanese could understand 'the illegal way' that Britain and the USA were using local proxies to implement an 'imperialist policy' of divide and rule along racial lines in order to maintain neocolonial power. The report added that the CIA continued this 'dangerous policy' through agents who were 'spread out across the country'. Rather than a plan of action, the report sounded like a regretful farewell. That year also saw the StB shelve its file on British Guiana. Burnham cut off relations with Czechoslovakia and every other communist country. He began to move leftwards in 1970, and established relations with Czechoslovakia in 1975.[34]

As for Latin America, in November 1966, the CCP reported that the problems identified in 1964 had metastasized. Castro was out of control, attacking some communist parties as 'pseudo-revolutionary' and accusing the Soviet bloc of viewing the 'revolutionary struggle' through a 'mercantile perspective'. The Chinese were adding confusion, US imperialism continued to gain strength, the 'revolutionary wave' that had followed in the wake of the Cuban Revolution receded, and Latin America's revolutionary forces had proven themselves unprepared to take power. Unmentioned in this analysis were Czechoslovak economic reverses, which had hobbled its efforts across the Third World. The CCP reached the glum realization that Latin America was no longer in 'an imminent revolutionary situation'.[35]

Conclusion

Czechoslovakia's relationship with British Guiana demonstrates several important but heretofore hidden facets of Czechoslovak and Guianese foreign policy. In British Guiana, as in Latin America in general, the Czechoslovaks showed an impressive determination to support and vindicate the Soviet Union's international goals. They pushed the Soviets to arm the Cubans in 1959, and their work in British Guiana from 1962 to 1964 was thorough and ideologically correct. The greater freedom in conducting their Latin American policy after the StB's 1961 summit with the KGB suggests that the Soviets recognized their expertise and granted them greater independence in executing foreign policy. This was seen when the Soviets inquired if the Czechoslovaks had a means of communicating directly with the PPP during the 1963 general strike: the KGB had loosened its grip over the StB in British Guiana so much that it did not know this basic yet crucial fact.

The Czechoslovaks were ostensibly interested in trade relations with British Guiana, but the way in which they conducted the relationship suggests that Czechoslovak business was ancillary to espionage. Both of the trade representatives who visited British Guiana were StB agents working under cover, and the key figure in the trade delegation that followed them was a high-ranking StB officer. Likewise, when the British vetoed Cheddi Jagan's proposal to open a Czechoslovak trade consulate, the Eastern bloc was prevented from setting up an intelligence outpost. Shortly thereafter, Cuba sent two intelligence agents to British Guiana, apparently filling that need, and the StB closed its file on the colony. The relative importance of intelligence versus diplomacy can also be seen in the Czech National Archive. The StB file for British Guiana is thick and filled with analyses of Guianese politics and personalities, while the country files for the Ministry of Foreign Affairs are thin.

The Czechoslovak documents also go a long way towards answering one of the important and vehemently argued questions from Guianese history: were the Jagans preparing to align British Guiana with the Soviet bloc? Cheddi Jagan's repeated requests to meet with Czechoslovak intelligence agents, his government's secret request for money to conduct the 1961 election, Janet Jagan's request for weapons from Fidel Castro in 1962, her apparent request for Soviet Communist Party funding for the PPP in 1962 and 1963, and the government's secret request for Czechoslovak weapons in 1964 all suggest that the PPP was preparing a covert alliance with the Soviet bloc.

Although the Jagans never turned against the Soviet Union and its satellites in word or deed, their defeat in the 1964 election left the Soviet bloc with the same result. The loss in British Guiana was the latest defeat for Soviet bloc foreign policy in the region, but it was by no means the key reason that the Czechoslovaks decided to reassess and conclude that the Latin American revolution was not imminent. Much more important were Fidel Castro's ferocious turn against the mercenary and stodgily anti-revolutionary East, US success in using the Alliance for Progress to put counter-revolutionary regimes on the offensive and a lack of money to provide aid thanks to the failure of Czechoslovakia's five-year economic plan. But the PPP's defeat did reinforce the idea that US imperialistic power was back in the ascendancy and Latin America's revolutionary moment had passed, at least for the moment.

Notes

1. Work on this project was supported by the European Regional Development Fund Project, "Creativity and Adaptability as Conditions for the Success of Europe in an Interrelated World" (No. CZ.02.1.01/0.0/0.0/16_019/0000734).

The authors would like to thank Professor Catherine Albrecht for assisting with translations.

2. For an overview of Czechoslovakia's Cold War relationship with Latin America, see Josef Opatrný, 'Czechoslovak-Latin American Relations 1945–1989', *Central European Journal of International and Security Studies* [hereafter, *CEJISS*] 7 (3) (2013), pp. 12–37, available at http://www.cejiss.org/static/data/uploaded/1393887975565903/cejiss_7.3_eJournal_1.pdf (accessed September 2017); and Josef Opatrný, Michal Zourek, Lucia Majlátová and Matyáš Pelant, *Las relations entre Checoslovaquia y América Latina 1945–1989 en los archives de la República Checa* [Relations between Czechoslovakia and Latin America 1945–1989 in the archives of the Czech Republic] (Prague, 2015).

3. 'The Conception of relations between Czechoslovakia and Latin America', November 23, 1962, f. 1261/044, box 5, Novotný Papers II, Czech National Archives, Prague, Czech Republic [hereafter, NA], Appendix III, p. 5; 'The Conception of relations between Czechoslovakia and Latin America', 23 June 1959, f. 1261/044, box 5, Novotný Papers II, NA, Appendix III, pp. 15–16.

4. 'The Conception of relations between Czechoslovakia and Latin America', 23 June 1959, f. 1261/044, box 5, Novotný Papers II, NA, Appendix III, pp. 3, 5–6.

5. Ibid., pp. 5–6, 8–9. For the difficulties faced by African students in Czechoslovakia, see Muehlenbeck, *Czechoslovakia in Africa* (New York, 2015), pp. 168–73. For the difficulties faced by Cuban students in Czechoslovakia, see Hana V. Bortlová, *Československo a Kuba v letech 1959–1962* [Czechoslovakia and Cuba in the years 1959–1962] (Prague, 2011), p. 152. For a novelistic portrayal of the problems faced by international students in the Soviet bloc, written by one of the earliest Guianese scholarship students in Czechoslovakia, see Jan Carew, *Moscow is Not My Mecca* (London, 1964).

6. Aleksandr Fursenko and Timothy Naftali, *'One Hell of a Gamble': Khrushchev, Castro, and Kennedy, 1958–1964* (New York, 1997), pp. 12–13, 22–5.

7. On Cheddi Jagan, Colin A. Palmer, *Cheddi Jagan and the Politics of Power: British Guiana's Struggle for Independence* (Chapel Hill, NC, 2010) is sympathetic; a more critical perspective is presented by Clem Seecharan, *Finding Myself: Essays on Race, Politics & Culture* (Leeds, 2015). There is no biography of Janet Jagan, but books are in the early stages of research by Gaiutra Bahadur and Robert Anthony Waters Jr.

8. Christopher Andrew, *Defend the Realm: The Official History of MI5* (New York, 2009), pp. 459–60.

9. A copy of the letter can be found at http://digitalarchive.wilsoncenter.org/document/121125. The letter is part of a Cold War International History Project [hereafter, CWIHP] e-Dossier. Other documents on Czechoslovak–Guianese relations are included in the dossier, along with an essay: Jan Koura and Robert Anthony Waters Jr, 'Cheddi Jagan and Guyanese Overtures to the East: Evidence from the Czech National Archives', 7 October 2014. Available at https://www.wilsoncenter.org/publication/cheddi-jagan-

and-guyanese-overtures-to-the-east-evidence-the-czech-national-archives (both accessed September 2017).
10. See, for example, Stephen Rabe, *U.S. Intervention in British Guiana: A Cold War Story* (Chapel Hill, NC, 2005), pp. 33–46; Jagan, *Forbidden Freedom: The Story of British Guiana* (Milton, ON, 1954).
11. The Russian version of *Forbidden Freedom* can be found at http://books.google.ru/books/about/Forbidden_Freedom_Свобода_под.html?id=xs-NMwEACAAJ&redir_esc=y (accessed September 2017); 'Communist parties leaders list', n.d. (between 1950 and 1955 – most likely, 1955), Russian State Archive of Social and Political History [hereafter, RGASPI], Fond 575, Inventory 1, File 440, pp. 15–18; Malov, 'A List of Communist Party leaders', March 28, 1955, RGASPI Fond 575, Inventory 1, File 440, pp. 19–24.
12. See, for example, Rabe, *U.S. Intervention in British Guiana*, pp. 52–3.
13. Fursenko and Naftali, *'One Hell of a Gamble'*, p. 21; Christopher Andrew and Vasili Mitrokhin, *The World was Going Our Way: The KGB and the Battle for the Third World* (New York, 2005), pp. 36–7. See also, Hana V. Bortlová, 'Czech Tractors, Cuban Oranges: Economic Relations between Socialist Czechoslovakia and Revolutionary Cuba', *CEJISS* 7 (3) (2013), pp. 77–95, available at http://www.cejiss.org/static/data/uploaded/1393887975565903/cejiss_7.3_eJournal_1.pdf (accessed September 2017). See also Albert Manke, 'Waffen für ein revolutionäres Kuba. Kuba und die Tschechoslowakei: Der Beginn einer neuen tranatlantischen Allianz im Kalten Krieg' [Weapons for a revolutionary Cuba. Cuba and Czechoslovakia: The beginning of a new alliance in the Cold War], in Albert Manke and Kateřina Březinová (eds), *Kleinstaaten und sekundäre Akteure im Kalten Krieg. Politische, wirtschaftliche, militärische und kulturelle Wechselberziehungen zwischen Europa und Latein Amerika* [The small countries and other secondary actors in the Cold War. Political, economic and cultural relations between Europe and Latin America] (Bielefeld, Germany, 2016).
14. 'Minutes of the meeting between the KGB at the Council of Ministers of the USSR and the Ministry of Interior of the CSSR about results and further expansion of cooperation in the coordination of intelligence and counter-intelligence measures and for the joint implementation of these measures, Prague, 26 to 30 June 1961', Archiv bezpečnostních složek [hereafter, ABS], Sbírka mezinárodních smluv. A copy of this document can be found at http://www.ustrcr.cz/data/pdf/projekty/mezinarodni-spoluprace/sssr/spoluprace05.pdf or http://digitalarchive.wilsoncenter.org/document/113217 (both accessed September 2017).
15. Ibid., pp. 4–5. In the Soviet lexicon, 'active measures' can refer to collection of intelligence or political activities by the KGB, including everything from propaganda and disinformation to assassination.
16. Bortlová, *Československo a Kuba v letech*, pp. 136–7, 105; Fursenko and Naftali, *'One Hell of a Gamble'*, pp. 36, 46, 50, 166, 374–5, fn. 42 (the warning is noted in pp. 374–5, fn. 42).

17. 'The Conception of relations between Czechoslovakia and Latin America', 23 November 1962, f. 1261/044, box 5, Novotný Papers II, NA, Appendix III, pp. 8, 15, Appendix IV, pp. 4–8, 3–4, 5. The analysis was prepared for, and approved by, the Central Committee by unknown analysts who probably worked for the foreign ministry.
18. Ibid., Appendix III, pp. 8, 15, 4, Appendix IV, pp. 4–9.
19. Archival copies and translations of these documents from the Czech National Archives can be found at http://digitalarchive.wilsoncenter.org/document/121119 and http://digitalarchive.wilsoncenter.org/document/121120 (both accessed September 2017). The author of the report transcribed Bhagwan's name as Bhagvert Mozes. In an interview, Bhagwan did not recall asking communist parties for campaign assistance; indeed, he said his tour of the communist world turned him away from orthodox communism. Bhagwan email to Waters, 9 September 2013.
20. See, for example, Rabe, *U.S. Intervention in British Guiana*, pp. 87–8; A. J. E. Longden, Senior Superintendent Head of Special Branch, British Guiana, 'Intelligence Report for the Month of June, 1962', p. 1, Colonial Office {hereafter, CO} 1031/3714, British National Archives, Kew, England {hereafter, BNA}.
21. Jagan to Chairman, Economic Commission for Contacts with Foreign Countries, 2 January 1961, Fond 365, Inventory 2, File 338, RGASPI [Jagan misdated the year]; 'PPP Relations with Communists, Communist Fronts, and Communist Bloc', 14 June 1962, 741D.00/16–1462, box 1668, RG 59, US National Archives {hereafter, USNA}; O.V. Adams to A.E.D. Chamier, 25 January 1962, CO 1031/3912, BNA; 'Mrs. Jagan in Prague', *Rudé Právo* (detailed summary), n.d. [interview held 19 January 1962], CO 1031/3912, BNA. Koura searched the Czech National Archives but could not find documents memorializing Jagan's meetings with Czechoslovak officials.
22. [Ambassador David] Bruce to Department of State, 'Subject: British Guiana: Janet Jagan', 3 February 1962, 741D.00/2–362, box 1668, RG 59, USNA.
23. An archival copy and translation of the document regarding this exchange can be found at http://digitalarchive.wilsoncenter.org/document/121112 (accessed September 2017); Tom Stacey, 'Violent Prelude to British Guiana Poll', *Sunday Times* (London), 26 April 1964; Stacey email to Waters, 25 July 2006.
24. For the subvention to the PPP, see Waters and Gordon O. Daniels, 'Striking for Freedom? International intervention and the Guianese Sugar workers' strike of 1964', *Cold War History* 10 (4) (2010), p. 551. There was no data for Communist Party assistance in 1964.
25. Grey to N. B. J. Huijsman, 12 February 1962, CO 1031/3912, BNA; Chargé d'Affaires [Mexico], 'Informational report on the situation in British Guiana', 10 December 1962, 3418/62, 1667, Ministry of Foreign Affairs, NA. On the 1962 general strike, which may have been supported by the USA, see Rabe, *U.S. Intervention in British Guiana*, pp. 92–4; and Gordon O. Daniels and

Waters, 'The British Guiana Trades Union Council Strike of 1962', paper presented at the North American Labor History Conference, Detroit, Michigan, 21 October 2005. Archival copies and translations of these documents can be found at http://digitalarchive.wilsoncenter.org/document/121112; http://digitalarchive.wilsoncenter.org/document/121114 (both accessed September 2017).

26. An archival copy and translation of this document can be found at http://digitalarchive.wilsoncenter.org/document/121112 (accessed September 2017).
27. An archival copy and translation of the document concerning this matter can be found at http://digitalarchive.wilsoncenter.org/document/121115 (accessed September 2017). Scholars have proven that the 1963 strike was funded by the USA: see Waters and Daniels, 'The World's Longest General Strike', *Diplomatic History* 29 (2005), pp. 279–307. On the Cuban agents in British Guiana, see Waters and Daniels, 'Striking for Freedom?'.
28. On Castro's anger over the missile crisis, see, for example, Sergo Mikoyan, in Svetlana Savranskaya (ed.), *The Soviet Cuban Missile Crisis: Castro, Mikoyan, Kennedy, Khrushchev, and the Missiles of October* (Stanford, CA, 2012), pp. 191–234; 'Report on implementation of the conception of relations between Czechoslovakia and Latin America', 4 January 1964, f. 1261/044, box 5, Novotný Papers II, NA, Appendix III. On problems with Soviet economic assistance, see Oscar Sanchez-Sibony, *Red Globalization: The Political Economy of the Soviet Cold War from Stalin to Khrushchev* (New York, 2014), pp. 211–12, 212, fn. 27 and 25. On Operation Manuel, see Michal Zourek, 'Operation MANUEL: When Prague was a Key Transit Hub for International Terrorism', *CEJISS* 9 (3) (2015), pp. 132–52, available at http://static.cejiss.org (accessed September 2017); Prokop Tomek, 'Akce Manuel' [Operation Manuel], in *Securitas Imperii, Sborník k problematice zahraničních vztahů čs. komunistického režimu* [Collection on foreign relations of the Czechoslovak Communist regime], 9 (Prague, 2002), pp. 326–33; Daniela Spenser, 'Operation Manuel: Czechoslovakia and Cuba', CWIHP e-Dossier (with translated documents from the Czech National Archives), 7 July 2011, available at https://www.wilsoncenter.org/publication/operation-manuel-czechoslovakia-and-cuba (accessed September 2017).
29. 'Report on implementation of the conception of relations between Czechoslovakia and Latin America', 4 January 1964, f. 1261/044, box 5, Novotný Papers II, NA, Appendix III.
30. Waters and Daniels, 'Striking for Freedom?'.
31. Vladimír Pavlíček, 'Special report about government, political parties and trade unions in British Guiana', pp. 1, 3, 5–6, ABS, 1. Správa Sbor národní bezpečnosti [hereafter, SNB], sign. I-SF-0101-15-26; 'Extract from the report from Havana of 27 June 1964', ABS, 1. Správa SNB, sign. I-SF-0101-15-26.
32. An archival copy and translation of the document concerning this proposal can be found at http://digitalarchive.wilsoncenter.org/document/121118

(accessed September 2017); 'Information about People's Progressive Party of British Guyana', 15 June 1965, NA, Archiv Ústředního výboru Komunistické strany Československa [hereafter, AÚV KSČ], 02/1, sv. 111, aj. 115, b. 20, Appendix III, p. 9.
33. 'Information about People's Progressive Party of British Guyana', 15 June 1965, NA, AÚV KSČ, 02/1, sv. 111, aj. 115, b. 20, Appendix III, pp. 6, 9.
34. An archival copy and translation of the document regarding this termination of relations can be found at http://digitalarchive.wilsoncenter.org/document/121116 (accessed September 2017). Unfortunately, the Czech National Archives for the period 1970–85, during which time Burnham turned to the left and eventually opened relations with Czechoslovakia, are in too much disarray to uncover anything significant.
35. Ibid.; 'Report on new phenomena in the national liberation movements in Latin America', 4 November 1966, NA, AÚV KSČ 02/1, sv. 14, aj. 15, b. 3, Appendix III, pp. 7, 13, 16–17. For Czechoslovak economic reverses, see Muehlenbeck, *Czechoslovakia in Africa*, pp. 173–8.

CHAPTER 4

THE THIRD WORLD AS STRATEGIC OPTION: ROMANIAN RELATIONS WITH DEVELOPING STATES

Larry L. Watts

Over the course of 1955–75 the non-aligned developing 'Third World' evolved from a zone with which Bucharest had little contact to an area of primary foreign- and security-policy focus and a central pillar of Romanian soft power. Economic ties with the Third World kept pace with this strategic reorientation, becoming greater in number and diversity than those of any other Eastern European member of the Warsaw Pact. As of 1971, it had established diplomatic relations with 86 states, and economic and commercial relations with more than 100.[1]

These ties were facilitated by a corresponding growth in capacities, including construction of a merchant navy of more than 170 ships by 1975.[2] This expansion also held true for both trade and assistance, particularly in areas of comparative advantage. By the end of the 1960s, for example, Romania was 'the world's third largest manufacturer' and 'second largest' exporter of petroleum equipment, almost entirely to developing countries.[3] Between 1955–75, it accounted for more than half of all Eastern European petroleum development assistance from the Soviet bloc. By the end of that period, Romania was the largest donor of non-military aid among the Eastern European countries (contributing US$260 million in 1974).[4]

Remarkably little of this was coordinated with the other members of the Warsaw Pact. Despite the considerable leeway allowed bloc members in choosing economic partners, Romania exercised observably greater 'independence in making individual commitments' in the Third World than the rest of the Pact, whose aid patterns exhibited a 'high degree of complementarity' with Moscow.[5] As US intelligence noted at the end of the decade, while other bloc members provided 'support to Third World nations and insurgent movements, often in close cooperation with the USSR', Romania pursued 'objectives vis-à-vis the Third World that differ[ed] radically from those of the USSR and that do not purposely serve Soviet interests'.[6] This situation was evident regarding military aid as well, where aspirations to 'play the larger international role of mediator, as opposed to partisan' made Romania a marginal contributor in comparison with all the other Pact members.[7]

Soviet–Romanian peer competition in the developing world had a particularly sharp edge to it, with the former going 'so far as to dog the steps of Romanian commercial representatives in Arab countries (and in Latin America) and deliberately underbid them, even to the point of giving away free goods and services'.[8] This discordance reflected a fundamental difference between the autonomy exercised by the other Eastern European members of the Soviet alliance in the post-Stalin period and the independence with which Romania acted.[9] While the autonomy of the other bloc members remained dependent on Soviet approval and conformity with the Moscow line, Romanian behaviour often resembled not so much autonomy as mutiny.[10]

This was most evident in Romania's efforts to enlist other members of the Warsaw Pact, together with developing socialist countries outside of it, in order to counter Moscow's hegemonic tendencies within the alliance.[11] Bucharest sought to roll back that dominance by obstructing Soviet unilateralism within the Pact, empowering the non-Soviet allies vis-à-vis Moscow and/or dissolving the alliance altogether, prompting constant complaints concerning its attempts to 'paralyze', 'subvert', 'obstruct', 'weaken' and even cause the Warsaw Pact to 'disintegrate'.[12] In this endeavour, Romania saw in the Third World a natural ally.

Small-State Theory and Third World Activism

Bucharest began this campaign after the Cuban Missile Crisis, when Moscow almost drew it into a nuclear conflict without its foreknowledge.[13] As part of its effort to avoid a repetition of that near-catastrophe Bucharest overhauled the Soviet concept of 'peaceful coexistence', the state of permanent political and ideological struggle in the absence of military conflict, and reformulated it as the pursuit of a durable peace and expanded cooperation between states regardless of ideology (or 'social order', in Romanian parlance). Seeking to obstruct Moscow's military unilateralism, it declared negotiation to be the only legitimate method for resolving international tension and stressed the responsibility of all states for regional and global security, regardless of size.[14] While it set forth the mediation of tension and conflict as the 'sacred obligation' of all states, Bucharest explicitly called upon small and medium-sized states to cross the ideological divide in the service of peace. Thus, it argued, 'negotiations with any capitalist country on this basis in no way implies abandonment of principles; rather, it means serving the interests of peace.'[15]

Tactically, the removal of ideology from interstate relations served to justify the expansion of Romania's relations with non-socialist countries. Strategically, it dealt a terrific blow to the main barrier across the East–West divide and between the First, Second and Third Worlds. Romanian policy used the terms 'Third World' and 'developing states' interchangeably, but focused on the more profound non-ideological cleavages between great and small powers and between the developed and developing worlds.

To enable this, Bucharest called for 'new-type relations' based on a set of principles that would empower smaller states vis-à-vis the force potentials of larger powers. It then relied upon this 'new code of international principles' to combat Moscow's attempts to create supranational organisms, assume the role of 'leading center' and otherwise impose Soviet control over the Warsaw Pact (and the Council for Mutual Economic Assistance). As it declared in 1964, 'There are no, and there can be no "parent" parties or "son" parties, no "superior" or "subordinate" parties; there is a great family of communist and workers' parties equal in rights; no party has or can have a privileged position, none can impose its line or opinions upon other parties.'[16] By extending this equality to states and placing it at the forefront of their foreign policy, Romania's Communist Party leaders defended their own interests and positioned their country as a champion of the 'little guy', drawing support from all three 'worlds' and especially from the developing Third World.

For example, party leader Nicolae Ceaușescu called upon small and medium-sized states to struggle for security by opposing the 'imperialist policy of force, diktat, and interference'.[17] 'Since all peoples are interested in the achievement of security,' he argued, 'all of them are called upon to contribute to its realization' because security 'cannot be the result of an agreement reached among several states or among existing blocs', but could only be achieved when all states concerned reached understanding 'by virtue of their equal rights'.[18]

The 'new type relationship' on which Bucharest insisted excluded 'the use of force and the threat of the use of force', and guaranteed 'that no state can fall victim to aggression,' and all states could 'develop freely in accordance with their own volition and be able to cooperate without obstacles in an atmosphere of mutual understanding and full equality'.[19] A secure world, the Romanian leadership explained, presupposed that capitalist and socialist states 'must live peaceably side-by-side and will establish normal relations with each other irrespective of their social order'.[20] 'Acting in this spirit,' Ceaușescu reiterated, Romania approached 'its relations with every country in the world on a broad spectrum, regardless of other countries' social order, and actively participating in the implementation of the new policy based on the principle of equality among states'.[21]

In essence, Romania was recruiting members outside the closed socialist community dominated by Moscow on the basis of its interpretations of Marxism–Leninism, and drawing them into a much broader community of independent actors. It advocated for the empowerment of small states and against their submission to great-power hegemons. Unsurprisingly, Moscow and its loyalist allies saw this as a fundamental challenge to Soviet foreign policy and security architecture. According to the East Germans, Romanian policy now 'deviated' from the policy of the other Pact members 'on every important international issue'.[22] As the East German State Security reported,

Starting from the theory that small and medium-size states should play an independent role in international relations in order to create an atmosphere of collaboration, it has in fact refused the Soviet Union its role in the active peace policy of the socialist countries. The class character of socialist foreign policy is erased entirely [when Romanian officials advocate] that small and medium sized countries of Europe must develop contacts and collaboration with a view to transcending the Cold War regardless of their military, political or philosophical leanings.[23]

East Germany and Hungary repeatedly denounced 'the well-known Romanian thesis on sovereignty and the role of small nations' in their internal reports as 'directly' supporting 'anti-Sovietism'.[24] Budapest warned small states of dire consequences should they engage in foreign relations outside the framework of their alliances, claiming that their disregard of class considerations served the 'enemies of the working class', undermined the 'international class struggle' and threatened to unravel the socialist world system.[25] The Romanians were likewise censured for their 'reactionary ideas', for serving the interests of 'great power policy' and 'nationalistic separatism', and for creating an 'unprincipled bloc' of small states that disregarded class character and ignored 'the realities of world affairs'.[26]

To such attacks Bucharest countered that European security depended upon guarantees of equality, sovereignty and independence, principles that were 'universal in the sense that they are equally binding on all states and they protect all states with the same firmness' despite differing political systems or alliances.[27] Only thus could 'the "right" of the strongest, the "right" of the fist, and the law of the jungle' be eliminated, and only thus could 'the rule of law and the power of right' be established. Security would not be achieved through ideological imposition, for what was 'prohibited by general international law cannot be permitted in the relations of any continent, region, or group of states with any particular state'.[28]

Ignoring the battle lines of East–West and regional competition often led Romania into sensitive and dangerous territory. For instance, there were inherent contradictions between its advocacy of small-state independence and equality, its status as a Soviet ally and its special relationship with the USA. But rather than attempting to conceal these contradictions, the Romanians 'owned' them, as Ceaușescu showed during a 1974 meeting with Palestinian organizations, explaining that

> Severing diplomatic relations does not help to solve problems between states. Moreover, [the] existence of such relations does not entail total or even partial agreement with their policies [...] But it does assist in search for solutions to various problems, solutions based on peaceful coexistence.[29]

If the dangers and vulnerabilities of such a policy were evident, so too were the rewards. As spokesperson for small and medium-sized states Bucharest acquired a good deal of insight regarding developing-world problems and interests, and its relations with the Third World grew correspondingly.[30] Within a year after the period covered by this chapter, Romania was accepted as an observer in the Non-Aligned Movement (NAM), gaining a level of influence within it that occasionally rivaled that of NAM's official leadership.[31] Romanian advocacy at the United Nations, within the Warsaw Pact, and in bilateral dealings for a new approach to the developing world and the problems of underdevelopment (specifically regarding the ownership of raw materials and fair exchange), gained it leverage and even some protection.

Romanian 'mediation' in the Third World was spurred by the same fear that motivated its change of strategy after the Cuban Missile Crisis: that of nuclear war caused by great-power unilateralism. Thus, in South East Asia, Bucharest was concerned that US troops might be sent into North Vietnam near the border with the People's Republic of China, and that Beijing's reaction might trigger the use of nuclear weapons.[32] Alternatively, it feared that an exhausted and frustrated US administration, nearing the end of its rope in an unwinnable war, might perceive the nuclear option as its salvation.[33]

The thousands of Soviet military personnel deployed in the Middle East likewise represented a potential catalyst that could trigger nuclear war if Soviet-backed Arab forces seriously threatened Israel, or if the USSR's Arab allies suffered such a catastrophic military defeat that Soviet personnel and prestige came under serious threat. As Ceaușescu warned Egyptian President Anwar Sadat in 1972, the attempt to impose a military solution would almost certainly draw in the USA and the USSR with 'unfathomable consequences'.[34] Romanian fears of nuclear escalation were hardly fanciful. According to the US Department of State, the October War of 1973 brought 'the United States closer to a nuclear confrontation with the Soviet Union than at any point since the Cuban missile crisis'.[35]

Romanian 'small state theory' sought to empower regional states to act on their own, without having to rely on 'sponsors' or 'middle-men'. The problem with third parties, Ceaușescu announced to all who would listen, was that 'no matter what you want, it is always difficult to find intermediaries that are quite so disinterested and that do not seek to draw certain uses' from their involvement.[36] In Vietnam, Bucharest repeatedly parried Soviet efforts to use its 'assistance' to compel North Vietnam into what Hanoi considered an unfavourable peace. In the Middle East, the Romanians cautioned Sadat that 'certain countries' gave aid and assistance 'only so that they can gain a position of influence'.[37] The same advice, to disembarrass itself of Soviet tutelage, had been proffered to the leadership of Gamal Abdel Nasser as well.[38]

The Six Day War and its Aftermath

Vietnam revealed the very different directions of Romanian and Soviet policy in the Third World. But the conflict in the Middle East represented the sharp edge of Romanian–Soviet security contestation. In Vietnam, Bucharest and Moscow shared a common central goal: ending the war. Moscow might have preferred greater influence on how that conflict ended but, given the limitations of its influence over Hanoi and Beijing's antagonistic involvement, Romanian divergence had not become a source of major contention.

The Middle East was something else altogether. Negotiation and peace there were neither necessary nor desirable for the purposes of Soviet power projection. Tension and strife – not mediation – invited military influence. And Moscow and Bucharest each sought to limit the influence and access of the other in this region.

For Romanians, Soviet intentions were unambiguous and not at all helpful to a long-lasting resolution of the conflict. They had a 'front-row seat' for the extraordinarily risky provocations that the Kremlin launched in Berlin (1959/1961) and Cuba (1962). Within the alliance, they repeatedly faced down exaggerated Soviet threat assessments based on manipulated statistics and fabricated intelligence and aimed, they believed, at more completely subordinating the other allies to Soviet command. Soviet prophecies of imminent war, Romania's Foreign Minister reported, were made in order 'to justify the so-called emergency course, namely, that in case of emergency, the command of the troops of the Warsaw Pact member states should be transferred to the Soviet General Staff', giving Moscow 'the possibility of interfering in the internal affairs of our countries'.[39]

The Romanians observed first-hand how Moscow manipulated its Arab clients and encouraged tensions, systematically supporting Arab radicalism in the run-up to the 1967 Six Day War and goading Nasser with false intelligence into actions that provoked the conflict.[40] As to whether this was intended, Bucharest had no doubts.[41] The Kremlin had done this before, in 1966, driving its Syrian and Egyptian clients together and frightening them into taking countermeasures by delivering the same sort of fabricated intelligence: that Israel was amassing its forces on their borders for an imminent attack.[42] Given the circumstances, it was hardly surprising that Bucharest shared the view that 'instead of adopting a constructive position to prevent the war and maintain peace', the USSR proved 'the catalytic factor which instigated Egypt against Israel'.[43]

Nor was there anything in the denouement of the war to shake Bucharest in its assessment. The crushing defeat delivered by Israeli forces to Egypt and its allies seemed a blow to Moscow's position, given that the Arab armies were Soviet-supplied and Soviet-trained. Paradoxically, however, the ruinous defeat proved a tremendous near-term boon for Soviet influence in the region as a panicked Nasser abandoned non-alignment as 'no longer sustainable' and requested a 'direct military agreement with the socialist countries'.[44]

In fact, Nasser was handing over his entire armed forces to the USSR. Syria likewise 'begged' for Soviet military personnel and equipment, proclaiming that the Arab countries would now follow the 'socialist road' and form 'an alliance with the socialist countries'.[45] While the Kremlin avoided assuming direct responsibility for the Arab armies, it did establish a massive military footprint in the area (some 20,000 personnel in Egypt alone). Soviet advisors were posted throughout the armed forces, pro-Soviet officers were appointed to command posts and

Nasser publicly declared his 'total' reliance on Egypt's Soviet military comrades.[46] The flailing Egyptian President went further still, initiating a purge of the armed forces, dismissing and arresting officers known to harbour pro-Western or anti-Soviet feelings, and promoting 'cadres who had studies [sic] in the USSR'.[47]

Brezhnev and Moscow's loyalist allies immediately saw an opportunity to capture the region for socialism.[48] According to Bulgarian leader Todor Zhivkov, the defeat handed the Soviet bloc 'the means necessary to help the three Arab countries' – the UAR [Egypt], Syria and Algeria – along 'their non-capitalistic road, in their social transformation', and to press that advantage elsewhere in the Third World.[49] Nasser's delivery of Egypt may have been unexpected. But it is difficult to imagine a more ringing endorsement of the Romanian assessment regarding the Soviet use of tension, crisis and conflict to expand its influence than the statement made during the Budapest meeting of loyalist bloc leaders in July 1967:

> In general we think that there are premises to transform the military defeat of those countries into our political success. To strengthen our position and our influence there. It would also have great significance in terms of our influence on Turkey, Iran and the African countries. We should not dramatize the defeat, but use the emerging situation for increasing our influence in the region.[50]

This threatened Romanian policy at a fundamental level. As Prime Minister Ion Gheorghe Maurer informed President Lyndon B. Johnson in the last week of June 1967, international crisis and tension endangered his country's efforts 'to be master in its own house' because Moscow invariably told the other bloc members 'to get together, to renounce some of their sovereignty and some of their independence and to obey the command of another state'. This, the Prime Minister explained, was what motivated Romania 'to interfere in problems which really are beyond her and to try to settle them'.[51]

The Romanian reaction was almost diametrically opposite that of the Soviet Union and the rest of the bloc, particularly in its advocacy of direct talks.[52] East German Politburo members complained to North Korean leaders that while French President Charles De Gaulle aligned with the Soviet position on the issue of direct talks, 'Romania currently stands to the right of France', demanding 'that Israel and the Arab nation negotiate directly with one another and that in this manner the UN [read: the USSR] be excluded from the process'.[53] GDR officials pointed out the irony of the situation. Foreign Minister Couve de Murville, 'a French nobleman,' supported Moscow's position while 'a member of the Communist Party', Romanian Foreign Minister Corneliu Manescu, opposed it.[54] Romania's position on the withdrawal of forces conformed to Western European opinion, on the issue of direct talks it stood in advance of some (e.g., France), and it went beyond most others in proposing a means of transforming current antagonisms into cooperative relationships over time.

These, however, were by no means the main points over which Bucharest and Moscow contended. When the Six Day War broke out, the Romanians refused to follow the rest of the Warsaw Pact in breaking off relations with Israel and condemning the USA. According to Brezhnev, they were even 'using their veto' in the CMEA to block alliance assistance to the Arab allies of Moscow.[55] Worse still, Romania denied permission to the Soviet Union and the other Pact allies to use its roads and railways, or overfly its territory, for military-supply operations to Soviet client states in the Middle East.

At the July 1967 Soviet bloc meeting in Budapest, to which Romania was pointedly not invited, Soviet leader Leonid Brezhnev informed the other Pact leaders and Yugoslavia's Josef Broz Tito of the open break with Bucharest. After approvingly reporting Iraq's appeal 'to the Arab world to cut off diplomatic relations with the Romanians and [for] inclusion of Romania on the "black list"' alongside the 'USA, England [sic] and the FRG, because they are helping Israel', he turned to Bucharest's other 'hostile' activities.[56] The Romanians, he said, had opposed the Soviet line at the UN General Assembly's special session and held unapproved talks in New York while neither 'contacting other socialist countries, nor informing them' of the content of their discussions. They had visited Beijing while 'skipping Moscow,' without bothering to 'inform comrades from other socialist countries about the results of that visit' either. Romania's membership in the alliance and its commitment to the common defence was, in Brezhnev's words, 'a façade' because 'everything indicates that they intend to finally break relations with our camp' and leave the Warsaw Pact.[57]

Soviet activities in the Middle East had pushed Romania towards the USA, with which, Bucharest felt, it shared a 'similarity of views'.[58] Expressing his country's assessment that the USA had 'a reasonable stand' towards the conflict and 'an equitable solution for peace', Maurer told Johnson that a 'large measure of responsibility for the provocation of the conflict in the [Middle] East rests with the Soviet Union' and 'does not rest with the United States'. The Prime Minister underlined the fact that 'Romania could not rally to Moscow's position' because it was pursuing a 'dangerous policy in that part of the world and is interfering in a rude manner in the internal affairs of Arab countries'.[59]

The prospects for countering Soviet inroads in the Middle East and advancing the peace process after June 1967 appeared rather dismal. To many, Moscow had won – game, set and match. A myth of Israeli military invincibility was created that made compromise even more difficult for Tel Aviv. And the humiliation inflicted upon Cairo (and Damascus) obscured the difference between negotiation and capitulation, and would continue to do so until Egyptian (and Syrian) pride and reputation could be restored.

A number of intervening events also appeared to diminish Bucharest's leverage with Moscow and key Arab states. In 1968, Romania was compelled to deploy forces to deter a possible Soviet military intervention after it publicly condemned the Soviet-led invasion of Czechoslovakia.[60] Within a year, Syria, Iraq and Sudan broke off relations with Bucharest (and Egypt recalled its Ambassador) after Romania upgraded its diplomatic relations with Israel. In 1971 and 1972, Romanian state security foiled several Palestinian terrorist attacks against the Israeli Ambassador in Bucharest and the visiting Prime Minister Golda Meir.[61]

Ironically, by 1970 Nasser was reconsidering the subordinate position into which he had led his country by throwing its security into the hands of the USSR following the Six Day War. In his public appeal of 1 May 1970, Nasser opened the door to discussions with the USA (and Israel), and to an eventual amelioration of Soviet predominance in Egypt, for which he had been directly responsible.[62] Shortly thereafter, he reached out to Bucharest for assistance.[63]

Ceaușescu already knew that Tel Aviv was interested in direct talks because Israeli Prime Minister Levi Eshkol had asked Prime Minister Maurer to facilitate Israeli–Egyptian contacts in 1969, renewing a request first made by the government of David Ben-Gurion back in 1956, during the Suez Crisis.[64] In October 1970, the Romanian leader discussed this with Prime Minister Golda Meir when both attended the jubilee session of the UN General Assembly in New York.[65] As he later recounted to Sadat, the Israeli prime minister 'told me that she wants a political solution, that she is ready to make concessions and [find] an acceptable understanding'.[66]

At the end of 1971, Sadat requested greater Romanian involvement in facilitating Egyptian–Israeli relations.[67] Consequently, officials from Bucharest quietly met with a number of officials from Tel Aviv and Cairo over the next several months. Ceaușescu's remarks to Sadat during their meetings in April 1972 suggest that Israel responded favourably, and Sadat affirmed his 'full confidence' and 'complete faith' in his Romanian interlocutor with whom he professed to share 'the same opinions on all issues discussed'.[68]

Ceaușescu had stressed the need for a 'new initiative' of a political rather than military character 'to get things moving' towards direct talks:

> [A] way must be found to start discussions. Maybe one can consider confidential discussions [...] They [the Israelis] want to talk any place and under any condition. An inflexible position is not the best choice. Secret negotiations could be carried out [...] [T]he idea of secret negotiations should not be excluded; if not for now, at least in the future.[69]

The following month, during the Israeli prime minister's visit to Bucharest in May 1972, Ceaușescu provided what Meir described as 'the best news I have heard for many years': that her Egyptian counterpart was 'ready to meet with an Israeli'.[70] Unfortunately, for reasons probably related to internal Egyptian considerations, Soviet–Egyptian relations, and the Romanian preoccupation with the upcoming Helsinki (Commission on Security and Cooperation in Europe; CSCE) talks, no further moves were made by Cairo before the year's end.

Less than two months later, in July, Sadat invited the approximately 20,000 Soviet military personnel in Egypt to leave, informing the Soviet Ambassador that Egypt would now 'dispense with the services of all Soviet military experts'.[71] Dissatisfaction with the large Soviet presence on the part of both Cairo and Moscow had been observable since 1970, but as the CIA reported, 'the decision was unquestionably an Egyptian, not a joint one'.[72] Sadat also reached out to the US administration, then distracted by Watergate, anti-war protests and an electoral campaign.[73] By now, what Bucharest had been telling Sadat privately, Washington and Israel were stating publicly – 'that the Russian presence in Egypt was an obstacle to resolution of the Arab-Israeli problem' – suggesting that their departure might offer 'a potential break in the no-war-no-peace situation existing between Cairo and Tel Aviv'.[74]

Before and After the October War

By the 1970s, Romanian policy towards the Third World began acquiring more substance, with Bucharest championing a 'new world economic order' that would permit underdeveloped states to improve their lot as a matter of global security. As Prime Minister Maurer cautioned in April 1973, the 'ultimate consequences in international disturbance' resulting from the 'tendency of [the] US, USSR, and developed countries to disregard needs of great masses of people living in radically sub-standard conditions in underdeveloped countries' would 'dwarf' all other threats, causing 'grave damage to 'civilized countries and their values'.[75] Ceauşescu made the same point within Warsaw Pact councils.

At the alliance's summit in April 1974, the Romanian leader argued that only fair exchange would 'help underdeveloped countries develop more rapidly':

> Establishing just relations between [countries exporting] raw materials and finished products is an important question. Its resolution would accelerate the progress of the underdeveloped states. We must respect the right of peoples to be the masters of their own natural resources. The complex nature of these questions makes it necessary for all countries to participate in the discussion of them on the basis of equality.[76]

Romania also continued its campaign to diminish the military clout of the Warsaw Pact and Moscow's ability to wield that clout unilaterally. It sought to mobilize all Pact members to call for the 'simultaneous dissolution of NATO and the Warsaw Pact', it advocated 'less stress on the military and more on the political component of the Warsaw Pact', it called for unilateral disarmament and troop and budget reductions and it refused to drop older proposals for the rotation of all Pact command posts.[77] Bucharest was remarkably candid with Washington about the aims of its 'deviant' small-state policy and interest in spreading that deviation further afield:

> Romania pursues policy based on principles, rather than on dominance of military and economic strength, both to advance its own national interest and because it sees successful pursuit of policy as benefiting peoples of other countries and ultimately contributing to a more secure and just framework of international relationships. If Romania can succeed, others (Eastern European countries) will be encouraged to try same course according to their possibilities.[78]

The Romanians shared the mid-1973 CIA assessment that Moscow had failed in the Middle East because its geopolitical interests had 'little in common with the interests of the countries of the area', and that it failed in Egypt specifically because conflict between the Arabs and Israelis was 'the initial source – and still the main basis – of the Soviet position in the area'.[79] The bottom line for Kremlin strategists was that, despite the risks of direct involvement in the war, 'peace would remove a major reason for their presence in the Arab world'.[80]

In typical fashion, the Kremlin knew of the planned attack on Israel some two days before the start of the October War but did not bother passing that information on to Romania. Nevertheless, Bucharest moved rapidly out of the starting gate, informing Moscow once again that it would neither provide military assistance to the belligerents nor allow other Pact members to use its roads or railways for that purpose, and it 'would not allow Soviet planes to overfly Romanian territory with military supplies for Arab countries' either.[81]

Bucharest also sent three notes to Moscow and Washington proposing a 'five kilometer zone between Arab and Israeli forces where UNEF [the United Nations Emergency Force] would be stationed and offered Romanian participation in force'.[82] On 14 October 1973, before the Arab armies faced serious defeat, it sent messages to Egypt, Syria and

Israel 'to abandon hostilities and engage in negotiations'.[83] After the Third Egyptian Army was surrounded by Israeli forces, on 22 October, Cairo asked Bucharest to intercede with Tel Aviv, and Foreign Minister Abba Eban was invited to Romania for 'urgent talks'.[84]

In response to Moscow's declaration that it 'reserved the right to act unilaterally' in the region (despite the opposing decision of the UN Security Council), and to Washington's subsequent placing of the US Armed Forces and nuclear arsenal on alert, the Romanian Communist Party (RCP) leadership called for a Romanian–Soviet or Warsaw Pact summit specifically to discuss the 'dispatch of troops to the area and the risks of direct involvement'.[85] Ceauşescu placed considerable store by Romanian participation in the new United Nations Emergency Force (UNEF II), noting to the RCP leadership on 26 October that 'we are the only country accepted by both parties and, in this way the troops of the socialist countries would be present in the Middle East'.[86]

Moscow did not respond to the request for a summit. Since the nuclear crisis was averted within 24 hours, Bucharest did not continue to pursue it. However, the Kremlin did reject Romania's participation in UNEF in no uncertain terms.[87] Bucharest was told 'not to participate in the Middle East Peace-Keeping Force' since only loyalist allies (in this case, Poland) would be accepted, and warned that if it did not withdraw the offer then the Soviet representative on the UN Security Council would veto it anyway, creating more scandal further damaging to bilateral relations.[88] Romania's Ambassador in Washington admitted to an American interlocutor that same evening (2 November 1973) that 'withdrawal had been at Soviet behest' and that this move against Romanian participation in UNEF was not an 'isolated case of Soviet pressures on Romania' but rather part of 'a Soviet policy of isolating Romania in all fora, 'from Vienna to New York'.[89]

Moscow held no comparable leverage over Romanian moves within the region. Eban's visit (4–7 November) was given 'heavy coverage' in the Romanian news media, which described it as 'an important contribution in strengthening efforts in the direction of [a] just and equitable political solution to Middle East crisis'.[90] Praising Romania's policy of maintaining contact with all sides, the Israeli Foreign Minister declared that all problems could be dealt with in 'free, sovereign, sincere negotiations' with 'flexibility and realism, not necessarily shaped by Great Powers'.[91] Bucharest then sent delegations (during 12–28

November) to Egypt, Syria, Jordan, Morocco and Sudan. Israeli Defence Minister Moshe Dayan later reported that Bucharest continued mediating between Tel Aviv and Cairo in more covert fashion, persuading both to continue talks between emissaries of their intelligence services in Romania and Morocco in spite of the war.[92]

Bucharest considered its efforts a safety net for the high-wire shuttling of Henry Kissinger, 'providing both an indirect means of communication between the parties and a back-up possibility for continuing efforts at accommodation if other efforts (like those of the US) ran into difficulties'.[93] According to US observers, Romania benefited from its involvement 'by again demonstrating its independence of view, its attachment to the principle of direct negotiations between parties as the only proper method to resolve disputes, and its even-handedness toward both Israel and the Arabs which might allow it to play a useful role in the future'.[94] But it also incurred serious costs ranging from Arab boycotts and sabotage by the other Pact members to terrorist attacks by Palestinian radicals.[95]

Just how close to the wind Romania was sailing is suggested by the exchange between Soviet Defence Minister Andrei Grechko and GDR leader Erich Honecker in mid-November 1973. Marshal Grechko, known to be a '"major domestic critic" of détente and [a] hawk on [the] Middle East', was already spoiling for a fight with the Romanians after they cancelled the Warsaw Pact Committee of Defence Ministers meeting scheduled to take place ten days hence in Bucharest, allegedly because their defense minister had 'more important tasks to fulfill'.[96] For Grechko, this was 'an insult and a crass provocation, just one among numerous examples of the impertinence with which the Romanian comrades recently behave'.[97]

Adding injury to insult, Bucharest refused to participate in the bloc's joint operations in the Middle East during and after the 1973 October War. As in June 1967, Grechko complained, 'only Romania' refused military assistance and denied the use of its military facilities, territory and airspace to allied forces for conveying military aid to Moscow's Arab clients.[98] This, the Soviet Marshal underscored, contradicted the policy of every other Pact member as well as Yugoslavia, all of which had 'accorded active assistance to the Arab states during the aggression'.[99]

The final straw was Bucharest's demonstration of 'insolence and effrontery of the meanest sort' by inviting the Israeli Foreign Minister to

Romania 'as if there were no war in the Middle East'. According to the notes taken by the East German Chief of the General Staff, the Soviet Defence Minister then claimed that he and Brezhnev agreed that military intervention in Romania was required, operational plans for which had already been approved and prepared.[100] Fortunately, cooler heads prevailed and Grechko was held in check.

By 1975, Western observers viewed Romania as moving towards the Third World and the Middle East as some sort of haven offering protection from the USSR.[101] Relations and coordination with all small and medium-sized states were indeed important elements of Romanian soft power. But the Middle East was a central battlefield in which Romanian and Soviet world views and interests repeatedly clashed, and Bucharest was playing the long game. Here, Romania was a strategic actor rather than an opportunistic tactician.

The Third World in Romanian Strategy

The stark nature of Romanian–Soviet competition in the region was indicated during the visit of the Egyptian War Minister to Bucharest in April 1976, when Ceauşescu underlined the fact 'that small and medium-sized countries must unite to avoid being "swallowed up" by the Soviet Union'.[102] Ceauşescu and his Defence Minister then 'praised Egypt's abrogation of the friendship treaty with the USSR, and both candidly described Bucharest's efforts to fend off Soviet pressure'.[103] In Romanian eyes, this represented a major victory against Soviet hegemony and for the empowerment of small and medium-sized states, one that was superseded only by Sadat's meeting with his Israeli counterpart in Tel Aviv – also brokered by Bucharest – the following year.

Within the Soviet bloc, the justifying principles for such activity had to be constantly defended. Thus, Bucharest declaimed efforts at 'twisting Marxist-Leninist doctrine to advance Soviet hegemony' and protested the misuse of '"proletarian internationalism" to mean that anyone who defends his nation's independence violates communist theory'.[104] Now, however, with the reorientation that had been under way for more than a decade, it could rely on Third World support. That same April, after quoting Lenin in defence of his country's position, Ceauşescu 'went on to warn the Soviets that they themselves cannot be free if they oppress others', that 'true' proletarian internationalism was 'based on the defense of national sovereignty', that 'many developing countries share Romania's position and that they, too, reject efforts to write the role of the nation out of communist theory'.[105]

By the end of the decade, Kremlin authorities were regularly denouncing Romania for seeking to roll back Soviet influence within the Pact and globally, especially in the developing world. According to a Communist Party of the Soviet Union (CPSU) Central Committee official responsible for the country, the USSR and other Pact members were exasperated by Romania's single-minded efforts to 'cut off the USSR from the socialist countries and from those in the course of development'.[106] Within the socialist community, Bucharest persisted in its attempts 'to draw to its side, in anti-Soviet actions, the leaderships of Bulgaria, Poland, and the GDR', and it did much the same amongst small and medium-sized states throughout the Third World.

In Africa, Bucharest denounced 'the "intervention of foreign troops" in Angola and called for cessation of "any kind of foreign intervention" (which would include Cubans and Soviets)'.[107] It even assisted Angola's National Liberation Front (FNLA), which opposed that country's main Soviet client (the MPLA; the Popular Movement for the Liberation of Angola) during 1974–5.[108] This 'seriously negative' policy changed little in the years that followed, with Romania insisting that African problems 'must be resolved by the Africans, without any outside intervention', and protesting 'against the presence of Cuban troops in Ethiopia'.[109] And Soviet Central Committee authorities were infuriated with Romania's characterization of the 'fraternal assistance accorded by socialist Cuba to the people of Ethiopia' as 'an act of aggression'.[110]

According to Fidel Castro, in Latin America, the Romanians were 'brainwashing' leftist leaders in Mexico and encouraging 'rousing distrust toward the Soviet Union and breaking up the movement'.[111] Moscow likewise bemoaned Romanian refusals to support to its policies in Nicaragua.[112] As one observer noted, Romania desired to 'avoid anything that might upset the international situation or permit Nicaragua to slip into the Soviet orbit'.[113]

Particularly egregious in Moscow's view was the Muslim delegation that Bucharest sent to Ayatollah Khomeini after the fall of the Shah of Iran. According to Soviet officials, 'the delegation tried to warn Khomeni [sic] not to invite specialists of the USSR into Iran, underscoring, at the same time, that the interests of the great powers are all encompassing and do not coincide with the interests of the small and medium-sized countries'.[114] Perhaps more galling still were the 'anti-Soviet overtures' that Romania made to the Ambassador of Afghanistan in Moscow while the Soviets were preparing operations to overthrow the Afghan leadership.[115]

Due to fundamental policy differences, Romanian cooperation with the Warsaw Pact in the Third World became the exception rather than the rule over the course of 1955–75. Although difficult for either of the great powers to perceive clearly at the time, Romanian policies in the developing world were not driven merely by the need to counter Soviet (or US) hegemony. Nor did Bucharest turn towards the Third World merely to avert or balance Soviet hostility because of Romania's relations with the West. They had a logic and dynamic of their own.

Romanian policies were aimed at creating a world in which there was safety in numbers, where great powers were constrained from employing force unilaterally, and where small and medium-sized states had access to and influence over discussions and decisions at the international level that directly affected them. In other words, Romania's policy towards the Third World, despite its membership in the Warsaw Pact, was not so much a variation on a theme as it was a different story altogether.

Notes

1. Romanian Foreign Ministry Archives (hereafter, AMAE), fond Israel/1970, problema 220, vol. I, f. 181.
2. Constantin Georgescu and Monica Tudor Georgescu, 'Romania's Merchant Fleet', *Knowledge Horizons – Economics*, vol. 6, no. 4 (2014), pp. 167–70.
3. CIA, 'Communist Aid to the Third World Oil Industries (ER RP 73–12)', 1 June 1973, pp. 1–3, 19. All of the CIA documents referenced herein are available at https://www.cia.gov/library/readingroom/home.
4. CIA, 'Intelligence Report: Communist Aid to Less Developed Countries of the Free World, 1974 (ER IR 75–16)', 1 June 1975, pp. 2–3.
5. 'Coordination and instruments for direction of Soviet and East European aid programs within and outside CEMA', in CIA, 'Relationship Between Soviet and East European Economic Aid Programs in LDCs (SOVA [Office of Soviet Analysis])', 26 September 1975, pp. 1–3.
6. CIA, 'National Intelligence Estimate: Soviet Military Capabilities to Project Power and Influence in Distant Areas (NIE 11-10-79)', 1 October 1979, pp. 21–2.

7. See Table 6: 'East European Military Assistance to Third World Countries, 1955–1977', in ibid., p. 21. For details on the Bulgarian case, see Jordan Baev, 'East-East Arms Trade: Bulgarian Arms Delivery to Third World Countries, 1950–1989', *Global Cold War*, Parallel History Project on Cooperative Security at http://www.php.isn.ethz.ch/lory1.ethz.ch/collections/index.html (hereafter, PHP), 18 September 2006.
8. 'Memorandum of Conversation between Emil Bodnaras and Harry G. Barnes, U.S. Ambassador to Romania', Bucharest, 17 May 1974, Cold War International History Project (CWIHP) Digital Archive. Available at http://digitalarchive.wilsoncenter.org/document/110457 (accessed September 2017).
9. Larry L. Watts, *With Friends Like These: The Soviet Bloc's Clandestine War Against Romania* (Bucharest, 2010), pp. 162–207. See also Larry L. Watts, 'Divided Loyalties: Romanian Objection to Informal Soviet Control, 1963–1964', CWIHP e-Dossier No. 42, Washington, DC, Woodrow Wilson International Center for Scholars, 1 October 2013. Available at https://www.wilsoncenter.org/publication/divided-loyalties-within-the-bloc-romanian-objection-to-soviet-informal-controls-1963 (accessed September 2017).
10. Hungary, for example, 'needed to keep itself to the line defined by Moscow' in order to 'pursue its own interests as well'. Csaba Békés, László J. Nagy and Dániel Vékony, 'Bittersweet Friendships: Relations between Hungary and the Middle East, 1953–1988', CWIHP e-Dossier No. 67, Wilson Center, 5 November 2015. See also Anna Locher, 'Shaping the Policies of the Alliance – The Committee of Foreign Ministers of the Warsaw Pact, 1976–1990', May 2002, and Christian Nünlist, 'Cold War Generals: The Warsaw Pact Committee of Defense Ministers, 1969–1990', May 2001, both in *Warsaw Pact Records*, PHP (accessed October 2017).
11. Bucharest tried to do the same in the Council for Mutual Economic Assistance (CMEA). See Elena Dragomir, 'Cold War Perceptions: Romania's Policy Change Towards the Soviet Union, 1960–1964', doctoral dissertation, University of Helsinki, 2014, pp. 131–4, 153.
12. See, for example, Jan Sejna, *We Will Bury You* (London, 1982), p. 75–6; Vojtech Mastny, *Learning From The Enemy: NATO as a Model for the Warsaw Pact* (Zurich, 2001), p. 22; PHP. See also 'Hungarian Minutes of Politburo Meeting on Summit in Bucharest', 12 July 1966, and 'Report to the Hungarian Party Politburo and Council of Ministers on the PCC Meeting', 9 March 1968; and 'On the Position of the Socialist Republic of Romania: Additions to the Speech by the East German Head of State (Erich Honecker), 4 April 1974' – all in *Party Leaders*, PHP (accessed October 2017).
13. See, for instance, Larry L. Watts, 'Romanian Security Policy and the Cuban Missile Crisis', Cold War International History Project e-Dossier No. 38, February 2013, https://www.wilsoncenter.org/publication/romania-security-policy-and-the-cuban-missile-crisis.
14. *Scânteia*, 26 April 1964 (*Scânteia* was the principal daily newspaper.) This 'declaration of independence' was officially entitled *The Declaration with Regard*

to the Position of the Romanian Workers' Party on the Problems of the International Communist and Workers' Movement.
15. Ibid.
16. Ibid.
17. Agerpres (national news agency of Romania), 6 May and 28 June 1971; Robert R. King, 'Rumania and European Security', *Rumania*/13, Radio Free Europe Research (hereafter, RFER), 20 July 1972, Open Society Archives (OSA), Box 114, Folder 2, Report 266, pp. 12–13. Ceaușescu told US officials not to take anti-imperialist attacks personally, since the charge had a wider application.
18. *Scânteia*, 26 July 1971.
19. 'Speech by the General Secretary of the Romanian Communist Party (Nicolae Ceaușescu) at the January 1972 PCC Meeting in Prague', *PCC Meetings 1970– 1990, Party Leaders*, PHP (accessed October 2017).
20. Ibid.
21. 'Minutes of 14 April 1974 PCC Meeting, Including Speeches', Warsaw, April 17, 1974', in *PCC Meetings 1970–1990, Party Leaders*, PHP, pp. 36, 39–42 (accessed October 2017).
22. 'Situation of the Socialist Republic of Romania and the Imperialist Influence on This Country, February 7, 1969', Hauptverwaltung A (HVA) report, BStU, MfS, ZAIG 5481, f. 1–38; Document 5 in Georg Herbstritt and Stejaru Olaru, *Stasi si Securitatea* [The Stasi and (Romanian) State Security] (Bucharest, 2005), pp. 276–7.
23. BStU, MfS, ZAIG 5481, f. 1–38; Herbstritt and Olaru, *Stasi si Securitatea*, p. 276.
24. See, for example, 'Minutes of the Joint Meeting of the Central Committee and the Ministers' Council, August 04, 1971', History and Public Policy Program Digital Archive, Hungarian National Archives, Budapest (MOL), MOL M-KS-288 f. 4. cs. 113. o. e. http://digitalarchive.wilsoncenter.org/document/110268; 'Evaluation by the East German Embassy in Bucharest on Ceausescu's Visit to China, June 11, 1971', in *China and Eastern Europe from the 1960s to the 1980s: International Conference, Beijing, 24–26 March 2004, Global Cold War*, PHP (accessed October 2017), pp. 1–3. 'Analysis of Romanian-Chinese Relations by the East German Embassy in Bucharest, 18 December 1972', in ibid., p. 3; and 'Analysis of the Romanian Attitude Toward Maoism, 1974', in ibid., pp. 2–3.
25. King, 'Rumania and European Security', pp. 10, 13; Tamas Palos, 'Small Countries – Big Policy', *Népszava*, 20 August 1971; K. K., 'Hungary and Her Southern Neighbors', *Hungary*/14, RFER, 26 August 1971, p. 9. See also Charles Andras, 'European Security and the Security of Europe', *East-West Relations Background Report*/1, RFER (EERA [East Europe Region Analysis]), March 1970.
26. K. K., 'Hungary and Her Southern Neighbors', p. 10; Robert R. King and William F. Robinson, 'Rumanian-Hungarian Relations: Friendship with Reservations?' *Eastern Europe*/5, RFER, 10 March 1972, p. 7.

27. Nicolae Ecobescu and Edwin Glaser, 'European Security and International Law', *Lupta de Clasa*, no. 3 (March 1972), pp. 51–62 in Joint Publications Research Service, No. 55958, 10 May 1972, pp. 43–55; King, 'Romania and European Security', pp. 13–14.
28. Ecobescu and Glaser, 'European Security'.
29. Telegram #2092, Subject: Ceausescu Visit To Lebanon, From American Embassy Beirut (Houghton) to Secretary of State, Washington, February 20, 1974. Ceauşescu met with PLO Chairman Yasir Arafat, Fatah's Farouq Qaddumi, Saiqa's Zohayr Muhsen and the PDFLP's Yasir Rabdrabbu.
30. See, for instance, Dusko Doder, 'Ceausescu Moves Romania Toward Third-World Role', *St. Petersburg Times*, 30 May 1975.
31. Romania thus attended the NAM conference in Colombo, Sri Lanka, in 1976, and was admitted to the UN's Group of 77 developing nations (the G77) the same year.
32. 'Conversation between Governor Harriman and President [of the Council of Ministers] Maurer of Romania regarding Vietnam and Middle East', 28 November 1967, US Library of Congress, Manuscript Division, Harriman Papers, Box 557, Folder 4, Document 11, pp. 12–14. US arguments against 'no first use' proposals in the Nonproliferation Treaty referenced the overwhelming conventional Chinese threat. 'Transcript of Discussions Held on the Occasion of the Reception by Comrade Nicolae Ceausescu of Richard Nixon, Former Vice-President of the U.S.A.', Bucharest, 22 March 1967, Romanian National Archives (hereafter, ANR), Fond C.C. al P.C.R., Secţia Relaţii Externe, dosar 15/1967, f. 4, 16–20. See also Document 34 in Larry L. Watts, *Mediating the Vietnam War: Romania and the First Trinh Signal 1965–1966*, CWIHP Working Paper No. 81, Wilson Center (July 2016). Available at https://www.wilsoncenter.org/sites/default/files/cwihp_wp_81_larry_watts_july_2016.pdf (accessed September 2017).
33. Romanian Prime Minister Ion Gheorghe Maurer and North Vietnamese Prime Minister Pham Van Dong discussed the threat of US employment of nuclear weapons in Vietnam after that scenario appeared in *L'Express* in October 1966. Maurer admitted he 'did not know' whether it was genuine. Document 30 in Watts (2016). The danger of US nuclear escalation was also discussed with the Soviets. 'Transcript of Senior-Level Discussions Between the Communist Party of the Soviet Union and the Romanian Communist Party', Moscow, 17–18 March 1967, ANR, Fond C.C. al P.C.R., Secţia Relaţii Externe, dosar 14/1967, f. 7–8.
34. 'Memorandum of Conversation between Nicolae Ceausescu and Anwar El-Sadat', Cairo, 3 April 1972, ANR, Fond C.C. al P.C.R., Secţia Relaţii Externe, dosar 19/1972, ff. 37–43 (hereafter, Ceauşescu–Sadat Conversation I). This translation from Mircea Munteanu, 'CWIHP Launches New Middle East Initiative', *Cold War International History Project Bulletin*, no. 16 (2008) p. 541.

35. US Department of State, 'The Arab-Israeli War 1973', available at https://history.state.gov/milestones/1969–1976/arab-israeli-war-1973 (accessed September 2017).
36. Document 41 in Watts (2016).
37. Ceauşescu–Sadat Conversation I, in Munteanu, 'CWIHP Launches', p. 541.
38. See, for example, 'Note of Conversation of Nicolae Ceausescu with ad interim charge d'affaires of the United Arab Republic, Fikry Mahanny Nakhla, in Bucharest, Accompanied by a Copy of the Appeal Addressed by President Gamal Abdel Nasser to U.S. President Richard Nixon', 12 May 1970, ANR, Fond C.C. al P.C.R., Secţia Relaţii Externe, dosar 15/1970, f. 1–20.
39. 'Stenographic Transcript of the Meeting of the Consultative Political Committee of the Central Committee of the Romanian Communist Party', 24 November 1978, in Dennis Deletant, Mihail E. Ionescu and Anna Locher, 'Romania and the Warsaw Pact: Documents Highlighting Romania's Gradual Emancipation from the Warsaw Pact, 1956–1989', March 2004, PHP.
40. CIA, 'Intelligence Report: Soviet Policy and the 1967 Arab-Israeli War' (Reference Title: CAESAR XXXVIII), 16 March 1970, pp. 3–6, 53–8.
41. Although Moscow provided false intelligence to its Arab clients that contributed to the outbreak of war, controversy continues as to whether it provoked Egypt and Syria intentionally or inadvertently. Regardless of the final verdict on this debate, it is worth noting that interpretations stressing inadvertence rely substantially on arguments of dysfunctional civil–military competition within the Kremlin at the time. Given that such competition would have been largely opaque to anyone outside the inner circle, it is unreasonable to expect that contemporary observers could have perceived Soviet actions as representing anything other than Soviet policy. For the interpretation of inadvertence, see Guy Laron, *The Six-Day War: The Breaking of the Middle East* (New Haven and London, 2017).
42. Isabella Ginor, 'The Cold War's Longest Cover-Up: How and Why the USSR Instigated the June 1967 War', *MERIA* (Middle East Review of International Affairs), vol. 7, no. 3 (September 2003), pp. 34–59. See also Isabella Ginor and Gideon Remez, 'The Six-Day War As A Soviet Initiative: New Evidence And Methodological Issues', *MERIA*, vol. 12, no. 3 (September 2008).
43. 'Telegram from Valeriu Georgescu, Extraordinary Envoy and Plenipotentiary Minister of Romania in Tel Aviv, Regarding the Position of the Israeli Communist Party vis-a-vis the [Israeli] conflict with Arab Nations', 20 June 1967, History and Public Policy Program Digital Archive, Archive of the Ministry of Foreign Affairs, Bucharest, Telegrams, Tel Aviv, vol. 1. 1/1967. Available at http://digitalarchive.wilsoncenter.org/document/113619 (accessed September 2017); James G. Hershberg, 'The Soviet Bloc and the Aftermath of the June 1967 War: Selected Documents from Polish and Romanian Archives', CWIHP e-Dossier No. 13, Wilson Center, 7 July 2011. Available at https://www.wilsoncenter.org/publication/the-soviet-bloc-and-the-aftermath-the-june-1967-war (accessed September 2017).

44. 'The Visit of the Czechoslovak President's Special Envoy, V. Koucki, to the UAR', 28 June 1967, CWIHP History and Public Policy Program Digital Archive, available at http://digitalarchive.wilsoncenter.org/document/112572 (accessed September 2017); 'Polish Record of Meeting of Soviet-bloc leaders (and Tito) in Budapest (excerpts)', 11 July 1967, CWIHP History and Public Policy Program Digital Archive, available at http://digitalarchive.wilsoncenter.org/document/113622 (accessed September 2017).
45. Ibid.
46. 'Polish Record of Meeting of Soviet-bloc leaders (and Tito) in Moscow', 9 November 1967, CWIHP History and Public Policy Program Digital Archive, available at http://digitalarchive.wilsoncenter.org/document/113629 (accessed September 2017); 'Polish Record of Meeting of Soviet-bloc leaders (and Tito) in Budapest (excerpts)', 11 July 1967.
47. 'Polish Record of Meeting of Soviet-bloc leaders (and Tito) in Moscow', 9 November 1967.
48. 'Record of Conversation between Polish Politburo member Zenon Kliszko and Soviet Leader Leonid Brezhnev', Moscow, 24 June 1967, History and Public Policy Program Digital Archive, KC PZPR, Archiwum Akt Nowych, Warsaw. Available at http://digitalarchive.wilsoncenter.org/document/113621 (accessed September 2017).
49. 'Polish Record of Meeting of Soviet-bloc leaders (and Tito) in Budapest (excerpts)', 11 July 1967.
50. Ibid., Interestingly, Yugoslavia's Josef Broz Tito also attended, and adhered to, the Moscow line.
51. 'Memorandum of Conversation', Subject: 'Call of Romanian Prime Minister on President Johnson,' Washington, 26 June 1967, Document 157, *Foreign Relations of the United States, 1964–1968*, Volume XVII, Eastern Europe, US Department of State, at https://history.state.gov/historicaldocuments/frus1964-68v17/d157.
52. *Scânteia*, 11 June 1967.
53. 'Memorandum on a meeting with a delegation from the Supreme People's Assembly of the DPRK on 3 July 1967', Document No. 4, in Bernd Schäfer, 'Weathering the Sino-Soviet Conflict: The GDR and North Korea, 1949–1989', in 'New Evidence on North Korea', *Cold War International History Project Bulletin*, Issue 14/15 (2003–4), p. 45.
54. Ibid.
55. See 'Polish Record of Meeting of Soviet-bloc leaders (and Tito) in Budapest (excerpts)', 11 July 1967. See also Dumitru Preda (ed.), *Romania-Israel: Documente Diplomatice* [Romania–Israel Diplomatic Documents], vol. 1, 1948–69 (Bucharest, 2000).
56. 'Polish Record of Meeting of Soviet-bloc leaders (and Tito) in Budapest (excerpts)', 11 July 1967; TASS (USSR press agency), 12 July 1967.
57. Polish Record of Meeting of Soviet bloc leaders (and Tito) in Budapest (excerpts), 11 July 1967.

58. 'Memorandum of Conversation', Washington, 26 June 1967, Document 157, *Foreign Relations of the United States, 1964–1968*, Volume XVII, Eastern Europe.
59. CIA, 'Rumanian Reaction to the Johnson-Maurer Meeting of 26 June 1967', 1967, p. 1. See also CIA, 'Intelligence Information Cable, Romanian Diplomats' Comments on Relations with the United States and the Communist World', 1967.
60. See, for instance, former Warsaw Pact Chief of General Staff, A. I. Gribkov, *Sud'ba varshavskogo dogovora: Vospominania, Dokumenty, fakty* [Part of the Warsaw Pact: Recollections, Documents, Facts] (Moscow,1998), pp. 75–6, 119–47.
61. Watts, *With Friends Like These*, pp. 579–81.
62. See, for example, *U.S. News & World Report*, 2 May 1970. See also 'Memorandum From the President's Assistant for National Security Affairs (Kissinger) to President Nixon', Washington, 12 May 1970, Subject: 'Nasser's "Appeal" to You – A New Diplomatic Initiative', Document 115 in *Foreign Relations of the United States, 1969–76*, vol. XXIII, Arab-Israeli Dispute, US Department of State, at https://history.state.gov/historicaldocuments/frus1969-76v23/d115.
63. 'Note of Conversation of Nicolae Ceausescu with ad interim charge d'affaires of the United Arab Republic, Fikry Mahanny Nakhla, in Bucharest, Accompanied by a Copy of the Appeal Addressed by President Gamal Abdel Nasser to U.S. President Richard Nixon', 12 May 1970, ANR, Fond C.C. al P.C.R., Secţia Relaţii Externe, dosar 15/1970, f. 1–20.
64. Ion Calafeteanu and Alexandru Cornescu-Coren, *România i criza din Orientul Mijlociu* [Romania and The Crisis in the Middle East] *(1965–1971)* (Bucharest, 2002), p. 82; AMAE, fond Telegrame Varsovia, dosar no. 25/1956, telegram no. 29017, 15 November 1956; Mihai Retegan, *In the Shadow of the Prague Spring: Romanian Foreign Policy and the Crisis in Czechoslovakia, 1968* (Iaşi, 2000), p. 25.
65. Ceauşescu was in the USA during 8–28 October 1970. After New York, he and Prime Minister Meir met separately with President Nixon and attended the same White House dinner for UN delegates in the East Wing on October 24, 1970.
66. Ceauşescu–Sadat Conversation I, in Munteanu, 'CWIHP Launches', pp. 541, 543. See also, Anwar el-Sadat, *In Search of Identity: An Autobiography* (New York, 1978), pp. 230–1.
67. 'Transcript of Conversation on Occasion of the Reception by Nicolae Ceausescu of the First Vice-President of the United Arab Republic Council of Ministers, Dr Aziz Sedki, Regarding Romanian-Egyptian Relations and the Situation in the Middle East (13 December 1971), Accompanied by the Letter of Mohamed Anwar El-Sadat (President of Egypt) addressed to Nicolae Ceausescu and a Note Referring to the Conversations', ANR, Fond C.C. al P.C.R., Secţia Relaţii Externe, dosar 107/1971, f. 1–24. Sedki was appointed prime minister one month later.

68. 'Memorandum of Conversation Between Nicolae Ceausescu and Anwar El-Sadat', Cairo, 6 April 1972, ANR, Fond C.C. al P.C.R., Secția Relații Externe, dosar 19/1972, f. 45–56 (hereafter, Ceaușescu–Sadat Conversation II), in Munteanu, 'CWIHP Launches', p. 543.
69. Ceaușescu–Sadat Conversation I, in Munteanu, 'CWIHP Launches', p. 541; and Ceaușescu–Sadat Conversation II, in Munteanu, 'CWIHP Launches', p. 543.
70. Kenneth W. Stein, *Heroic Diplomacy: Sadat, Kissinger, Carter, Begin and the Quest for Arab-Israeli Peace* (New York, 1999), pp. 63, 185.
71. Sadat (1978), pp. 230–1.
72. CIA ONE (Office of National Estimates), 'Memorandum: The Russian Ouster – Causes and Consequences', 22 August 1972, p. 1.
73. William B. Quandt, *Camp David: Peacemaking and Politics* (Washington, DC, 1986), pp. 22–3.
74. CIA ONE, 'Memorandum: The Russian Ouster', pp. 4–5.
75. Telegram #1413, Subject: Call on Prime Minister Maurer, From American Embassy, Bucharest to Secretary of State, Washington, 18 April 1973, Central Policy Files, US National Records And Administration (hereafter, NARA). Available at https://aad.archives.gov/aad/createpdf?rid=5193&dt=2472&dl=1345 (accessed September 2017).
76. 'Minutes of 14 April 1974 PCC Meeting, Including Speeches', Warsaw, April 17, 1974', in *PCC Meetings 1970–1990, Party Leaders*, PHP, p. 42.
77. Ibid., pp. 36, 39–40.
78. Telegram #1413, Subject: Call on Prime Minister Maurer, From American Embassy, Bucharest to Secretary of State, Washington, 18 April 1973, NARA.
79. CIA, 'Intelligence Memorandum: Soviet Policy in the Middle East', May 8, 1973, pp. 1, 6.
80. Ibid., See also CIA, 'Soviet Policy Toward the Middle East (SOV 86-10048X)', 1 December 1986, CIA, Appendix B, 'Moscow and the Arab-Israeli Peace Process', p. 83.
81. Telegram #28218, From American Embassy, Paris (Irwin) to Secretary of State, Washington, 31 October 1973. Public Library of US Diplomacy (Wikileaks), available at https://wikileaks.org/plusd/cables/1973PARIS28218_b.html.
82. Ibid.
83. *Scânteia*, 25 October 1973; Petre Otu, 'Romania's Position Towards The Arab-Israeli War of 1973', in Shaul Shay and Orly Woland (eds), *The Cold War and the Arms Race in the Middle East*, Proceedings of the Israeli-Romanian International Seminar, Tel-Aviv, Israel, 19–23 May, 2002, p. 53.
84. Otu, 'Romania's Position', p. 54; CIA, 'Romania-Israel-USSR', in CIA, *The President's Daily Brief*, 6 November 1973, p. 3.
85. Otu, 'Romania's Position', p. 56.
86. ANR, Fond C.C. al P.C.R., Secția Cancelarie, dosar 149/1973, f. 4.
87. Paradoxically, Romania's offer of peacekeeping forces during the Suez Crisis in 1956, although agreed by Egypt and the UN Secretary General, had been rejected by the USA.

88. See, for instance, Telegram #3987, Subject: Soviet Opposition to Romania Participation in Middle East Peace-Keeping, From American Embassy, Bucharest (GS Martens) to Secretary of State, Washington, 1 November 1973, NARA.
89. Telegram #4491, Subject: UNEF, From US Mission United Nations (USUN), New York (Bennett), to Secretary of State, Washington, 6 November 1973, NARA.
90. *Scânteia*, 6 November 1973.
91. Ibid; Telegram #4063, Subject: Eban Visit to Romania, From American Embassy, Bucharest (Martens) to Secretary of State, Washington, 6 November 1973, NARA.
92. Interview with Moshe Dayan, Jerusalem Domestic Television Service, 5 October 1977, in Foreign Broadcast Information Service, Daily Report – 'Middle East and North Africa', 6 October 1977, p. N2. See also, Stein, *Heroic Diplomacy*, pp. 184–5.
93. Telegram #4117, Subject: An Unofficial Romanian View of the Abba Eban Visit, From American Embassy, Bucharest (Martens) to Secretary of State, Washington, 10 November 1973, NARA.
94. Ibid.
95. See, for example, CIA, 'Arab States – Romania', in United States Intelligence Board (hereafter, USIB), *National Intelligence Bulletin*, 30 August 1975, p. 11. Bucharest avoided boycotts of its airline TAROM, which flew to Tel Aviv, Beirut, Cairo and Algiers, in 1967 and 1974, but not August 1975.
96. *Pravda*, 8 October 1973; Victor Zorza, 'The Middle East War: A Boost for Soviet Hawks', *Washington Post*, 16 October 1973.
97. 'Minute regarding the meeting between Comrade Erich Hoenecker and Comrade Marshal Grechko', 17 November 1973, BStU, MfS, SdM 1577, S. 50–56 – reproduced: Document 12, in Herbstritt and Olaru, *Stasi si Securitatea*, pp. 314–15.
98. Ibid.
99. Ibid.
100. Ibid; Otto Wenzel, 'The Soviet Defense Minister Suggests the Military Occupation of Romania', *Zeitschrift des Forschungsverbundes S.E.D.-Staat an der Freie Universitat Berlin* [Journal of the Socialist Unity Party (East German Communist Party)-State Research Association at the Free University of Berlin], nr. 6 (1998), p. 94.
101. 'Romania', in USIB, *National Intelligence Bulletin*, 26 April 1975, p. 12. According to the CIA, Ceauşescu was 'pushing hard for closer association with the nonaligned world and possibly for a seat at the Geneva talks on the Middle East', because of a belief 'that by inserting himself into the Middle East picture and by improving relations with key nonaligned nations, he [would] be better able to resist Soviet pressure'.
102. CIA, 'Romania-Egypt', in USIB, *National Intelligence Bulletin*, 22 April 1976, p. 8.

103. Ibid; 'Transcript of Conversations on the Occasion of the Reception by Nicolae Ceaușescu of General Mohamed El-Gamasy, Chief of the Egyptian Military Delegation', 16 April 1976, ANR, Fond C.C. al P.C.R., Secția Relații Externe, dosar 32/1976, f. 1-10.
104. CIA, 'Romania-USSR', in USIB, *National Intelligence Bulletin*, 28 April 1976, p. 6.
105. Ibid., These remarks were made to the Congress of Romanian Trade Unions on 26 April 1976.
106. 'Conspect of Conversations with Cde. V. I. Potapov, Head of Romania Sector of CPSU CC Section', May 16, 1979, Document 4, in Larry Watts, 'The Soviet-Romanian Clash Over History, Identity and Dominion', CWIHP e-Dossier No. 29, 31 January 2012. See also Document 5 in ibid.
107. Telegram #6545, Subject: Romanian Foreign Policy: Ceausescu's Year-End Review, From American Embassy, Bucharest (Barnes) to Secretary of State, Washington, 19 December 1975, NARA.
108. Odd Arne Westad, 'Moscow and the Angolan Crisis, 1974–1976: A New Pattern of Intervention', *CWIHP Bulletin*, nos 8–9 (Winter 1996), p. 25, 31, footnote 42; Raymond L. Garthoff, *Détente and Confrontation* (New York, 1994), p. 558.
109. See 'Conversations with Cde. V. I. Potapov, Chief of Romanian Sector of CPSU CC Section', 27 October 1978, Document 3 in Watts, 'The Soviet-Romanian Clash'. See also Documents 2–5 in ibid.
110. 'Exposition of the Conversations with Cde. V.I. Potapov, Chief of the Romanian Sector of the CPSU CC', 27 June 1978, Document 2 in ibid. Bucharest was also attacked for its allegedly pro-NATO and pro-Beijing attitude towards Zaire.
111. 'Minutes of the Meeting between Todor Zhivkov and Fidel Castro in Sofia', 11 March 1976, History and Public Policy Program Digital Archive. Available at http://digitalarchive.wilsoncenter.org/document/112241 (accessed September 2017).
112. These complaints were voiced by Brezhnev and Soviet Central Committee expert on Romania, V.I. Potapov, during 1978–9. See Documents 3, 4, 5 in Watts, 'The Soviet-Romanian Clash'.
113. Sebastian Garcia, 'El Rey defiende las libertades en su visita oficial a Rumanía' {King Defends Freedoms During his Official Visit to Romania}, *El País*, 21 May 1985. Romania had similarly mediated with the military junta in Portugal in 1975, to 'head off a radical swing to the left that could bring Portugal under considerable Soviet influence'; CIA, 'Romania: Ceaușescu's remarks during visit to Portugal bound to irk Kremlin', in USIB, *National Intelligence Bulletin*, 3 November 1975, p. 8.
114. Document 5 in Watts, 'The Soviet-Romanian Clash'.
115. Ibid.

PART II

'INTERMEDIARIES': SPIES, JOURNALISTS, DOCTORS, TEACHERS AND DIPLOMATS IN THE THIRD WORLD

CHAPTER 5

COLD WAR ON THE CHEAP: SOVIET AND CZECHOSLOVAK INTELLIGENCE IN THE CONGO, 1960-3

Natalia Telepneva

In July 1960, the chairman of the Soviet Committee on State Security (KGB), Alexander Shelepin, hosted a high-level delegation from the Czechoslovak State Security (StB; *Státní Bezpečnost*) headed by the Czechoslovak minister of the interior, Rudolf Barák. A former head of the Soviet Youth Organization (Komsomol) and a protégé of the first secretary of the Central Committee of the Communist Party of the Soviet Union (CC CPSU), Nikita Khrushchev, Shelepin was a rising star in the Party. So was Barák, an ambitious and dynamic man who had a taste for foreign affairs and was rumoured to harbour ambitions to supersede Antonín Novotný as first secretary.[1]

As minister of the interior, Barák presided over the StB's First (Intelligence) Directorate that, alongside its Soviet equivalent (the First Directorate of the KGB), was responsible for foreign intelligence.[2] Not much is known about Shelepin's personal relations with Barák, but we do know that the latter's term as minister of the interior ushered in a new era of cooperation between the KGB and the Czechoslovak Ministry of the Interior on a number of issues, including joint intelligence operations in the Third World. In fact, the July 1960 meeting was the first instance of the StB and the KGB coordinating joint intelligence operations across the world against the USA – the 'main adversary' in KGB parlance.[3] The KGB and StB had developed close ties since the Soviet-sponsored takeover of the country by the Communist Party of Czechoslovakia (CPC) in 1948. However, the meeting of July 1960 was extraordinary because it ushered in a new era of cooperation between the StB and the KGB in the Third World. The timing was not coincidental, since 1960 witnessed the crisis in the Congo during which rival intelligence services – the Soviet KGB, the American Central Intelligence Agency (CIA) and the British MI6 – played a key role.

The crisis in the Congo was one of the most important moments in the history of postcolonial Africa. The Belgian Congo, with its colonial-era capital in Léopoldville, a country two-thirds the size of Western Europe and rich in mineral resources, was set on a path to independence in 1959. On 13 January of that year, after a series of violent protests in its main cities, Belgian King Baudouin announced his intention to 'lead the people of Congo' towards independence. The announcement led to a proliferation of political parties, many of which rooted in regional ethnic groups. Following the Roundtable Conference held in January and February 1960 in Brussels, the Belgian Government agreed to hold general elections and transfer political power to the Congolese. The two parties that did best in the elections were the Alliance of Bakongo (ABAKO; Alliance des Bakongo) and the Congolese National Movement (MNC; Mouvement National Congolais). Thus, on 30 June 1960, ABAKO's leader, Joseph Kasavubu, became the first president of the Congo, while MNC's Patrice Lumumba became its first prime minister.

Only five days later, a major crisis erupted in the country. On 5 July, Congolese soldiers mutinied over pay and the presence of Belgian officers in the army. The revolt was quickly followed by a workers' strike; general chaos ensured, including sporadic, yet widely reported, violence against white residents. On 11 July, Brussels decided to send in paratroopers, seemingly to restore law and order. The following day, the leader and strongman of Katanga, Moïse Tshombe, announced the secession of the resource-rich province. The Belgians stationed the bulk of their forces in Katanga, ostensibly to protect its citizens but in fact their aim was to safeguard Western companies and economic interests. Lumumba appealed to the United Nations to intervene and prevent the secession of Katanga, but frustration with Western inaction led him to turn to the Eastern bloc.

By August, Washington believed that Lumumba was dangerously close to the Soviets and planned for his removal. On 14 September, the army chief of staff, Joseph-Désiré Mobutu, arrested Lumumba and eventually transported him to Katanga province, where he was brutally murdered on 17 January 1961. The struggle for the Congo was not yet over, however. A group of Lumumba's supporters, originally led by Antoine Gizenga, fled to the MNC's stronghold in Stanleyville in eastern Congo, from where Gizenga attempted to launch an armed offensive against the Léopoldville government. Having failed to achieve a military breakthrough, Gizenga half-heartedly agreed to a power-sharing arrangement negotiated at the Lovanium Conference in July 1961. The arrangement lasted only until the end of 1963, when various actors opposed to the central government launched an offensive in yet another round of the civil war, known as the 'Simba Rebellion', which would last until their final defeat in 1965.

While the role of Western intelligence in the Congo Crisis has been the subject of substantial public and historical interest, we know little about the roles of Soviet and Eastern European intelligence personnel. While early literature focused on the role of the West, the declassification of archival materials has begun to establish the Congo Crisis as a multi-dimensional, multi-actor story that had a profound effect on the Cold War.[4] The story of Lumumba's murder still grips both historiographical and public debates.[5] The recent publication of the *Foreign Relations of the United States* (FRUS) book series focused attention on the role of the US and the CIA in particular, showing that in the Congo, the CIA engaged in one of its largest covert actions, costing US$90–150 million at today's money, not counting the military assistance provided by the Department of Defense.[6] Even so, we still know little about the role of Soviet and, especially, Czechoslovak intelligence in the Congo. Bar a general overview by the journalists Petr Zídek and Karl Sieber, as well as a few oral testimonies, the only account that deals with the Czechoslovak role is Philip Muehlenbeck's *Czechoslovakia in Africa*. Muehlenbeck argues that in the Congo, as elsewhere in Africa, Prague was not simply subservient to Moscow's will but instead tried to pursue its commercial, ideological and strategic interests in Africa in line with its own national objectives.[7] Nonetheless, our understanding of the Soviet and Czechoslovak intelligence presence in the Congo remains patchy. Did US officials in the country really overestimate the extent of the communist threat, and what was the role of Czechoslovak intelligence in this story? This chapter aims to answer these questions.

Czechoslovakia had a long-standing presence in the Congo. One of the Czechoslovak diplomats stationed in Léopoldville before independence, Josef Virius, had relationships with Congolese nationalist politicians. He shared information with his Czechoslovak superiors, who then, most likely, informed their Soviet counterparts. In 1960, the KGB and StB launched their first joint operation to monitor events in the Congo, but it was cut short by Lumumba's arrest. When Antoine Gizenga moved to Stanleyville, Czechoslovak intelligence advocated increased support for his military offensive, but the Soviet leadership soon realized the limits of its involvement in a faraway conflict. Based on largely overlooked records of the StB, this chapter reveals that even after Gizenga's government agreed, at Lovanium, to a compromise solution to the standoff with Léopoldville, Czechoslovak intelligence entertained ambitious plans for operations in the Congo. While this optimism subsided a few months later, Czechoslovak intelligence still pushed for its station in Léopoldville to gather information, recruit informants and agents of influence, and undertake so-called 'active operations' to discredit Western powers in the Congo right up until the expulsion of Soviet embassy staff from the country in November 1963, and even afterwards. As a reflection of policy, an examination of Soviet and Czechoslovak intelligence in the Congo helps to clarify foreign-policy objectives hidden from view, as well as the substantial role played by Czechoslovakia, Moscow's so-called 'junior partner'. Lacking in essential knowledge, resources and alliances in the region, and unwilling to face a major showdown with the US, Soviet and Czechoslovak spies in the Congo played key roles as policy intermediaries – a 'cheap' weapon in the Cold War in Africa.

The KGB–StB Mission in Léopoldville, 1960

Czechoslovakia's visibility in Africa was linked to changes in the foreign policy of the Soviet Union. The CC CPSU first secretary, Nikita Khrushchev, turned to the Third World in the mid-1950s, as a wave of decolonization swept through the formerly colonized territories in Africa and Asia. Khrushchev was hopeful that the Third World could offer a new frontier for the peaceful spread of socialism. During his momentous tour of Asia in 1955, he famously challenged the West to 'compete without war', as he believed that the newly independent nations could see the benefits of Soviet-style modernization.[8] Keen to portray the Soviet Union as champion of the anti-imperialist struggle, Khrushchev became increasingly willing to respond to demands for assistance, including arms. A major exporter of small arms, Czechoslovakia was set to benefit economically as well as politically from the new openness to the Third World. When, in September 1955, news emerged that Czechoslovakia had made a deal with the president of the United Arab Republic (UAR), Gamal Abdel Nasser, to supply US$250 million-worth of modern Soviet weaponry, Prague emerged as a key ally of the Soviet Union in Africa.[9]

Czechoslovakia had long-standing connections with the Congo. Its consulate in Léopoldville functioned from 1929 until 1939 and then reopened in 1948. In the early 1950s, the consulate was affected by communication difficulties and personal feuds, with two members of its staff arrested – one of whom was shot – and a third refusing to return to Prague.[10] Only in 1955 did the Czechoslovaks manage to obtain a permanent presence in the Congo with the dispatch of Consul Josef Virius, most likely an StB officer with the code name DIPLOMAT.[11] In charge of selling Czechoslovak Škoda cars in Léopoldville, Virius established connections with a number of Congolese politicians, one of whom was Pierre Mulele, one of the founders of the left-leaning African Solidarity Party (PSA: Parti Solidaire Africain). The PSA's co-founder, Cléophas Kamitatu, stated that Virius organized ideological classes in Léopoldville, with Mulele as one of the attendees. Mulele and Virius were friends, and in 1959 the consul persuaded Kamitatu to buy a Škoda – 'the cheapest on the market' – for the PSA.[12] According to Virius himself, his best contact was with Antoine Gizenga.[13]

The story of initial Soviet contacts with Patrice Lumumba is well known. Lumumba had been trying to establish contact with the Soviets since 1959, when he approached the Soviet Embassy in Guinea. However Moscow was initially sceptical as they believed his party, the MNC, was 'more moderate' than ABAKO.[14] Yet it is also possible that there was some exchange between Czechoslovak and Soviet officials about the situation in the Congo, and that Virius's good relations with Gizenga had something to do with the latter's invitation to Moscow in January 1960, just as the Roundtable Conference was in session. In conversations with the Soviet Solidarity Committee, Gizenga tried to secure support for ABAKO and the PSA and their plan for the Congo as a federation of six independent states, criticizing Lumumba and alleging that he had connections with the Belgian administration. He also asked for a meeting with Nikita Khrushchev for financial assistance and for weapons to launch a liberation struggle if the Belgians refused to grant independence. However, Gizenga did not make much of an impression on his hosts, who believed that he was opportunistic, and recommended that the CPSU should refrain from considering his requests but should learn more about Congolese politicians.[15]

Soviet opinions of Lumumba started to change in early 1960, partly under the influence of the Belgian Communist Party (BCP). The BCP leader, Albert de Coninck, believed that the Congo presented the best conditions for the expansion of Marxism because of a relatively high level of urbanization and who argued that Lumumba was a 'progressive' politician under the influence of Guinean President Sékou Touré.[16] With the BCP acting as intermediary, on 19 February, the first secretary of the Soviet Embassy in Brussels, Boris Savinov, met Lumumba, who expressed his willingness to form a union with a number of small Congolese parties. One of them was the African Regroupment Party (CEREA; Centre de Regroupment Africain), an organization whose leader, Anicet Kashamura, wanted to establish a communist party in the Congo and maintain close links with the BCP. On the basis of the conversation, Savinov reported to Moscow that Lumumba, who enjoyed 'enormous popularity', deserved serious attention from Moscow.[17]

The Belgian intervention on 11 July 1960 thrust the Congo into the Cold War. Lumumba interpreted the intervention as a neocolonial coup rather than a rescue mission, and requested military assistance from UN Secretary-General Dag Hammarskjöld. However, frustrated by Western inaction, Lumumba appealed to Nikita Khrushchev to closely watch developments in the country. Sensing an opportunity to curry favour with newly independent African leaders, Khrushchev responded with a strong statement in support of Lumumba. On 16 July, the Soviet Union pledged 2.5 million roubles of economic aid, agreed to send 10,000 tonnes of food to the Congo and provided 26 aeroplanes and six helicopters to support the UN mission. In comparison, the USA provided 100 planes for the UN effort.[18] The Soviet Union also pushed for the support of Lumumba's position at the United Nations; however, Lumumba's overtures to Moscow made him dangerous in the eyes of the US administration. The CIA chief of station in the Congo, Larry Devlin, writes that in July and August 1960, 'several hundred Soviet personnel' entered the Congo, and the CIA assumed that most if not all of these men were Soviet intelligence officers.[19] By September, Washington was convinced that Lumumba was in the pay of the Soviets and that he had to be replaced by a more moderate, pro-Western government, by force if necessary.[20]

The CIA exaggerated the size of the Soviet intelligence presence in the Congo. The KGB operation there started fairly late, in August 1960, and was limited in its size and scope. On 6 August, Soviet Ambassador Mikhail Yakovlev and a small group of KGB officers led by chief of the KGB station, Leonid Podgornov, arrived in Léopoldville. Their mission, according to Oleg Nazhestkin, who was part of the team, was fairly limited; they were to collect information about Congolese politicians and find out about 'Western plans' for the country.[21] The reasons for the missions lay in Khrushchev's growing frustration over Western inaction in the Congo. In particular, he believed that UN Secretary-General Hammarskjöld had colluded with the US administration, turning a blind eye to Katanga's secession.[22] When Lumumba's trip to the USA in July 1960 brought no results, Khrushchev was particularly annoyed and authorized a plan for an intelligence mission in the Congo.[23] The KGB had a very limited intelligence presence in sub-Saharan Africa before 1960, and only in August did the KGB's First Directorate establish their first eight-man desk to specialize in intelligence operations in Africa.[24] The KGB mission in August was therefore in many ways the first of its kind in sub-Saharan Africa.

Prague was also interested in providing support for the new government. In fact, Czechoslovakia was the first to establish full diplomatic relations with the newly independent Congo. Since the late 1950s, Prague had maintained an official presence in Léopoldville, with the consul, Josef Virius, acting as an intermediary, receiving requests from local politicians and passing them onto Prague. On 18 August, a Czechoslovak delegation arrived carrying the second tranche of assistance in the form of food and medicine worth Kčs2 million (Czechoslovak crowns).²⁵ In Léopoldville, the delegation met with Virius, who explained to them that his best contact, Gizenga, had passed a request for Prague to dispatch security instructors and one military attaché, who would clandestinely provide counsel to the government. When the Czechoslovak officials spoke to Lumumba, they also discovered that the prime minister required, above all, weapons and means of transportation to defeat Tshombe's forces in Katanga.²⁶

Henceforth, Prague moved quickly to provide military assistance. It dispatched two intelligence officers and started a process of negotiation to supply weapons to Lumumba's government, culminating in another delegation arriving in Léopoldville on 5 September, led by Deputy Foreign Minister Karel Klima.²⁷ Prior to the trip, Czechoslovak officials held consultations over support for the Congo in Moscow. The Soviets had encouraged their colleagues to undertake 'maximum initiative' in responding to Congolese requests, but Moscow had agreed to take upon itself the task of supplying weapons and equipment for the Congolese Army. Meanwhile, Czechoslovakia was to specialize in providing security assistance for the new government. In fact, Klima's delegation included a special security advisor who was to provide 'on-site' assistance to the government. It is most likely that a high-ranking officer such as security advisor and head of the Afro-Asian Department, Josef Janouš, was to propose some organizational changes to the Congolese.²⁸

However, any advice came too late, as the political crisis in the Congo reached its crescendo. On the same day that the Czechoslovak delegation landed in Léopoldville, President Kasavubu dismissed Lumumba and replaced him with Joseph Ileo. Lumumba refused to accept the decision and a constitutional crisis ensued before, eventually, on 14 September, Joseph-Désiré Mobutu apprehended Lumumba and placed him under house arrest. At the same time, he ordered Soviet and Czechoslovak embassy staff to leave the country within 24 hours. When Khrushchev learned about events in Léopoldville while on a boat to New York, where he was to give a speech at the UN, he was distraught.²⁹ Speaking at the UN's General Assembly, he lashed out at the West and at UN Secretary-General Hammarskjöld personally for conspiring to overthrow Lumumba. He also proposed an overhaul of the UN's governing body.³⁰ Meanwhile, Antoine Gizenga fled Léopoldville to a stronghold in Stanleyville, from where he appealed, in the name of Lumumba's government, for support from the Eastern bloc.

Arms for Gizenga, 1961

News of Lumumba's arrest and Gizenga's appeal for assistance led to a new bout of Soviet–Czechoslovak dialogue on the Congo in early 1961. On 9 January that year, a Czechoslovak delegation arrived in Moscow for a two-day consultation with their Soviet counterparts. The Soviet deputy foreign minister, Yakov Malik, informed them that Khrushchev had promised all necessary assistance to Gizenga as soon as possible, and that it was merely a matter of execution. This time, the Soviets were ready to offer infantry equipment for 5,000 men, 20 trucks, ten planes, cars, food, medication, a radio transmitter and US$500,000 with weapons to be delivered via the UAR with Sudan's approval. Both sides also decided to send a special mission to Stanleyville, consisting of advisors on defence, security, technical administration and economic matters, with Prague taking upon itself the role of organizing the security component.

The issue of arms was also on the agenda. The Soviet side suggested that their Czechoslovak counterparts should deliver weapons to Stanleyville using all routes (through the UAR or alternatives) as soon as possible. The Soviets also recommended that the Czechoslovaks establish an airline, with pilots and technical crew from the UAR or with Czechoslovak pilots, to deliver supplies to Stanleyville.[31] On 24 January, the Central Committee of the CPC approved a donation of small arms for 2,500 men, four aeroplanes, 60 tonnes of food and pharmaceuticals and £25,000 in cash to the Stanleyville government. The Czechoslovaks also pledged to send their diplomats to Stanleyville and establish an airline that would deliver supplies to Gizenga's capital.[32]

The Soviets soon discovered that the delivery of matériel posed a serious problem. The key obstacle lay in the unwillingness of the Sudanese Government to allow any transportation of assistance to Gizenga's forces in Stanleyville. Other leaders sympathetic to Lumumba's plight, such as the president of the UAR, Gamal Abdel Nasser, were also cautious about becoming entangled in the conflict. On 31 January 1961, the Soviet deputy prime minister, Vladimir Semenov, held a long conversation with Nasser on his way to Sudan. Nasser conveyed a sense that the Gizenga government was critically short on supplies and promised that the UAR contingent in the Congo would leave behind half of its weapons for the regime. He admitted that neither the UAR nor Ghana had succeeded in convincing the Sudanese Government to allow the passage of supplies through its territory. When Semenov explained that the Soviet Government had decided to send a group of experienced diplomats, including from the military, to help Gizenga, Nasser dismissed the suggestion with a joke, saying that the only way would be by parachuting the group into Stanleyville.[33]

News of Lumumba's death, announced on Katangese radio on 13 February, sent shockwaves around the world and strengthened support for Gizenga, who now proclaimed himself the successor of the slain prime minister. One of the African leaders deeply affected by the murder was Ghana's first president, Kwame Nkrumah. Only one day after the announcement, Nkrumah invited Leonid Brezhnev, the chairman of the Presidium of the Supreme Soviet of the Soviet Union, who was on a state visit to Guinea at that time, to Ghana for talks. The Congo was the main point of conversation when Brezhnev arrived in Accra. Nkrumah argued that the only solution to the Congo Crisis would be the replacement of the UN contingent with an African command consisting of troops from the Casablanca Group of African states. Nkrumah also discussed various ways to deliver arms to Stanleyville. One possible route lay via the Central African Republic. Moreover, argued Nkrumah, Lumumba's murder might have changed the stance of the Sudanese Government on the transportation of supplies through their territory. Brezhnev also discussed the Congo with King Hassan II of Morocco, who proposed to transfer weapons via that country's UN contingent. Nkrumah posited a similar scheme for the Ghanaian contingent. In a letter sent to Moscow during his trip, Brezhnev urged the Soviet Central Committee to consider the delivery of light weapons and ammunition to Gizenga's government via Ghana and Morocco.[34] Moscow and Prague continued their support for Gizenga, but did not want the crisis to escalate into a major international incident.

The Soviet view can be detected in the discussions held between Pierre Mulele, now a representative for Gizenga's government, and a group of high-level Soviet officials, including Deputy Foreign Minister Vasiliy Kuznetsov and Minister of Defence Rodion Malinovskiy, in Moscow in March 1961. Describing a difficult financial situation, and especially their inability to pay soldiers, Mulele stressed the importance of delivering supplies and asked for assistance in establishing a Congolese commercial airline, arguing that the UN would not object.

To that, Malinovsky stated that not only would the UN object to the passage of planes, but would actually shoot them down.[35]

Czechoslovakia was likewise concerned about the safety of its aircraft, and was unwilling to provide assistance without prior authorization from the UN and Sudan. When a representative from Gizenga's government, Antoine Mandungu, spoke to the Czechoslovak officials again in June 1961 about the delivery of arms, the deputy foreign minister, Ján Bušniak, stressed that Czechoslovakia had only recently brought planes for long-haul flights to Accra and did not have any trained pilots. But, more importantly, they would not risk flying planes without permission because they would have to fly over West Germany, where there was risk of such a plane being shot down by 'American military forces', citing a recent incident in which a Czechoslovak plane was shot down over Nuremberg, allegedly by the Americans, who suspected that it was carrying weapons to Africa.[36] With neither Sudan nor the UAR giving permission for Czechoslovak planes to fly over their territory, plans to establish an air route to Stanleyville failed.[37] The CIA also provided a continuous obstacle. When a CIA contact working with Pierre Mulele found out that the Soviets had handed US$500,000 to the Congolese to be transferred via Sudan to Stanleyville, the agency hatched a plan to steal the suitcase full of cash at Khartoum Airport.[38]

Meanwhile, Soviet–US relations deteriorated to the point of a major crisis over the status of West Berlin in the summer of 1961. The long-term causes of this crisis dated back to the division of Germany and Berlin into zones of occupation after World War II. In his first series of meetings with the newly elected president, John F. Kennedy, in Vienna on 3 and 4 June 1961, tensions flared up again as Nikita Khrushchev declared the Soviet Union would sign a separate peace treaty with the German Democratic Republic, terminating Western access rights to West Berlin.[39] Khrushchev's provocation stimulated an outflow of East Germans to the West, eventually leading to the construction of the Berlin Wall in August. This was the context in which the KGB and the StB met for their second four-day meeting in Prague on 26 June 1961. The result of the consultations was a lengthy document that yet again outlined spheres of cooperation in the Third World.[40] KGB Chairman Alexander Shelepin pitched a version of the plan to Khrushchev as a series of measures to distract the attention of the USA and its allies during the settlement of the Berlin Crisis, and on 1 August the CC CPSU signed its approval.[41]

The June 1961 KGB–StB agreement on the Congo shows that the Soviets did not give up on finding a way to transfer arms to Gizenga's government in Stanleyville. The agreement consisted of four parts. First, both sides pledged to establish possible ways to deliver arms, ammunition and food supplies, accepting the use of illegal methods and private trading companies from capitalist and neutral countries. Second, the KGB and Czechoslovak intelligence decided to establish joint channels for sourcing reliable information about the situation in the Congo. The third part of the plan included the publication of articles to help undermine US and Belgian efforts to destroy Gizenga's government. Finally, both sides agreed to undercut the 'protégés of the colonisers' – Kasavubu, Mobutu, Ileo and Bomboko.[42] While we do not know how certain parts of the plan were executed, at least one goal was to re-establish a Soviet intelligence presence in the Congo. In July 1961, Podgornov's team reached Stanleyville after a long and torturous journey.[43]

The main mission of the KGB team in Stanleyville was to facilitate a consensus between the authorities in Léopoldville and Lumumba's supporters in Stanleyville. The framework was a meeting of various political parties on 22–23 July at the University of Lovanium, about 20 km from Léopoldville, convened under UN pressure to select a new government. One of Podgornov's team, Oleg Nazhestkin, writes that their mission did 'a lot of work' to encourage compromise between the rival groups in the Congo.[44] The CIA's chief of station in the Congo, Larry Devlin, also writes that Podgornov and his men tried to convince Gizenga to come to Lovanium, as they believed he would be elected the new prime minister.[45] While Gizenga did not attend, the Lovanium Conference elected him deputy prime minister *in absentia*. Meanwhile, Devlin used bribes to ensure that Cyrille Adoula – his ally, known as a moderate – was elected the new prime minister. While other Lumumba supporters, such as Christophe Gbenye, also entered the government, key posts remained occupied by members of the so-called 'Binza Group' (a group of Mobutu's allies named after the prosperous suburb where its members lived), which included Foreign Minister Justin-Marie Bomboko, Head of the Security Services Victor Nendaka and Central Bank Director Albert Ndele. Yet, the Soviet Union recognized Adoula's new government and re-established diplomatic relations with Léopoldville. Doing so allowed Podgornov's group to return to the Congolese capital in September 1961.

Czechoslovak Plans for the Congo, 1962–4

Conditions for the Soviet and Czechoslovak embassies and their staff upon their return to Léopoldville proved difficult. Oleg Nazhestkin recalls that their team encountered stiff opposition from the Congolese Ministry of Foreign Affairs, which refused to recognize the status of their diplomatic mission. From Moscow, the situation looked so hopeless that at one point the Soviet Ministry of Foreign Affairs sent a telegram questioning whether it would be more reasonable to shut the mission. Their team persevered, writes Nazhestkin, and, with support of the minister of the interior, Christopher Gbenye, 'a friend', the Adoula government officially approved the restoration of diplomatic relations with the Soviet Union, Czechoslovakia, Poland and Belgium.[46] While Adoula initially required Podgornov to return to the USSR to relaunch diplomatic relations 'according with procedure', he never required this of the Czechoslovak chargé d'affaires, an attitude that Prague wished to use as a precedent to ease Soviet re-entry to Léopoldville.[47]

With the KGB and StB back in Léopoldville, Prague drew up extensive plans for intelligence work in the Congo. On 19 December 1961, the StB compiled a 19-point plan for their intelligence station in Léopoldville that was to be staffed by four intelligence officers working under diplomatic cover. The four men were to gather information on all Congolese politicians, members of the UN apparatus, the political composition of parliament and the 'strength of the progressive forces'. On the operational side, they were to develop channels of communication with Gizenga in case he remained in a powerful position at Stanleyville, establish safe houses and develop pre-existing intelligence contacts. Prague also instructed the intelligence team to provide assistance for Léopoldville-based organizations fighting for the independence of Angola, Portugal's largest colony in Africa and Congo's southern neighbour.[48] Despite these myriad tasks, Prague knew the StB station would operate in a hostile environment and thus warned that the team should not give the 'reactionary forces' any excuse to expel the diplomatic mission from the Congo.[49]

One of the key goals of Soviet and Czechoslovak intelligence in Léopoldville was to develop a network of confidential informers. According to an StB report of 25 January 1962, the Czechoslovak network allegedly contained 50 people. The majority were members of the 'Lumumbist parties', such as the MNC, PSA and CEREA. Besides this, Czechoslovak intelligence also allegedly had two contacts in the central government, two amongst the UN personnel and one in a foreign embassy. The key aim of developing the network was to obtain information about the activities of Western powers in the Congo and about internal developments. This information could also be used for 'active measures' to strengthen the positions of the socialist countries in the Congo and Africa in general. While members of the 'progressive parties' were to be used to engage in joint actions on ideological or financial bases, Prague instructed its agents in Léopoldville to recruit contacts amongst the UN apparatus, and for the Czechoslovaks living in the Congo to infiltrate their 'most qualified' personnel into Western-dominated institutions in the government administration and the military. The intelligence team was also to follow the activities of Western intelligence services and developments in Angola, but also in Rwanda and Burundi. For that reason, the Czechoslovak Ministry of the Interior proposed to establish a strong Czechoslovak intelligence station in Léopoldville and to gradually strengthen it by increasing the number of intelligence officers in Katanga, Kasai and the Orientale province.[50] The sheer volume of tasks shows that the Ministry of the Interior was still very ambitious about its capacity for action in the Congo and beyond.

However, the implementation of these ambitious plans proved very difficult. In early 1962, Antoine Gizenga was arrested because he would not return to Léopoldville from Stanleyville. While many of the former supporters of Patrice Lumumba retained their government posts, the activities of the socialist countries and of groups associated with them, such as the Angolan MPLA (the Popular Movement for the Liberation of Angola), were closely monitored, with the Czechoslovak and Soviet embassies being attacked in the press and under constant threat of expulsion. The Czechoslovak Ministry of the Interior thus instructed the intelligence team in Léopoldville to focus operational attention on officials in Adoula's government, situational analysis and providing support for Angolan nationalists resident in the Congolese capital.[51]

Moreover, difficult working conditions meant that the whole Czechoslovak station in Léopoldville comprised only one man – StB agent Zdeněk Černý.

Nonetheless, Prague still demanded of Černý that he should develop extensive contacts both within the government and also amongst the leaders of opposition parties, and chastized him for failing to deliver on these aims. On 3 September 1962, Černý's senior officer in Prague, Stanislav Turnovsky, gave an overwhelmingly negative evaluation of the former's work. He argued that Černý did little to develop contacts with the Congolese, acted with little initiative or concrete plans and did not provide adequate analysis about the situation in the country. While Prague asked Černý to limit contact with Lumumbists, Turnovsky also argued that Černý had made an error when he had abandoned communication with them, leaving Prague without adequate knowledge of politics, plans or prospects of the 'friendly camp'.[52] It is most likely that Turnovsky's reference to the 'friendly camp' signifies those men and women who had been linked to Patrice Lumumba and the MNC and who either remained in parliament following the consensus reached at the Lovanium Conference or who left the Congo for neighbouring countries, especially Brazzaville in the Republic of the Congo.

Prague continued to blame Černý for his failure to deliver on its ambitious plans over the course of the following year. On 17 June 1963, the StB determined that Černý had failed to fulfil his tasks as he had not provided adequate information about the USA, Adoula's government or the UN in the Congo. Prague also criticized Černý for failing to develop confidential contacts with persons of interest and failing to undertake a single 'active operation' to discredit the USA and its allies in the Congo. While Prague acknowledged that Černý worked under very difficult conditions, he was still responsible for failing to develop a single trusted contact who could provide accurate information on Adoula's government. The only positive aspect was his work with the Angolan nationalist movement and the provision of information about the aims of opposition parties.[53]

The Soviet KGB station in Léopoldville followed a similar strategy on instructions from Moscow. One of the KGB team, Oleg Nazhestkin, recalls that in late 1962 the CC CPSU International Department instructed the newly appointed head of the KGB in the Congo, Boris Voronin, to maintain contacts with members of the pro-Lumumbist opposition, many of whom had relocated to neighbouring Brazzaville, located only a ferry ride away across the Congo River. According to Nazhestkin, Voronin believed that this policy pursued by the International Department would not end well and would distract attention from the main tasks of recruiting agents amongst the representatives of Western countries and obtaining information about their activities in the Congo.[54] The CIA noticed. Larry Devlin recalled that Soviet Ambassador Sergei Nemchina had had a difficult task in providing assistance to Prime Minister Adoula in order to undermine the Congo's dependence on the UN and the Western powers while, at the same time, wooing Adoula's leftist opposition with money and advice. Devlin boasts that his response to the Soviet 'wooing' strategy was to install listening equipment at the Soviet Embassy and recruit a *féticheur* (a medicine man) to put a curse on anybody who entered the property.[55]

Boris Voronin had genuine reasons to doubt the practicability of the Soviet strategy that potentially endangered the Soviet presence in the Congo. While the Lovanium consensus lasted as long as the Adoula–Kasavubu government was fighting against Katanga's secession, the agreement unravelled after the authorities finally managed to end, with UN support, Moïse Tshombe's bid for independence by the end of 1963. In September, the Adoula–Kasavubu government dismissed parliament on the pretext that it was no longer effective, causing opposition leaders, such as Christopher Gbenye and Bocheley Davidson, to move to Brazzaville, where they established the National Liberation Council (NLC), which was one of the groups behind an uprising that would be known as the 'Simba Rebellion'. The KGB's contacts with opposition leaders thus became increasingly dangerous.

In November 1963, the Soviet presence in the Congo came to its dramatic conclusion. One the evening of 19 November, Boris Voronin and Soviet attaché Yuriy Myakotnykh were on their way back to Léopoldville from a routine trip to neighbouring Brazzaville. The two cities were linked by a ferry across the Congo River, and on that day, their Fiat car, with its diplomats' number plates, carried household staff as well as documents that testified to Voronin's contacts with members of the NLC residing in Brazzaville. When their ferry docked at Léopoldville, Voronin and Myakotnykh were suddenly surrounded by government officials and gendarmes, who dragged them out of the vehicle, beat them up and threw them into the back of a jeep. The two men were driven first to the headquarters of the Congolese security services for questioning and then to the Ndolo prison where they were subjected to a staged mock execution orchestrated by the powerful chief of the army, Joseph-Désiré Mobutu.[56] While both were released the following day, the Congolese authorities claimed that they had found evidence of the Soviets plotting against their government. The embassy staff, for the second time in three years, were ordered to leave the country within 48 hours. With the Soviets expelled, the Czechoslovak officer, Zdeněk Černý, stayed behind, and thus became a valuable source of intelligence in the country. In the first half of 1964, Černý dispatched for Prague 45 notes and one document including analysis about the reasons for the expulsion of the Soviet embassy, which was passed on to the 'comrades'.[57]

The struggle for the Congo was not over, however. Faced with a rapidly deteriorating military situation, in July, President Kasavubu appointed Moïse Tshombe, the former leader of the Katanga secessionists responsible for Lumumba's murder, as the new prime minister. Tshombe's appointment increased support for the anti-government rebellion amongst those African leaders who had previously supported Lumumba. In October, Algerian President Ahmed Ben Bella asked for Czechoslovak assistance in the provision of planes to transport 40 tonnes of military matériel to Christopher Gbenye in Stanleyville, one of the leaders of the 'Simba Rebellion'.[58] Černý believed that Prague should satisfy Ben Bella's request, and so did the head of intelligence, Josef Houska. The Czechoslovak Foreign Ministry, however, seems to have been against the initiative.[59] A Czechoslovak official of the Ministry of Foreign Trade had a number of low-level discussions in Moscow about Ben Bella's request, and he was apparently told that his colleagues would not be able to refuse such a request if asked. Upon his return and following further discussions, the Central Committee came to a compromise decision: Czechoslovakia would not fly the planes, but would provide the necessary armaments directly to Ben Bella, who would then transport them to Stanleyville.[60] On 30 October 1964, the Central Committee of the CCP approved the provision of arms worth Kčs 1.5 million, yet we do not know if these ever reached the Congo.[61] Nonetheless, Prague remained the main source of information for events in the Congo, with the Soviet Ministry of Foreign Affairs relying on its colleagues, since diplomatic relations were not formally re-established until 1968.[62]

Conclusion

Czechoslovakia and its StB emerged as the key Eastern bloc actor in the Congo Crisis of 1960–3. The Czechoslovak presence predated that of the Soviets in the Congo, with Josef Virius acting as the only official representative of the Eastern bloc before independence. He played an important role as a point of contact between Czechoslovak officials and the Congolese, with the possibility that early Soviet views of Patrice Lumumba were at least partly shaped by information coming from Virius, who had been in close contact with Antoine Gizenga. We also know that there was extensive Soviet–Czechoslovak cooperation in the Congo from the beginning on an official and, most likely, operational level. While we still do not know all the details surrounding this, it would be fair to say that the unsuccessful attempt to provide support for Lumumba and his followers was the first major Soviet–Czechoslovak operation in sub-Saharan Africa. While cooperation did exist, there is no particular evidence that Czechoslovakia followed Moscow's diktat. In fact, using its connection to Virius, Prague was in many ways equally, if not more, enthusiastic in pursuing assistance first to Lumumba and then to Gizenga, with Prague providing specific advice in the security area. The grandiosity of Czechoslovak plans for their intelligence operations in 1961 shows that Prague envisioned this role as that of a substantial actor in Africa and a key Soviet partner. Ben Bella's request for the provision of Czechoslovak planes shows that by the early 1960s, Prague had become a prominent player in Africa in its own right. In fact, Zdeněk Černý remained the only source of information on the Congo after the Soviet embassy was expelled in 1963 as far as we know. Prague continued to be involved in the Congo after these events, but its appetite for action subsided in the following years.

Secret intelligence played a key role in the Congo due to Soviet weakness in sub-Saharan Africa. The KGB had no presence in the region before 1960, and very little knowledge about local politics and actors. The hurried dispatch of the team in August 1960 was a response to Soviet inability to influence the situation via diplomatic means. While the Soviets were keen to support first Lumumba's and then Gizenga's government with arms and money, they were not prepared to risk a showdown with the West. Newly available documents prove once again that the absence of long-range aircraft and trained crews, as well as real fears of planes being shot down, provided a major obstacle for weapons to Stanleyville. Nonetheless, the Soviets believed that forces opposed to the authorities in Léopoldville still had a chance. Given logistical problems and power realities on the ground, it was down to secret intelligence to fulfil tasks such as the delivery of weapons to Stanleyville in a clandestine way. It remains unclear to what extent the Soviet and Czechoslovak intelligence were successful in this endeavour. The KGB and StB relied on intelligence agents on the ground not only to obtain information about ongoing events but also to develop confidential contacts in a country in the midst of civil war. Lacking effective ways to support their allies in the Congo, Moscow and Prague relied overwhelmingly on their few intelligence officers to bolster first Antoine Gizenga and then other members of the opposition deemed 'progressive'. Even after Lumumba's murder, Moscow and Prague still harboured very ambitious plans for the Congo, whereby spies were to gather information, maintain contacts with members of the opposition and, crucially, recruit agents and confidential contacts within the government. That was a daunting and dangerous task in the Congo, and the story of Voronin and Myakotnykh's arrest in 1963 clearly revealed the risks. Soviet and Czechoslovak spies thus played a crucial role as 'mediators' in the Congo. While the Soviets would build up their naval and aerial technology to project power over long distances, human intelligence still remained one of their key weapons in Cold War Africa. While many KGB documents are still unavailable, a re-examination of Soviet and Czechoslovak intelligence in the Congo shows that the CIA definitely overhyped the Soviet threat. In the Congo and elsewhere, where Western influence was historically much stronger or confrontation too dangerous, the Soviets and their allies used secret intelligence to wage the 'Cold War on the cheap'.

Notes

1. František August and David Rees, *Red Star Over Prague* (London, 1984).
2. The StB's First Directorate is mostly referred to as 'Czechoslovak intelligence' in this chapter.
3. For details, see: Pavel Žázek, 'Czechoslovak and Soviet State Security Against the West Before 1968', paper presented to the conference *The Contours of Legitimacy in Central Europe: New Approaches in Graduate Studies*, European Studies Centre, St Antony's College Oxford, 24–26 May 2002, p. 2.

4. Madeleine G. Kalb, *The Congo Cables: The Cold War in Africa – from Eisenhower to Kennedy* (New York, 1982); Sergey Mazov, *Kholodnaya Voyna v 'Serdze Afriki'. SSSR i Kongolezskiy Krizis, 1960–1964* [Cold War in the 'Heart of Africa'. USSR and the Congo Crisis, 1960–1964] (Moscow, 2015); Lise Namikas, *Battleground Africa: Cold War in the Congo, 1960–1965* (Stanford, 2013); and Alessandro Iandolo, 'The Rise and Fall of the "Soviet Model of Development" in West Africa, 1957–64,' *Cold War History*, 12 (4) (November 2012), pp. 683–704.
5. Ludo de Witte, *The Assassination of Lumumba* (London, 2002); Emmanuel Gerard and Bruce Kuklick, *Death in the Congo: Murdering Patrice Lumumba* (Cambridge, MA, 2015).
6. Stephen Weissman, 'What Really Happened in Congo: The CIA, the Murder of Lumumba, and the Rise of Mobutu', *Foreign Affairs* (July/August 2014), pp. 14–24.
7. Petr Zídek and Karl Sieber, *Československo a Subsaharská Afrika v Letech 1948–1989* [Czechoslovakia in Sub-Saharan Africa, 1948–1989] (Prague, 2007); Philip E. Muehlenbeck, *Czechoslovakia in Africa, 1945–1968* (New York, 2015).
8. Alexander Fursenko and Timothy Naftali, *Khrushchev's Cold War: The Inside Story of an American Adversary* (New York, 2006), p. 57.
9. For a full story of the Egyptian–Czech arms deal, see: Muehlenbeck, *Czechoslovakia in Africa*, pp. 91–5.
10. Zídek and Sieber, *Československo*, pp. 127–8.
11. This comes from the database of the StB agents located on the website of the StB archive, Archiv Bezpečnostních Složek [hereafter, ABS] at http://www.abscr.cz/en/searching-in-the-archival-finding-aids (accessed September 2017).
12. See comments of Cléophas Kamitatu in *The Congo Crisis, 1960–1961: A Critical Oral History Conference* [transcript of conference], Woodrow Wilson International Center for Scholars, 23–24 September 2004, p. 34.
13. Report of a Conversation with the Prime Minister of the Congo, Lumumba, about the Situation in the Congo, National Archives of the Czech Republic, Records of the Communist Party of Czechoslovakia [hereafter, NA-UV KSC], Inv. 566, Ka. 230.
14. Mazov, *Kholodnaya Voyna*, p. 23. The Guinean Ambassador in the Soviet Union also apparently expressed support for Gizenga. See: A. Safronov, 'Otchet o Prebyvanii v SSSR Predsedatelya parti Afrikanskoi solidarnosti Kongo A. Gizenga', Gosudarstvennyi Arkhiv Rossiiskoi Federatsii [hereafter, GARF], Fond (F.) 9540, Opis (Op.) 2, Delo (D.) 29, p. 8.
15. Ibid., pp. 3–11.
16. Notes of conversation with the secretary of the CC Communist Party of Belgium [Albert] de Coninck regarding the Congo, 9 May 1959, in *A Cold War International History Project* (CWIHP) Document Reader compiled for the international conference 'The Congo Crisis, 1960–1961', Washington, DC, 23–24 September 2004, Document 2.

17. Memo of conversations with the leader of the National Congolese Movement (MNC), Patrice Lumumba, on 19 February 1960 and 26 February 1960, in ibid., Document 9.
18. Muehlenbeck, *Czechoslovakia in Africa*, p. 66.
19. Larry Devlin, *Chief of Station, Congo: A Memoir of 1960–67* (New York, 2007), p. 23
20. 'Memorandum of Discussion at the 456th Meeting of the National Security Council', in *Foreign Relations of the United States (FRUS), 1958–1960, Africa, Volume XIV* (Washington, DC, 1992), pp. 422–4. Larry Devlin writes that he received direct instructions for Lumumba's physical assassination, and that President Eisenhower personally authorized it. See: Devlin, *Chief of Station*, p. 95.
21. The CIA and the MI6 posts are generally called 'stations', while those of the KGB are referred to as 'residentura'. The head of the 'residentura' is referred to as 'resident'. The term KGB 'station' is used here for simplicity.
22. Sergey Khrushchev, *Nikita Khrushchev: Creation of a Superpower* (University Park, PA, 2003), p. 405.
23. Namikas, *Battleground Africa*, pp. 85–6.
24. Vadim Kirpichenko, *Razvedka: Litsa i Lichnosti* [Intelligence: People and Personalities] (Moscow, 1998), p. 89.
25. Zídek and Sieber, *Československo*, p. 130.
26. Report of a Conversation with the Prime Minister of the Congo, Lumumba, about the Situation in the Congo, NA-UV KSC, Inv. 566, Ka. 230.
27. Zídek and Sieber, *Československo*, p. 130.
28. Note [Attachment III], NA-UV KSC, Inv. 566, Ka. 230.
29. Fursenko and Naftali, *Khrushchev's Cold War*, pp. 315–17.
30. On Khrushchev's campaign at the UN, see Alessandro Iandolo, 'Imbalance of Power: The Soviet Union and the Congo Crisis, 1960–61', *Journal of Cold War Studies*, 16 (2) (June 2014).
31. Report about Consultation of Assistance to the Congo in the USSR, 12 January 1961, NA-UV KSC, Inv. 566, Ka. 2.
32. Muehlenbeck, *Czechoslovakia in Africa*, p. 81.
33. Transcript of the talk between deputy foreign minister of the USSR, V. S. Semenov, and president of the United Arab Republic, Gamal Abdel Nasser, 31 January 1961, in CWIHP Document Reader, pp. 9–12.
34. Mazov, *Kholodnaya Voyna*, pp. 134–5.
35. Transcript of the talk between deputy foreign minister of the USSR, V. V. Kuznetzov, and minister of education and arts in the Gizenga government, Pierre Mulele, 8 March 1961, in CWIHP Document Reader, p. 6.
36. Minutes of negotiation with the representative of the government of the Republic of the Congo, Mr Antoine Niatti Mandungu, at the ministry of foreign affairs, on 15 June 1961, NA-UV KSC, Inv. 566, Ka. 230.
37. Transcript of the talk between the deputy foreign minister of the USSR, A. A. Slobber, and the ambassador of Czechoslovakia in Moscow, G. R.

Dvorzhak, February 6, 1961, in CWIHP Document Reader, pp. 13–14; Transcript of the talk between the deputy foreign minister of the USSR, N. P. Firkin, and the ambassador of Czechoslovakia in Moscow, G. R. Dvorzhak, March 9, 1961, in CWIHP Document Reader.
38. Devlin, *Chief of Station*, pp. 141–2.
39. On the deterioration of Soviet-US relations in early 1960, see: Jeffrey Sachs, *To Move the World: JFK's Quest for Peace* (New York, 2013).
40. Record of proceedings between the Soviet KGB and the Interior Ministry of the Czechoslovak Socialist Republic on the expansion of intelligence cooperation, June, 1961, History and Public Policy Program Digital Archive, ABS. Available at http://digitalarchive.wilsoncenter.org/document/113217 (accessed September 2017).
41. For a detailed discussion of Shelepin's plan, see: Vladislav Zubok, 'Spy vs. Spy: The KGB vs. the CIA, 1960–1962', *CWIHP Bulletin*, 4 (1994), pp. 28–9. The author was unable to obtain a copy of the plan that Shelepin presented to Khrushchev, but there are multiple similarities that lead to the conclusion that it was based on the StB–KGB consultation of June 1961.
42. Ibid.
43. Nazhestkin, 'Gody', pp. 158–9.
44. Ibid., p. 159.
45. On the Lovanium Conference and the CIA's role, see: Devlin, *Chief of Station*, pp. 156–9.
46. Nazhestkin, 'Gody', p. 159.
47. Prague, 25 September 1961, NA-UV KSC, Inv. 566, Ka 230.
48. Oleg Nazhestkin, 'Superderzhavy i Sobytiya v Angole' [Superpowers and Events in Angola], *Novaya i Noveyshaya Istoriya* 4 (2005), pp. 30–50. On the connection between the Congo and the Angolan liberation movement, see: Natalia Telepneva, 'Our Sacred Duty: The Soviet Union, the Liberation Movements in the Portuguese Colonies, and the Cold War, 1961–1975', PhD dissertation, London School of Economics, 2015.
49. Long-Term Developments in the Congo, 17 November 1961, ABS, 80717/000, pp. 52–9.
50. Work of the 9th Department, 25 January 1962 ABS, 80717/000.
51. Evaluation of the StB station in Léopoldville, Prague, 3 September 1962, ABS, 80717/00.
52. Ibid.
53. First Directorate, 8th department, Prague, 17 June 1973, ABS, 80717/000.
54. Nazhestkin, 'Gody', p. 160.
55. Devlin, *Chief of Station*, p. 195.
56. The eyewitness account of these events is taken from: Nazhestkin, 'Gody', pp. 160–1.
57. Evaluation of the Implementation of Plans for the KGB station in Léopoldville, 1.1-30.6.1964, 14 July 1964, ABS, 80717/000, pp. 116–17.

58. On Ben Bella's Request for Assistance in the Congo, 4 November 1964, ABS, 80717/000, pp. 147–51.
59. Ibid.
60. Report on the Request of the President of the People's Democratic Republic of Algeria, Ben Bella, about the Provision of the Special Material for the Government of the People's Republic of the Congo in Stanleyville [Attachment III], NA-UV KSC, Inv. 566, Ka. 230, pp. 1–5.
61. CC CCP Resolution: Assistance to the Congolese People's Republic in Stanleyville [Attachment I], 30 November 1964, NA, Inv. 566, Ka. 230. Also see: Zi'dek and Sieber, *Československo*, p. 137.
62. Information on consultations with MID officials on issues related to Congo-Kinshasa and other African countries in Prague during 19–23 August this year, 28 August 1966, ABS, 11566/000, pp. 47–53.

CHAPTER 6

PRESS, PROPAGANDA AND THE GERMAN DEMOCRATIC REPUBLIC'S SEARCH FOR RECOGNITION IN TANZANIA, 1964–72

George Roberts

Amongst the member states of the Warsaw Pact, the German Democratic Republic (GDR) had a unique goal in the Third World. As Lorena De Vita explains in her contribution to this volume, while it shared the task of advancing the cause of Marxism with its Eastern European allies, its foreign policy was transfixed on obtaining diplomatic recognition from the states of the Global South. Shut out by its Western neighbours in Europe, the GDR looked to the decolonizing and non-aligned states of the Third World to provide the legitimacy it craved. The Federal Republic of Germany (FRG) tried to prevent exactly this recognition. Bonn's foreign policy became tied to the tenets of the so-called Hallstein Doctrine, through which it threatened to cut diplomatic relations and sever bilateral aid agreements with any state that recognized the GDR. The consequence was the globalization of the inter-German Cold War, as the two rival states waged a diplomatic struggle across myriad locations. In fighting against the Hallstein Doctrine, the GDR pursued policies which, though mostly supported by the Soviet

Union, often privileged its own particular interests above those of the Warsaw Pact bloc.[1]

The case of Tanzania is an anomalous, yet consequently instructive instance of the inter-German Cold War in the Third World. As explained below, a chain of events in East Africa in 1964 created a situation in which, after a protracted political struggle, Dar es Salaam became the first sub-Saharan capital to house diplomatic representatives of both German states, to Bonn's anger. Using this foothold, the GDR pushed for full, official recognition from the Tanzanian Government. This chapter builds on existing work on the diplomatic and development-aid aspects of the GDR's relationship with Tanzania in order to explore the networks of information politics through which East Berlin waged Cold War in Dar es Salaam.

As historians of empire have shown, network-focused approaches offer a means of escaping restrictive core–periphery frameworks and provide a bridge between the 'local' and the 'global'.[2] This chapter reapplies this approach to the global Cold War, paying attention to the structures of politics 'on the ground'. It thereby refocuses debate away from superpower diplomacy and instead shows how such rivalries were embedded in local politics. This does not reject the significance of top-down approaches to international affairs, but rather throws them into relief through floodlit illumination from below. As Paul Boyer writes, 'heightened sensitivity to local effects and implications can enrich and deepen the macro-level analysis of foreign relations, adding complexity and human texture to the enterprise'.[3] Odd Arne Westad suggests that the global Cold War bears analogy to an elephant, capable of being studied from multiple perspectives via diverse methodologies. An examination of the elephant's hidden entrails may enable us to understand better its larger constitution.[4] Through analysis of the GDR's press and propaganda activities, this chapter explores the micropolitical relationships that lay beneath the surface of high diplomacy.

The Inter-German Cold War Comes to Tanzania

On 12 January 1964, the Government of Zanzibar was overthrown in a coup d'état. The islands, which lie a short distance off the East African coast, had become independent from Britain the previous month.

The 1964 revolution was rooted in long-standing ethnoracial tensions amongst the islands' cosmopolitan population, which had been catalysed into partisan grievances in the run-up to independence.[5] However, the West seized on the presence of a number of Marxists in the revolutionary government of President Abeid Karume as evidence of a communist-backed plot. Britain, the USA and West Germany therefore delayed recognizing the Karume regime, leaving open the door for an influx of communist aid to the islands. Abdulrahman Mohamed Babu, a Marxist with connections to Beijing, became the first foreign minister in the non-communist world to extend full recognition to the GDR.

As Zanzibar appeared to be entering the orbit of the communist world, Karume feared that the Marxist faction, particularly Babu, represented a threat to his own grip on power. On mainland Tanganyika, which became independent from Britain in 1961, President Julius Nyerere also looked on events in Zanzibar with alarm. Just days after the revolution on the islands, the weakness of his own government had been exposed by an army mutiny in Dar es Salaam that forced him to summon British military support to restore order. Nyerere was also a leading African voice amongst the non-aligned group of Third World states, and felt that developments in Zanzibar threatened to introduce destabilizing Cold War competition to East Africa. In April 1964, Nyerere and Karume therefore secretly signed an act of union, with brought together their respective states to form the country that became known as the United Republic of Tanzania.[6]

The question of the GDR's position in the new Tanzanian state stood out as a problematic issue. As union president, Nyerere ordered all diplomatic missions in Zanzibar to be downgraded to consular status. Fully fledged embassies were to move to Dar es Salaam.[7] However, under the terms of the Hallstein Doctrine, the FRG would not tolerate the transfer of the GDR's Zanzibar Embassy to the mainland. For its part, the GDR was unwilling to concede the prized victory that it had obtained in Zanzibar. This accident – a collision between regional politics and global Cold War rivalries – therefore confronted the new union government with 'one of the thorniest diplomatic problems in the modern world', as the newspaper of the ruling Tanganyika African National Union (TANU), the *Nationalist*, put it.[8] The situation was aggravated by the pressure that the GDR apparently placed on Tanzania. In June, an editorial in the *Nationalist* claimed that it had 'evidence that the East Germans are attempting to destroy our Union in the interests of their own desires [...] Through intrigue and sharp practice they are trying to secure, through the Union, a diplomatic status in Africa which has up to now being denied them.'[9] After lengthy diplomatic negotiations, in February 1965 Nyerere offered a compromise: the GDR would maintain its presence in Zanzibar at a consular level and be permitted to open a low-status consulate-general in Dar es Salaam. This explicitly did not constitute full recognition. The GDR reluctantly accepted the deal but the FRG reacted angrily, withdrawing a military training team from Tanzania. In a striking demonstration of his non-alignment, Nyerere declared that Tanzania would forgo *all* aid agreements already reached with Bonn, worth around US$32.5 million.[10]

The consequence of this turbulent diplomatic struggle thrust Dar es Salaam into the frontline of East–West German rivalry in the Third World. Although the GDR continued to concentrate its development-aid projects in Zanzibar, East Berlin recognized that in order to win *de jure* recognition from Tanzania, it had to press for support from the government in Dar es Salaam. Despite its third-rate diplomatic status, the GDR therefore became a prominent actor on the city's diplomatic scene. Writing in 1969, the French Ambassador noted that amongst the Warsaw Pact states, after the Soviet Union, it was the GDR which played the 'preponderant role' in Tanzania.[11] Moscow provided some support for the GDR's search for recognition. For example, when serving as Dean of the Diplomatic Corps in 1968, the Soviet Ambassador pleaded with the Tanzanian authorities to allow the GDR to be invited to official diplomatic receptions – a recurring bone of contention in East–West German relations in Dar es Salaam.[12] Largely, however, the GDR pursued its task alone: there is no evidence from the East German archives of it acting under close Soviet supervision.

The bulk of the literature on East Germany's experience in Tanzania focuses either on the diplomatic saga[13] or its development schemes.[14] The latter represented prominent forms of propaganda, as the incarnation of the GDR's socialist philosophy. Its flagship project in Zanzibar was a major housing development, which bore the concrete imprint of East Berlin's vision of socialist modernity.[15] Seeking to complement this literature, this chapter focuses on the GDR's public information work in Dar es Salaam. *Öffentlichkeitsarbeit* ('publicity work') was a key plank in the GDR's strategy for building influence amongst the political elite. As historians of the inter-German rivalry elsewhere in the world have shown, East Germany sought to exploit every opportunity to denigrate Bonn and parade its own socialist virtues. These activities took diverse forms, from international trade-fair exhibitions and documentaries exposing the crimes of Western imperialism, to embassy handouts and face-to-face meetings with local officials and politicians.[16]

In Tanzania, the propaganda and contact-building operations involved in *öffentlichkeitsarbeit* both contributed to and tapped into the political environment of Dar es Salaam. The city emerged in the early 1960s as a 'nodal point'[17] of global affairs in sub-Saharan Africa, primarily because Nyerere offered refuge to exiled liberation movements from those territories still under white minority rule. The guerrilla leaders established offices in the Tanzanian capital. Like other socialist states, the East Germans used their presence in the city to cultivate relationships with these potential governments-in-waiting, which were generally of a leftist persuasion. Dar es Salaam became a locus of political gossip, allegations of espionage, and talk of coups: Nyerere himself referred to his capital as 'Rumourville'.[18]

The GDR ran a propaganda campaign in Dar es Salaam of a size disproportionate to its small mission there. Even before the Zanzibar Revolution, East Berlin had attempted to cultivate a relationship with the Tanganyikan media: in June 1962, two East German radio experts had visited the country.[19] While much of the material that the GDR circulated and placed in the local press attempted to showcase the East German 'socialist paradise', more controversial stories denigrated their capitalist rivals across the Berlin Wall. In particular, as Katrina Hagen has demonstrated in a case study of the Congo, the GDR tried to draw connections between Germany's imperialist past and its contemporary policy in Africa. This propaganda presented the FRG as the successor to the colonial Second Reich and the fascist Third Reich, culpable of racially motivated genocide in both Africa and Europe. In Tanzania, such parallels were expected to resonate with memories of the German colonial period, playing on the example of the brutal repression of the Maji Maji rebellion of 1905–7.[20] The GDR drew connections between these histories and West Germany's relationship with states upholding white minority rule in Africa – especially Portugal, Bonn's valued

NATO ally. Even before the GDR established a diplomatic presence in the region, it played on these tensions to audiences in Tanganyika and Zanzibar. In 1963, the GDR's German–Africa Society distributed a pamphlet claiming that 'when Portuguese airplanes with their West German machine guns hunt down peaceful people in Angola and Mozambique and shoot them like deer, officials in West Germany do not waste a single word on the topic [...] These are the same forces that in the years before 1945 plunged our people and the whole of Europe into distress by unleashing an imperialist war.'[21]

In December 1965, the West German Embassy complained to the Tanzanian Government about a publication entitled *Brown Book: War and Nazi Criminals in West Germany*, which was in circulation in Dar es Salaam. Distributed around the world by the East Germans, the book largely consisted of a list of prominent West German politicians and officials who had associations with the Nazi regime. It alleged that 15 ministers and junior ministers; 100 generals and admirals; 828 lawyers, judges and high judicial officials; 245 diplomats; and 297 police and security officials had played significant roles in the Nazi Party.[22] The *Braunbuch* stated that Heinrich Lübke, the West German president, had been involved in the construction of a concentration camp. There was some truth in this, though the *Braunbuch*'s authors exaggerated the charges.[23] After the FRG received no response to the complaint, it approached the Tanzanian Ambassador in Bonn, demanding that Gottfried Lessing, the GDR consul-general, be expelled from the country.[24] Nyerere himself ordered the Tanzanian Ministry for Home Affairs to ban the *Braunbuch*.[25] After the acrimonious rift with Bonn over the question of East German representation in Tanzania, Nyerere was in no mood to tolerate such antagonistic material.

In an early indication of the Tanzanian Government's exasperation with the GDR's propaganda activities, the consulate-general was reprimanded over the *Braunbuch* affair.[26] The government subsequently tried to pull in around 1,000 copies of the pamphlet – an indication of the scale of the GDR's propaganda operations in Dar es Salaam.[27] Shortly afterwards, in 1966, the Tanzanian Government issued a notice to diplomatic representations in the city, warning them that their publications 'should primarily serve to appraise and elucidate problems and facts related to their own respective countries'. The government would 'take serious note and exception to the circulation of publications in which accounts of the political views of a foreign country contain attacks upon a third state'.[28] 'We will have to be more cautious and reserved from now on', wrote an East German diplomat, tellingly.[29]

The ADN and the *Nationalist*

As James Brennan explains, the activities of international news agencies were enmeshed in the politics of the global Cold War.[30] Newspaper editors in decolonizing Africa were dependent on externally sourced agency material to fill their foreign-affairs columns. The state-controlled communist agencies – the Soviet TASS and Novosti, China's Xinhua, Cuba's Prensa Latina and Czechoslovakia's Četeka – all had bureaux in Dar es Salaam. These performed the dual function of gathering news from Tanzania and furnishing the local media with content from abroad, carrying their own ideological and political slant. However, they faced a challenge from the established British agency, Reuters, which was the preferred option of the English-language newspapers.[31]

Aware of the limits of blatant propaganda like the *Braunbuch*, the GDR looked to the Allgemeine Deutsche Nachrichtendienst (General German News Service, ADN) as an intermediary in its relations with the Tanzanian media and government. The ADN was founded in 1946 as an organ of the ruling Socialist Unity Party of Germany (Sozialistische Einheitspartei Deutschlands, SED). It set up its first offices abroad in Bucharest, Budapest and Prague two years later. Decisions to open bureaux were taken mainly on political rather than economic or geographical grounds: able to operate in countries where the GDR had no official representation, its reporters were instructed to emphasize the GDR's anti-imperialist credentials in the push for international recognition. According to Deba Wieland, the director of the ADN from 1952 to 1977, 'the first people to struggle for the sovereignty and recognition of the GDR were the [ADN's] correspondents [...] They were pioneers.' In 1964, the ADN dipped its toes into the news economy of eastern Africa by establishing offices in Nairobi and Zanzibar. Like the employees of other state-owned communist news agencies, ADN correspondents often also worked for the East German intelligence services, the Stasi. Their cover offered ample scope for intelligence gathering, but the tactic also risked embarrassment. In November 1965, the ADN's Dieter Dahlke was expelled from Kenya; another unnamed correspondent was thrown out the following February.[32]

From the opening of the consulate-general in 1965 until 1970, Peter Spacek served as the ADN's correspondent in Dar es Salaam, where he doubled-up as a journalist for the newspaper *Neues Deutschland*. Trained in radio broadcasting, Spacek had been working in Iraq when revolution broke out in Zanzibar in 1964. At his own suggestion, he was sent to Zanzibar immediately after the coup, where he helped the revolutionary government establish a radio network.[33] In Dar es Salaam, Spacek worked alongside Horst Schlegel, who also wrote for *Neues Deutschland*. The GDR believed that the ADN's bulletins would have greater leeway in attacking the FRG, since it could be argued that they did not represent the 'official' voice of the State. The ADN would therefore have greater scope to criticize the FRG's 'revanchism, militarism, and neocolonialism'.[34] Nevertheless, the ADN had to tread carefully. For example, four issues of its Tanzanian bulletin were pulled in 1968 due to their explicit attacks on West German politicians. After an issue elicited complaints from the West German Embassy in 1969, the Tanzanian Ministry of Foreign Affairs reminded the GDR of the 1966 circular. 'Tanzania is no arena for other states to hold their boxing matches', it warned.[35]

The ADN focused its activities on inserting pro-GDR (and anti-FRG) articles into the Tanzanian media. They had no success with the radio, which was brought under state control in 1965 and relied on Reuters. The directors of Radio Tanzania were reportedly under strict instructions not to broadcast any material provided by the GDR without government permission.[36] Instead, the ADN concentrated on the printed press, especially the two newspapers owned by TANU: the English-language *Nationalist* and its Swahili sister-publication, *Uhuru* ('Freedom'). Founded in 1964, the *Nationalist* struggled to establish itself – its circulation was just 10,000 in 1965 – and was heavily dependent on government subsidies. Yet as a party publication, it remained a key source of information for the political elite, Asian business community and foreign expatriate population in Dar es Salaam.[37]

Both German states vied for influence over the *Nationalist*. In 1965, the GDR Consulate-General reported that the West German Ambassador was a regular visitor to the newspaper's offices. The GDR believed that its own network of contacts amongst the *Nationalist* staff was 'not systematic enough'.[38] However, it took comfort from the presence of a number of perceived pro-Eastern bloc radicals on the newspaper's management. Both the editor-in-chief, Joel Mgogo, and the managing editor, Stephen Mhando, had spent time at the University of Leipzig, where Mgogo had studied on a GDR-sponsored course and Mhando had taught Swahili. The editor, James Markham, had previously written alongside Kwame Nkrumah for the *Evening News* in Accra, worked for the Anti-Colonial Bureau of the Asian Socialist Conference in Rangoon and represented the Gold Coast at the 1955 Bandung Conference.[39] Another *Nationalist* journalist, Nsa Kaisi, wrote articles for a local Chinese magazine, *Vigilance Africa*.[40] Although owned by the governing party, the *Nationalist* was plugged into global networks of anticolonialism, pan-Africanism and internationalist Marxism that transcended Tanzanian affairs.

The radicals amongst the *Nationalist* staff were also well connected to the country's political elite. Abdulrahman Mohamed Babu had been transferred from Zanzibar to the mainland government as part of the union arrangement in 1964. He wrote a pseudonymous weekly column, in which he propounded his Marxist world view and savaged the USA's foreign policy. The TANU secretary-general and – until September 1965 – minister for foreign affairs, Oscar Kambona, maintained an influential role over the newspaper's content. As a law student in London in the late 1950s, Kambona moved in radical circles in Britain, the Eastern bloc and elsewhere in Africa. During this time, he corresponded with Mgogo (described by British intelligence as 'a young man of extreme views'), who was then also studying in Prague.[41] In November 1964, Kambona used his influence on the *Nationalist* to publish copies of documents obtained by the Tanzanian Ambassador to Kinshasa, which purported to show evidence of an American- and Portuguese-backed plot to overthrow Nyerere. This led to an outpouring of anti-American sentiment at a demonstration in Dar es Salaam, and to a minor diplomatic crisis. The letters were subsequently recognized as forgeries, but the episode was a blow to Tanzania's relationship with Washington.[42]

The GDR looked to exploit these connections between the radical press and the apparatus of the party-state. The ADN correspondent Schlegel developed a strong working relationship with Mhando, who also edited the trade-union newspaper *Mfanyakazi* ('The Worker'), which carried numerous East German propaganda handouts.[43] Kambona's relationship with the GDR dated back to 1962, when he had been introduced to the authorities in East Berlin by the Kenyan socialist Oginga Odinga.[44] On arrival in Dar es Salaam as an ADN correspondent in 1965, Peter Spacek was instructed to make contact with Kambona, whom the East Germans dubbed 'Red Oscar'.[45] When the GDR sent a printing press to the *Nationalist* in January 1963, it arrived on an East German cargo ship in crates addressed to Kambona himself.[46]

However, the radical approach of the *Nationalist* sat uneasily with Nyerere's own attempts to stake out a non-aligned position in the Cold War world. Over the course of 1964–5, Tanzania fell out with its three largest bilateral aid donors: West Germany, over the imbroglio outlined above; the USA, over the 'letter plot' and another espionage scandal, which resulted in the withdrawal of the US Ambassador; and Britain, when Nyerere severed relations after Rhodesia's Unilateral Declaration of Independence in November 1965.[47] The aggressive anti-imperialism of publications like the *Nationalist* risked further endangering these strained relations. Nyerere therefore sought to temper the stream of attacks on British policy in southern Africa and the US intervention in Indochina. In April 1966, Markham was replaced as editor; in August, Mgogo and Mhando also lost their jobs. Nsa Kaisi remained on the staff, but told a GDR diplomat that the changes had been encouraged by conservative forces within the government, who considered the newspaper 'more Vietnamese than the Vietnamese'.[48] Markham's replacement as editor was Benjamin Mkapa, later the third president of Tanzania. Mkapa confirmed to an American diplomat that he had ended 'the virulent, anti-Western hyperbole of his predecessor' and that the *Nationalist* would henceforth 'pursue a more truly non-aligned policy, less dependent on communist propaganda handouts'.[49]

The GDR perceived a shift towards an editorial line in the *Nationalist* that was more amenable to the West. The consulate-general reported a rise in the number of pro-West German articles and duly took steps to combat this: in early 1967, GDR diplomats held meetings with members of the *Nationalist* team, including Mkapa and Kaisi, at which they stressed the progressive credentials of East German policy in Africa, vis-à-vis neo-imperialist West Germany.[50] Over time, the *Nationalist* reverted to a more radical stance, under the influence of the likes of Babu and Kaisi. Later in 1967, Mkapa told a British doctoral researcher that he was under constant pressure to move the editorial line further to the left.[51] However, the newspaper's orientation was more pro-Chinese than favourable to the Eastern bloc. This development paralleled the strengthening of Tanzania's relations with China, which climaxed in Beijing's agreement to provide financial and technical assistance to build the 'freedom railway' between the port of Dar es Salaam and the copper belt of landlocked Zambia.[52] Although the GDR continued to press material onto the *Nationalist*, it struggled to develop any real influence with the newspaper.

Tanzanian Politics, Cold War Interventions and the GDR

At the same time, the GDR's own standing in Tanzania suffered a series of setbacks. In February 1967, Nyerere issued the 'Arusha Declaration' – a landmark party document that set out TANU's vision for Tanzania's socio-economic development. This eschewed Soviet-style Marxist–Leninist doctrine in favour of a more flexible African socialism, grounded in the supposed communal traditions of the Tanzanian peasantry and based on the philosophy of *ujamaa* ('familyhood'). The Arusha Declaration was followed by a swathe of nationalizations, but the centrepiece of *ujamaa* socialism was a massive resettlement of the rural population into collectivized villages, with ultimately disastrous economic consequences.[53]

Although, as Nyerere emphasized, the Arusha Declaration rejected a Marxist path to modernity, the Eastern bloc greeted developments positively. Writing in *Izvestiya*, the Soviet commentator on Africa V. K. Kudryavtsev declared that Tanzania had 'entered a new stage in the building of its state' and 'embarked on the road of socio-economic transformation based on the principles of scientific socialism'.[54] Sensing an opportunity, the GDR ratcheted up its propaganda activities in Dar es Salaam. The ADN introduced a new Swahili-language version of its news bulletin, *Urafiki* ('Friendship'), circulating 120–150 copies to media outlets and government departments.[55] GDR diplomats gave Tanzanian officials and politicians copies of articles clipped from the West German press that displayed scepticism about the Arusha Declaration.[56] Gottfried Lessing, the consul-general, also sought to strengthen the GDR's ties with 'progressive politicians' in Tanzania, including Babu and Kambona.[57]

However, the Arusha Declaration set in motion domestic political forces that the GDR could neither predict nor comprehend. Many politicians and bureaucrats were concerned at the inclusion of a 'code of conduct', which prevented them from holding private assets and property. Amongst this discontented faction was Kambona, who already had a tense relationship with Nyerere. In July 1967, Kambona fled Tanzania to London, where he became an outspoken critic of the Nyerere government. He was rumoured to have received money from the Eastern bloc, especially the GDR. Other individuals earmarked as potential allies by the GDR were also either imprisoned or forced into exile. The result was not only the GDR's loss of key contacts among the political elite but also a soiled reputation in the eyes of Nyerere and his supporters.[58]

The visit of the West German federal minister for expellees, Kai-Uwe von Hassel, to Tanzania in July–August 1968 brought simmering tensions to the surface. Von Hassel told Tanzanian journalists that Nyerere had privately confirmed that he would never recognize the GDR.[59] Just prior to von Hassel's arrival, a mysterious pamphlet entitled *Outlook from the Pamirs* had appeared in Dar es Salaam. It represented a vicious assault on China, comparing it to Nazi Germany and describing Mao as a 'Socialist Genghis Khan'.[60] Two other flyers appeared at the same time, criticizing the government and making a scurrilous attack on Nyerere's private life.[61] The GDR was suspected of being behind these publications, potentially working in cahoots with the exiled Kambona. There is no indication that this was the case, however, and the consulate-general denied any involvement. It believed they had been deliberately timed to denigrate the GDR ahead of von Hassel's trip.[62] Nonetheless, such assumptions demonstrated the reputation that East Germany had developed for malicious propaganda in Tanzania.

The Tanzanian Government's response came in the form of a *Nationalist* editorial, which was widely held to have been written by Nyerere himself.[63] Entitled 'Hands off', it warned the Eastern bloc against interfering in Tanzanian affairs. 'We did not fight the Western colonialists to become the playthings of any Eastern country', it stated.[64] Diplomats in Dar es Salaam from both sides of the Cold War divide believed that it was targeted at the GDR.[65] GDR and FRG diplomats subsequently exchanged bitter correspondence in the Letters to the Editor pages of the *Standard*, a then independently owned newspaper. Lessing took issue with von Hassel's comments that the GDR was spreading 'lies' about Bonn's cooperation with South Africa, prompting a counterattack from the West German Embassy. Further correspondence was swiftly closed.[66] Just as Dar es Salaam's fiercely contested public sphere was fertile terrain for the GDR to stir up opposition to the FRG, its West German enemies and Tanzanian sceptics could turn the same environment to their own advantage in smearing and criticizing East Germany.

The Warsaw Pact invasion of Czechoslovakia on 21 August was a major blow to the GDR's standing in Tanzania. The Nyerere regime was amongst the most outspoken African critics of the Soviet-led intervention, which it condemned as a violation of state sovereignty and an act of neo-imperialism. The *Nationalist* followed the government's lead in castigating Moscow. In his pseudonymous column, Babu accused the Soviet Union and its allies of 'proceeding from a deep-seated and dangerous conception' that they were 'the appointed defenders of socialist development'.[67] On 23 August, a protest organized by students and TANU's youth wing turned into a raucous affair, at which the demonstrators – led by two government ministers – vaulted the walls of the Soviet Embassy and vandalized its grounds.[68]

The well-oiled Dar es Salaam propaganda machines of the Warsaw Pact lurched into action. The Soviet Embassy received instructions from Moscow 'to strengthen elucidative work', 'expose Western propaganda' and explain the 'underlying reasons' for the invasion.[69] Its Swahili-language weekly, *Urusi Leo* ('Russia Today') set out Moscow's interpretation of events and claimed that the Soviet Union, in conjunction with other socialist states, 'took steps to safeguard socialist society in Czechoslovakia, together with the peace and security of its people'.[70] The Czechoslovak Embassy, which stood beside Alexander Dubček's government, issued a series of information bulletins, *Habari Katika Czechoslovakia* ('News from Czechoslovakia'), which carried the defiant statements of politicians in Prague.[71] The GDR initially kept a low profile, but later distributed a pamphlet to government officials on the 'Counterrevolutionary Developments in the Czechoslovak Socialist Republic', though such material found little sympathy amongst the Tanzanians.[72]

This nadir in relations between the Eastern bloc and Tanzania paradoxically heralded an unexpected upturn in the GDR's position in the country. Nyerere was concerned about maintaining a balanced non-aligned stance, which some foreign observers had called into question as Tanzania appeared to move closer to China. The embarrassing events at the Soviet Embassy pushed him into recalibrating the public face of Tanzania's foreign policy. In November 1968, Nyerere made the surprising decision to appoint Stephen Mhando, the former teacher and newspaper editor, as minister of state for foreign affairs.[73] The move was clearly designed to appeal to Eastern bloc sensibilities and reaffirm Nyerere's non-aligned credentials.

As I set out elsewhere, Mhando worked closely with the GDR to promote its interests in Tanzania. He paved the way for the signing of the first intergovernmental agreements between the two states in 1971. Horst Schlegel, the ADN correspondent, played an especially important role as an intermediary between the consulate-general and the Minister of State. 'Comrade Schlegel has good connections with Mhando', wrote a GDR diplomat, 'He can call on him any time without an appointment.'[74] The relationship between Schlegel and Mhando stretched back to 1965, when the latter had served on the editorial board of the *Nationalist* and *Mfanyakazi*. Although Mhando's attempts to secure full diplomatic recognition of the GDR failed in the face of Nyerere's implacable opposition, the genuine improvement in GDR–Tanzania relations demonstrates again the significance of political networks in Dar es Salaam, in which domestic affairs, diplomacy and media circuits all overlapped.[75]

In January 1969, Mhando and the GDR were at the centre of another murky local 'black literature' controversy, when a pamphlet entitled *China and the Devil Slaves* fell into the in-trays of officials, politicians and newspaper editors in Dar es Salaam. According to its title page, it was written by Walter Markow, an East German Africanist, 'assisted by Stephen Mhando'. The publisher was named as the German–African Society of the German Democratic Republic. Like *Outlook from the Pamirs*, it was a scathing attack on Beijing: a deliberate challenge to the bonds of Afro–Asian solidarity between China and Tanzania. It described how the Chinese have 'for many centuries' regarded Africans as 'inferior beings' – 'suitable only for slavery, or to be sterilised, or to be wiped off the face of the earth'.

The tract offered a batch of 'historical' examples to support these wild accusations.⁷⁶

The GDR immediately disowned any involvement in *China and the Devil Slaves*. Erich Butzke, who had replaced Lessing as consul-general, told Mhando that it was clearly a West German production. Mhando in turn informed Schlegel that Nyerere regarded the pamphlet as 'nonsense' and did not think that the GDR was behind it. 'The inclusion of Stephen Mhando in the forgery is regarded as the first official reaction among imperialist circles to his appointment as minister of state', wrote Schlegel. The only public word on the matter came from a TASS correspondent, who described the pamphlet as a 'provocation' by West German 'revanchists'. Carrying out their own private inquiry in Dar es Salaam, the Americans were told by a West German diplomat that the pamphlet was part of a double-bluff operation, in which the GDR had produced a forgery so crude it would be assumed to be a plant by West Germany. But he also admitted that he could not be '100 per cent sure' it had not been produced by his own country. When State Department experts carried out tests on a specimen, they traced the pamphlet's paper and staples to North Korea, which only muddied the waters further still.⁷⁷ Once again, the GDR's reputation for smear attacks continued to complicate its operations in Tanzania.

Exploiting West German Policy in Southern Africa

The GDR's propaganda was most successful when its message resonated with a key pillar of Tanzania's foreign policy and national self-image: the commitment to the liberation of southern Africa. As Rui Lopes argues, Bonn's prioritization of European Cold War *Realpolitik* over the principle of decolonization meant that it kept strong relations with the Portuguese *Estado Novo* (Second Republic), despite Lisbon's refusal to give up its African territories. West Germany continued its military cooperation with Portugal into the 1970s.⁷⁸ Bonn also maintained ties with South Africa, especially in terms of trade, which the West German Government avowed was a separate matter to political relations.⁷⁹

Bonn's soft approach to the white minority regimes was low-hanging fruit for the GDR. Criticism of Bonn's *Afrikapolitik* was a common refrain in the GDR Consulate-General's handouts. In a rare interview with Nyerere in August 1967, for example, Lessing gave the president a pamphlet entitled 'Bonn/Pretoria', produced by the GDR's Afro–Asian Solidarity Committee.[80] Playing on a Tanzanian sensitivity to any evidence of Western neo-imperialist support for Portugal and South Africa, the GDR was also prepared to twist truths in order to maximize the damage done to the FRG's image. In 1968, a *Nationalist* article made unfounded accusations that 17,000 West German troops were fighting in Mozambique and that 2,000 ex-Wehrmacht officers were training South African forces. While there is no evidence that the piece was produced by the GDR, it is likely to have fed the false information to the newspaper.[81] Against these accusations, the GDR could point more positively to its own commitment to the liberation struggle, especially as it increased its support for the Mozambican Liberation Front (Frente de Libertaçaõ do Moçambique, FRELIMO) in the late 1960s.

The nationalization of the *Standard* in 1970 opened up a new channel for the GDR's efforts to denigrate West Germany and its foreign policy in Africa. Under the African socialist principles of *ujamaa*, the foreign- and privately owned *Standard* had stuck out as an anomaly in Dar es Salaam's congested public sphere. In February 1970, its front page suddenly announced that the *Standard* was 'appearing for the first time as the official newspaper of the Government of Tanzania'.[82] As Nyerere wrote in an accompanying editorial, it was 'clearly impossible for the largest daily newspaper in independent Tanzania to be left indefinitely in the hands of a foreign company. In a country committed to building socialism, it is also impossible for such an influential medium to be left indefinitely in the control of non-socialist, capitalist owners.'[83]

However, the *Standard*'s nationalization did not turn it into an obedient government mouthpiece. Rather, the editorial team appointed by Nyerere transformed the newspaper into a radical organ, connected to a transnational revolutionary left. Nyerere appointed Frene Ginwala as the *Standard*'s new editor. Ginwala was a South African of Asian descent who supported the African National Congress, which was amongst the liberation movements operating out of Dar es Salaam. The staff that she assembled was a radical mix of foreigners and Africans. The *Standard* pursued an internationalist editorial line, particularly critical of Western 'imperialism' in Africa.[84]

While the *Standard* was under private ownership, the GDR had had little success in influencing the newspaper's position or inserting material into its pages. However, after the paper's nationalization, its realignment under Ginwala gave it significant political overlap with the GDR's own propaganda agenda. Although the East German archival holdings beyond 1969 become scarce, there are hints elsewhere at a more proximate relationship between the *Standard* under Ginwala and the GDR Consulate-General (and the Eastern bloc representations more generally). In February 1971, the *Standard* published two articles which alleged that West Germany, along with Israel, was providing military support to rebels in southern Sudan. According to the accompanying caption, one was abridged from a bulletin of the Soviet Union's Sudan Afro–Asian Solidarity Committee; the other, attributed to the ADN, concerned the activities of a West German mercenary, Rudolf Steiner.[85] The West German Embassy alleged that they were fundamentally identical in content to articles appearing in the local East German bulletins, *GDR News* and *Urafiki*. Again, this seemed to contravene the Tanzanian Foreign Ministry's own rules on attacks on third-party states, through a government-owned newspaper.[86]

In early 1971, however, West Germany's chief concern in Africa was defending itself against damaging charges that it had been involved in events in Guinea-Conakry the previous year. In October 1970, a force of undercover Portuguese troops, mercenaries and local opponents of Guinean President Ahmed Sékou Touré's regime invaded the country from neighbouring Guinea-Bissau. The operation was intended by Lisbon to free Portuguese prisoners of war and destroy the assets of Amilcar Cabral's African Party for the Independence of Guinea and Cape Verde (Partido Africano da Independência da Guiné e Cabo Verde, PAIGC), which was based in Conakry. Although the intervention was unsuccessful, it drew bitter criticism across Africa.[87] As a state which also sheltered liberation movements, Tanzania had even more reason to fear than others. Ginwala's *Standard* dubbed the invasion 'an object lesson to Africa and the whole world as to the extent to which imperialist and colonialist nations will go to try to dominate and dictate'.[88]

Naturally, Africa's – and Tanzania's – anger was directed primarily against Lisbon, but Portugal's NATO allies also came under fire. The FRG was accused of involvement in the invasion. Touré demanded that Bonn replace its ambassador to Conakry, who was formally charged with complicity in the plot. By the end of 1970, the Touré government had expelled the West German expatriate community from Guinea-Conakry. On 26 January 1971, it then severed relations with Bonn. The Guinean

Government issued a 'white paper', which included charges against the West German Government. In a response set out in July, Bonn alleged that Touré had been misled by the GDR, which it claimed had fabricated the connection between the FRG and the invasion of Guinea-Conakry through falsified documents.[89]

Seeking to clear its name, West Germany stressed to African governments that allegations made in the Guinean 'white paper' rested on fabricated evidence. Tanzania's ambassador to Bonn told the West German Foreign Office that he fully agreed that the documents had been falsified. Other representatives of the Tanzanian Government assured the West German Embassy that the matter would not have a negative impact on relations between the two countries.[90] However, the Tanzanian media continued to disseminate wild stories about the West German Government's participation in Portuguese colonial operations. In February, the *Sunday News* (the Sunday edition of the *Standard*) reproduced a Guinean report under the title 'Germans and Portuguese took part in Guinea raid'.[91] In a complaint to the Tanzanian Ministry of Foreign Affairs, the FRG alleged that the article 'creates the impression for the Tanzanian reader that the German participation is an established fact'. The situation was made more problematic by the West German Embassy's poor relationship with the *Standard*, which prevented the former from submitting clarifying statements to Ginwala.[92]

Ginwala's editorship provided a brief window in which the GDR relocated the focal point of its engagement with the Tanzanian press from the *Nationalist* to the previously avoided *Standard*. Having pinpointed the soft underbelly of West German foreign relations in Africa, the GDR latched on to the *Standard*'s radical turn in order to further its own propaganda war against Bonn. At a meeting of Eastern bloc press and cultural attachés in Dar es Salaam, the Soviet representative countered the scepticism of his Czechoslovak and Bulgarian colleagues by arguing that Ginwala – with contacts in the South African Communist Party – was a potential ideological ally in Tanzania.[93] However, the *Standard*'s radicalism was short-lived: in August 1971, Ginwala and several of her more vituperative staff members were dismissed from their positions. The decision followed a series of Western embassy complaints about the newspaper, but was triggered by a particularly aggressive editorial regarding the persecution of communists in Sudan, which threatened to damage a regional alliance between Dar es Salaam and Khartoum.[94]

Conclusion

Tanzania and the GDR eventually opened formal diplomatic relations on 21 December 1972. The Tanzanian Government's change of heart owed nothing to the GDR's own policies in Africa, however. Rather, the agreement took place amid a slew of recognitions of the East German state across the Third World, coming days after Bonn and East Berlin signed the 'Basic Treaty', under which the two German states recognized each other's sovereignty.[95] This development essentially normalized the coexistence of the GDR and FRG in Dar es Salaam, although the propaganda wars continued unabated. West German representatives monitored in depth the stream of attacks on Bonn in GDR news bulletins, which repeatedly returned to the FRG's policy towards South Africa.[96]

The GDR's propaganda tactics did far more damage than good in its mission to gain full recognition in Dar es Salaam. The attacks on the FRG's support – exaggerated or otherwise – for Portugal and South Africa were well received by the more radical elements of the press and political elite, but had little effect on the government itself. Cruder propaganda efforts like the *Braunbuch* were met with disdain, and created precedents which meant that when even more disreputable 'black literature' surfaced in the city, East Germany was assumed to be a prime suspect. The East German experience in Zanzibar, where its ill-considered development projects and pushy approach contributed to the island's government preferring Chinese aid, also discouraged Tanzania's support for the GDR's cause.[97] East Germany's pursuit of influential contacts amongst the overlapping networks of the Tanzanian media and political establishment largely backfired.

Mostly, however, the GDR's entanglement in Tanzanian affairs reveals how its own policies were contingent on shifting political dynamics in the country. While the GDR claimed some support from the Soviet Union in its attempt to gain recognition in Tanzania, its near subordination of all other policy to its unique cause led it to become utterly transfixed on its competition with Bonn. Marginalized in terms of diplomatic relations with the Nyerere regime, the GDR turned to media networks as a means of currying favour in Tanzania. But this entwined the East German struggle for recognition with the labyrinthine world of Tanzanian politics and the government's attempts to marshal the postcolonial public sphere. Here, in the entrails of Odd Arne Westad's anecdotal Cold War elephant, the intersection of local and global political dynamics demonstrated the relative weakness of the GDR on the world stage. Starved of opportunities to develop a meaningful, constructive relationship with the Tanzanian Government, the GDR became a scavenger state, seeking to feed off every opportunity that arose to advance its cause, in a sometimes reckless manner.

Notes

1. Werner Kilian, *Die Hallstein-Doktrin: der Diplomatische Krieg zwischen der BRD und der DDR, 1955–1973* [The Hallstein Doctrine: The Diplomatic War between the FRG and the GDR, 1955–1973] (Berlin, 2001); William Glenn Gray, *Germany's Cold War: The Global Campaign to Isolate East Germany, 1949–1969* (Chapel Hill, NC, 2003).
2. Gareth Curless, Stacey Hynd, Temilola Alanamu and Katherine Roscoe, 'Editors' introduction: networks in imperial history', *Journal of World History*, 26 (2015), pp. 705–32. See also Frederick Cooper, 'Networks, moral discourse, and history', in Thomas Callaghy, Ronald Kassimir and Robert Latham (eds), *Intervention and Transnationalism in Africa: Global-Local Networks of Power* (Cambridge, 2001), pp. 23–46.
3. Paul Boyer, 'Foreword: bringing diplomatic history home', in Jeffrey A. Engel (ed.), *Local Consequences of the Global Cold War* (Washington, DC, 2007), pp. xi–xvi, here xvi.
4. Odd Arne Westad, 'Exploring the histories of the Cold War: a pluralist approach', in Joel Isaac and Duncan Bell (eds), *Uncertain Empire: American History and the Idea of the Cold War* (Oxford, 2012), pp. 51–9.
5. Jonathan Glassman, *War of Words, War of Stones: Racial Thought and Violence in Colonial Zanzibar* (Bloomington, IN, 2011).
6. Issa G. Shivji, *Pan-Africanism or Pragmatism? Lessons of the Tanganyika-Zanzibar Union* (Dar es Salaam, 2008), pp. 69–99; Ethan R. Sanders, 'Conceiving the Tanganyika-Zanzibar Union in the midst of the Cold War', *African Review*, 41 (2014), pp. 35–70.
7. 'Govt. statement on Z'bar missions', *Nationalist*, 26 June 1964, p. 1.
8. 'Understanding friends', editorial, *Nationalist*, 25 June 1964, p. 4.
9. 'Were we wrong?', editorial, *Nationalist*, 26 June 1964, p. 4.
10. Heinz Schneppen, 'Sansibar und die Hallstein-Doktrin' [Zanzibar and the Hallstein Doctrine], *Deutschland Archiv*, 32 (1999), pp. 409–19; Ulf Engel, *Die Afrikapolitik der Bundesrepublik Deutschland, 1949–1999: Rollen und Identitäten*

[The Africa Policy of the Federal Republic of Germany, 1949–1999: Roles and Identities] (Hamburg, 1999), pp. 117–45; Kilian, *Die Hallstein-Doktrin*, pp. 171–214; Ulrich van der Heyden, '"I will not recognise East Germany just because Bonn is stupid". Anerkennungsdiplomatie in Tansania, 1964 bis 1965' [The diplomacy of recognition in Tanzania, 1964 to 1965], in Ulrich van der Heyden and Franziska Benger (eds), *Kalter Krieg in Ostafrika: Die Beziehungen der DDR zu Sansibar und Tansania* [Cold War in East Africa: The GDR's Relations with Zanzibar and Tanzania] (Berlin, 2009), pp. 9–30.
11. Naudy to Direction Afrique-Levant, Ministère des Affaires Étrangères [MAE-DAL], 5 August 1969, Centre des Archives diplomatiques, Nantes [hereafter, CADN], 193PO/1/26 AII22.
12. Lessing to Kiesewetter, 18 January 1968, Bundesarchiv, Berlin [hereafter, BA], Stiftung Archiv der Parteien und Massenorganisationen der DDR [SAPMO], DY 30/IV A 2/20/970, pp. 389–91.
13. Helmut Matthes, 'Zur Entwicklung außenpolitischer Grundlagen der Beziehungen zwischen der Deutschen Demokratischen Republik und der Vereinigten Republik Tansania bis Mitte der siebziger Jahre' [On the development of the foreign-policy foundations in relations between the German Democratic Republic and the United Republic of Tanzania up to the mid-1970s], in van der Heyden and Benger (eds), *Kalter Krieg*, pp. 55–97.
14. Sara Lorenzini, *Due Germania in Africa: la cooperazione allo sviluppo e la competizione per i mercati di materie prime e tecnologia* [The Two Germanys in Africa: Development Cooperation and Competition for Markets in Raw Materials and Technology] (Florence, 2003), pp. 189–205; Hubertus Büschel, *Hilfe zur Selbsthilfe: Deutsche Entwicklungsarbeit in Afrika, 1960–1975* [Helping People Help Themselves: German Development Work in Africa, 1960–1975] (Frankfurt, 2014); Young-Sun Hong, *Cold War Germany, the Third World, and the Global Humanitarian Regime* (Cambridge, 2015), pp. 300–14.
15. Garth Andrew Myers, *Verandahs of Power: Colonialism and Space in Urban Africa* (New York, 2003), pp. 106–34; Ludger Wimmelbücker, 'Architecture and city-planning projects of the German Democratic Republic in Zanzibar', *Journal of Architecture*, 17 (2012), pp. 407–32; Büschel, *Hilfe zur Selbsthilfe*, pp. 452–81; Hong, *Cold War Germany*, p. 305.
16. Katherine Pence, 'Showcasing Cold War Germany in Cairo: 1954 and 1957 industrial exhibitions and the competition for Arab partners', *Journal of Contemporary History*, 47 (2011), pp. 69–95; Gerd Horten, 'Sailing in the shadow of the Vietnam War: the GDR government and the "Vietnam bonus" of the early 1970s', *German Studies Review*, 36 (2013), pp. 557–78.
17. I take the expression from Andrew Ivaska's exploration of cultural politics in the city: *Cultured States: Youth, Gender, and Modern Style in 1960s Dar es Salaam* (Durham, NC, 2011).
18. George Roberts, 'The assassination of Eduardo Mondlane: FRELIMO and the politics of exile in Dar es Salaam', *Cold War History*, 17 (2017), pp. 1–19.
19. Deschamps to MAE-DAL, 5 February 1963, CADN, 193PO/1/26 AII23.

20. Katrina M. Hagen, 'Crimes against humanity in the Congo: Nazi legacies and the German Cold War in Africa', in Philip E. Muehlenbeck (ed.), *Race, Ethnicity, and the Cold War: A Global Perspective* (Nashville, TN, 2012), pp. 166–99.
21. Quoted in Hong, *Cold War Germany*, p. 294.
22. Michael F. Scholz, 'Active measures and disinformation as part of East Germany's propaganda war, 1953–1972', in Kristie Macrakis, Thomas Wegener Friis and Helmut Müller-Enbergs (eds), *East German Foreign Intelligence: Myth, Reality and Controversy* (London, 2010), pp. 113–33.
23. Pagenstert to Auswärtiges Amt, 2 December 1965, Politisches Archiv des Auswärtiges Amt, Berlin [hereafter, PAAA], B34, 606; de Bourdeille to MAE-DAL, 22 February 1966, CADN, 193PO/1/26 AII23; Hong, *Cold War Germany*, p. 294.
24. Kilian, *Die Hallstein-Doktrin*, pp. 219–20.
25. Pagenstert to Auswärtiges Amt, 10 February 1966, PAAA, B34, 671.
26. GDR Consulate-General, Dar es Salaam, to Kiesewetter, 18 January 1966, BA, SAPMO, DY 30/IV A 2/20/963, p. 184.
27. Pagenstert to Auswärtiges Amt, 10 February 1966, PAAA, B34, 671.
28. Tanzanian Ministry of Foreign Affairs, 21 May 1966, BA, SAPMO, DY 30/IV A 2/20/957, p. 234.
29. Scholz to Abteilung Information, Ministerium für Auswärtige Angelegenheiten [hereafter, MfAA], 1 June 1966, BA, SAPMO, DY 30/IV A 2/20/957, pp. 230–3.
30. James Brennan, 'The Cold War battle over global news in East Africa: decolonization, the free flow of information, and the media business, 1960–1980', *Journal of Global History*, 10 (2015), pp. 333–56.
31. George Roberts, 'Politics, decolonisation, and the Cold War in Dar es Salaam, c. 1965–1972', PhD dissertation, University of Warwick, 2016, pp. 68–9.
32. Michael Minholz and Uwe Stirnberg, *Der Allgemeine Deutsche Nachrichtendienst (ADN): Gute Nachrichten für die SED* [The General German News Agency: Good News for the SED] (Munich, 1995), esp. pp. 284, 293.
33. Peter Spacek, 'Die Anfänge in Sansibar und Dar es Salaam' [The beginning in Zanzibar and Dar es Salaam], in van der Heyden and Benger (eds), *Kalter Krieg*, pp. 169–83.
34. Fischer to Abteilung Presse, MfAA, 6 April 1967, BA, SAPMO, DY 30/IV A 2/20/970, p. 121.
35. Wendlandt, 14 October 1969, BA, SAPMO, DY 30/IV A 2/20/958, pp. 522–5.
36. Junghahns, 1 November 1968, BA, SAPMO, DY 30/IV A 2/20/964, pp. 231–41.
37. Martin Sturmer, *The Media History of Tanzania* (Mtwara, 1998), pp. 108, 110.
38. 'Jahresbericht 1965', 3 January 1966, BA, SAPMO, DY 30/IV A 2/20/963, pp. 108–83.
39. Sturmer, *Media History*, 107; Robert Vitalis, 'The midnight ride of Kwame Nkrumah and other fables of Bandung (Ban-doong)', *Humanity*, 4 (2013), pp. 261–88, here 275.

40. Gordon to State Dept, 5 December 1964, National Archives and Records Administration, College Park, MD [hereafter, NARA], Record Group [hereafter, RG] 59, Subject Numeric Files [SNF] 1964–6, Box 1561, CSM TANZAN.
41. Director of Special Branch, Tanganyika, to Harris, 30 June 1960, National Archives, Kew, London [UKNA], FCO 141/17768/17.
42. Paul Bjerk, *Building a Peaceful Nation: Julius Nyerere and the Establishment of Sovereignty in Tanzania* (Rochester, NY, 2015), pp. 236–46.
43. Junghahns, 1 November 1968, BA, SAPMO, DY 30/IV A 2/20/964, pp. 231–41.
44. Odinga to Secretary, Zentralkommitee, SED, 2 April 1962, BA, SAPMO, DY 30/IV A 2/20/957, p. 5; Abt. Aussenpolitik und Internationale Verbindungen, SED, 16 April 1962, BA, SAPMO, DY 30/IV A 2/20/957, pp. 7–9.
45. Spacek, 'Anfänge', pp. 174–5.
46. Deschamps to MAE-DAL, 22 January 1963 and 5 February 1963, CADN, 193PO/1/26 AII23.
47. Cranford Pratt, *The Critical Phase in Tanzania, 1945–1968* (Cambridge, 1976), pp. 139–52.
48. Scholz, 23 August 1966, BA, SAPMO, DY 30/IV A 2/20/966, pp. 330–2.
49. Burns to State Dept, 4 June 1966, NARA, RG 59, SNF 1964–6, Box 428, PPB TANZAN.
50. Fischer to Zibelius, 5 April 1967, BA, SAPMO, DY 30/IV A 2/20/970, pp. 117–20.
51. Graham Mytton, interview with Benjamin Mkapa, 3 November 1967, Papers of Graham Mytton, Institute for Commonwealth Studies, London, ICS 115/1/4.
52. Jamie Monson, *Africa's Freedom Railway: How a Chinese Development Project Changed Lives and Livelihoods in Tanzania* (Bloomington, IN, 2008).
53. The literature on *ujamaa* socialism is vast. See Priya Lal, *African Socialism in Postcolonial Tanzania: Between the Village and the World* (New York, 2015).
54. Quoted in 'Tanzania: Soviet views on the Arusha programme', *Mizan*, 9 (1967), pp. 197–201, here 200.
55. Fischer to Abteilung Presse, MfAA, 6 April 1967, BA, SAPMO, DY 30/IV A 2/20/970, pp. 122–4; Jäntsch to Korrbüro-Ausland, 25 August 1967, BA, SAPMO, DC 900/4134.
56. Fischer to Zibelius, 5 April 1967, BA, SAPMO, DY 30/IV A 2/20/970, pp. 117–20; Fischer, 6 April 1967, BA, SAPMO, DY 30/IV A 2/20/970, p. 121.
57. Lessing to Kiesewetter, 14 February 1967, BA, SAPMO, DY 30/IV A 2/20/970, pp. 58–69.
58. Roberts, 'Politics', pp. 48–56, 88–91.
59. 'FRELIMO aid claim denied: West German minister gives assurances', *Standard*, 10 August 1968, p. 5. Von Hassel was born in German East Africa in 1913, and had worked in British Tanganyika during the interwar years.

60. Enclosed in Burns to State Dept, 20 March 1969, NARA, RG 59, CFPF 1967–9, Box 1511, CSM TANZAN. The pamphlet's text was based on articles appearing in the 27 September and 4 October 1967 issues of *Literaturnaya Gazeta*, a Soviet literary journal. Rogers to US emb., Dar es Salaam, NARA, RG 59, CFPF 1967–9, Box 1511, CSM TANZAN; Ernst Henri, 'A view from the Pamirs', *Survival*, 10 (1968), pp. 28–30.
61. Enclosed in Burns to State Dept, 8 August 1968, NARA, RG 59, CFPF 1967–9, Box 2513, POL 2 TANZAN.
62. MfAA, 26 September 1968, BA, SAPMO, DY 30/IV A 2/20/964, pp. 219–25.
63. Burns to State Dept, 16 August 1968, NARA, RG 59, CFPF 1967–9, Box 2513, POL 2 TANZAN; Phillips to Stewart, 2 January 1969, UKNA, FCO 31/442/17.
64. 'Hands off', editorial, *Nationalist*, 13 August 1968, p. 4.
65. MfAA, 26 September 1968, BA, SAPMO, DY 30/IV A 2/20/964, pp. 219–25.
66. Lessing, 'G.D.R. policy', letter to the editor, *Standard*, 15 August 1968, p. 2; Pullen, 'G.D.R. policy', letter to the editor, *Standard*, 19 August 1968, p. 2.
67. [A. M. Babu], 'The so-called world's policeman', *Nationalist*, 23 August 1968, p. 4.
68. On the protest and its fallout, see Roberts, 'Politics', pp. 143–6.
69. Arkadi Glukhov, 'The fateful August of 1968: hot summer in Dar es Salaam', in Russian Academy of Sciences Institute of African Studies, *Julius Nyerere: Humanist, Politician, Thinker*, trans. B.G. Petruk (Dar es Salaam, 2005), pp. 42–9, here 45.
70. 'Hali ya Czechoslovakia' [The situation in Czechoslovakia], *Urusi Leo*, 8 September 1968, pp. 1, 4.
71. Enclosed in NARA, RG 84, Dar es Salaam, UCSF, 1965–75, Box 9, POL 27.
72. Zielke, 23 September 1968, BA, SAPMO, DY 30/IV A 2/20/970, pp. 514–16.
73. Nyerere himself retained the full foreign-affairs portfolio.
74. MfAA, 5 December 1968, BA, SAPMO, DY 30/IV A 2/20/964, pp. 262–3.
75. Roberts, 'Politics', pp. 101–108.
76. Enclosed in Burns to State Dept, 20 March 1969, NARA, RG 59, CFPF 1967–9, Box 1511, CSM TANZAN.
77. Burns to State Dept, 20 March 1969; Rogers to US emb., Dar es Salaam, 18 April 1969: both in NARA, RG 59, CFPF 1967–9, Box 1511, CSM TANZAN.
78. Rui Lopes, *West Germany and the Portuguese Dictatorship, 1968–1974: Between Cold War and Colonialism* (Basingstoke, 2014).
79. Reinhard Rode, *Die Südafrikapolitik der Bundesrepublik Deutschland, 1968–1972* [The South Africa Policy of the Federal Republic of Germany, 1968–1972] (Munich, 1975); Tilman Dedering, 'Ostpolitik and the relations between West Germany and South Africa', in Carole Fink and Bernd Schaeffer (eds), *Ostpolitik, 1969–1974: European and Global Responses* (New York, 2009), pp. 206–31.
80. Lessing, 10 August 1967, BA, SAPMO, DY 30/IV A 2/20/970, pp. 195–200.

81. 'NATO's tentacles are all over Africa', *Nationalist*, 16 May 1968, p. 3.
82. 'Government takes over "The Standard"', *Standard*, 5 February 1970, p. 1.
83. Julius K. Nyerere, 'A socialist paper for the people', *Standard*, 5 February 1970, p. 1.
84. Sturmer, *Media History*, pp. 120–6; Roberts, 'Politics', pp. 191–3.
85. 'The "Anyanya"'; 'Rudolf Steiner' – both in *Standard*, 13 February 1971, p. 2. The articles appeared shortly after the Tanzanian press carried allegations of Israeli involvement in the coup d'état that had brought Idi Amin to power in Uganda. Tanzania, along with Sudan, opposed the coup. Nyerere refused to recognize Amin as president of Uganda.
86. Memcon (Namfua, Hebich), 19 February 1971, PAAA, NA 13465.
87. Lopes, *West Germany*, p. 25.
88. Editorial, *Standard*, 24 November 1970, p. 1.
89. Lopes, *West Germany*, pp. 26–8, 33.
90. Memcon (Namfua, Hebich), 19 February 1971, PAAA, NA 13465.
91. 'Germans and Portuguese took part in Guinea raid', *Sunday News*, 14 February 1971, p. 6.
92. Memcon (Namfua, Hebich), 19 February 1971, PAAA, NA 13465.
93. Hollender, 29 March 17971, PAAA, MfAA, C 759/74.
94. Roberts, 'Politics', pp. 193–6.
95. Kilian, *Die Hallstein-Doktrin*, p. 226.
96. See the documents in PAAA, NA 13473.
97. Lorenzini, *Due Germania*, p. 203; Hong, *Cold War Germany*, pp. 313–14.

CHAPTER 7

MEDICINE, ECONOMICS AND FOREIGN POLICY: EAST GERMAN MEDICAL ACADEMICS IN THE GLOBAL SOUTH DURING THE 1950S AND 1960S[1]

Iris Borowy

This chapter explores the policies of the German Democratic Republic (GDR) in the field of medical academia in countries in the Global South, a small but revealing sector of East German foreign policy. During 40 years of its existence, between 1949 and 1989, the GDR engaged in an active policy of cooperation with low-income countries in the field of medicine in general and in medical research and teaching in particular. Financially, it was not a particularly large field of medical-development cooperation. According to a 1980 East German study, GDR authorities spent DDM 43.84 million on activities related to medical education, teaching and research between 1965 and 1979, roughly 10 per cent of total expenditures on 'solidarity support in the medical field'. By contrast, almost DDM 300 million were spent on drugs and medical supplies.[2]

However, academic cooperation was significant far beyond what its expenses suggest. Unlike practising doctors, academic professors moved in circles of universities and research institutions, typically in urban areas near the national political centres of their respective countries.

They met members of the elite group rather than patients, and their perspectives tended to be more attuned to the macro view of the development of the country in question and its relationship with the GDR. In addition, medical specialists working in academic institutions, including university hospitals, frequently acted in an informal consulting capacity regarding purchases of medical supplies and equipment, an issue of tangible relevance to the GDR's foreign relations. As such, the activities of academics provide a glimpse into the sphere of medical policy in low-income countries between the top-down perspective of government plans and the bottom-up perspective of grassroots medicine.

The topic forms part of a small but growing historiography on East German interactions with the Global South. Even while the GDR existed, East German 'solidarity' aid to low-income countries was the subject of studies both by West German[3] and East German[4] scholars – the latter as part of a governmental survey. After 1989, as primary diplomatic sources became available, a growing body of scholarship pointed to the highly politicized nature of East German policies in the Global South but also to the degree to which these policies were subject to local rationales and circumstances.[5] Several of these studies have taken a comparative approach – pointing to differences, but also to far-reaching similarities, between East and West German attitudes to low-income countries, born largely from the way in which attitudes germane to industrialized countries and local dynamics complemented Cold War rationales.[6] Though health regularly represents a large part of industrialized countries' engagement in the Global South, only relatively few studies have thus far addressed the medical sector of GDR 'solidarity' policies either in specific studies[7] or as a component of German policies in the medical field.[8] So far, studies have focused on medical experts as practitioners, largely ignoring their important role as academics, teachers and researchers. This omission is noteworthy, since the practice and theoretical education of medicine are closely intertwined. Medical education inevitably includes practical therapeutic work, and hospitals and medical schools routinely cooperate. Health-related 'development' or 'solidarity' work would inevitably involve the academic component of teaching and researching medicine.

This chapter is based on primary sources of the East German Ministry of External Affairs (Ministerium für Auswärtige Angelegenheiten) and of the Ministry of Health (Ministerium für Gesundheit), as well as a series of interviews with East German doctors who taught medicine or engaged in research cooperation while on assignment in a Global South country.[9] It argues that these activities had certain characteristics that set them apart from other 'development' or 'solidarity' work in the health field: they involved different political and economic repercussions; different risks and chances; and also, to some extent, a different set of people. This analysis, therefore, seeks to unravel the specific role played by medical academics within the larger context of East German foreign policy. What role did professors, lecturers and researchers play for relations between the GDR and low-income countries in the Global South, and which factors affected the successes or failures of their efforts?

Official Policy and Personal Motivation

Officially, the purpose of East German policies in and with these countries, most of which were former colonies, was to support peoples emerging from imperialist domination as part of international socialist solidarity.[10] However, though this approach – one of socialist idealism – played a role in the motivation of individual doctors and medical professors, overall policy decisions were more complex, determined often by considerations of material possibilities, by windows of opportunities in often hostile international territory and by political and economic self-interest within the overall circumstances that the GDR faced at various times.

Above all else, the activities of its medical academics in low-income countries were determined by the foreign-policy interests of the GDR – notably, an intense desire of the East German Government to break out of its international isolation. After its emergence as one of the German successor states of the pre-war German Reich, the GDR competed with the Federal Republic of Germany (FRG) for recognition as the legitimate representation of Germany – or for any recognition at all. This situation was accentuated during the 1960s, when the independence of numerous former colonies created a large number of potential allies for both German states. Development assistance did not originally form part of East German foreign-policy plans, however; it emerged almost inadvertently in response to the Korean War. In 1950 the National Front, an association of parties and mass organizations, created a Korea Assistance Commission, designed to coordinate aid programmes while denouncing 'US imperialism'. Until 1953, this commission provided DDM 16 million worth of aid, including some 136,000 kilograms (300,000 pounds) of drugs and two ambulances.[11] This event provided the model through which further activities in the Global South would be conceptualized as acts of 'solidarity' with its people against perceived Western aggression. During the following years, health activities evolved into a regular part of GDR foreign policy. A position paper of the Ministry of Health (MOH), written in the mid-1950s, listed a variety of measures to be used in this context – health agreements, the participation of East German medical experts in conferences, the treatment of foreign patients in hospitals in the GDR and 'foreign propaganda in the field of health' ('außenpolitische Propaganda auf dem Gebiete des Gesundheitswesens') – all to be used as means to strengthen the position of the Soviet bloc in the Cold War in general, and the position of the GDR in relation to West Germany in particular.[12] Though the Ministry of External Affairs (MEA) endorsed and encouraged this policy as a form of soft power, its implementation and funding remained MOH responsibility, which became a source of tension between the two ministries. Thus, the position paper complained that the MEA was clearly interested in maximizing the number of health agreements regardless of whether such agreements made sense with regard to health work in the countries concerned or whether they were within the financial means of the MOH.[13]

In addition, this strategy was complicated by the domestic situation. The proximity of West Germany acted like a standing invitation to those who were disillusioned with life in the GDR. Around 2.6 million people left the GDR between 1949 and 1961, out of a population of 18.4 million in 1946.[14] The emigrant group included at least 7,500 doctors, and possibly over 8,700, so that the country suffered a painful loss of precisely those people who would be most needed not only for domestic medical care but also for medical assistance to low-income countries.[15] This situation turned the sending of doctors to low-income countries for medical projects into a problematic affair. Sometimes, therefore, the GDR had to cancel or curtail projects for lack of suitable medical experts.[16] While the construction of the Berlin Wall in 1961 substantially reduced the loss of manpower, it increased the political risk of sending East German specialists to countries in the Global South.

Working in low-income countries now became a rare opportunity to leave the GDR for good and to move to a Western country. This was more than a theoretical risk – as became clear when, after the construction of the Berlin Wall, the gynaecologist Dr Andrae and the dentist Dr Rost chose to become West German citizens while they were working in Yemen.[17]

With regard to lecturers and biomedical researchers, both the scarcity and the risk of embarrassing defections were less pronounced. Though, in 1950, the Dean of the Charité, the medical department of Berlin's Humboldt University, declared that only 12 out of 24 positions of full professors at his department were filled, circumstances were better regarding the lower ranks: 25 out of 29 positions of adjunct professors and 211 out of 252 positions for assistant professors were taken.[18] These numbers reflected the position of medical academics. Lecturers and scientists had a privileged position in East German academia, which often came with opportunities to travel, since the authorities acknowledged, reluctantly, that international exchange formed part of science. While practising doctors often felt professionally constrained in the GDR because the East German authorities aimed at a medical system without private practices – which, traditionally, doctors coveted – a comparable conflict did not exist in teaching and research. Besides, while practising doctors could realistically hope to continue their work in West Germany, diverging networks and qualifying profiles in East and West made it more difficult for East German professors of medicine to gain an attractive academic position in the West. At the same time, for academics, work experience in a foreign country was a clear career advantage after their return to the GDR, since having foreign experience was an asset for becoming a full professor. Thus, medical scientists had more to lose and less to gain by defecting via a country in the Global South than did practising doctors.[19]

There were other advantages in employing scientists in international cooperation in medicine and health. Ideologically, academia formed a link to a reputation of Germany as a place of science and learning, a rare connection to past German prestige politically open to the GDR. East German officials explicitly recommended claiming the legacy of medical scientists like Robert Koch[20] and Ferdinand Sauerbruch[21] (ignoring their ambivalent roles during colonialism or National Socialism) when medical academics lectured in low-income countries.[22] Thus, in 1963, a 'Robert-Koch-Week', involving an exhibition and talks, was used to introduce a cooperative GDR–Egyptian project on tuberculosis.[23] The founder and director of the Tbc-Research Berlin-Buch, Professor Paul Steinbrück, opened the week with a lecture on Koch's life and work and on contemporary tuberculosis policies of the GDR.[24] A year later, Steinbrück also formed part of the commission in charge of negotiations for a GDR–Egyptian agreement on cooperation in the health field. Apparently, the organizers valued the participation of scientists even for programmes that, as in this case, did not have a large academic component.[25]

Universities in low-income countries often acted as natural places of contact for East German scientists and as natural platforms for scientific presentations. Sometimes, this played out in practical terms, as when universities offered premises for the display of exhibitions of the Hygiene Museum of Dresden – as the University of Jakarta did in 1957.[26] More importantly, within the small elites of low-income countries emerging from colonial rule, politicians and academics often originated from the same thin layer of people with higher education. Sometimes, the link between medical academic cooperation and diplomatic relations could be very direct. For example, in the 1950s the professor for surgery at the University of Rangoon was the father-in-law of the head of the military government of Burma. Similarly, numerous medical students and doctors who received specialized training at the university clinic in Rostock later occupied senior government positions in their home countries.[27] Generally, access to academia was tantamount to access to higher political positions, and academics were those most likely to have the language skills necessary to communicate with GDR officials. At other times, academic institutions could provide an entry into a country whose government was hostile to socialist countries. Thus, in September 1961, the visit of a delegation of Argentinian communist physicians and university lecturers to the GDR, arranged by the 'circulo de los amigos de la R.D.A.' ('circle of friends of the GDR'), was expected to open the way to further contacts in Argentina, for which other opportunities via State- or Church-controlled hospitals were limited.[28] Thus, the seemingly apolitical framework of health care promised political prospects not easily available elsewhere.

Besides, cooperation between academic institutions could be financially beneficial. Sometimes, when authorities in East Berlin considered support for university education in low-income countries particularly important for political or humanitarian-developmental reasons, the East German Government gave financial support for lecturers and scientists. But more frequently, the work of lecturers, professors and co-examiners was paid for by the receiving countries. Usually, payment went into the East German state budget rather than to the individuals, who would then often, though not always, receive payment from the East German authorities. Similarly, students receiving medical education in East Germany could be financed by East German solidarity funds but, increasingly, students of privileged background were accepted for payment to the GDR Government.[29]

Medical professionals, on the other hand, had reasons of their own to be interested in scientific cooperation with low-income countries. To begin with, it provided rare opportunities to travel to exotic countries. Beyond that, motives differed and included various combinations of the wish to help, curiosity about life in foreign cultures and a certain sense of adventure, but also scientific interest and professional challenge and opportunity. Some viewed their work as a contribution to the health system of the country as well as to East German foreign policy. Those who travelled to low-income countries as doctors, Red Cross staff or diplomats also perceived a genuine need for medical education, and sometimes recommended the engagement of East German academics as part of development assistance.[30] In that vein, it was easy to see humanitarian value in work at medical departments that were clearly deficient in teaching staff, whose staff were often unfamiliar with existing technology (including equipment already bought) and whose students were eager to learn.

On the other hand, not all university staff members were eager to teach in low-income countries. Living and hygienic conditions were frequently so different from East German standards that they required a sense of adventure, which not everybody possessed. Assignments also entailed separation from family members, who were often forced to stay behind. Wives were only allowed to join their husbands for stays of a year or more, and even then it was not certain that all children could accompany them. By contrast, some doctor–scientists who were eager to work in the Global South were refused for political reasons, despite their comparatively low defection risk. Local expectations were usually high, requiring sound professional and language skills, including profound and extensive knowledge about their field, broadly conceived. Often, academics prepared their stays for up to year by taking language lessons – often in English, but, as the case might be, possibly also in Swahili, etc. – or by reading up on their field in English-language textbooks.[31] Though engagement in medical academia was manifold – including teaching, exam taking, providing publications and exchanging students – two fields stand out for their direct political and economic relevance: medical research and trade in pharmaceutical products.

Medical Research

Medical research as part of East German policy towards the Global South was initially hampered by the fact that the GDR possessed competent and prestigious medical institutes but none that specialized in the specific needs of the target countries. This situation was considered problematic for several reasons. On a practical level, cooperation with the Global South entailed East German citizens coming into contact with diseases that no longer existed in the GDR, and having a place prepared for specialized therapy increasingly seemed like a prerequisite for intensifying relations with those countries. In addition, a certain expertise in this field appeared necessary in order to be considered a serious partner for low-income countries in health cooperation. Specifically, the absence of a tropical-medicine institute left the GDR unable to compete with West German institutions and forced East German agencies to send their scientists to West Germany for training in tropical diseases. Finally, a lack of knowledge in this field specifically limited the work of the Dresden Museum of Hygiene: its exhibitions could have been valuable showcases of East German medical knowledge, but their usefulness was limited if they could inform only about health topics pertaining to Germany but not about questions of particular interest in the Global South. Thus, medical officials were forced to seek basic information in exactly those fields in which they would have preferred to act as experts.[32] For a while, there were plans to acquire the relevant expertise through participation in international projects, which would have justified further cooperation. Thus, in 1956 the MEA declared that it intended to contribute to the organization of a hospital in North Vietnam, which had been established with the support of the Soviet Union, Poland and the People's Republic of China. In the process,

East German doctors were expected to gain urgently needed knowledge about tropical diseases.[33] But it soon became clear that such projects could not replace a permanent tropical institute in the GDR.

The vicinity of an international harbour and the model of the Hamburg Institute determined the choice of Rostock as one of the GDR's centres for tropical medicine. Following the appearance of some imported cases of smallpox in Heidelberg and Berlin in 1958, a working group in tropical medicine was established at the Rostock institute of microbiology. Those present included hygienist and microbiologist Professor Klaus-Dietrich Rudat and a young doctor, Kurt Ziegler, who would become the long-time director of the institute. Ziegler was immediately dispatched to attend a course on tropical medicine in Hamburg and, in 1960, to China, to gain some first-hand experience of patients with tropical diseases.[34] In later years, Ziegler was happy to have the opportunity to cooperate with an Egyptian institute regarding research on schistosomiasis, establishing the life cycle of the parasite at his institute, and to explore a little-known subspecies in Laos.[35]

Establishing research cooperation met with a number of difficulties, however. To begin with, a fragile research infrastructure was apt to become the victim of political upheaval. Soon after the establishment of a centre of tropical medicine in Rostock, Professors Rudat and Harald Dutz tried to promote scientific cooperation through a two-month stay at the microbiological institute at Hanoi in 1960, where they initiated research in medicinal plants in Vietnam and believed they had found anti-biotically active substances in the papaya plant. Frustrated by what they perceived as lack of official support for this goal, they forcefully emphasized that academic cooperation with a country in a tropical or subtropical region was in East German interests, for scientific as well as educational reasons, notably in the fields of hygiene and microbiology as well as for political and economic reasons. They also urged for more education of doctors from the Global South at East German universities.[36] Apparently, some cooperation was under way in 1960 with projects regarding virus infections.[37] In 1965, two senior scientists of the Institute for Sera- and Vaccine Control (Institut für Serum- und Impfstoffprüfung) in Berlin were getting ready to study virological experimentation using monkeys as models at a recently founded research institute in Northern Vietnam. But shortly afterwards, the outbreak of the war put an end to these plans.[38] Eight years later, Vietnamese authorities judged their scientific potential to be inadequate for the needs of modern times.[39]

Thus, effective research cooperation between the GDR and the Global South required a combination of propitious circumstances, as the case of cooperation with one Brazilian institution demonstrates. The case concerned the Tuberkuloseforschungsinstitut (Tuberculosis Research Institute) in Berlin-Buch and the Instituto Brasileiro para Investigação da Tuberculose (IBIT), a private research institute in Salvador da Bahia. This cooperation followed the visit by the director and founder of IBIT, José Silveira, to East Berlin in 1959, but it also benefited from propitious circumstances. Brazil experienced a dynamic period during the presidency of Juscelino Kubitschek de Oliveira (1956–61), whose administration initiated a phase of accelerated modernization and high economic growth rates, placing 'at the top of his sanitary agenda the control of mass diseases, particularly rural endemic diseases'.[40] In 1960, the MEA decided that Brazil constituted a country of special interest in Latin America, and cooperation between institutes and scientists was considered necessary in order to strengthen relations with Brazil.[41]

Consequently, Dr A. Krebs spent 15 months at IBIT in 1961–2. He took an active part in its laboratory work and its broad spectrum of research projects, ranging from the analysis of drug resistance to a typology of isolated mycobacteria, comparisons of methods of cell culture work, and in-vitro and animal experimentation with various vaccines. At the time, IBIT consisted of a dispensary; a small clinic; departments of radiology, bacteriology, pathology and biochemistry; a library; and several specialized laboratories. Its activities included research on tuberculosis and similar illnesses, the training of medical specialists, the treatment of TB patients, and prevention activities and social support for affected families. Its extensive work was impeded by practical difficulties ranging from cuts in electricity to water scarcity, lack of funding and difficulties in importing chemicals from other countries.[42] His stay produced some tangible results for both sides: Krebs succeeded in getting the institute at Berlin-Buch to offer a steam-coagulator to IBIT; provided the publishing house, *VEB Verlag Volk und Gesundheit*, with an evaluation of the possibilities for selling scientific literature on the Brazilian market; and supplied names of colleagues who might be receptive to further information about the country.[43] He also added two titles to his list of publications.[44]

Cooperative research provided valuable contact with foreign countries at a time when the GDR was suffering from diplomatic isolation. More than just an avenue for some interaction, tangible biomedical expertise constituted an important prerequisite for the GDR's recognition as an attractive partner in a field that was of obvious importance to countries of the Global South, poor in medical infrastructure. Additionally, medical research came with economic implications in that it provided a link to the trade in pharmaceutical products.

Trade in Pharmaceutical Products

Pharmaceutical production was a sensitive issue for East Germany. After 1945, the country possessed little in terms of a pharmaceutical industry since the big companies were clustered along the Rhine River in the West. And when the Soviet administration dismantled more than 1,000 industrial companies, including those in the chemical industry, this further weakened the GDR's pharmaceutical industry.[45] Since importing drugs from the West required spending scarce foreign currency, its government developed a domestic industry. The export of pharmaceutical drugs never became a mass phenomenon, accounting for only a small percentage of the GDR's trade with low-income countries.[46] Nevertheless, it was both economically and politically significant: exporting drugs offered a valuable way to offset some production costs and earn some foreign currency, while being able to supply pharmaceuticals and equipment was something that low-income countries expected from the Northern world. This capacity, therefore, was essential to being accepted as a modern, industrialized country. When the GDR proved unable to send relatively simple devices to Egypt in 1963, this situation proved politically embarrassing and placed the country a disadvantage in its competition with West Germany which, though politically less welcome, clearly had superior capacities to supply the desired medical material.[47]

In the GDR, pharmaceutical research mainly took place in an academic setting, which gave medical researchers a central role in production.[48] Medical professionals also played an important part in marketing, as they used their lectures and contacts with colleagues at foreign universities and clinics to present East German pharmaceuticals, lending their scientific credentials to tangible commercial purposes.

Thus, lecture tours by scientists were sometimes coordinated by GDR governmental trade agencies. Indeed, foreign trade formed an important component of East German medical cooperation through academia from the beginning – and even before the end of the country's political isolation in 1970, these efforts spread beyond economic and ideological divides.

Efforts to gain commercial benefits from cooperation in pharmaceutical research were not always successful, as demonstrated by early contacts with China. The People's Republic of China (PCR) was a logical early partner for the GDR in the medical field. Established in 1949 as a communist state, it formed part of the Soviet bloc and was therefore open to relations with the GDR while also being perceived as a partner deserving socialist solidarity. It was also a poor country, which had emerged from a period of semi-colonial foreign domination, war with Japan and civil war, and which stood on the threshold of rapid socioeconomic development along socialist lines. Health formed an important component of this process, and despite disastrous setbacks from – largely politically induced – famines during the Great Leap and upheaval during the Cultural Revolution, China was beginning to make spectacular gains in life expectancy after 1950.[49]

Efforts at East-German–Chinese cooperation in the pharmaceutical field were triggered by the research of Professor Hans Knöll. Despite long-time membership of the German National Socialist Party (NSDAP) before World War II, Knöll became professor of bacteriology at the University of Jena in 1950. Until 1952, he also acted as director of the newly established pharmaceutical production company Jenapharm, a successor to the Glaswerke (Glass Factories) Schott, which Knöll had founded. As an expert on tuberculosis and the father of the production of penicillin in the GDR, he was clearly an important figure in East German medical research.[50] In the early 1950s, Jenapharm was preparing the production of tebethion, an anti-tuberculosis drug thought of as also being an effective leprosy treatment. At the time, leprosy was no longer an issue in the GDR and even tuberculosis was declining rapidly.[51] Both diseases, however, were major concerns in low-income countries, providing the ground for a mixture of humanitarian and commercial interests both for Knöll and the GDR Government. In the absence of leprosy patients in the GDR, Knöll sought and found partners for clinical tests in China, where leprosy was prevalent.

In late 1951, the PRC's Ministry of Health informed the East German Embassy about very positive results in the treatment with tebethion of a leprosy patient at the dispensary of Chilu University in Shangdong province between June and October of that year. As a result, the embassy handed over more tebethion for further clinical tests, urging the Chinese side to provide detailed information about the results.[52] In April 1952, Knöll suggested conducting parallel tests in clinics in geographically and climatically different regions.[53] A few weeks later, he proposed additional tests with isonicotinic acid hydracide (INH), a drug that had recently been introduced into anti-tuberculosis therapy and which also showed promise for anti-leprosy treatment. Knöll hoped that it might be useful, especially for cases in which tebethion had remained ineffective, and offered to provide samples of INH for clinical tests on selected patients in China.[54]

Initially, therefore, prospects for GDR-PRC cooperation in pharmaceutical research seemed to warrant optimism. Chinese officials turned down the suggestion for extended tebethion tests at different locations, but asked for samples of tebethion and INH, which Jenapharm supplied in May 1953.[55] But eventually, Knöll's and the East German Government's hopes were dashed. Chinese officials had promised information about test results, but apparently never sent any beyond those regarding the earliest case. Worse still, though the PRC ordered and received a sizable quantity of tebethion in 1952 on a commercial basis, by the end of the year an East German delegation observed that tebethion and INH were being produced in the PRC itself, so that, presumably, it no longer needed to import material for experimentation.[56] Jenapharm did not benefit from seeking scientific cooperation; in fact, it may have supplied blueprints to its own competition.

However, promotion activities did not necessarily involve research – as was demonstrated by the activities of Professor Richard Kirsch. As head surgeon and professor at the cancer clinic of the Charité at Humboldt University in the 1950s, Kirsch took a leading role in the establishment of an East German hospital in Hanoi, North Vietnam in 1956/7, the first large project of this kind and politically a prestigious one.[57] Some years later, he expanded his efforts into neighbouring countries. In 1959, he attended a medical conference in Rangoon, Burma, traveling as part of a mission of the governmental trading company DIA (Deutscher Innen- und Außenhandel; German Domestic and Foreign Trade) together with a delegate of Jenapharm and a translator. The explicit purpose of this trip was to determine the possibility of increasing the export of medical-pharmaceutical products.

Kirsch established contact with Burmese colleagues both at the conference and at the University of Rangoon, the only institution of tertiary education in the country. He found that Burmese doctors were very much oriented towards the USA, but were open to contacts with the GDR once the first barrier was broken. In this context, he benefited from the fact that some of the older doctors had been educated in Germany or Austria before World War II. For instance, the head of the surgery department, U Ban, had worked as Sauerbruch's assistant in Berlin during the interwar years. He was also the father-in-law of the prime minister. According to Kirsch, the Burmese were very interested in acquiring medical equipment – from single objects, like artificial eyes, to entire hospital interiors. Kirsch also reported a perceived need for antibiotics, hormone and vitamin preparations, anaesthetics and drugs required for cancer chemotherapy. Generally, he insisted that the participation of a doctor–scientist in such a trip opened trade opportunities that were not available to a businessperson alone.[58] On his return to the GDR, he supplied a list of 87 Burmese medical professors and lecturers, their positions and specialties for further contact, much to the delight of both the East German trade representation in Rangoon and the Foreign Ministry.[59] The results of these efforts are unclear, but the sources suggest that they were decidedly limited. When Kirsch visited Burma again in early 1961, no high-ranking politician was prepared to meet him and the East German deputy minister for foreign and domestic trade, Gerhard Weiß, voiced criticism that Kirsch was reaching beyond his competency.[60]

It is possible that Kirsch's reports suffered from his penchant for self-aggrandizement and promised more than was realistically possible. However, the constant concern of the GDR authorities about limiting expenses, which comes across strongly in the sources, might present another explanation. It also lends plausibility to Kirsch's analysis that the unwillingness of the East German Government to invest sufficiently in contacts in the Global South placed it at a disadvantage compared with other Northern countries – even those within the Soviet bloc. After all, the GDR was hardly the only player on the international scene and competition demanded the ongoing cultivation of contacts. Thus, Kirsch complained that while the East German Government had limited its involvement in North Vietnam to the donation of a single hospital, Czechoslovakia, Hungary, Romania, Bulgaria and the Soviet Union had kept doctors' delegations in that country on a long-term basis, thus retaining the ability to promote drugs and medical machinery from their countries. The Czechoslovak Government, in particular, had not only donated a superior hospital but had also retained an active part in the training of doctors and midwives, which enabled it to market its pharmaceutical products in ways that were beyond East German reach.[61]

This image of a certain half-hearted or inept engagement on the part of the East German Government is corroborated by Dr Krebs, head of the urological clinic in Berlin. In 1960, he travelled to Egypt in order to promote East German cystoscopes (instruments used for bladder examinations) on behalf of the German Export-Import Society (Export- und Importgesellschaft) for Precision Mechanics. However, upon his arrival in Cairo he found that nothing had been prepared. The university, understandably, showed little inclination to allow a perfect stranger to give lectures clearly designed to market a foreign product. The problem was only solved when doctors who had worked in Halle vouched for his scientific credibility. But, obviously, their insistence that Krebs was a serious scientist rather than a travelling salesman could not fully gloss over the fact that the central point of his visit was commercial rather than medical. Similarly to Kirsch in Asia, he saw substantial potential for East German exports of medical equipment to Egypt, or even of entire clinics, provided a medical scientist remained in Cairo on a long-term basis.[62] Such a permanent presence was expensive, and apparently never materialized.

Instead, the GDR continued to rely on short-term missions to jump-start trade relations. This strategy was hardly ideal, but nor did it result in a constant series of failures. If nothing else, such missions offered a way to open doors into areas that were not firmly within the Soviet bloc but where political developments offered windows of opportunity. A case in point was Brazil, the country that promised to be a point of entry for Latin America. In April/May 1963, four East German delegates travelled through Brazil on a seven-week mission. In addition to Kirsch, the group consisted of three representatives of scientific/technical centres producing various types of medical equipment. The purpose of the trip was explicitly to study the Brazilian health and university systems, to undertake a 'market analysis' of Brazilian production and imports, to evaluate the export potential for East German products, to establish an export network and to conduct sales negotiations. Remarkably, the products that the GDR could offer seemed to have little to do with the principal health priorities in Brazil. According to the final report of the delegation, the Brazilian Government was focused on acting against a series of diseases (malaria, trachoma, Chagas disease, goitre, helminth diseases, smallpox, TB and cancer), the reduction of infant mortality rates and the creation of milk-powder production. Nevertheless, the group decided that there was substantial potential for the export of laboratory equipment, clinical technology (precision surgery and X-ray machinery), ophthalmological devices by Zeiss, blood-drying and powderization equipment, and dental material.[63]

Kirsch's role in this mission was to establish contact with prominent scientists, thereby opening doors otherwise closed to GDR trade representatives. He was also to advise GDR traders on the scientific aspects of commercial negotiations and to spread a positive image of his country, if necessary by contradicting propaganda emanating from West Germany. In this vein, he visited universities and major research hospitals in Rio de Janeiro, São Paulo, Florianopolis, Pôrto Alegre, Brasilia, Belém and Recife; presented lectures; and discussed medicine, politics and trade with professors and doctors.[64] Though Kirsch's enthusiastic descriptions of his successful negotiations must be taken with a pinch of salt, the sheer number of places that received him and the rest of the delegation indicates a certain level of interest. The rise of the right-wing military dictatorship in Brazil in 1964 may explain the lack of records on any subsequent trade outcome. But these activities formed a model for similar activities in the 1970s and 1980s.

By that time, the GDR was exporting its medical equipment through Intermed, a governmental agency in charge of trade in medical products. The export potential was inhibited by the limited spectrum, particularly of sophisticated medical appliances produced in East Germany. Machinery could also be offered as a package, whereby East German equipment would be supplemented by components from Western companies. Remarkably, this type of cooperation was entirely market oriented. Thus, Intermed products were successfully sold to universities and hospitals in a number of countries with little political affinity to

East Germany. In these instances, providing scientific expertise in high-tech medicine opened the way to consultancies regarding the import of expensive machinery from the GDR. In this respect, highly qualified specialists, such as Horst Klinkmann – head of the Internal Medicine Clinic at the University of Rostock between 1974 and 1992 and internationally renowned specialist in nephrology, dialysis and artificial organs – were valuable actors in East Germany's foreign policy in medicine. In the 1970s, he promoted Intermed products in Latin America, including Cuba, as well as in Colombia and Brazil, integrating machinery from Swedish companies.[65] His role would have been unthinkable without an adequate scientific reputation, earned through presentations, research and teaching.

Conclusion

When reviewing the role of medical academics as part of East German relations with the Global South, probably the most striking finding is the disconnect between the declared East German allegiance to the socialist world and worldview and the strictly nationalist real-life agenda. There was neither apparent coordination with Soviet agencies nor attempts to convert cooperating countries to a socialist health system. Though a few position papers paid lip service to the need to integrate health-related 'solidarity work' into the long-term agenda of the Soviet bloc, these considerations played no role in definitions about tangible activities. As far as the East German Government was concerned, the two dominant purposes of the engagement of medical academics was to improve the international standing of the GDR and to stimulate international trade in pharmaceutical and medical products. This fixation on diplomatic recognition and trade resulted in a remarkable lack of ideology. Again, this finding is at odds with the rhetoric, particularly with regard to frequent references to West Germany and the perceived need to stand up to and, if possible, defeat West German influence in the countries with which the GDR cooperated. But these comments entailed not so much ideological competition as a specific national rivalry – above all, a strong desire to gain recognition as a sovereign state. In fact, this craving for recognition overpowered any ideological reservations that the government might otherwise have had, since any cooperation with any of the large number of countries with whom the GDR had no diplomatic relations represented a de facto recognition of sorts and was, therefore, a political victory.

Consequently, the GDR cooperated with any country and anybody that was willing to do so, regardless of political orientation. And any matter that made other countries engage in any form of contact with the GDR was an asset in this policy. Clearly, medicine was one such matter. This context explains why the MEA was eager to encourage cooperation in the health field with any country that showed an interest.

In this context, medical academics were valuable since they supplied three crucial elements: the standing required to be recognized as a modern, scientifically and technologically successful state, with which it was worthwhile establishing contacts; the knowledge to develop and produce exportable pharmaceutical and medical products; and an inside access to those people in the Global South who were most likely to decide about relevant purchases while also being connected to political leadership. In as much as medical academics were also among the least likely to engage in politically embarrassing defection, they were valuable instruments of foreign policy.

However, in real life, such research and trade cooperation was difficult and expensive to sustain. It involved an attractive offer of expertise and products, a patient cultivation of connections and also a certain degree of luck. Thus, the outcome of cooperation projects often depended primarily on circumstances and interests in the Global South. Contacts could vanish with revolutions or peaceful changes of political allegiance. Local agents might look for other, more attractive offers of cooperation and acquire necessary capacities themselves. This means that medical academics were crucial to initiate valuable contacts, but without support both in Berlin and in the recipient countries they were powerless to turn these contacts into political and/or economic successes. In the context of the Cold War, authorities in the Global South had options on both sides of the political divide, and the GDR faced competition not only from West Germany but also from allies within the Soviet bloc. The attitude of the East German Government thus often remained contradictory, as was reflected in frequent quibbles between consulates, embassies, the MEA and the MOH about funds and priorities, and in an apparent lack of willingness to engage in long-term commitments; to offer tailor-made products to recipient countries; and, perhaps most importantly, to invest in high-quality pharmaceutical production. Academic promotion of pharmaceutical and medical goods was helpful, but did not compensate for a restricted product range.

This raises a question about the role of the other actors in this field of cooperation. The medical experts were far from passive executioners of governmental policies, but they had only limited room for manoeuvre. They could propose but could not decide on projects or initiatives in other countries, and for the most part they entered into cooperative projects by answering to governmental offers that were relayed through their superiors in institutes or ministries. However, when in low-income countries of the Global South – especially when they worked as the only, or as one of few, East German expert(s) – they frequently enjoyed a freedom of action that was rare in the GDR. As the interviews demonstrated, researchers/lecturers often gained highly fulfilling experiences both as professionals and as people. Their institutions, likewise, enjoyed the benefits of the opportunities offered towards an international world of academia, to which they otherwise had only limited access. In all but a few cases, the advantages probably outweighed the cost of temporarily losing an employee.

The benefits for recipient countries are, however, most difficult to assess. They certainly benefited from the knowledge transfer entailed in both research and teaching, but it is unclear to what extent this was any different from cooperation with any other country. There is little in the sources that appears specific to medical academic cooperation with the GDR, and in the absence of in-depth considerations of which type of knowledge was useful to particular countries there was some danger of ill-suited specialization. However, this risk was manageable in most medical disciplines, and the very fact that the GDR represented one player among many offering medical expertise that was – or could be made to be – useful to medical education was of advantage.

Notes

1. The author would like to thank Walter Bruchhausen, Institute for the History, Theory and Ethics of Medicine, University of Aachen, for valuable input and for making work on this project possible.
2. Eberhard Kaschel, 'Stand, Möglichkeiten und Grenzen solidarischer Unterstützung der DDR für national befreite Staaten sowie Anforderungen an ihre

planmäßige Gestaltung, untersucht am Beispiel des Gesundheitswesens' [State, possibilities and limitations of solidarity support of the GDR for liberated states as well as prerequisites for their planned implementation: the case study of publich health], PhD Hochschule für Ökonomie 'Bruno Leuschner', Berlin, 1980, p. 122.

3. Hans Havemann et al., *Handbuch für Entwicklungshilfe* [Manual for development aid] (Baden-Baden, 1969), June 1969 and follow-up papers; Jörg Bärschneider, 'Die Entwicklungspolitik der DDR – gegenseitiger Nutzen oder einseitiger Vorteil?' [The development aid of the GDR – mutual benefit or unilateral advantage?], in Hannsgeorg Beine (ed.), *Die Entwicklungspolitik unserer Nachbarn* [Our neighbours' development aid] (Münster, 1985), pp. 25–47; Hans-Joachim Spanger und Lothar Brock, *Die beiden deutschen Staaten in der Dritten Welt* [The two German states in the Third World] (Opladen, 1987).

4. Kaschel, 'Stand, Möglichkeiten und Grenzen'.

5. Rainer A. Blasius, '"Völkerfreundschaft" am Nil: Ägypten und die DDR im Februar 1965. Stenographische Aufzeichnungen aus dem Ministerium für Auswärtige Angelegenheiten über den Ulbricht-Besuch bei Nasser' ['People's friendship' at the Nile: Egypt and the GDR in February 1965. Stenographic reports from the Ministry of External Affairs about Ulbricht's visit to Nasser], *Vierteljahrshefte für Zeitgeschichte* [Quarterly for Contemporary History], vol. 46, issue 4 (October 1998), pp. 747–805; Harald Möller, *DDR und Dritte Welt. Die Beziehungen der DDR mit Entwicklungsländern – ein neues theoretisches Konzept, dargestellt anhand der Beispiele China und Äthiopien sowie Irak/Iran* [The GDR and the Third World. The relations of the GDR with developing countries – a new theoeretical concept, based on case studies] (Berlin, 2004); Haile Gabriel Dagne, *Das entwicklungspolitische Engagement der DDR in Äthiopien* [The developmental engagement of the GDR in Ethiopia] (Münster, 2004); Hans-Joachim Döring, 'Es geht um unsere Existenz.' Die Politik der DDR gegenüber der Dritten Welt am Beispiel von Mosambik und Äthiopien. 'Entwicklungspolitik und Solidarität in der DDR, dargestellt an Beispielen der staatlichen Zusammenarbeit mit Mosambik und Äthiopien und der entwicklungsbezogenen Bildungsarbeit unabhängiger Gruppen' [Development policies and solidarity in the GDR, a study based on case studies regarding state cooperation with Mozambique and Ethiopia and regarding developmental educational initiatives of independent groups], PhD thesis, University of Berlin, 2007; Ulrich van der Heyden and Franziska Benger (eds), *Kalter Krieg in Ostafrika. Die Beziehungen der DDR zu Sansibar und Tansania* [The Cold War in East Africa. The relations of the GDR with Zanzibar and Tanzania] (Berlin, 2009).

6. Quinn Slobodian, 'Bandung in Divided Germany: Managing Non-Aligned Politics in East and West, 1955–63', *Journal of Imperial and Commonwealth History*, 41 (4) (2013), pp. 644–62; Hubertus Büschel, *Hilfe zur Selbsthilfe* [Help towards self-help] (Frankfurt and New York, 2014).

7. Young-Sun Hong, 'The Benefits of Health must Spread Among All', in Katherine Pence and Paul Betts (eds), *Socialist Modern. East German Everyday Culture and Politics* (Ann Arbor, MI, 2008), pp. 183–210; Young-Sun Hong, 'Kalter Krieg in der Ferne. Dekolonisierung, Hygienediskurse und der Kampf der DDR und der USA um die Dritte Welt' [The Cold War far away. Decolonization, the sanitary discourse and the competition of the GDR and the USA about the Third World], in Uta Balbier und Christiane Rösch (eds), *Umworbener Klassenfeind: das Verhältnis der DDR zu den USA* [Coveted class enemy: relations between the GDR and the USA] (Berlin, 2006), pp. 77–95; Iris Borowy, 'Medical Aid, Repression and International Relations The East German Hospital at Metema', *Journal of the History of Medicine and Allied Sciences* 71 (2016), pp. 1, 64–92; Iris Borowy, 'The Hospital Carlos Marx – the Politics of Solidarity between Biomedicine and Primary Health Care', *História, Ciências, Saúde – Manguinhos* 24 (2) (2017) 2, pp. 411–28.
8. Walter Bruchhausen, Helmut Görgen and Oliver Razum (eds), *Entwicklungsziel Gesundheit* [Health as a development goal] (Frankfurt am Main, 2011).
9. Interviews with Horst Konrad (13 June 2014), Siegfried Akkermann (11 June 2014), Kurt Ziegler (21 February 2014); communication to author by Gerhard Asmussen (23 June 2014), Horst Klinkmann (12 June 2014), Walter Dummler (27 June 2014).
10. Benger, 'Die Entwicklungszusammenarbeit der DDR in Sansibar / Tansania' ['The Development Cooperation of the GDR in Zanzibar/Tansania'], in Ulrich van der Heyden and Franziska Benger (eds), *Kalter Krieg in Ostafrika. Die Beziehungen der DDR zu Sansibar und Tansania* [Cold War in East Africa. The relations oft he GDR to Zanzibar and Tansania], Berlin: LIT Verlag, 2009, pp. 341–89, 341; Young-Sun Hong, 'The Benefits of Health', pp. 183–210, 184–5.
11. Spanger and Brock, *Die beiden deutschen Staaten*, p. 215; Charles K. Armstrong, '"Fraternal Socialism": The International Reconstruction of North Korea, 1953–62', *Cold War History*, 5 (2) (2005), pp. 161–87, 164.
12. Ministry of Health (MOH) position paper, untitled, undated, written approximately 1957, BArch [Bundesarchiv] DQ 1/1955, quote, p. 4.
13. Ibid., p. 3.
14. Hermann Weber, *Geschichte der DDR* [History of the GDR] (Munich, 1999) (note 5), pp. 220, 53.
15. Anna-Sabine Ernst, *Die beste Prophylaxe ist der Sozialismus* [Socialism is the best prophylactic] (Münster, 1997), p. 55.
16. See, for example, Kulturabteilung Sektion II to Handesvertretung in Accra [Department of Culture, Section II, to Traderepesentation in Accra], 8 September 1964, Politisches Archiv des Auswärtigen Amtes (PAAA), MfAA. A.16959.
17. Correspondence BArch, DQ 1/3643.
18. Sabine Schleiermacher and Udo Schagen, 'Rekonstruktion und Innovation' [Reconstruction and innovation], in Johanna Bleker and Volker Hess (eds),

Die Charité. Geschichte(n) eines Krankenhauses [The Charité. The history of a hospital] (Berlin, 2010), p. 208.
19. Interviews with Horst Klinkmann (12 June 2014), Siegfried Akkermann (11 June 2014) and Kurt Ziegler (21 February 2014).
20. Robert Koch (1843–1910) was a professor at Berlin University. He became famous for discovering the specific causative agents of tuberculosis, cholera and anthrax and for establishing four postulates that became the basis for determining the causes of infectious diseases. He was awarded the Nobel Prize for Medicine in 1905. Koch travelled repeatedly in Africa, and took advantage of colonial structures for his research.
21. Ferdinand Sauerbruch (1875–1951) was a surgeon and head of the surgical department of the Charité at Berlin University from 1928 to 1949. While not a member of the National Socialist party, he had ties to National Socialist personalities and was a fervent nationalist.
22. Trade representation Rangoon to MfAA, 15 February 1959, PAAA, MfAA A, 14983.
23. Krause to Sefrin, 13 November 1963, Bundesarchiv (BArch), DQ 1/4303; Weitz, Aktenvermerk, 24 October 1963, PAAA, MfAA A, 16764.
24. Weitz and Scharf, GDR consulate in the UAR, 29 December 1963, PAAA, MfAA A, 16764; Consulate GDR Cairo, Information über die Teilnahme einer Ärztedelegation [Information about the Participation of a Doctors' delegation], 29 December 1963, PAAA, MfAA A, 16761.
25. Bericht über Verhandlungen [Report about Negotiations], 14–22 April 1964, undated, PAAA, MfAA A, 16764.
26. W.-A. Spengler, report on visit to Indonesia Nov to Dec 1957, PAAA, MfAA A, 10014.
27. Kirsch, Bericht über eine im Auftrage der DIA-Chemie durchgeführte Reise nach Burma und Indien [Report about a Mission to Burma and India, conducted at the request of DIA-Chemistry], 2 February 1959, PAAA A, 14983; interview with Klinkmann (12 June 2014).
28. Delegationsbericht argentinischer Ärzte [Delegation report of Argentinian doctors], 10 January 1962; Abschlußbesprechung mit argentinischer Ärztedelegation [Final Discussions with Argentinian Doctors], 27.9.1961 – both PAAA, MfAA.A.3119.
29. Interviews with Klinkmann and Akkermann (12 and 11 June 2014).
30. W.-A. Spengler, report on visit to Indonesia November to December 1957, PAAA, MfAA A, 10014.
31. Interviews with Konrad (13 June 2014), Akkermann (11 June 2014), Ziegler (21 February 2014); communication to author by Gerhard Asmussen (23 June 2014); Kurt Ziegler, *Zum 50jährigen Bestehen der Tropenmedizin an der Universität* [To the 50th anniversary of tropical medicine at the university] (Rostock, 2008), p. 23.
32. Hong, 'Kalter Krieg', p. 90.

33. Simons, MfAA, to embassy GDR in Hanoi, 31 July 1956, PAAA, MfAA A, 8.340.
34. Ziegler, *Zum 50jährigen* (note 24), pp. 13–19.
35. Interview with Ziegler (21 February 2014).
36. Profs. Dutz and Rudat, Report on mission to Vietnam 22 November–1 January 1960, 21 January 1960, PAAA, MfAA A, 8408.
37. Embassy GDR in Hanoi to MfAA, 23 February 1959, PAAA, MfAA A, 8408.
38. MfG to embassy GDR in Hanoi, 3 March 1965; Bergold to Tautz, 1 April 1965, PAAA, MfAA A, 16951.
39. Thümmel, Information über die gegenwärtige Lage im Gesundheitswesen der DRV [Information about the Present State of the Health System oft he DRV], 2 May 1973, PAAA, MfAA C, 5432.
40. Gilberto Hochman, 'From Autonomy to Partial Alignment: National Malaria Programs in the Time of Global Eradication, Brazil, 1941–1961', Canadian Bulletin of Medical History, 25 (1) (2008), pp. 161–92, 163; Sheldon Maram, 'Juscelino Kubitschek and the Politics of Exuberance, 1956–1961', *Luso-Brazilian Review*, 27 (1) (1990), pp. 31–45.
41. MfAA to Kroll, MfG, 2 September 1960, BArch, DQ 1/2493.
42. Krebs, 'Bericht über eine 15-monatige Tätigkeit in Brasilien' [Report about my 15 months' work in Brazil] 28 January 1963, BArch, DQ 1/2493.
43. Ibid.
44. A. Krebs et al., 'Untersuchungen nicht-klassifizierter Mykobakterien in Bahia', *Rev.Nac.Tub* (Rio de Janeiro) 30 (1962), pp. 87–95; A. Krebs, 'Kampf gegen Tuberkulose in Brasilien', *Humanitas*, 6.3.63.
45. Weber, *Geschichte der DDR* (note 5), pp. 53–4.
46. For example, medical exports accounted for 4.5 per cent of overall trade in 1967. See Hans Havemann et al., *Handbuch für Entwicklungshilfe* [Handbook for development aid] (Baden-Baden, 1969), IID03, p. 6.
47. Kosser, Aktennotiz [File note], 31 October 1963, PAAA, MfAA A, 16764.
48. Ulrich Meyer, '"Man sollte die Entwicklung nicht hemmen" – Fritz Hauschild (1908–1974) und die Arzneimittelforschung der DDR' ["You should not obstruct development"– Fritz Hauschild (1908–1974) and pharmaceutical research in the GDR] *Pharmazie* 60 (6) (2005), pp. 468–72.
49. Zhongwei Zhao, 'Unequal Health Care Access, and Mortality in China', *Population and Development Review*, 32 (3) (September 2006), pp. 461–83, 464.
50. Hans Knöll, biographical data bank. Biographical information from the handbook 'Wer war wer in der DDR?' [Who was who in the GDR?], available at http://bundesstiftung-aufarbeitung.de/wer-war-wer-in-der-ddr-%2363%3B-1424.html?ID=1777 (accessed September 2017); JENAPHARM, *50 Jahre Jenapharm* (Jena, 2000), pp. 26–36.
51. Xiang-Sheng Chen et al., 'Leprosy in China: epidemiological trends between 1949 and 1998', *Bulletin of the World Health Organization*, 79 (2001), pp. 306–12.

52. Dipl mission GDR to Chinese For Off, 27 December 1951 and Chin For Off to Dipl mission GDR, 29 February 1952, PAAA, MfAA.A, 9896.
53. Keilson, MfAA, to Diplo mission GDR, 3 April 1951, PAAA, MfAA.A, 9896.
54. Dipl Mission GDR to Chin For Off, 30 June 1952, PAAA, MfAA.A, 9896.
55. Chin For Off to MfAA, 3 March 1953 and MfAA to dipl miss GDR, 20 May 1953, both PAAA, MfAA.A, 9896.
56. Kulitzka, MfAA, to embassy GDR, 19 November 1953 and Grüttner, embassy GDR, to MfAA, 3 December 1953, both PAAA, MfAA, A, 9896.
57. Heinz David, '... es soll das Haus die Charité heißen ... ' [The house shall be called Charité] (Berlin, 2004), p. 633.
58. Kirsch, Bericht über eine im Auftrage der DIA-.Chemie durchgeführte Reise nach Burma und Indien [Report on a trip to Burma and India conducted at the request of the DIA], 9 February 1959, PAAA, MfAA A, 14983.
59. Trade representation Rangoon to MfAA, 15 February 1959; Lämmel to trade representation, 24 February 1959 – both PAAA, MfAA A, 14983.
60. Consulate Rangoon to MfAA, 31 January 1961; Thun to MfAA, 22 February 1961; Note by Kirsch, 23 February 1961; Weiss to MfAA, 29 March 1961 – all PAAA, MfAA A, 14983.
61. Travel report Prof. Dr. Kirsch to Vietnam and Korea, 13 July 1959, PAAA, MfAA A, 8.408.
62. Krebs to Deutsche Export- und Importgesellschaft, 23 December 1960, BArch DQ 1/22006.
63. Abschlußbericht der Dienstreise 'Brasilien' vom 10.4. bis 30.5.1963 [Final report of the business trip to Brazil from 10 April to 30 May 1963], BArch, DQ 1/2493.
64. Ibid., Anlage 1: Kirsch, Bericht über meine Reise nach Brasilien [Report about my Journey to Brazil, BArch, DQ 1/2493.
65. Interview with Klinkmann (12 June 2014).

CHAPTER 8

LOST ILLUSIONS: THE LIMITS OF COMMUNIST POLAND'S INVOLVEMENT IN COLD WAR AFRICA

Przemysław Gasztold

In November 1971, Ryszard Frelek, the newly appointed director of the International Department within the Central Committee of the Polish United Workers' Party (CC PUWP) prepared a one-page memo for Secretary of the CC Stanisław Kania, who was then responsible for the supervision of the state-security apparatus:

> The transfer of medical equipment already decommissioned by the Ministry of Defence would be highly appreciated by freedom movements as our humanitarian gesture. We need to take into account, that Poland so far has supported those groups in a smaller scale than other socialist countries. The need to increase our aid for the African national liberation movements also results from our economic relations with Portugal. The most controversial issue is related to sales of vessels which, according to freedom movements, are used by the colonial regime as a tool for dispatching their troops and military hardware. But after very detailed analysis of mutual Polish-Portuguese turnover, we decided that the agreement of selling 3 ships to Lisbon is clearly justified on

economic grounds and should proceed. That deal should give us approximately 900 thousand USD. In this situation it seems that a visible increase of aid intended for freedom fighters would minimalize [sic] the threat from them of using the sale of ships for propaganda action against our country. Taking into consideration all those circumstances I suggest sending freedom fighters decommissioned medical equipment.[1]

This short report bluntly presents the Polish communists' two-pronged approach towards the decolonization of Africa. Without unnecessary ideological appeals to Marxism–Leninism, Frelek points out that economic factors played the predominant role within Polish foreign policy in so-called Third World countries, and that Warsaw's support for anti-colonial movements had its limits. His attitude not only reflects behind-the-scenes decision making during Edward Gierek's rule as the first secretary of the PUWP (1970–80) but also mirrors the imponderables of the previous Polish position towards African countries.

Based on archival documents, some recently declassified, from the Archive of the Ministry of Foreign Affairs, the Archive of the Institute of National Remembrance and the Central Archive of Modern Records, this chapter argues that the Polish approach towards Africa had deep limitations and was frequently inconsequential and restrained. Authorities in Warsaw were usually circumspect and faintly aloof in 'bringing the light of revolution' to newly created postcolonial states. Just like other members of the Warsaw Pact, Poland supported decolonization, sent humanitarian aid and provided economic assistance, but its policy was not primarily determined by ideological goals. In reality, official proclamations; factors such as cost-effectiveness; the profitability of investments; and, particularly, a focus on safeguarding European interests dictated rather limited Polish activity in Cold War Africa. Taking into account the country's population size and level of industrialization within the Soviet bloc, Poland's involvement in Africa was low compared with that of other countries in the Warsaw Pact.

Warsaw's relations with Africa during the Cold War can be viewed in three overlapping phases. Between 1956 and 1970, under Władysław Gomułka as general secretary of the PUWP, policy was shaped by a pragmatic attitude towards international relations, as Warsaw underlined Poland's efforts to secure the stability of its western border.

In the early 1960s, Poland aimed to become more active and visible on the African continent. The involvement was based on establishing diplomatic relations, opening embassies and trade offices, signing first agreements and contracts and exchanging official visits.[2] However, after a few years any anti-colonial enthusiasm had receded due to a lack of expected economic profits, and Polish involvement in some fields decreased. The second phase started under Gomułka's successor, Edward Gierek, who placed greater emphasis on activity within the United Nations and on developing relations with Western countries as well as with African national-liberation movements. In 1973, the Political Bureau of the PUWP adopted a resolution on the coordination of Polish external relations, which highlighted solidarity with national movements and progressive organizations.[3] In the 1970s, Warsaw was thus quite active in supporting various guerrilla groups, sending them weapons and/or providing humanitarian aid. At the time, fruitful relations were also established with countries by no means perceived as 'progressive'. This change in foreign policy was enabled by the reception of foreign loans, which bolstered the Polish economy and thus allowed Warsaw to conduct a more active policy in the international arena. This was the time when the regime spread the myth that Poland was the tenth-most developed country in the world, based on gross domestic product.[4]

Poland's centrally planned economy in fact proved difficult to modernize. The loans were mostly used for expanding heavy industry, and levels of debt rose rapidly after the 1973 oil crisis. In the late 1970s Poland's economy became stagnant, which laid the groundwork for social unrest and the establishment of the 'Solidarity' movement. After the introduction of martial law in December 1981, the military government tried to engage more strongly and highlight the Polish presence in Africa – sometimes in a spectacular way. However, such efforts failed due to a weakening economy.[5] During this third phase of Warsaw's relations with Africa, many of Poland's embassies and consulates in the continent were shut down for economic reasons. In the era of General Wojciech Jaruzelski's rule (1981–90), the driving force of Polish relations with Africa was economic profit, which mostly supplanted Marxist ideology.

In Africa, Poland maintained the most active relations with the Maghreb countries and Egypt.[6] The authorities in Warsaw usually did not consider the Maghreb as part of their 'African' policy, but rather separately focused attention on the Arab-speaking world. This distinction, however, did not relate to various border conflicts and clashes – as, for example, between the Polisario front (the national-liberation movement struggling for independence in Western Sahara) and Morocco.[7] In 1979, the Polish Foreign Ministry listed Algeria, Angola, Libya, Morocco, Egypt and Nigeria as the group of most significant countries on the continent, while Tunisia and Sudan were listed as the second tier. Relations with the first group featured more active and frequent political, economic and scientific contacts, while there was only limited cooperation with the second group. In a separate category were 'ideological' partners: Libya, Algeria, Angola, Mozambique, Ethiopia and Benin.[8] Although appreciated for their pro-socialist attitude, these countries were not viewed as potential partners for establishing fruitful economic relations.

Gomułka's Phase: Economic Opportunities vs. Ideological Principles

Poland was subjected to the forcible introduction of the Soviet-style system known as 'Stalinization' immediately after World War II ended in 1945. Polish foreign policy was thus quickly subjected to the Kremlin's goals, yet its scope was limited to Europe.[9] However, after Joseph Stalin's death in March 1953, a political 'thaw' in the Soviet Union followed through to 1956, culminating in October when Władysław Gomułka again took the post of the first secretary of the CC PUWP.[10] The internal changes within the country resulted in an increasing range of freedoms, which included the expulsion of the Soviet 'advisors' and a reduction in Moscow's influence on Poland's policy-making process. Soviet leaders still criticized the country's private agriculture and the strong position of the Catholic Church, but in practice the Kremlin reluctantly accepted this 'Polish specificity'.[11] To some extent, Moscow's domination was also reduced in foreign policy, which allowed Gomułka to set his own tasks and conduct more 'individual' actions in the international arena, so long as they did not violate Marxists precepts. The Polish Government was especially interested in securing international recognition of the country's western borders. The Oder–Neisse line was treated by NATO countries as part of the status quo, but no official confirmation was voiced to assure the inviolability of the border.[12] This was why most of Warsaw's efforts, apart from developing relations inside the Soviet bloc, were concentrated on relations with Germany – but also with France, Great Britain and the USA. Polish diplomacy also tried to gain support from African countries for final confirmation of its border, but most of these attempts failed. Non-aligned countries were unfamiliar with the intricacies of the Polish–German borders, and did not want to damage their relations with West Germany by openly backing Warsaw.[13]

In the late 1940s and mid-1950s, Poland had little involvement in Africa besides publicly voicing its support for decolonization.[14] Those Poles who happened to live in Africa were mostly war refugees, who had found safe haven in the British colonies of Tanganyika, Uganda and South Africa.[15] Polish involvement was restrained, especially when Warsaw had a chance to attain important goals in Europe at the expense of its support for decolonization. For example, in 1958 the Polish Government was even ready to withdraw its recognition of the Algerian government in exile, in exchange for a French endorsement of Poland's western border.[16] Gomułka felt that efforts to secure Poland's own particular interests in Europe outweighed the potential benefits of increasing Polish influence in Africa. Nonetheless, that same year Poland took part in a covert mission conducted by Vietnamese communists to transport captured French weapons from Indochina to the Algerian National Liberation Front. Warsaw provided a ship, which successfully transferred the military equipment to North Africa – with commercial goods used as cover.[17]

The dawning of 1960, known as the 'Year of Africa', marked the beginning of Warsaw's new approach towards the continent. The employees of Department V within the Ministry of Foreign Affairs took over all matters related to Africa and the Middle East.[18] In June 1965, a Polish Committee of Solidarity with Asian and African Nations was established. Its main goal was to maintain international relations with communist or 'progressive' national movements and non-state actors from around the world.[19] As officially a 'public organization' that was officially sponsored by the general populace[20] the committee was used by the Polish Government for transfers of humanitarian aid, hosting wounded guerillas and providing scholarships. Also at this time, an African Studies programme was developed at Warsaw University.[21]

Africa's decolonization also affected Polish society in some ways. The initial idea of establishing an organization focused on promoting the history and culture of Africa appeared only in 1958. A group of people from Łódź submitted a request to the authorities asking permission to create an association dedicated to African affairs. The Ministry of the Interior rejected the idea, but shortly thereafter received many letters from ordinary citizens interested in the struggle against colonialism. The government wanted to have full control over such initiatives and enforce its communist, anti-imperialist line.[22] This was the main reason that the Polish–African Friendship Association was created in 1962. Members of the association organized exhibitions, lectures and meetings with African students and diplomats. In 1963, they organized special courses at the Aviation Training Centre in Krosno for 21 people from Angola, Togo and Algeria. The Red Cross strongly needed experienced crews, and 13 of these students were trained to be pilots while the other eight were trained to be aircraft mechanics.[23] Because the organization was fully subordinated to the authorities, who aimed through it to fulfil political goals, the Polish–African Friendship Association was not flexible enough and failed to change the stereotypical image of Africa within Polish society.[24] The majority of Poles still did not know much about Africa, and the continent remained *terra incognita*. Yet, because information on the outside world was strictly limited, from the late 1950s onwards African students aroused great interest on grey, sad and ethnically homogeneous Polish streets.[25]

From the 1960s, Warsaw backed many resolutions in the United Nations General Assembly supporting national-liberation movements in Africa, usually in accordance with guidelines sent from the Kremlin. Some evidence comes from the analysis of conferences and seminars organized by the Afro-Asian People's Solidarity Organisation (AAPSO) in which the Soviet Solidarity Committee was perceived – at least, by Polish delegations – as a coordinator of policy towards national-liberation movements. When multilateral talks during official summits came to an end, the Soviets always arranged unofficial meetings and gathered members of other socialist solidarity committees to summarize and recapitulate the debate. This was the moment when the Soviets presented their opinions and suggestions for further actions, which were usually taken into consideration by other delegations.[26] The communists were aware that newly independent African countries could provide more pro-Soviet votes in the UN, which later could be used for ideological purposes.[27]

The Polish regime generally preferred to operate under a policy called 'aid through trade', which involved closer cooperation with those countries that could offer natural resources or other goods useful for the Polish economy.[28] Newly created states were very poor and needed loans for establishing long-term cooperation, but the Polish Government could not provide these to all interested countries. An emphasis was also placed on scientific and technical relations, and the use of Polish specialists. Poland thus prioritized economic goals over ideological factors. Relations with Guinea and Ghana showcased Gomułka's approach.

Warsaw's economic involvement in Guinea was limited. In July 1959, Poland established diplomatic relations with the country and opened its embassy in the capital, Conakry, the following year.[29] Politicians from both sides exchanged visits and signed several agreements, but these contacts did not boost economic turnover. The newly independent country needed military and economic assistance. After the USA refused to provide such aid, the government of Ahmed Sékou Touré sought support from Poland and other communist countries. A Guinean delegation visited Poland in February 1959, just a few months before the protocol establishing diplomatic relations was signed. The Guineans sought non-refundable support in economic and military areas.[30] Touré expected that communist countries would willingly transfer expertise and provide guidance with the implementation of economic reforms.[31] While Czechoslovakia provided Conakry with much aid, Poland did not.[32] According to the Ministry of Foreign Affairs, Warsaw could not afford to build a dam and power station in Guinea in exchange for bananas and pineapples, offered at a price 30-per cent more expensive than on world markets – as the Soviets agreed to do.[33] Neither did Warsaw provide arms or counter-intelligence training to the Guinean Army – in contrast to the USSR and Czechoslovakia.[34] The fate of a joint Polish–Guinean fishing company, 'Soguipol', shows that entering African markets was not as easy as policy makers in Warsaw initially thought. The enterprise was established in 1961, but only after two years was shut down due to large economic losses. Vessels were sold to Guinean authorities, but only a few Polish specialists remained in Conakry providing assistance in developing the fishing industry.[35]

Closer cooperation was established with Ghana. In January 1959, a Polish delegation visited Conakry and held talks with Ghana's first president, Kwame Nkrumah, about potential cooperation. Polish diplomats concluded that Ghana had interesting prospects for economical involvement; however, due to continuing British influence and corruption, the possible partnership had its limitations.[36] The Polish Embassy was opened there in 1961, followed by the establishment of the Ghanaian Embassy in Warsaw the following year. In July 1961, Nkrumah visited Poland, becoming the first high-level African political figure to visit Warsaw after World War II. He met with Chairman of the State Aleksander Zawadzki and Prime Minister Józef Cyrankiewicz and signed an agreement to buy industrial equipment on credit terms. A couple of months later, during the non-aligned countries' conference in Belgrade, Nkrumah gave clear support to Polish demands urging the final confirmation of its western borders, which could be perceived as a simple quid pro quo exchange. The conference's public resolution on this matter was not adopted due only to West Germany's tempting offers of economic aid, made to several African countries.[37] Nonetheless, this issue would remain a significant aspect of Polish diplomacy in Africa. When Ethiopian Emperor Haile Selassie paid a visit to Poland in September 1964, he was also thoroughly briefed on the matter.[38] The Ghanaian Embassy in Warsaw was quietly shut down in 1967; the decision probably had to do with Nkrumah's overthrow in a military coup of the same year.[39]

Beyond economic collaboration, the Polish authorities developed cultural and scientific exchange with Ghana.[40] In January 1964, several scholars from Warsaw University received scholarships to deliver public lectures and conduct research at the University of Ghana. In return, students and academics from Ghana were hosted by Polish institutions, which provided assistance and guidance on film production and the functioning of state theatres.[41] However not all Polish scholars wanted to teach Marxist–Leninist theory to foreign students, thus rousing the concern of Polish diplomats. In December 1963, Eugeniusz Kułaga, the Polish ambassador to Ghana, held a meeting with all Polish scholars working there, at which he encouraged them to be more 'socialist':

'Mechanical objectivism' could not be perceived as a guideline for our scholars. They represent the politically involved science and that has to be underscored in their moral approach and lectures. It concerns particularly the economy and political science, so fields where Poles held important positions. We must work skillfully: in the Institute of Cadres, prof. Perczyński should openly teach Marxism with [a] strong critique of Western economic theories. The situation at Accra University is a little bit different. We need to keep an impartial approach but also try to choose material in the way that students would not have any doubts about the superiority of Marxist thought.[42]

Jan Drewnowski was one of the few professors who did not fit into this ideological framework. Born in 1908, he defended his PhD in 1936 at Warsaw School of Economics (Szkoła Główna Handlowa, SGH). As a prisoner of war, he was held at Oflag Murnau from 1939 to April 1945. He returned to Warsaw the following year, joined the Polish Socialist Party (which in 1948 'merged' with the Communist Party) and started to work as a director at the Central Planning Office. He was expelled from the Communist Party in 1950 under the suspicion of having 'right-wing views' and for teaching 'bourgeois economics'. After the October 'thaw' of 1956, he continued to work as a professor at the Main School of Planning and Statistics (Szkoła Główna Planowania i Statystyki – the successor to the SGH) and travelled regularly to Western countries. In the early 1960s, he was chosen by the authorities to be sent as a scholar to Ghana. During the decision making process, no one apparently took into consideration the fact that his political beliefs were not strictly communist. Only when President Nkrumah frequently expressed his displeasure at Drewnowski, claiming that he was an outspoken 'reactionary' and supporter of Western economic thought, did the fact become known to the Polish Embassy in Accra.[43]

Other opinions gathered by Ambassador Kułaga also confirmed the professor's ideological neutrality. According to Allan Nun May – a British scientist who had supplied the USSR with US and British atomic secrets during World War II, and who was acting vice-chairman of the Ghanaian Academy of Science at that time – Drewnowski shared certain economic attitudes with the British, and that is why they did not treat him as a 'communist' obstacle.[44] Indeed, Kułaga was forced to conclude that Professor Drewnowski was an exceptionally good manager, and an experienced and skilful teacher, but by no means was he a Marxist. When Drewnowski was asked to teach in Ghana, nobody required him to have a strong ideological background and nobody vetted his political beliefs or commitment to communism. Nevertheless, the Embassy rapidly removed him following Nkrumah's stinging critique. Drewnowski was promptly sent back home.[45]

The case of Polish scholars in Ghana demonstrates that PUWP authorities did not pay much attention to ideology. It was not only Drewnowski who failed to hide scepticism towards the implementation of socialist solutions within the African economy.[46] Some evidence comes from a collaborator with the Polish security services codenamed 'Przybył', who worked in Guinea as a specialist in the fishing industry between 1964 and 1969. According to his report, the majority of the Poles living in Conakry befriended Western citizens and became involved in illegal trade on the black market. Some of them were focused only on earning hard currency.[47]

The PUWP's policy also focused on economic profit. The emphasis placed on financial factors led to burgeoning Polish–South African economic relations, which flourished in the late 1950s.[48] In 1960, the Polish Government even seriously took into consideration the possibility of establishing mutual diplomatic relations with South Africa. The idea was abandoned after the Sharpeville massacre (March 1960), when police officers killed 69 black protestors in cold blood.[49] But later, Polish ships used South African seaports, where they bought oil and supplies, and in 1983 chartered flights between Warsaw and Cape Town were opened.[50]

The opinions of Lucjan Wolniewicz, the chairman of the Polish Solidarity Committee, reflect Poland's sceptical approach. At the first joint meeting of the Eastern bloc solidarity committees held in June 1966 in East Berlin, Wolniewicz voiced doubts about prospects in Africa. During discussions, he was openly critical of Warsaw Pact policy in the continent as he questioned the ideological background of many anti-colonial 'progressive' organizations and national leaders that he had recently met on a tour of East Africa. He admitted to being a 'little shocked' because he was concerned whether those groups really represented 'the people'. According to Wolniewicz, communist countries should have been more careful in choosing their African partners because some movements used a pro-socialist line as a 'veil' in order to procure financial and military support. He wanted to avoid myopic measures, and concluded, 'I am not a pessimist. I just want to see what is really happening on this continent.'[51] He also underlined doubts in a report on a meeting of AAPSO that he had attended in December 1967. He voiced mistrust as he described a three-hour-long discussion as a 'fantastic lesson of collaboration with African and Asian countries', because Arabs, Africans and Indians 'throw off their European personality' and showed their 'real face'. All the participants wanted to speak at the same time and no one agreed with anyone, reported Wolniewcz.[52]

Moscow often took advantage of Warsaw's ideological blindness. In the early 1960s, Soviet Foreign Minister Andrei Gromyko had some problems in establishing official contacts with Madagascar, so the Soviet authorities encouraged Warsaw to develop relations. Moreover, the Soviets politely asked Poland to open an embassy in Senegal and intensify activity in Morocco because they believed that Warsaw was perceived as less hostile than the USSR.[53] Relations with Ivory Coast may also serve as a good example for illustrating Poland's highly flexible approach towards Africa. The Soviets saw Félix Houphouët-Boigny of Ivory Coast as 'reactionary' and pro-Western.[54] Mutual diplomatic relations between Moscow and Abidjan were not established until 1967, and were severed two years later. Meanwhile, Warsaw established diplomatic relations with Ivory Coast in 1974, during which time Soviet–Ivorian relations were still frozen (they remained so until 1986). This may demonstrate that the Poles were used as a Soviet proxy. Warsaw's policy in Africa, aimed more at achieving economic goals than promoting communist ideology, might have been used by Kremlin authorities as a key for opening doors in several African states ruled by right-wing governments. For example, one can observe this in Polish relations with Liberia. In 1956, Warsaw did not establish diplomatic contacts with Monrovia because its Ministry of Foreign Affairs wanted to wait for the Soviet Union to do so first.[55] They sent a permanent trade delegation to Monrovia in 1964, but did not establish diplomatic relations with Liberia until 1973. Moreover, when Liberia broke off its relations with Moscow in 1985, it was Poland who took over the representation of Soviet interests.[56]

By the late 1960s, Polish officials became increasingly disappointment with the outcomes, and thus their enthusiasm for Africa declined. In 1969, an official of the Polish Ministry of Foreign Affairs concluded, 'After the period of socialist states' active involvement in African events in the early 1960s, when new countries emerged there, socialist states, including Poland, have recently weakened their attention towards this continent.'[57] Leaders of the Polish Solidarity Committee were also to some extent disappointed. Five years after establishment of the organization they came to this conclusion:

> There is a need for a more effective 'outcome' of Polish initiatives in the international arena and a more secure 'acknowledgement' of the receipts of the material assistance that is provided by us. It still happens that our material assistance is spent without any political benefits to our government, or goes to the wrong people. Equally important matter is a further development of our cooperation with the Solidarity Committees from socialist countries, the need to better coordinate our cooperation and eradication of all forms of 'competitiveness,' which unfortunately inform our contacts, especially in economic relations with the so called Third World countries[58]

The situation started to change in December 1970 when Gomułka was overthrown and replaced by Edward Gierek. The new First Secretary wanted to increase Poland's international prestige, and this agenda influenced the country's approach towards Africa.

Gierek's Phase: Support for Anti-Colonial Movements and the Development of Economic Ties

In November 1971, Kwiryn Grela, the general secretary of the Polish Committee of Solidarity with Asian and African Nations, sent to the International Department of the Central Committee of the PUWP a confidential report about the Warsaw Pact's support for African national-liberation movements. He stated that in comparison with other Eastern European countries, Poland's involvement in economic and military assistance was perceived as unworthy of its position and capabilities, particularly when it came to backing anti-Portuguese resistance movements in Angola and Mozambique. In particular, he referred to a case in which the leaders of the national-liberation movements criticized Warsaw for selling Polish ships to Lisbon. Such occurrences undermined Poland's image as a state that supported the anti-colonial struggle. The national-liberation movements had good access to publishing houses; they printed many bulletins, journals, and leaflets; and took part in international conferences. They could therefore, argued Grela, influence the news, constructing an image of Polish–Portuguese collusion.[59]

Warsaw's reputation as an anti-colonial state was poor in the 1960s. In 1969, the leader of the Mozambique Liberation Front (FRELIMO), Eduardo Mondlane, complained that Poland was the only country among socialist states that did not support his movement.[60] Moreover, in June 1970 António Alberto Neto, a member of the Popular Movement for the Liberation of Angola (MPLA), met with representatives of the Polish Solidarity Committee and complained that Polish ships were used to transport Portugal's troops from Europe to its colonies.[61] Grela's report of November 1971 thus suggested activating contacts with the MPLA, FRELIMO and the African Party for the Independence of Guinea and Cape Verde (PAIGC). Prior to this, Polish support for PAIGC had been limited and boiled down to providing medicine (1967, 1971) and clothes (1969). This was why Warsaw increased its total value of aid, delivering 300–500 automatic pistols with ammunition to each of the organizations and inviting some of their leaders – such as the PAIGC commander, Amilcar Cabral – to Poland.[62]

Figures show that the Polish authorities genuinely improved their support for the liberation movements. While in 1971, PAIGC received 28 boxes of medicine (2,532 kg/5,580 lb), MPLA 17 boxes (1,389 kg/3,060 lb) and FRELIMO 4 boxes (537 kg/1,180 lb), the next year Polish aid increased to 970 boxes with medicine, clothes and technical equipment for PAIGC (75,000 kg/165,000 lb), 406 boxes (31,427 kg/69,280 lb) for MPLA and 488 boxes (39,113 kg/86,230 lb) for FRELIMO.[63] Such an increase in assistance for these movements represented an attempt to preserve Poland's anti-colonial reputation in a relatively inexpensive way. Beginning in 1973, the level of support to PAIGC dropped to previous levels and included machetes, medical equipment and medicines.[64] However, other Warsaw Pact states continued to play a much bigger role in supporting the liberation movements, and Poland's support for the PAIGC and FRELIMO remained pragmatic.[65] The same was true for Polish relations with the MPLA. Mutual contacts flourished in the 1970s, with Warsaw providing the Angolans with large quantities of military equipment. In 1978 the MPLA's leader, Agostinho Neto, visited Poland and the following year the Polish chairman of the state, Henryk Jabłoński, paid a return visit to Luanda, where an inter-party agreement was signed.[66]

During Gierek's rule, Poland was more active in the international arena and joined the United Nations Council for Namibia in 1972.[67] This is why the South West Africa People's Organization (SWAPO) was one of the national-liberation movements that maintained quite active and multidimensional relations with Poland.[68] Contacts dated back to 1962, when SWAPO had received two scholarships for students to study medicine. One was given to Libertina Amathila, who in 1969 became the first African woman to have graduated as a doctor of medicine in Poland and was to became the first female doctor in the history of Namibia. She moved to Tanzania, where in 1970 she became the deputy secretary for health and welfare on the SWAPO Central Committee and director of the SWAPO Women's Council.[69] In the 1970s, Warsaw provided SWAPO with medicine, weapons, ammunition, tents, four trucks and hosted 60 wounded fighters for medical treatment until 1986.[70] SWAPO's leader, Sam Nujoma, visited Poland twice. In the 1980s, the frequency of relations largely decreased and scholarships remained the only important element of Polish support. As of 1986, 13 members of this organization were hosted in hospitals in Warsaw and other Polish cities.[71] However Warsaw's assistance to other African organizations – such as the African National Congress, the Tanzanian Party of the Revolution and the Liberation Front in Algeria – was limited.[72]

At the same time, Gierek's government was also developing economic ties with African countries that were not perceived by the Soviet bloc as 'progressive'. During the 1970s, the Polish Government maintained fruitful relations with Nigeria, which was then developing its relations with Western countries.[73] This collaboration was not motivated by ideology but instead purely limited to trade and investments, which might be the key to understanding its success. Early in the decade, the Polish Embassy even represented East German interests there for some time, because authorities in Lagos did not recognize that country in the international arena.[74] The number of specialists that Poland sent to Nigeria reached more than 400 in late 1970s.[75] Moreover, the amount of trade between the two countries was greater than what Poland enjoyed with any other African country.[76] In 1976, Poland signed with Nigeria a most-favoured nation clause, and the following year its exports there amounted to US$40 million while its imports barely existed. The majority of exports went through joint Polish–Nigerian companies like Daltrade, Polfa, Nigpol or Polconsult Associates, which covered the Nigerian fishing industry, construction business and pharmaceutical industry.[77] Over subsequent years, economic relations flourished, and in 1983 the number of Polish contract workers reached 800.[78] This development of economic relations had nothing to do with the promotion of Marxism; maybe that is why mutual cooperation was so efficient.

In the 1970s, Poland tried to stay out of Ethiopia. At that time, Poland relied on foreign loans and maintained relatively favourable relations with the West. It wanted to avoid helping to build a repressive system in Ethiopia, and feared that their involvement would spark unnecessary criticism and lead to the reduction of Western loans. In 1977, the Ethiopian Ministry of Internal Affairs asked for support in establishing an advanced penitentiary system. The idea was discussed in detail within the directorate of the Polish Ministry of Internal Affairs. A handwritten comment by a high-ranking official indicates that Deputy Minister Mirosław Milewski personally opposed the prospect of Poland's involvement. This opinion was shared by Colonel Józef Chomętowski, director of the Ministry of Internal Affairs' Cabinet, who wrote to the Fifth Department of the Ministry of Foreign Affairs, 'We believe that it would be inadvisable for Poland to provide assistance in this matter.' Accordingly, the Poles politely rejected the offer.[79] At the same time, however, PUWP officials did not hesitate to supply the Ethiopian Army with light military hardware and medical equipment.[80] Sending several dozen boxes of ammunition and AK-47s was a much easier task than providing the sort of long-term assistance implicit in sending qualified advisors. In 1978, the Council for Mutual Economic Assistance (CMEA) appointed Poland to develop particular branches of the Ethiopian economy, especially the textile and leather industry. Warsaw offered cooperation, but Addis Ababa lacked foreign currency, and thus economic relations remained limited.[81]

Meanwhile, providing scholarships remained the principal way in which Poland supported African states and national-liberation movements. In the 1967/8 academic year, among the 1,679 foreign students in Poland, 463 came from Africa.[82] In 1974/5, among 3,876 foreign students, there were 533 Africans.[83] By 1979, their number had increased to 1,100.[84] The most important institution responsible for hosting guests from abroad was the School of Polish for Foreigners, established in 1952 in Łódź. Nearly every foreign student who was given a scholarship was sent there first to learn basic Polish. The school provided education to approximately 30,000 students from Europe, Africa, the Middle East, Asia and Latin America during the Cold War.[85] Between 1956 and 1975, 1,145 Africans completed the programme, accounting for 23 per cent of all graduates.[86]

Warsaw used scholarships as a simple, easy, inexpensive and useful tool for showcasing support for Africa. The provision of scholarships was often the only aspect of cooperation between Poland and some African countries – as for example, with Ethiopia, with the number of students from that country increasing from two in 1961 to 20 in 1965.[87] When PUWP officials recognized some regime or national movement as 'friendly' but did not want to spend a lot of money on investment projects, they simply offered scholarships. To promote relations with Sudan, the PUWP leadership decided to provide a large number of scholarships, with more than 300 Sudanese graduating from Polish universities by 1986 – most of them with a medical degree.[88] Scholarships also formed the major form of cooperation with Zambia, with students receiving education in medicine, engineering, architecture, regional and economic planning, and agriculture in Poland.[89] However, Polish assistance in scholarships remained at much lower levels as compared with other countries of the Warsaw Pact. In 1979, Poland provided only 18 scholarships to Benin.[90] At the same time, Bulgaria offered 30 scholarships for ideological training in Sofia alone, while the GDR organized a six-week-long seminar about 'socialist management' for 200–300 people, providing assistance with shaping Benin's university-level scholar education.[91]

Conclusion

Several key factors drove the scope and complexity of the Polish approach towards developing relations with African countries. First, economic conditions did not allow Poland to conduct a wider and more fruitful policy in Africa, and the government was aware that spending public money on international support for so-called Third World countries would not gain much popularity amongst the Polish public. The same situation dissuaded the authorities from providing much-needed loans and made long-term cooperation difficult. A high rate of civil unrest known as the 'Polish months' of June 1956, March 1968, December 1970, June 1976 and August 1980 also made it difficult for the government to transform Africa into an interesting and important goal for Polish diplomacy.

Second, the PUWP's leadership was moderately interested in improving its rather modest contribution to the decolonization process. Apart from backing anti-colonial resolutions at the UN or announcing public statements and resolutions condemning 'racist' or 'imperialist' Western policy, Warsaw did not engage as deeply on the 'ideological' field as other Eastern bloc members. Poland did not provide or sell as much military equipment as Czechoslovakia, nor did it help with Marxist education for local African cadres or provide as much security training as the GDR.[92] One should mention that the state's economic and political interests were strictly limited and focused mostly on Europe. Polish authorities did not have to seek international recognition as did the GDR, nor assert its presence or exert influence to mark its importance within the communist bloc, as did Bulgaria or Romania. Gomułka did not perceive Africa as a place where Warsaw could prove its importance within the Soviet bloc. Conversely, Poland's ideological flexibility allowed Moscow to often use Warsaw to facilitate cooperation with those countries where relations were strained for ideological reasons.

Poland's involvement was not unconditional, had its limits and vacillated over time. Mostly restrained during Gomułka's rule, it became more active in the 1970s, which saw substantial support to anti-Portuguese resistance and to Angola after independence. However, the PUWP leadership wanted at the same time to back 'socialist' or 'progressive' paths of modernization, develop economic cooperation and generate financial profits. These combined goals were often difficult to achieve because assistance was provided on a non-refundable basis or required complementary support from the USSR or the GDR. Warsaw was also unable to become a powerful player in Africa because of internal instability, and the PUWP did not try to compete with other members of the Warsaw Pact in this respect. Describing Polish–Cameroonian relations, Jacek Knopek concluded that both partners expected from each other more than they could offer.[93] This opinion might be extrapolated into the whole Polish attitude towards Africa during the Cold War. The initial optimistic expectations of the early 1960s turned into 'realpolitik' based on beneficial relations with countries like Nigeria, which were far from being perceived as Marxist. Pragmatism ruled the Polish approach to Africa.

Notes

1. Archiwum Akt Nowych (hereafter, AAN), KC PZPR, LXXVI-503, Ryszard Frelek to Secretary of Central Committee of the PUWP Stanisław Kania, November 1971.
2. Jacek Tebinka, 'Dyplomacja popaździernikowa (1957–1960)' [Post-October Diplomacy (1957–1960)], in Wojciech Materski and Waldemar Michowicz (eds), *Historia Dyplomacji Polskiej* [History of Polish Diplomacy. Volume VI (1944/1945–1989)] (Warsaw, 2010), pp. 579–80.
3. AAN, KC PZPR, sygn. LXXVI-32, Resolution of the Polish Political Bureau of CC PUWP on coordination and organization the Polish external relations, January 1973, p. 4.
4. Marcin Zaremba, 'Propaganda sukcesu. Dekada Gierka' [The Propaganda of Success] in Piotr Semków (ed.), *Propaganda PRL. Wybrane problemy* [The Propaganda of the Polish People's Republic. Selected Problems] (Gdańsk, 2004), pp. 29–30.
5. From 1985 to 1987, the Polish helicopter squadron (Polish Relief Helicopter Squadron in Ethiopia) took part in a relief operation in famine-stricken areas of Tigray and Northern Wollo. The contingent consisted of 22 persons, including ten highly trained pilots who flew three helicopters. The squadron was responsible for selecting and preparing drop zones as well as carrying out airdrops in remote areas.
6. Wanda Jarząbek, *PRL w politycznych strukturach Układu Warszawskiego w latach 1955–1980* [The Polish People's Republic in the Political Structures of Warsaw Pact, 1955–1980] (Warsaw, 2008), pp. 87–8; Jacek Knopek, 'Stosunki Polski z Afryką arabską po II wojnie światowej' [Polish relations with North African Arab countries after World War II], *Forum Politologiczne*, vol. 3 (2006), pp. 139–71; Przemysław Gasztold-Seń, *PRL wobec państw Maghrebu 1970–1989* [The Polish People's Republic towards the Maghreb Countries, 1970–1989], *Olsztyńskie Studia Afrykanistyczne*, vol. 1 (2010), pp. 141–51.
7. Archiwum Ministerstwa Spraw Zagranicznych (hereafter, AMSZ), Department V, 26/86, w-1, 10-4-82, 22-2-82, K. Baliński's Memo on Minister J. Czyrek's talks with Algerian Foreign Minister Achmed Taleb Ibrahimi, 2 June 1982.

8. AMSZ, Departament V, 26/86, w-6, 023-50-82, The Party-Technical Meeting in the Department V, 4 January 1979.
9. Wanda Jarząbek, *Polska Rzeczpospolita Ludowa wobec polityki wschodniej Republiki Federalnej Niemiec w latach 1966–1976. Wymiar dwustronny i międzynarodowy* [The Polish People's Republic towards the East Policy of the Federal Republic of Germany. Bilateral and International Dimension] (Warsaw, 2011), p. 23.
10. From 1943 to 1948, he had been General Secretary of the Polish Workers' Party, but was removed from the post on charges of supporting 'right-wing nationalist deviation' and imprisoned in 1951 during internal purges; he was released in 1954.
11. Andrzej Paczkowski, '1956 rok – XX Zjazd. Polski Październik. Walka o autonomię' [1956–XX Congress. Polish October. The Struggle for Autonomy] in Adam Daniel Rotfeld and A.V. Torkunow (eds), *Białe plamy-czarne plamy. Sprawy trudne w polsko-rosyjskich stosunkach 1918–2008* [The Blank Spots-Black Spots. Difficult Issues in Polish-Russian Relations, 1918–2008] (Warsaw, 2010), p. 492.
12. Andrzej Skrzypek, *Dyplomatyczne dzieje PRL w latach 1956–1989* [Diplomatic History of Polish People's Republic, 1956–1989] (Pułtusk-Warsaw, 2010), pp. 38–9.
13. Piotr Madajczyk, 'Dyplomacja polska w latach sześćdziesiątych' [Polish Diplomacy in the 1960s], in Wojciech Materski and Waldemar Michowicz (eds), *Historia dyplomacji polskiej. Tom VI. 1944/1945–1989* [The History of Polish Diplomacy Volume VI, 1944/1945–1989] (Warsaw, 2010), p. 619.
14. Jacek Knopek, *Stosunki polsko-zachodnioafrykańskie* [Polish-West African Relations] (Toruń, 2013), pp. 124–34, 171.
15. Anna Hejczyk, *Sybiracy pod Kilimandżaro. Tengeru, Polskie osiedle w Afryce Wschodniej we wspomnieniach jego mieszkańców* [Sybiracy at Kilimanjaro. Tengeru, Polish Resettlement Camp in East Africa in the Memories of its Inhabitants] (Rzeszów-Kraków, 2013).
16. Jacek Tebinka, *Uzależnienie czy suwerenność? Odwilż październikowa w dyplomacji Polskiej Rzeczpospolitej Ludowej 1956–1961* [Dependency or Sovereignty? The October Thaw in the Diplomacy of the Polish People's Republic, 1956–1961] (Warsaw, 2010), p. 256.
17. Merle Pribbenow, *Vietnam Covertly Supplied Weapons to Revolutionaries in Algeria and Latin America*, CWIHP e-Dossier No. 25. Available at https://www.wilsoncenter.org/publication/vietnam-covertly-supplied-weapons-to-revolutionaries-algeria-and-latin-america#sthash.sjaTNk6O.dpuf (accessed September 2017).
18. Krzysztof Szczepanik, *Organizacja polskiej służby zagranicznej 1918–2010* [The Organization of Polish Diplomacy, 1918–2010] (Warsaw, 2012), p. 219.
19. AAN, KC PZPR, LXXVI-503, Draft Memo on providing support to national movements in Africa, November 1971.

20. Archiwum Instytutu Pamięci Narodowej (hereafter, AIPN), 1585/20320, The Statue of Polish Committee of Solidarity with Nations of Asia and Africa, 1970, p. 12.
21. Konrad Czernichowski, Dominik Kopiński and Andrzej Polus, 'Polish African Studies at Crossroads: Past, Present, Future', *Africa Spectrum* (2012), vols 2–3, pp. 171–2.
22. Błażej Popławski, 'Z dziejów pewnego towarzystwa. O początkach działalności Towarzystwa Przyjaźni Polsko-Afrykańskiej w Warszawie' [The History of Some Association. Beginnings of the Polish-African Friendship Association], in Patryk Pleskot (ed.), *Cudzoziemcy w Warszawie 1945–1989. Studia i materiały* [Foreigners in Warsaw 1945–1989. Studies and Documents] (Warsaw, 2012), pp. 189–92.
23. AIPN Rz, 055/8, The Head of Division VII of 2. Department of Ministry of Internal Affairs to Head of II Division within the Citizen's Militia headquarters in Rzeszów, 1 July 1963, pp. 3–4.
24. See Maciej Ząbek, *Biali i czarni. Postawy Polaków wobec Afryki i Afrykanów* [White and Black. Poles towards Africa and Africans] (Warsaw, 2007).
25. Popławski, 'Z dziejów pewnego towarzystwa', pp. 189–202.
26. AAN, Polski Komitet Solidarności z Narodami Azji Afryki i Ameryki Łacińskiej [Polish Committee of Solidarity with the Nations of Asia, Africa, and Latin America] (hereafter, PKSzNAAiAŁ), Report from the X. Session of OSAA Steering Committee, 1971.
27. Danuta Eitner, Tadeusz Łętocha and Jerzy Prokopczuk, *Państwa Afryki w ONZ 1960–1962* [African Countries in UN, 1960–1962] (Wrocław, 1967).
28. Madajczyk, 'Dyplomacja polska w latach sześćdziesiątych', pp. 617–18.
29. Krzysztof Szczepanik, Anna Herman-Łukasik and Barbara Janicka (eds), *Stosunki dyplomatyczne Polski. Informator. Tom IV. Afryka i Bliski Wschód 1918–2009* [The Diplomatic Relations of Poland. Directory. Volume IV. Africa and Middle East 1918–2009] (Warsaw, 2010), pp. 81–3.
30. Director General's circular on the visit of Guinean Delegation, 18 February 1959, in Piotr Długołęcki (ed.), *Polskie Dokumenty Dyplomatyczne 1959* [Polish Diplomatic Documents 1959] (Warsaw, 2011), pp. 128–9.
31. Dale C. Tatum, *Who Influenced whom? Lessons from the Cold War* (Lanham, MD, 2002), p. 84.
32. Philip E. Muehlenbeck, *Czechoslovakia in Africa, 1945–1968* (New York, 2015).
33. Tebinka, *Uzależnienie czy suwerenność?*, p. 257.
34. Muehlenbeck, *Czechoslovakia in Africa*, p. 57.
35. AIPN Gd, 003/29, Plan of operational actions for a case codename 'Aweni' on West African seaports, 21 January 1964, pp. 29–30.
36. Memorandum of the Director of Department V on visit of governmental delegation in African countries, March 1959, in Długołęcki, *Polskie Dokumenty Dyplomatyczne*, pp. 174–6.

37. Tebinka, *Uzależnienie czy suwerenność?*, p. 262.
38. Degefe Gemechu, 'Stosunki polsko-etiopskie. Zarys problematyki' [Polish-Ethiopian Relations: Outline of the Problem], *Forum Politologiczne*, vol. 3 (2006), pp. 180–1.
39. Szczepanik, Herman-Łukasik and Janicka, *Stosunki dyplomatyczne Polski. Informator*, p. 76.
40. Lukasz Stanek, 'Architects from Socialist Countries in Ghana (1957–67): Modern Architecture and Mondialisation', *Journal of the Society of Architectural Historians*, 74 (4) (December 2015), pp. 416–42.
41. AIPN, 1585/1942, Plan of implementation of the agreement between Polish People's Republic and Ghana on cultural cooperation for 1965 (undated, but 1965), pp. 5–9.
42. AIPN, 1585/1910, Copy of Eugeniusz Kułaga's Note, 1963, pp. 193–4.
43. Ibid., Memorandum about Jan Drewnowski, 9 June 1964, pp. 187–8.
44. Keith Jeffery, *The Secret History of MI6, 1909–1949* (New York, 2011), pp. 658–9.
45. AIPN, 1585/1910, Eugeniusz Kułaga's Note, 1964, pp. 191–212.
46. W. Scott Thompson, *Ghana's Foreign Policy, 1957–1966: Diplomacy Ideology, and the New State* (Princeton, NJ, 1969), p. 277.
47. AIPN Gd, 003/29, Copy of information obtained from source codenamed 'Przybył' about Poles in Guinea, 1969, p. 164–7.
48. Jerzy Prokopczuk, *Afryka. Likwidacja kolonializmu i neokolonializm* [Africa. The Liquidation of Colonialism and Neo-Colonialism] (Warsaw, 1963), pp. 138–9.
49. Tebinka, *Uzależnienie czy suwerenność?*, p. 258.
50. AIPN, 0449/1 vol. 5, Urgent Note on arresting Polish charter plane by Zambian authorities, 8 January 1987, pp. 84–5.
51. Bundesarchiv-Stiftung Archiv der Parteien und Massenorganisationen der DDR, DZ8/32, Consultation Meeting between the representatives of the Afro-Asian Solidarity Committee of the European Socialist countries, 28–29 June 1966, p. 57 (I am grateful to Natalia Telepneva for sharing this document with me).
52. AAN, PKSzNAAiAŁ, sygn. 66, Report of Polish Solidarity Committee with Nations of Asia and Africa's Delegation from OSAA Conference in Cairo, 27–29 December 1967.
53. Madajczyk, 'Dyplomacja polska w latach sześćdziesiątych', p. 620.
54. Jerzy Prokopczuk, *Problemy ruchu komunistycznego i narodowo-wyzwoleńczego na Bliskim Wschodzie i w Afryce* [The Problems of Communist and National-Liberation Movements in the Middle East and Africa] (Warsaw, 1970), p. 49.
55. Knopek, *Stosunki polsko-zachodnioafrykańskie*, pp. 182–3.
56. Szczepanik, Herman-Łukasik and Janicka, *Stosunki dyplomatyczne Polski. Informator*, p. 176.
57. W. Jarząbek, 'Dyplomacja polska w warunkach odprężenia (styczeń 1969–lipiec 1975)' [Polish Diplomacy in a Period of Detente (January 1969–July 1975)], in Materski and Michowicz, *Historia dyplomacji*, pp. 720–1.

58. AAN, PKSzNAAiAŁ, sygn. 19, General remarks to evaluation, 1970, p. 37.
59. AAN, KC PZPR, LXXVI-503, Draft Memorandum on providing support to national movements in Africa, November 1971.
60. AAN, PKSzNAAiAŁ, sygn. 66, Jerzy Prokopczuk's report on the 'International Conference in Support of the People of Portuguese Colonies and Southern Africa', which was held in Khartoum, 18–19 January 1969.
61. AAN, PKSzNAAiAŁ, sygn. 66, Note on talks with MPLA's Antonio Alberto Neto, 1970.
62. AAN, KC PZPR, LXXVI-503, Draft Memorandum on providing support to national movements in Africa, November 1971; AAN, KC PZPR, LXXVI-512, Note on sending delegation to Guinea, 1972.
63. Deputy Director of Department V Włodzimierz Paszkowski to International Organizations' Department on support revolutionary movements in Africa, 27 January 1973, in Piotr Majewski (ed.), *Polskie Dokumenty Dyplomatyczne 1973* [Polish Diplomatic Documents 1973] (Warsaw, 2006), pp. 31–2.
64. AAN, KC PZPR, LXXVI-767, Report on Support for PAIGC 1956–1975, undated.
65. AAN, KC PZPR, LXXVI-449, Report on Africa, 1986.
66. AAN, KC PZPR, LXXVI-605, Agreement of Cooperation between The Popular Movement for the Liberation of Angola – Labour Party and Polish United Workers' Party, 1979–1980, undated.
67. Andrzej Abraszewski, *Polska w Organizacji Narodów Zjednoczonych (1945–1975)* [Poland in the United Nations, 1945–1975] (Warsaw, 1975), p. 150.
68. AAN, KC PZPR, LXXVI-592, Letter from President of SWAPO Sam Nujoma to the Secretary of Central Committee of the Polish Workers' Party in Warsaw, 4 December 1979; Arkadiusz Żukowski, *Polsko-południowoafrykańskie stosunki polityczne* [Polish-South African Political Relations] (Olsztyn, 1998), pp. 194–8.
69. Libertina Inaaviposa Amathila, *Making a Difference* (Windhoek, 2012). She also served as the Deputy Prime Minister of Namibia from 2005 to 2010.
70. AAN, KC PZPR, LXXVI-605, Letter from President of SWAPO Sam Nujoma to Comrade Ambassador of the People's Republic of Poland in Luanda about receipt of material aid, 15 December 1980.
71. AAN, KC PZPR, LXXVI-449, South West Africa People's Organization – memorandum prepared in the International Department of the Central Committee of the PUWP, 1986.
72. AAN, KC PZPR, LXXVI-577, Agreement on Establishing Permanent Representation of Zimbabwe Patriotic Front in Poland, 1979; AAN, KC PZPR, LXXVI-592, Evaluation of Polish Solidarity Committee with Nations of Asia and Africa, 1980; AAN, KC PZPR, LXXVI-452, Memorandum prepared in the International Department of the Central Committee of the PUWP on Secretary of the Central Committee of ZANU Nelson T. Mawema's visit in Poland, 8–11 December 1988, 14 December 1988; AAN, KC PZPR, LXXVI-449, The National Liberation Front – memorandum prepared in the

International Department of the Central Committee of the PUWP, February 1986; AAN, KC PZPR, LXXVI-449, African National Congress – note prepared in the International Department of the Central Committee of the PUWP, February 1986; AAN, KC PZPR, LXXVI-449, South African Communist Party – note prepared in the International Department of the Central Committee of the PUWP, 17 February 1986; AAN, KC PZPR, LXXVI-449, The revolutionary party in Tanzania, encyclopedic information, Relations with PUWP – memorandum prepared by the International Department of the Central Committee of the PUWP, February 1986; AAN, KC PZPR, LXXVI-449, Congolese Labor Party – note prepared in the International Department of the Central Committee of the PUWP, February 1986; AAN, KC PZPR, LXXVI-592, Program of cooperation between Central Committee of the Congolese Labor Party and PUWP for 1980–1981, undated.
73. See Machowski, 'Achievements of Poles Employed in Nigeria', in Zygmunt Łazowski (ed.), *Poland's Relations with West Africa* (Warsaw, 2004), pp. 155–6.
74. Knopek, *Stosunki polsko-zachodnioafrykańskie*, p. 182.
75. AAN, KC PZPR, LXXVI-577, Report on First Session of Polish-Nigerian Joint Committee on Economic, Scientific and Cultural Cooperation, 5 July 1979.
76. AAN, KC PZPR, LXXVI-577, Program of Cultural and Educational Cooperation between Polish People's Republic and Federal Military Government of Nigeria, 1979–1980, undated.
77. AIPN, 2602/26771, Report on external policy of Nigeria, undated, but 1979, p. 65.
78. AIPN, 01789/389/CD, Report to the Director of the 1st Department of the Ministry of Internal Affairs Fabian Dmowski, Warsaw, 6 May 1983, p. 9.
79. AIPN 1585/15315, Note from Colonel J. Chomętowski to Deputy Director of Department V Julian Sutor, 16 May 1977, pp. 8–9.
80. AAN, KC PZPR, LXXVI – 438, Current Situation in Africa and Polish projects – memorandum prepared in the Department V, May 1978.
81. AIPN, 0827/244, Note on Socialist Ethiopia, 1978, pp. 184–5.
82. AIPN, 2602/9853, General Mieczysław Bień to General Wojciech Jaruzelski, 12 March 1968, pp. 11–12.
83. AIPN, 003172/9 t. 6, Memorandum on foreign students in Poland, 10 July 1975, p. 71.
84. AIPN, 1585/1811, Memorandum on Polish relations with African countries prepared for a meeting of Parliamentary Commission of Foreign Affairs, 15 October 1979, p. 100.
85. AIPN, 1510/2283, Memorandum on the goals of II Division of Provincial Office of Internal Affairs in Łódź in the field of counteracting threats in The School of Polish for Foreigners. Captain Zbigniew Głowacki's Master of Arts written under supervision of Colonel Dr R. Głukowski in the Institute of Criminalistics and Criminology Academy of the Interior, 1989, p. 43.
86. AIPN, 1510/3609, The organization of counter-intelligence work among the students from non socialist countries in The School of Polish for Foreigners.

Captain Janusz Jasiński's Master of Arts written under supervision of Colonel Dr Zbigniew Więckiewicz in the Methodology of Counter-Intelligence Chair within the Institute of Criminalistics and Criminology Academy of the Interior, 1976, p. 64. Overall, by 2002, 3,791 African students had graduated from Łódź University.
87. Gemechu, 'Stosunki polsko-etiopskie', p. 185.
88. AAN, KC PZPR, LXXVI-449, The Republic of Sudan – memorandum, 11 February 1986.
89. National Archives of Zambia, Cabinet Office, CO 2/6/001, Political brief on Poland for use by the Right Honourable Prime Minister Mr K. S. K. Musokotwane when He meets the Polish Parliamentary Delegation on 4th May 1985 (I am grateful to Jodie Yuzhou Sun for sharing this document with me).
90. AAN, KC PZPR, LXXVI-576, Note prepared in the International Department of the Central Committee of the PUWP, 1 June 1979; AAN, KC PZPR, LXXVI-577, Report on the progress of implementation of the Protocol concerning the results of the talks between the delegations of Poland and Benin, 16 August 1979.
91. AAN, KC PZPR, LXXVI-577, Memorandum on relations between communist parties and socialist countries with the People's Revolutionary Party of Benin, 17 August 1979.
92. Garteth M. Winrow, *The Foreign Policy of the GDR in Africa* (Cambridge, 1990), p. 223.
93. Jacek Knopek, 'Stosunki polsko-kameruńskie: geneza, struktury, funkcjonowanie' [Polish-Cameroonian relations: origins, structures, and development], *Wrocławskie Studia Politologiczne*, no. 14 (2013), pp. 31–2.

PART III

MONEY AND INFLUENCE: DIPLOMACY, AID AND TRADE

CHAPTER 9

ROMANIA BLOCKS MONGOLIA'S ACCESSION TO THE WARSAW TREATY ORGANIZATION: THE ROOTS OF ROMANIA'S INVOLVEMENT IN THE SINO-SOVIET DISPUTE

Elena Dragomir

Drawing on recently declassified materials from the archive of the Central Committee of the Romanian Communist Party, this chapter argues that the July 1963 proposal regarding the admission of the Mongolian People's Republic (MPR) into the Warsaw Pact Organization (WPO) was blocked by Romania's opposition, an aspect rarely mentioned by the existing scholarship. Presenting Bucharest's reasons for this opposition, and the tactics that it used to secure its success, this study challenges the received wisdom regarding not only the ability of the USSR to control a junior ally such as Romania but also the capacity of the latter to successfully pursue its own interests, even when these contradicted the (perceived) common interest of the socialist camp or the USSR's (perceived) objectives. Generally, there is little information on Mongolia's attempted accession to the WPO, and the findings advanced by this study, corroborated with evidence from other Eastern European archives, could create a better understanding of the event, in general, and of Romania's independence (or autonomy) within the Warsaw Pact, in particular.

Introduction

Traditionally, scholars divide Romania's Cold War foreign policy into two main periods – one, from the end of World War II to the turn of the 1960s, in which Romania is seen as a docile satellite of the USSR with no independent interests or foreign-policy objectives, obediently and voluntarily following in its domestic and foreign policy any Soviet request or indication; and another, from the early 1960s to the end of the Cold War, when Romania, detaching from the USSR, practised a more independent or autonomous[1] policy from that of Moscow.[2]

Regarding the causes of Bucharest's detachment, scholars advance different interpretations, often seeing it as a reaction to either de-Stalinization or specialization attempts within the Council for Mutual Economic Assistance (CMEA). According to one interpretation, the Romanian leaders turned their back on Moscow because accepting de-Stalinization would have meant giving up their power. Desperate to preserve its political power domestically, so this line of argument goes, the leadership in Bucharest distanced itself from the Soviet leadership that had prompted de-Stalinization.[3] Another analysis contends that Romania's opposition was triggered by the attempted CMEA reformation drive towards specialization, which – if it had been allowed to occur – would have affected not only Romania's narrow economic interests but its general political interests as well, limiting its independence, sovereignty or territorial integrity.[4]

Although developing rather slowly, another body of research contests (more or less explicitly) Romania's voluntary subordination to the USSR, and argues that although publicly and officially Romania acted both domestically and internationally as a loyal satellite of the USSR, behind the scenes it tried to accommodate its own interests as opposed to the Soviet ones many years prior to the early 1960s. Contrary to the traditional dominant scholarship, this scholarly line observes, for instance, that as early as the late 1940s or early 1950s various political figures – such as Gheorghe Gheorghiu-Dej, Ion Gheorghe Maurer or even Ana Pauker – attempted to follow their country's interests in domestic or foreign policy-related matters[5] and that Romania's opposition to the USSR manifested itself earlier than is generally acknowledged.[6]

Although, occasionally, scholars claim that the Cuban Missile Crisis was the 'precipitating event';[7] the 'triggering event';[8] or, at least, a major factor that 'determined' Bucharest's detachment from Moscow',[9] nobody has thus far identified any archival document supporting this assertion. In other words, there is no 1962-dated document yet available with regard to how the Romanian leaders perceived or reacted to the crisis during its occurrence or immediately afterwards. Moreover, during various meetings of the politburo or of the Central Committee (CC) of the Romanian Workers' Party (RWP) held in 1963 or 1964, the Cuban Missile Crisis was often discussed but only as an example of how careless and unpredictable the Soviet leadership was, which, according to the Romanian interpretations, presented serious security risks for Bucharest as well. Refining Romania's policy towards the USSR in response to perceived CMEA threats, in 1963–4, the country's leadership did take into consideration the perceived Soviet unpredictability, carelessness and aggressiveness as proven during the Cuban Crisis, but there is as yet no archival evidence available to suggest that this crisis functioned as a trigger of Bucharest's detachment from the USSR[10] – an aspect that does, however, remain to be carefully determined by further research.

Bucharest's distancing from Moscow has been generally studied through two case studies: Romania's opposition to CMEA specialization and its divergent position towards the Sino–Soviet dispute, the latter being often seen either as a beneficial context that allowed the 'opportunistic' Romanian leadership to reach its CMEA-related goals[11] or as a cause, or even a model, of detachment.[12] Behind the scenes, however, in the early 1960s, Bucharest was beginning to contest Moscow within the Warsaw Pact framework as well, its opposition to Mongolia's membership being one example in this regard.

Despite its significance, Romania's resistance to Mongolia's admission to the WPO and its role in blocking this perceived Soviet proposal is a case that remains greatly understudied. Generally, most Romanian-authored studies dealing with Cold War Romania's foreign policy or with its opposition to the USSR completely ignored the event[13] or barely mention it.[14] More recent studies present a detailed account of the country's opposition, but they are generally descriptive and do not properly address the reasons behind Bucharest's opposition or the tactics that it employed to achieve its goal.[15] Until recently, foreign scholars noted that Romania had some sort of involvement in this case, but without access to the country's archival sources any in-depth analysis used to be rather difficult.[16] A notable exception in this regard is Laurien Crump's recent monograph on Warsaw Pact relations. Drawing from Romanian archival sources, Crump underlines Romania's 'concerns' about Mongolia's admission and observes that the available evidence 'suggests' that its criticism was one of the factors explaining why Soviet leader Nikita S. Khrushchev eventually dropped this proposal. According to Crump, the Mongolian application provided the Romanian leadership with the opportunity to use the Warsaw Pact as a tool to explore its room for manoeuvre and to expand its independence.[17] According to Cezar Stanciu, Romania opposed Mongolia's accession to the Warsaw Pact because it wanted to avoid the extension of defence guarantees to Mongolia by the WPO.[18] Focusing on Romania's role in blocking Mongolia's admission, this chapter sheds additional light on the reasons behind Bucharest's opposition, describes the tactics that ensured its success, presents new evidence that the initiative originated in Moscow and not in Ulan Bator, and contributes to the discussion of how Romania's opposition influenced Khrushchev's decision to renounce his initial position.

Until 1961, Romania's relations with the Asian socialist states existed within the Soviet system of alliances, at their basis being the proclaimed common struggle for the communist cause. Those relations had evolved within the framework provided by the treaties of friendship, cooperation and mutual assistance between Romania and the USSR (1948) and between the USSR and China (1950), whose stipulations were consolidated through the 1955 Warsaw Pact treaty. During the 1950s, when Sino–Soviet relations were rather cordial, Romania aligned with the Soviet policy towards Asia, expressing similar or common points of view towards problems such as the wars in Korea or Indochina, the liberation movements or decolonization.[19]

Compared with the situation in other Asian socialist states, after World War II, Romanian–Chinese relations had witnessed considerable improvement, although in absolute terms they remained rather modest. For instance, diplomatic relations between Romania and the People's Republic of China (PRC) were established in 1949, followed by the opening of the corresponding embassies in Beijing and Bucharest (in 1950), by the signing of a first commercial agreement (in 1953) and by the creation of an Association of Sino–Romanian Friendship (in 1958).[20] Romania's interest in other Asian socialist states was even more limited. For instance, Romanian–Mongolian diplomatic relations were established in April 1950, on the initiative of the latter party, and for more than a decade, the Romanian and Mongolian ambassadors in Moscow were to also hold the accreditation for, respectively, Mongolia and Romania. The two embassies were opened only in October 1963 in Bucharest and in January 1965 in Ulan Bator. Bilateral commercial trade was established in 1959, and the first multi-annual commercial agreement was signed in early 1963.[21]

China remained Romania's most prominent Asian partner, with mutual visits being organized at both party and state level during the 1950s and with a total value of bilateral trade reaching RUB60.2 million by 1960. However, given Bucharest's support for the Soviet side, as expressed during the Third Congress of the RWP in June 1960 and in the subsequent period, the following two years witnessed a deterioration of Romanian–Chinese political, economic and cultural relations, scheduled visits and cultural manifestations being cancelled at the request of the PRC, and the total value of bilateral trade decreasing by 1962 to RUB14 million.[22]

However, as Romanian–Soviet CMEA disagreements developed, in 1962–3, Romania began looking, within the camp, for allies to balance against the USSR. With this aim in mind, in 1963, Bucharest initiated a gradual rapprochement with Beijing. Thus, while the USSR was fostering CMEA specialization, using the argument that it was to the common benefit of the world socialist system, the Romanians were arguing that a world socialist system could not exist without the participation of the Asian socialist states, who should therefore be asked what they thought about the CMEA integration and about becoming full members of the Council. The Romanians knew that most likely China and other Asian states would not be interested in full CMEA membership, but they used the argument nevertheless in order to prolong and further complicate the integration debates, and to suggest to Moscow that, if its point of view on integration were not accommodated, Romania might slide towards China.[23]

As further detailed, Romania used a similar argument to block Mongolia's admission to the WPO, implying that if the Central Asian state's membership was necessary, so was the admission of other Asian socialist states, and that, given the implication of the move, all socialist countries should state their opinion, including Albania and the Asian states. From this point of view, the Romanian leadership masterfully juggled with (perceived) Soviet sensitivities towards the split within the communist movement.

Mongolia's Request for Admission

Throughout the Cold War, the relationship between the Asian socialist states and the WPO was influenced by the nature of the Sino–Soviet alliance.[24] As Albanian–Soviet and Sino–Soviet relations worsened, in the early 1960s, the socialist states began regrouping around Moscow and Beijing. In 1961, the Albanian leadership refused to attend the March meeting of the Political Consultative Committee (PCC) of the WPO, the August gathering of the WPO's first party secretaries or the October Congress of the Communist Party of the Soviet Union (CPSU) – all held in Moscow.[25] At that congress, Khrushchev severely criticized the Albanian leadership, with all the other WPO leaders following his lead. The Chinese delegation did not agree with this attack on a fraternal party and, eventually, left the congress early in protest. All other Asian socialist states, except Mongolia, allied with the Chinese delegation, refusing to denounce Albania,[26] and, as Laurien Crump phrased it, the socialist camp and the communist world 'suddenly seemed to have split in two, with the Asian leaders and Albania, on the one side, and the other Warsaw Pact leaders and Mongolia on the other'.[27]

During the final day of the CPSU's congress, on 31 October 1961, the leaders of the WPO member states (except Albania) jointly acted to exclude the Asian observers from the WPO's meetings. In a letter sent to the central committees of the parties from China, North Korea, North Vietnam and Mongolia, they argued that the Asian observers should be represented in the WPO meetings by their party and government leaders and not by low-ranking representatives. The letter notified its recipients that a 'conclusion had been reached' such that when the Asian socialist states were not represented at the highest level they would be 'directly informed' about the problems discussed in the PCC meetings, and that the presence of their observers was no longer necessary.[28] In its letter of response from 20 November, the Chinese leadership argued that it 'could not' and it 'must not' agree to allow other fraternal parties and states to decide the level of representation of the Chinese Party and State at any international gathering.[29] No other Chinese observer ever attended subsequent PCC meetings – an example followed by the other Asian socialist states, with the exception of Mongolia. As the Sino–Soviet split developed, the Asian socialist states were pressured to take sides, and gradually North Korea and North Vietnam sided with China and 'became virulently anti-Soviet', as historian Sergey Radchenko put it, while Mongolia 'unequivocally sided with Moscow'.[30]

During the 5–20 July 1963 Sino–Soviet talks in Moscow, the Soviet and Chinese leaderships attempted once more to tackle their ideological disagreements, but, with the Chinese representatives refusing to accept any form of cooperation between the socialist world and the USA, and with their Soviet counterparts defending the principle of peaceful coexistence, negotiations collapsed.[31] Propelled by this failure, on 16 July, Soviet–American–British negotiations on the Limited Test Ban Treaty (LTBT) resumed in Moscow, and on 25 July they concluded successfully.[32] The Chinese leadership fiercely denounced the LTBT, seen in Beijing as a Soviet–US attempt to maintain 'nuclear monopoly'.[33] According to a previous proposal, on 26 July, the WPO PCC should have decided on the Mongolian People's Republic's request to join the Pact – a proposal generally seen, by scholars and contemporaries alike, as another Soviet manoeuvre targeting China.[34]

Romania had received this request on 11 July 1963 in the form of a letter from Nikita Khrushchev. Dated 10 July and sent to the leaders of all WPO member states[35] excluding Albania, the missive called for consultations with regard to Mongolia's desire to be admitted into the WPO and announced that, given Mongolia's aspirations to world peace, the CPSU had a 'positive attitude' towards its request, which, therefore, deserved to be supported by all members of the Pact. Since Albania no longer participated in WPO meetings, Khrushchev contended, securing its consent was not an issue; he argued further that the admission of a non-European state into the Pact would probably necessitate a modification of Article 4 of the Pact's treaty. Mongolia's 1962 admission into the CMEA was used as an argument to support the enlargement of the WPO. The letter ended by stating that '[i]n case of a general agreement, Mongolia's admission could be accomplished' in July 1963, on the occasion of the CMEA conference, which was to bring all the WPO leaders together in Moscow.[36]

However, it was only several days later, on 15 July, that the Politburo of the Central Committee of the Mongolian People's Revolutionary Party (MPRP) formally decided to join the Warsaw Pact. The resolution adopted on that occasion argued that the American imperialists were using the treaty concluded in January 1960 between the USA and Japan 'to turn Japanese territory into their own military base' and to 'try to equip the Japanese army with nuclear weapons', thus 'creating a real threat to the freedom and sovereignty of the MPR and to the efforts of the Mongolian people to construct socialism'. Given 'the aforementioned threat', and 'noting the necessity of strengthening' Mongolia's 'defense capacity', the party politburo instructed Yumjaagiyn Tsedenbal, the president of the Council of Ministers of the MPR, to formulate the request regarding Mongolia's admission into the WPO. On the same day, Tsedenbal sent József Cyrankiewicz, the president of Council of Ministers of the Polish People's Republic, a letter 'announcing' Mongolia's 'desire to accede' to the Warsaw Pact and asking the Polish Government 'to request the consent' of the other member states. According to this missive, the admission was necessary because Mongolia 'needed to strengthen its defensive capabilities' against the American threat.[37]

On 15 July, Khrushchev sent another letter to the WPO leaders proposing the convening of the PCC after the conclusion of the CMEA conference.[38] Tsedenbal's letter, however, was never sent to Bucharest, a fact that displeased the Romanian leadership,[39] which therefore responded to Khrushchev's letter of 10 July. Generally, scholars argue that the Romanian response dates from 19 July (or even 20 July),[40] and that the RWP CC Politburo decided its approach to this matter in its 18 July meeting.[41] However, according to the minutes of the 18 July politburo meeting, by that time, the Romanian leadership had already transmitted its response to Moscow, through the intermediary of a 16 July letter and of talks with Ivan Kuzmich Zhegalin, the Soviet ambassador in Bucharest.

According to Gheorghiu-Dej and his politburo colleagues, the proposal was another Soviet anti-Chinese move that, if allowed to succeed, would further aggravate international tensions. Furthermore, according to perceptions and interpretations in Bucharest, strained international relations were not in Romania's interest. Thus, Romania was against Mongolia's admission into the WPO for several reasons.

First, according to the Romanian leaders, it was not in the country's interest to let itself become involved in the Sino–Soviet dispute, and accepting or rejecting Mongolia's request was, they believed, a way of doing precisely that. Moreover, they considered that it was also not in Romania's interest to allow Khrushchev to make declarations on its behalf. According to their perceptions, in the early 1960s, Romania's interests (security interests included) were threatened by the Soviet way of conducting international policy. Khrushchev was seen as unpredictable and reckless, manifesting a tendency to unilaterally involve its allies in the USSR's confrontations and disputes with third parties – whether Western or not. During the Cuban Missile Crisis, for instance, Romania had been on the verge of being bombed without even knowing why or by whom, Gheorghiu-Dej argued in a politburo meeting from February 1963 (and many times afterwards), because, amongst other things, Khrushchev used to make declarations on behalf of Moscow's allies without even consulting them. The same had happened, he observed, when the Soviet leaders fostered CMEA reformation through integration or bloc manoeuvres against the Chinese.[42] This perceived Soviet tactic infuriated Gheorghiu-Dej who, observing that 'there are attempts to introduce [in practice] things that have not even been discussed', considered that

> Nobody has the right, no matter who that would be, to make public declarations on our behalf. We did not give any mandate to anyone in this regard [...] We cannot accept such a thing, we cannot make declarations on behalf of any country, and absolutely nobody has the right to make declarations on our behalf.[43]

Observing that Sino–Soviet party relations had moved onto the level of state relations, pressuring other communist parties and socialist states to align with one or the other, the Romanian leadership often argued that Romania and the RWP supported neither of the two sides, which, it was emphasized, did not amount to being neutral. In 1963, the Romanians were particularly worried about rumours that the 'Chinese might break their relations with the Soviet Union', and interpreted the Soviet perceived initiative of bringing Mongolia into the WPO as a 'serious' act targeting China. What would the Chinese do if faced with such a 'provocative act'? Would it associate with North Vietnam and North Korea, and form its own military pact? Such an outcome would have been one of 'extreme gravity', the Romanian leadership believed, for all the countries of the socialist camp, including Romania.[44] Although much preoccupied with the issue, Romanian leaders were not able to reach any conclusion with regard to how the Soviets actually intended to use Mongolia's admission to the WPO. Did they fear that China would invade Mongolia? And if so, did the USSR want to use Mongolia's membership as a pretext to involve the WPO in military action against China? Were China and the USSR able to start a war against each other and to drag their allies into it?[45] The Romanians had no straight answer to such questions, but for them it was clear though that Mongolia's admission could only aggravate the international situation and that it was, therefore, not in Romania's interest either.[46]

Second, the Romanian leaders opposed the idea of collective (bloc) actions being taken against the Chinese because they feared the precedent that could be created in this way. A public condemnation of the Chinese within the CMEA or WPO frameworks or Mongolia's admission into the Pact were seen in Bucharest as coordinated anti-Chinese policies. If allowed to succeed, such a precedent would, the Romanian leaders feared, eventually affect Romania's interests as well: one day, the USSR might coordinate common actions against China; the next, it could be Romania's turn. According to the Romanian leadership, it was irrelevant whether the 'Chinese theses' were right or wrong, the only thing that mattered was that every state and every party had the right to choose its own domestic and foreign policy.[47] Later, in secret Romanian–Chinese talks, the Romanian leaders also presented their opposition to Mongolia's admission to the WPO as an unrequested favour to China,[48] being a way of obtaining Beijing's benevolence towards Romania's CMEA cause.[49]

However, from the moment it received news of Mongolia's request, the Romanian leadership knew that it had to block it – its concern being not if but rather how to stop another initiative (perceived as coming) from Khrushchev. In elaborating its reply, the Romanian leadership – as Ion Gheorghe Maurer phrased it – 'started from the premise that tactically it was not a good thing to say either yes or no' to Khrushchev.[50] This approach had a double meaning.

First, it was a reference to Romania's *neither–nor* position towards the Sino-Soviet dispute – i.e., neither with the USSR nor with the PRC; neither against the first nor against the second. Thus, between June 1960 and March 1962, the Romanians had periodically criticized and condemned the Chinese policy; subsequently, however, they no longer participated in the public anti-Chinese campaign, adopting instead a new position towards the Sino–Soviet dispute. Although these Romanian views were not published until August 1963, they were communicated from late 1962 onwards to the Soviets, the Chinese and their supporters (Indian, Yugoslav or Korean). In answer to the perceived pressures to choose a side, Romanian representatives were instructed to respond that Romania and the RWP 'holds neither with the Soviets, nor with the Chinese'. This stance was defined along the following lines: refusing to pick or support any side; avoiding discussing the substance of Sino–Soviet disagreements; arguing that all divergences that could arise amongst the communist parties and socialist states had to be tackled through, and only through (multilateral) negotiations and comradely talks in the common interest of the strengthening of the unity of the communist camp; and commitment to the stipulations of the 1960 Moscow Declaration.[51] Thus, according to the views of the Romanian leadership, accepting or rejecting the proposal regarding Mongolia's admission into the WPO was not in accordance with their *neither–nor* position towards the Sino–Soviet dispute.

Second, however, they believed that, 'tactically', it was not in Romania's interest to upset a neighbouring (albeit allied) great power. During the tense Romanian–Soviet negotiations on the CMEA reformation process, from March to June 1963, various Soviet representatives, Khrushchev included, had often implied or directly stressed that the USSR was a great power bordering a Romanian state that did not have the capability to defend itself against Soviet strength. They repeatedly emphasized that Romania had fought against the USSR during World War II and that its recent 'unfriendly' and 'anti-Soviet actions' could lead to the termination of the Romanian–Soviet friendship framework – i.e., the Treaty of Friendship, Collaboration and Mutual Assistance – which could once again be replaced, they argued or implied, with hostile relations and even with a state of war.[52] On 8 June 1963, for instance, complaining that the Romanian leadership had informed Party members about Romanian–Soviet disagreements over the proposed CMEA integration, Khrushchev was telling Nicolae Ceaușescu that

> [Ion] Antonescu's armies occupied Odessa, Crimea, and [they] even reached Stalingrad. Many of the people who remember this [fact] are still alive [in the USSR]. We [the Romanian and Soviet leaderships] must not allow the return of the [Romanian–Soviet] relations from Antonescu's time. The fact that you [Romania] appealed to the masses could encourage us [the USSR] to appeal to the masses as well.[53]

Such allusions were deciphered in Bucharest as threats: in Gheorghiu-Dej's words, as a Soviet attempt to 'intimidate' and to force Romania to 'exculpate' itself from the blame of having been a threat to the USSR's security interests.[54] Such threats – as well as other factors – convinced the Romanian leaders that it was not in Bucharest's interest to antagonize the USSR at any cost, and that 'we have the interest to maintain good relations with our Soviet comrades'.[55] However, they believed that, although possible, it was rather unlikely for the USSR to take any action to back up its threats because, in their view, for security, economic and prestige reasons it was not in the USSR's interest to break off its alliance with Romania.[56]

Secret Romanian–Soviet Talks

Given such perceptions and interpretations, when presented with (perceived) Soviet projects that they considered unacceptable, the Romanian leaders, instead of openly resisting them, preferred to use alternative opposition tactics – i.e., postponement, alteration, appealing to authority and even employing indirect threats. Thus, instead of openly agreeing or disagreeing with Khrushchev's perceived proposal of bringing Mongolia into the WPO, the Romanian leaders argued that, before taking any decision, the Pact members needed to thoroughly analyse it, in order to fully comprehend its juridical and political implications.[57]

Responding to the Soviet proposal, Romania's leaders claimed that 'it was not clear' how Mongolia's admission would affect the functioning of the WPO, and argued that before making any decision the member states had to examine its military, political and juridical aspects. First Secretary Gheorghe Gheorghiu-Dej implied that Bucharest would not agree to the modification of the treaty or to Mongolia's admission to the Pact, and that one might also raise the issue of admitting other Asian countries to the WPO. Given the complexity of the problem and its implications, Gheorghiu-Dej argued that the PCC would not have 'enough time to reach a definitive conclusion', implying thereby that Romania would not accept it.[58]

The Romanian leadership, however, considered that Khrushchev could not simply withdraw his proposal without looking weak, both domestically and abroad. Thus, seeking (legal and political) arguments to block his proposal, they were also thinking about what type of pretext the Soviet leader could accept and use to back down from his initial position, without appearing compromised. The Romanian delegation left for Moscow convinced that in its discussions with the Soviets, it would have to employ all the arguments it could think of to postpone the tackling, within the PCC, of the proposed Mongolian admission. The Romanians did not want a multilateral debate within the PCC framework; they wanted to address the problem bilaterally and secretly with the Soviets, hoping to obtain in this way a *sine die* postponement of addressing the issue in the PCC. They considered that their approach had a high chance of success and that, faced with their arguments and insinuations, the Soviets were most likely to drop their proposal.

However, they did not exclude the possibility that the Soviets would insist on addressing Mongolia's admission in the PCC framework, and for that situation the delegation was mandated to present to the PCC a different 'point of view of the Romanian part' – a document that was to be drafted in Moscow, if the situation demanded it. The Romanian delegation was also authorized to insist in its talks with the Soviets that there was no real imperialist threat against Mongolia, since this country had no border with any capitalist state; that Mongolia was not in need of military assistance, since it had treaties of mutual assistance concluded with both its neighbours; that Mongolia's admission into the WPO had the potential to obstruct US–Soviet negotiations on the LTBT; that 'Mongolia as a military force [did] not matter'; and that its admission would give satisfaction to the Americans, who could further criticize the WPO's policy. The delegation left for Moscow with the explicit mandate to end its line of argument with the 'request' that WPO members not hurry towards making any decision.[59]

The Romanian delegation to Moscow was formed of Gheorghe Gheorghiu-Dej (first secretary of the CC of the RWP and president of the State Council of Romania), Ion Gheorghe Maurer (member of the Politburo of the CC of the RWP and president of the Council of Ministers), Emil Bodnăraș (politburo member and vice-president of the Council of Ministers), Alexandru Bîrlădeanu (alternate member of the Politburo and vice-president of the Council of Ministers), Leonte Răutu (alternate member of the CC of the RWP and head of the Propaganda and Culture Section of the CC of the RWP), Nicolae Guină (member of the CC of the RWP and Romania's ambassador in Moscow) and a group of economic experts.[60] On 25 July, another, 'military', delegation – headed by Leontin Sălăjan, the minister of the armed forces – was to arrive in Moscow, in order to participate at the session of the PCC.[61]

The delegation thus left for the PCC meeting in Moscow with two aims in mind: to avoid any discussion of Mongolia's admission to the WPO and to avoid any additional expenses with regard to its military endowment – both of which aims were achieved. In July 1963, however, the delegates had arrived in Moscow prepared to oppose the USSR and its allies not only on these two aforementioned issues but also with regard to the perceived attempts to impose bloc coordination towards CMEA integration and towards condemning the Chinese. The Romanian leaders feared that the Soviets might have tried to use the CMEA and WPO gatherings to impose a common public condemnation of the Chinese. They even feared that Khrushchev might try to impose a common declaration condemning China's policy. Were something like that to happen, then the Romanian delegation was mandated to block it as well.[62]

On 23 July, Andrei Gromyko, the minister of foreign affairs of the USSR, met in Moscow with Gheorghiu-Dej, Maurer, Bodnăraș, Răutu and Bîrlădeanu, and addressed the issues that had been raised by the Romanians in their 16 July letter of response and in their talks with the Soviet Ambassador in Bucharest. Gromyko argued that Mongolia's admission was 'a reaction' to the 'aggressive' US policy in Asia, and that the capitalists could conduct airborne operations in Mongolia, which might transform it into a bridgehead to be used against socialist states in the region. Gromyko further stressed that the initiative of requesting

WPO membership belonged to the Mongolian leadership, 'without being influenced by anybody'. Regarding the accession of other socialist states from Asia to the Pact, such a problem did not exist, Gromyko argued, as China, North Korea and North Vietnam had formulated no request. But, if they 'will make requests to enter the organization, the Soviet part can have but a positive attitude'. The Soviet representative contended that the consent of all states was not necessary in this matter, and implied that if Romania, as a part of the WPO, 'did not comply with its obligations', it could be 'forbidden to use the rights' from which it benefited as a member state.[63]

Responding to Gromyko, Gheorghiu-Dej emphasized that, formulating its considerations, the Romanian part had in mind the 'desire' to think carefully and to avoid making a hasty decision that would 'sharpen even more the divergences existing within the communist movement'. The Romanian leadership was preoccupied not with what the capitalists might say, but with what the Albanian, the Chinese and even the Romanian people might say. 'Is there an imminent and direct danger that makes Mongolia's admission to the Warsaw Treaty necessary at right this moment?' the Romania leader asked rhetorically.[64] Gheorghiu-Dej, Maurer and Bodnăraş emphasized the fact that Mongolia's admission into the WPO was not in accordance with the general policy of the socialist states that had committed themselves to limit the expansion of military pacts and to strengthen peace. Such a move did not match with the ongoing negotiations regarding the limiting of the nuclear tests, they argued. 'If we strengthen this [Warsaw Pact] treaty through the admission of the Mongolian People's Republic, of the Chinese People's Republic, of the Democratic People's Republic of Korea and of the Democratic Republic of Vietnam wouldn't we increase the possibility of a general clash' instead of strengthening peace, the Romanian delegates asked – once again, rhetorically. They further argued that the danger of 'imperialist aggression' against Mongolia was 'small' because it would have to be done over the territory of the USSR or China. Implying that, in their opinion, the move was actually directed against China, the delegates contended that Mongolia's admission to the WPO would aggravate not only party relations, but also state relations within the communist camp.

In their discussion with Gromyko, the delegates also suggested that Romania could not officially respond to the proposal regarding

Mongolia's admission because its party and state forums, as well as the Romanian people, had not discussed the matter and had not yet made any decision. This was also an indirect threat towards making public Romania's opposition to Mongolia's admission. Insisting that such a move would break any possibility of negotiating an agreement with China, Gheorghiu-Dej ended the talks with Gromyko by appealing to the Soviets to postpone tackling the issue:

> Let us not transfer the divergences that have appeared at the level of parties [relations] to the level of states [relations]. Let us not precipitate, let us wait a little. We [Romanians] would desire to postpone the discussion of Mongolia's request for admission to the WTO.

How long should one postpone, Gromyko asked, and Gheorghiu-Dej responded that 'we did not think [of] a precise term'. Gheorghiu-Dej also emphasized that the Romanian delegation would like to present its considerations to Khrushchev directly.[65]

The indirect threat of making public Romania's dissenting position must be placed in the general context of Romanian–Soviet relations at the time. In March–June 1963, intense bilateral talks had been held with regard to the attempted CMEA integration. One of the tactics that the Romanians used to block this possibility comprised threatening the Soviets with making public Bucharest's opposition not only to the integration but also in matters related to the 'unity of the camp' – and not only domestically (in CC plenums, in regional party meetings) but internationally as well (in CMEA gatherings, in open letters, in newspaper articles or in party declarations). The Romanians were convinced that Moscow wanted to preserve the image of a united bloc, and that it therefore did not want additional public divergences with Bucharest. In the spring of 1963, the Romanian leaders began putting these threats into practice, by discussing Romania's opposition to the CMEA integration in the plenary session of the CC of the RWP from 5 to 8 March and in party meetings organized around the country, which led Khrushchev to accuse them of making 'the big secrets' public. Fearing that bloc integration might be forced on Romania at the July 1963 CMEA meeting, the country's leadership did take into consideration the possibility of escalating the issue – i.e., making its opposition public at the CMEA conference, in front of all the bloc leaders. If, despite this action, the integration pressures continued, then, the Romanian leadership decided, once returned to Bucharest, they could publish, in some form or another (article, open letter, party declaration) their opposition. However, presented with such threats, Khrushchev compromised and in late June 1963 a secret verbal agreement was reached, according to which the Soviets agreed to postpone the CMEA integration debates while the Romanians assented to refrain from making public their dissenting views. As Ion Gheorghe Maurer later put it, in June 1963, Romanian–Soviet divergences regarding the CMEA reforms were once again 'solved through postponement'. Observing the development of the Sino–Soviet dispute, in 1963, the Romanians believed that their tactic of threatening to publicize Romania's divergent viewpoint had a great chance of being successful,[66] and therefore they used it to block not only the CMEA integrations but also Mongolia's admission to the WPO.

However, appealing to the Central Committee of the RWP was not only about threatening to make Romania's opposition public. It was also about postponing the issue at hand and about appealing to the party authority. In the early 1960s, when it did not want to agree with a Soviet (or bloc) proposal, the Romanian leadership argued that it could not give a response as the CC of the RWP had not made a decision on the matter just yet. In this way, in an initial phase, addressing of the problem was prolonged by asking for time for the CC to reach a decision. In the following phase, however, the CC plenum would reject the proposal, which allowed the Romanian leaders to argue afterwards that they had no option but to comply with a party decision.[67]

In the case of Mongolia's admission, the Romanian leaders implied that the delegation in Moscow could take no official stance on the matter within the PCC since the RWP had not analyzed and had not made a decision in that respect. On 24 July, during the first break of the CMEA proceedings, Khrushchev came to the Romanian delegation to discuss Mongolia's request. Gheorghiu-Dej pleaded with him to not put the issue on the agenda of the PCC. In his own words, 'we insistently ask you [for it] to not be on the agenda, to be taken out, to be postponed.' According to Romanian sources, Khrushchev responded as follows:

I took note of your considerations. In a potential conflict, Mongolia's territory could become a bridgehead for launching airborne operations, but this is not the right moment for adhering. Today, the treaty on the banning of the tests with the nuclear weapon will be signed, which will have a great echo in the whole world. In this atmosphere of international détente, the strengthening of the Warsaw Treaty through the adhering of Mongolia will be incomprehensible. This is why I told Gromyko to discuss with comrade Tsedenbal, to explain him the situation and to ask him to postpone the request. I think the Mongolian comrades will understand.[68]

This response is evidence that Romania's opposition played a role in Khrushchev's decision to drop the proposal. According to the perceptions of the Romanian leaders, from the arguments that they used to block Mongolia's admission, Moscow had 'retained' the one that placed the initial proposal as far as possible from the Chinese problem – i.e., the idea that public opinion would not understand why, on the one hand, the WPO was strengthened through the admission of Mongolia, while, on the other, international détente was actively sought through the conclusion of the LTBT. However, the Romanian leaders considered that this was just a convenient pretext and that the Soviets had actually abandoned their proposal because, after the Sino–Soviet split, they wanted to avoid the emergence of another public divergence within the camp – this time, with Romania.[69]

The session of the PCC opened on 26 July. By that time, Moscow had already decided 'to not tease the Romanians' on the occasion of that meeting.[70] The available archival evidence on the talks held in this session is ambivalent,[71] but according to the minutes of the 31 July meeting of the Politburo of the CC of the RWP, and according to a document from the Hungarian archives, it appears that Mongolia's request was briefly discussed at the opening of session. According to the Hungarian report, 'the only negative reaction to it was [expressed] by the Romanians', who 'essentially said that they were not against it' but questioned its necessity, especially in that particular moment, when 'the nuclear test ban treaty had just been signed'. Khrushchev argued that there was a contradiction between Mongolia's admission to the Warsaw Pact, which implied the existence of a threat, and the concluding of the

LTBT, which signalled international détente. He also noted that 'it was still impossible to foresee which way the debate would go, as the preliminary reactions were mixed'. Then Tsedenbal spoke, asking for the decision on Mongolia's request to be postponed. The other participants agreed, and it was decided by the PCC not to discuss the matter.[72] In the 31 July politburo meeting, Gheorghiu-Dej briefly and vaguely summarized his intervention in the PCC session as follows:

> I came with the opinion regarding Mongolia. It was accepted immediately. You [the politburo members] should know that I made a declaration that 'we will stand by you, but we have the duty to draw your attention to what will happen.'[73]

Khrushchev's concern with the 'mixed preliminary reactions' suggests that he had changed his mind, influenced by the opposition expressed by the Romanians,[74] which challenges the scholarly conventional interpretation[75] that he was primarily concerned with the contradiction between the signing of the LTBT and the admission of Mongolia into the WPO.

Conclusion

Scholars sometimes argue that Romania's success in blocking Mongolia's admission to the Warsaw Pact 'marked a reorientation in Romanian foreign policy'[76] or that this was the first time that the country had opposed the USSR at all.[77] It was, however, just one example of Romania's opposition to (perceived) Soviet proposals – one amongst many that, behind the scenes in the early 1960s, were able to successfully oppose Soviet projects whether they concerned the WPO, the CMEA or the communist movement as a whole.[78]

This chapter has discovered that, in the complicated context of relations between Romania, the USSR and China, the Romanian leadership opposed the perceived Soviet proposal of bringing Mongolia into the WPO in order to avoid the anticipated (perceived) negative effects that Mongolia's membership would have had on Romania's interests (security interests included). This case points to the fact that Romania's opposition to the USSR was a reaction to a perceived threat, while its aim was to block or to eliminate that particular threat without causing additional tensions with the USSR. To spare the (perceived) sensibilities of the USSR, the Romanians preferred to formulate their opposition in secret bilateral talks, occasions on which they used a wide variety of tactics to reach their goals. Their opposition was indirect, the Romanians avoiding openly criticizing the Soviet proposal and choosing instead to discuss its 'legal and political implications'. In secret party meetings, the Romanians considered that the Soviet initiative of bringing Mongolia into the WPO was reckless and dangerous, with the potential to create additional international tensions. In bilateral (or even multilateral) talks, however, they did not openly oppose the proposal, asking instead for detailed studies on it and arguing that more time was needed for the RWP to reach a decision. Formally, the Romanians declared their accord with the proposal, but they also brought to the discussion additional questions and counterproposals that altered, complicated and therefore prolonged the original initiative. They even formulated indirect threats. One such threat was that Romania could make its secret divergences with the USSR public. The country's leaders were convinced that given the USSR's disputes with China and Albania, the superpower was particularly sensitive to the emergence of any additional intra-bloc or intra-camp public divergence, or to any Romanian–Chinese alignment.

This chapter also found that Romania's opposition to Mongolia's membership played a role in Khrushchev's decision to drop the proposal, and presented additional evidence that the initiative had in fact originated in Moscow and not in Ulan Bator. On a different level, this case study proves that in 1963 Romania had more room to manoeuvre in its relations with the USSR than has been observed by the dominant scholarship. It is not yet clear whether the Poles had also expressed their concerns with regard to Mongolia's admission but, regardless, by mid-1963 Romania had proved, in CMEA and WPO frameworks alike, that it had the will and the capacity to turn around a Soviet decision that had been accepted by all the other members of the bloc, while the USSR seemed unable to coordinate the policy of the bloc against the will of a single small ally. However, Romania opposed only those Soviet projects perceived as being dangerous and contrary to its interests. As Emil Bodnăraş later expressed it, 'despite all the differences we [Romania and the USSR] have, we [Romania] are interested to have good relations with a powerful neighbor' and for that reason 'anywhere we [Romanians] meet them [the Soviets], we say no to the problems we disagree with, but we seek the point where we can say yes'.[79] Once established in the early 1960s, this Romanian approach to the USSR remained valid for decades to come.

Notes

1. Regarding the independence vs. autonomy interpretations, see Elena Dragomir, 'The perceived threat of hegemonism in Romania during the second détente', *Cold War History*, 12 (1) (2012), pp. 111–15.
2. See, for instance, Vladimir Tismăneanu, *Stalinism for all Seasons. A Political History of Romanian Communism* (Berkeley, CA, 2003), p. 167; Gheorghe Ciobanu, *Relațiile internaționale ale României între anii 1948–1964* [Romania's international relations between 1948 and 1964] (Iași, 2006), p. 38; Dennis Deletant, 'Taunting the Bear: Romania and the Warsaw Pact, 1963–89', *Cold War History*, 7 (4) (2007), p. 496; Mioara Anton, *Ieșirea din cerc. Politica externă a regimului Gheorgiu-Dej* [Exit the circle. The foreign policy of Gheorghiu-Dej's regime] (Bucharest, 2007), pp. 17–31; Cezar Stanciu, *Devotați Kremlinului. Alinierea politicii externe românești la cea sovietică în anii'50* [Devoted to the Kremlin. The alignment of the Romanian foreign policy to the Soviet one in the 1950s] (Târgoviște, 2008), pp. 8–25.
3. See, for instance, Stelian Tănase, *Elite și societate. Guvernarea Gheorghiu-Dej, 1948–1965* [Elites and society. The government of Gheorghiu-Dej, 1948–1965] (Bucharest, 1998), pp. 123, 172, 192–9; Mihai Retegan, *In the Shadow of the Prague Spring: Romanian Foreign Policy and the Crisis in Czechoslovakia, 1968* (Iași, Oxford, 2000), pp. 19–22, 35–42.
4. For instance, see: Florian Banu and Liviu Țăranu, 'Studiu introductiv' [Introductory study], in Florian Banu and Liviu Țăranu, *Aprilie 1964. 'Primăvara de la București'. Cum s-a adoptat 'Declarația de independență' a României* [April 1964. 'The Bucharest spring'. How Romania's 'Declaration of Independence' was adopted] (Bucharest, 2004), VII–L; Brândușa Costache, 'Romania and Comecon. Principles of cooperation, 1949–1991', *Arhivele Totalitarismului* [Totalitarianism Archives], no. 1–2/2002, p. 168.
5. Robert Levy, *Ana Pauker. The Rise and Fall of a Jewish Communist* (Berkeley, CA, 2001), pp. 221–38; Banu and Țăranu, *Aprilie 1964*, XX–XXVI; Elena Dragomir, 'The Formation of the Soviet Bloc's Council for Mutual Economic Assistance. Romania's Involvement', *Journal of Cold War Studies*, 14 (1) (Winter 2012), pp. 34–47; Elena Dragomir, 'The Creation of the Council for Mutual Economic Assistance as seen from the Romanian Archives', *Historical Research*, 88 (240) (2015), pp. 355–79.
6. See, for instance, Liviu Țăranu, *România în Consiliul de Ajutor Economic Reciproc, 1949–1965* [Romania in the Council for Mutual Economic Assistance] (Bucharest, 2007), pp. 66–187; Elena Dragomir, 'Romania's Participation in the Agricultural Conference in Moscow, 2–3 February 1960', *Cold War History*, 13 (3) (2013), pp. 334–5.

7. Raymond L. Garthoff, 'When and why Romania distanced itself from the Warsaw Pact', in *Cold War International History Project Bulletin*, Issue 5 (Spring 1995), p. 111.
8. Mioara Anton, 'Introduction' in Mioara Anton, *România şi Tratatul de la Varşovia. Conferinţele miniştrilor afacerilor externe (1966-1991)* [Romania and the Warsaw Treaty. Conferences of the Foreign Ministers (1966-1991)] (Bucharest, 2009), p. XLVI.
9. Dan Cătănuş, 'România şi schisma sovieto-chineză, III. Criza albaneză' [Romania and the Sino-Soviet split, III. The Albanian Crisis], *Arhivele totalitarismului*, no. 3-4 (2000), p. 186.
10. Elena Dragomir, *Cold War Perceptions. Romania's Policy Change towards the USSR, 1960-1964* (Cambridge, 2015), pp. 241-2.
11. Mihai Croitor, *România şi conflictul sovieto-chinez (1956-1971)* [Romania and Soviet-Chinese conflict (1956-1971)] (Cluj-Napoca, 2009), pp. 16, 213.
12. Tismăneanu, *Stalinism for all Seasons*, pp. 178-81; Constantin Moraru, *Politica externă a României, 1958-1964* [Romania's foreign policy, 1958-1964] (Bucharest, 2008), pp. 77-8, 107; Dan Cătănuş, *Tot mai departe de Moscova: Politica externă a României, 1956-1965* [Further from Moscow. Romania's foreign policy, 1956-1964] (Bucharest, 2011), p. 31.
13. Anton, *Ieşirea din cerc*, pp. 166-77, Croitor, *România şi conflictul sovieto-chinez*, pp. 242-50.
14. Moraru, *Politica externă a României*, p. 51.
15. Corneliu Filip, *Tratatul de la Varşovia* [The Warsaw Treaty] (Târgovişte, 2006), pp. 47-9; Petre Opriş, 'Solicitarea R.P. Mongole de a deveni stat membru al Organizaţiei Tratatului de la Varşovia (15 iulie 1963)' [The request of the Mongolian People's Republic to become a member state of the Warsaw Treaty Organization (15 July 1963)], *Buletinul Arhivelor Militare Române* [The Bulletin of the Romanian Military Archives], 3 (2008); pp. 85-92; Mihai Croitor and Sanda Borşa, *Triunghiul suspiciunii. Gheorghiu-Dej, Hruşciov şi Tito (1954-1964)* [The triangle of suspicion. Gheorghiu-Dej, Khrushchev and Tito (1954-1964)], vol. I (Cluj-Napoca, 2014), pp. 119-22.
16. Lorentz M. Lühti, 'The People's Republic of China and the Warsaw Pact Organization, 1955-63', *Cold War History*, 7 (4) (2007), pp. 486-8; Vojtech Mastny, 'The 1963 Nuclear Test Ban Treaty. A Missed Opportunity for Détente?', *Journal of Cold War Studies*, 10 (1) (Winter 2008), p. 19; Sergey Radchenko, *Two Suns in the Heavens. The Sino-Soviet Struggle for Supremacy, 1962-1967* (Washington, DC, 2009), p. 85.
17. Laurien Crump, *The Warsaw Pact Reconsidered. International Relations in Eastern Europe, 1955-1969* (London, 2015), pp. 76-7.
18. Cezar Stanciu, 'Fragile Equilibrium. Romania and the Vietnam War in the Context of the Sino-Soviet Split, 1966', *Journal of Cold War Studies*, 18 (1) (Winter 2016), pp. 180-1, fn. 80.

ROMANIA'S INVOLVEMENT IN THE SINO-SOVIET DISPUTE 245

19. Romulus Ioan Budura, 'Studiu introductiv' [Introductory study], in Romulus Ioan Budura (coordinator), *Relațiile Romano-Chineze, 1880–1974. Documente* [Romanian-Chinese relations, 1880–1974. Documents] (Bucharest, 2005), pp. 13, 16.
20. Telegrams between Romanian and Chinese authorities in ibid., pp. 197–203, 254, 375.
21. *Notes* regarding Romanian-Mongolian relations, The (Romanian) National Central Historical Archives (ANIC), Central Committee of Romanian Communist Party (CC of RCP), Office, File no 48/1971, vol. I, 93–7.
22. *Notes* and *Reports* by the Romanian Embassy in Beijing, in Budura, *Relațiile Romano-Chineze*, pp. 399, 408–10.
23. Dragomir, *Cold War Perceptions*, pp. 143–8.
24. Lühti, 'The People's Republic of China and the Warsaw Pact Organization', pp. 479–94.
25. Crump, *The Warsaw Pact Reconsidered*, pp. 64–71.
26. Lorentz M. Lühti, *The Sino-Soviet Split. Cold War in the Communist World* (Princeton, NJ, 2008), pp. 205–208.
27. Crump, *The Warsaw Pact Reconsidered*, p. 71.
28. The letter of the Central Committees of communist and workers parties of the WPO members addressed to the Central Committees of the communist and workers parties from China, North Korea, North Vietnam and Mongolia, 31 October 1961, ANIC, CC of RCP, Foreign Relations, Alphabetic, File no 16U/1962, pp. 36–7.
29. Letter of the CC of the Chinese Communist Party, addressed to the CC of the Romanian Worker's Party (RWP), 20 November 1961, ANIC, CC of RCP, Foreign Relations, Alphabetic, 9C/1961–1964, pp. 8–11.
30. Sergey S. Radchenko, *The Soviets' Best Friends in Asia. The Mongolia Dimension of the Sino-Soviet Split*, Working Paper no. 42, Woodrow Wilson International Center for Scholars (Washington, DC, 2003), p. 2.
31. Odd Arne Westad, 'The Sino-Soviet Alliance and the Unites States', in Odd Arne Westad (ed.), *Brothers in Arms. The Rise and Fall of the Sino-Soviet Alliance, 1945–1963* (Washington, DC, 1998), p. 180.
32. Mastny, 'The 1963 Nuclear Test Ban Treaty', p. 18.
33. David Scott, *China Stands Up. The PRC and the International System* (London, 2007), p. 47; Crump, *The Warsaw Pact Reconsidered*, p. 75.
34. Radchenko, *Two Suns in the Heavens*, 2009, pp. 84–5; Crump, *The Warsaw Pact Reconsidered*, p. 75; *Minutes of the meeting of the Politburo of the CC of the RWP, 18 July 1963*, ANIC, CC of RCP, Office, File 39/1963, pp. 121–39.
35. Lühti, 'The People's Republic of China and the Warsaw Pact Organization', p. 487.
36. Thus far, this letter has not been located in the Romanian archives, but it is quoted in a *Note regarding the problem of Mongolia's admission into the Warsaw Treaty Organization, 14 December 1963*, ANIC, CC of RCP, Foreign Relations, File 16U/1963, p. 179.

37. Tsedenbal's letter to Cyrankiewicz, 15 July 1963, Parallel History Project on NATO and the Warsaw Pact (PHP), www.isn.ethz.ch/php, by permission of the Center for Security Studies at ETH Zurich and the National Security Archive at the George Washington University on behalf of the PHP network. Available at http://www.php.isn.ethz.ch/kms2.isn.ethz.ch/serviceengine/Files/PHP/16340/ipublicationdocument_singledocument/9d8f8235-12eb-4d4f-8f14-668952034f1a/en/letter_630715_Eng.pdf (accessed September 2017).
38. Lühti, 'The People's Republic of China and the Warsaw Pact Organization', p. 487; *Minutes of the Politburo meeting, 18 July 1963*, ANIC, CC of RCP, Office, File 39/1963, p. 122.
39. *Minutes of the Politburo meeting, 18 July 1963*, ANIC, CC of RCP, Office, File 39/1963, p. 122.
40. Opriş, 'Solicitarea R.P. Mongole', p. 87.
41. For instance, Lühti, 'The People's Republic of China and the Warsaw Pact Organization', p. 488; Radchenko, *Two Suns in the Heavens*, p. 85; Crump, *The Warsaw Pact Reconsidered*, p. 76.
42. *Minutes of the Politburo meeting, 26-27 February 1963*, ANIC, CC of RCP, Office, File 4/1963, pp. 23–135; *Notes of the talks with Y.V. Andropov over lunch, 2 April 1963*, ANIC, CC of RCP, Foreign Relations, File 13/ 1963, pp. 1–6.
43. *Minutes of the Plenum of the CC of the RWP, 5–8 March 1963*, ANIC, CC of RCP, Office, File 10/1963, pp. 5–8.
44. *Minutes of the Politburo meeting, 18 July 1963*, ANIC, CC of RCP, Office, File 39/1963, pp. 116–38.
45. In 1962, Nicu Gheorghe, Romania's military attaché in Beijing, was informing Bucharest that China would possess the nuclear bomb in a 'not very distant future'. *Note, 18 January 1962*, ANIC, CC of RCP, Administrative-Political Section, File 7/1962, p. 16.
46. *Minutes of the Plenum of the CC of the RWP, 17 February 1964*, in Dan Cătănuş, *Între Beijing şi Moscova. România şi conflictul sovieto-chinez, 1957–1965 (Documente)* [Between Beijing and Moscow. Romania and the Soviet-Chinese conflict, 1957–1965 (Documents)] (Bucharest, 2004), p. 284.
47. *Minutes of the Politburo meeting, 26–27 February, 1963*, ANIC, CC of RCP, Office, File 4/1963, pp. 23–135; *Minutes of the Politburo meeting, 18 July 1963*, ANIC, CC of RCP, Office, File 39/1963, pp. 121–39.
48. *Note of the talks between Gheorghe Gheorghiu-Dej and Liu Fang, the Chinese ambassador in Romania, 5 June 1964*, in Budura, *Relaţiile Romano-Chineze*, p. 476.
49. Dragomir, *Cold War Perceptions*, pp. 171–7.
50. *Minutes of the Politburo meeting, 18 July 1963*, ANIC, CC of RCP, Office, File 39/1963, pp. 122–37.
51. Dragomir, *Cold War Perceptions*, pp. 131–40, 162.
52. Khrushchev's *Letter to Gheorghiu-Dej, 23 May 1963*, annotated by Gheorghiu-Dej, ANIC, CC of RCP, Foreign Relations, File 18 U/1963, pp. 169–82; *Minutes of the meeting between the Romanian and the Soviet delegations, 3 June 1963*

and *Minutes of the Politburo meeting on 5 June 1963*, ANIC, CC of RCP, Office, File 24/1963, pp. 2–20; File 25/1963, pp. 1–28.
53. *Note on the talks between N. Ceaușescu and N.S. Khrushchev*, 8 June 1963, Moscow, ANIC, CC of RCP, Foreign Relations, 17U/1963, pp. 33–52.
54. Khrushchev's *Letter to Gheorghiu-Dej, 23 May 1963*, annotated by Gheorghiu-Dej, ANIC, CC of RCP, Foreign Relations, File 18 U/1963, pp. 169–82.
55. *Minutes of the meeting between the Soviet and the Romanian delegations, 26 May 1963*, in Mihai Retegan, *Războiul politic în blocul communist. Relații româno-sovietice în anii șaizeci (documente)* [Political war in the communist bloc. Romanian-Soviet relations in the nineteen-sixties] (Bucharest, 2002), p. 243.
56. *Minutes of the Politburo meeting from 5 June 1963*, ANIC, CC of RCP, Office, File 25/1963, pp. 13–18.
57. *Minutes of the Politburo meeting, 18 July 1963*, ANIC, CC of RCP, Office, File 39/1963, pp. 122–7.
58. Gheorghiu-Dej's *Letter to Khrushchev, 16 July 1963*, ANIC, CC of RCP, Foreign Relations, File 17U/1963, pp. 142–5.
59. *Minutes of the Politburo meeting, 18 July 1963*, ANIC, CC of RCP, Office, File 39/1963, pp. 123–6; *Minutes of the Politburo meeting, 31 July 1963*, ANIC, CC of RCP, Office, File 41/1963, pp. 15–21.
60. *Minutes of the CMEA meeting in Moscow, July 1963*, ANIC, CC of RCP, Foreign Relations, File 25/1963, vol. I, p. 10.
61. *Minutes of the Politburo meeting, 18 July 1963*, ANIC, CC of RCP, Office, File 39/1963, pp. 137–8.
62. Ibid., pp. 116–38.
63. *Note regarding the problem of Mongolia's admission into the Warsaw Treaty Organization, 14 December 1963*, ANIC, CC of RCP, Foreign Relations, File 16U/1963, pp. 182–6; *Note of the talks between Gheorghe Gheorghiu-Dej, Ion Gheorghe Maurer, Emil Bodnăraș, Leonte Răutu, Alexandru Bîrlădeanu, Andrei Gromyko, and N.S. Khrushchev, 23–24 July 1963*, ANIC, CC of RCP, Foreign Relations, File 24/1963, vol. II, pp. 82–9.
64. Ibid.
65. Ibid.; *Minutes of the Politburo meeting, 31 July 1963*, ANIC, CC of RCP, Office, File 41/1963, pp. 16–20.
66. Dragomir, *Cold War Perceptions*, pp. 87, 110–27.
67. Ibid., pp. 61–89.
68. *Note regarding the problem of Mongolia's admission into the Warsaw Treaty Organization, 14 December 1963*, ANIC, CC of RCP, Foreign Relations, Alphabetical, File 16U/1963, p. 186.
69. *Minutes of the Politburo meeting, 31 July 1963*, ANIC, CC of RCP, Office, File 41/1963, pp. 20–1, 48, 54–8.
70. Miller Center, *Minutes 107a of 23 July 1963*. Available at http://web1.millercenter.org/kremlin/63_07_23.pdf (accessed September 2017).

71. Leontin Sălăjan's *Report* (with *Annexes*) on the PCC session contained no reference to any discussions held about Mongolia's request. ANIC, CC of RCP, Foreign Relations, File no 24/1963, vol. II, pp. 106–19.
72. *Report on the 6th PCC Meeting (26 July 1963) by First Secretary of the Hungarian Socialist Workers' Party (János Kádár) to the Hungarian Politburo (31 July 1963)*. Available at PHP, http://www.php.isn.ethz.ch/kms2.isn.ethz.ch/serviceengine/Files/PHP/17907/ipublicationdocument_singledocument/eb0bdfdd-f938-4d90-8d73-7d317e8936a1/en/630731_Excerpts_Eng.pdf (accessed September 2017).
73. *Minutes of the Politburo meeting, 31 July 1963*, ANIC, CC of RCP, Office, File 41/1963, pp. 48–9.
74. Observing its 'political consequences', the Polish authorities too considered the proposal 'dubious and risky', directed against China, and risking triggering the creation of military pacts within the camp. Adam Rapacki's *Memorandum, 20 July 1963*. Available at PHP, http://www.php.isn.ethz.ch/kms2.isn.ethz.ch/serviceengine/Files/PHP/17905/ipublicationdocument_singledocument/afb9c738-3b70-4c98-98a2-3fbf7dc35f48/en/630720_Memo_Eng.pdf (accessed September 2017).
75. Radchenko, *Two Suns in the Heavens*, p. 85; Mastny, 'The 1963 Nuclear Test Ban Treaty', p. 19.
76. Crump, *The Warsaw Pact Reconsidered*, p. 77.
77. Filip, *Tratatul de la Varșovia*, p. 49.
78. Dragomir, 'Romania's Participation in the Agricultural Conference in Moscow', pp. 331–51, Dragomir, *Cold War Perceptions*, pp. 75–127, 179–85, 232–6.
79. *Minutes of the talks between Emil Bodnăraș and Zhou Enlai, 12 May 1966*, in Romulus Ioan Budura (coordinator), *Politica independentă a României și relațiile româno-chineze, 1954–1975. Documente* [Romania's independent policy and Romanian-Chinese relations, 1954–1975. Documents] (Bucharest, 2008), p. 283.

CHAPTER 10

CZECHOSLOVAK ASSISTANCE TO KENYA AND UGANDA, 1962–8

Philip E. Muehlenbeck

The colonies of British East Africa did not obtain their independence until a few years after the initial wave of independence hit the continent (Tanganyika, 1961; Uganda, 1962; Kenya, 1963). As a result, unlike the rest of Africa, where economic relations were paramount in Prague's relationships with newly independent African states, in British East Africa the Czechoslovak Socialist Republic (ČSSR) focused more on developing political relations with the future leaders of the decolonizing states.[1] In the late 1950s, although Czechoslovakia's economic relations with the region were limited, and Kenya and Uganda were still under British colonial rule, this did not prevent Prague from developing substantial contacts with the nationalist movements in both colonies in an effort to gain political capital in the soon-to-be independent states. In the months leading up to independence and for the first half-decade afterwards, political leaders in both African countries sought relations with Czechoslovakia as leverage against domestic political rivals as well as against their Western allies. This chapter will provide an overview of Czechoslovakia's involvement with Uganda and Kenya from 1962 to 1968, and explain how Czechoslovak aid allowed these African countries to gain a degree of autonomy from both their former colonizer and the Cold War superpowers while also playing a role in domestic political rivalries.

Czechoslovak Relations with Kenya Prior to Independence

Czechoslovakia first opened a diplomatic outpost in Kenya in 1937 in Mombasa.² However, following Czechoslovakia's occupation by Nazi Germany in March 1939, the majority of the Czechoslovak diplomatic offices around the world, including those in Africa, ceased to operate. A few, including the embassy in Cairo and consulates in Casablanca and Cape Town, continued functioning on behalf of the Germans. During World War II, the only remaining representation in Africa for the London-based Czechoslovak exile government was the honorary consulate in Kenya (which was based in Mombasa at the outset of the war, but moved its operations to Nairobi in 1942).³ Kenya therefore became the only country on the African continent in which Czechoslovakia had uninterrupted diplomatic representation from 1937 through to the 1960s.

As independence approached in the early 1960s, Kenya was also the colony that Czechoslovak officials believed held the most promise in British East Africa for orienting its foreign policies towards the Soviet bloc. This was largely because, like their counterparts in the West, Eastern bloc observers mistakenly viewed the Mau Mau uprising as communist-inspired. Prague therefore made an intensive effort to establish relations with Jomo Kenyatta's Kenyan African National Union (KANU) – and in particular with the party's left wing, which was led by KANU's vice-president, Oginga Odinga.

Kenyatta was a Kikuyu (Kenya's largest ethnic group) pan-Africanist intellectual who had studied social anthropology at University College London and the London School of Economics. While living in the United Kingdom, he had collaborated with pan-Africanists such as George Padmore, C. L. R. James and Kwame Nkrumah, and in 1945 helped organize the fifth Pan-African Congress, which took place in Manchester. He became active in Kenyan nationalist politics upon returning to Kenya in 1946, and was eventually arrested by British colonial authorities in October 1952 after accusations of being the mastermind behind the Mau Mau insurgency. The evidence linking Kenyatta to the Mau Mau rebellion was dubious and made his imprisonment a cause célèbre not only within Kenya but throughout Africa and the world, which served to greatly enhance his reputation and nationalist credentials. In May 1960, he was elected president of

KANU *in absentia*. After being released from prison in August 1961, he became the leading figure in Kenyan nationalist politics, winning the election as prime minister in June 1963 and becoming the first head of state of independent Kenya in December 1963.

In Cold War terms, Kenyatta was a moderate. On the one hand, he had briefly studied in Moscow, was linked to 'radical' pan-Africanists such as Padmore and Nkrumah, and was perceived to have been the leader of the violent anti-colonial Mau Mau uprising. On the other hand, he was Western-educated, had lived in the United Kingdom for over 15 years and encouraged white settlers to remain in independent Kenya. At the time of independence, Kenyatta was over 70 years old, so, given his age and moderation, both sides of the Iron Curtain sought to identify a younger Kenyan nationalist leader with whom they might be able to establish influence. The USA favoured Tom Mboya, while the Soviet Union, Czechoslovakia and communist China preferred Oginga Odinga.

Tom Mboya was an ethnic Luo (Kenya's second-largest ethnic group), who had studied industrial management at Ruskin College, Oxford before returning to Kenya in 1956 and engaging in nationalist politics. In 1958, he gained an international reputation when he served as conference chairman of the All-African Peoples' Conference taking place in Accra, Ghana. As a labour organizer, Mboya also formed close contacts with both governmental and non-governmental sources within the USA. In particular, he received support and funding from the International Confederation of Free Trade Unions (ICFTU).[4] The ICFTU was an organization created largely at the behest of the American Federation of Labor for Cold War purposes – to serve as a Western alternative to the Prague-based World Federation of Trade Unions (WFTU) – in order to recruit African and Asian labour unions to a Western-oriented global organization. In the late 1950s and early 1960s, Mboya made several visits to the USA and is believed to have been on the payroll of the US Central Intelligence Agency (CIA).[5] In 1960, Mboya joined KANU, became the party's secretary general, and led its delegation to the Lancaster House Conferences at which Kenya's constitutional framework and independence from the United Kingdom were negotiated. The USA funnelled both political and financial support to Mboya in the hope that he would be Kenyatta's successor as the leader of independent Kenya. Czechoslovakia considered

Mboya to be the greatest impediment to expanded Soviet bloc influence in Kenya, and as such he became the target of numerous Czechoslovak intelligence activities.[6]

Like Mboya, Oginga Odinga was also ethnically Luo but the two would eventually become political rivals due to the fact that they received support from opposite sides of the Iron Curtain.[7] Odinga studied at Makerere University in Uganda before returning to Kenya and becoming a highly successful and wealthy businessman. In 1948, he joined KANU and the Kenyan nationalist movement, and would become a political supporter of Kenyatta and one of the greatest advocates for the latter's release from British detention. Even prior to independence while Mboya was making frequent trips to the USA, 'Mr Double O', as the British called him, made several visits to communist countries.[8]

Initial links between Odinga and Czechoslovakia commenced in 1959 when Odhiambo Okello, a close confidante of Odinga and the head of KANU's Cairo office, approached Czechoslovak diplomats in the Egyptian capital with a request of support from Odinga. Okello later remembered that at the time 'the Czechoslovak anti-colonial stance was widely known, as was its willingness to support freedom fighters'.[9] Odinga's request was discussed at the highest levels of the Czechoslovak Government, and the politburo decided 'to orientate all its support to Oginga Odinga and his political wing within KANU' because it believed that Odinga, should he ascend to power, would position Kenya towards the socialist world.[10] Odinga first visited Prague in 1960, where he was promised financial and material assistance for KANU's office in Cairo. A follow-up visit by Okello resulted in the Czechoslovak Government granting 14 scholarships for Kenyan students, selected by KANU, to study in Czechoslovakia (from 1960 to 1964, between 150 and 200 Kenyans would attend university in Czechoslovakia).[11] After Czechoslovak officials met with Odinga at Tanganyika's independence celebrations in December 1961, KANU was awarded more scholarships for the training of two personal bodyguards for Kenyatta and Odinga and 20 officials who would be trained to become the nucleus of Kenya's ministries of interior and defence after independence.[12]

During the negotiations in London between British and KANU officials on setting a date for Kenyan independence in the spring of 1962, KANU representatives visited the Czechoslovak Embassy and requested funding to purchase a printing press and assistance to help fund its office in London. Czechoslovak officials were reluctant to buy KANU a printing press, suggesting instead that they themselves set one up in Dar es Salaam (Tanzania), which could then be used to publish materials for all of the national-liberation movements that they were supporting in eastern and southern Africa. The Czechoslovak Ministry of Foreign Affairs did, however, decide that because of the 'urgency and importance of assisting the Kenyan party KANU' that additional funding, originally earmarked for nationalist groups in Northern and Southern Rhodesia and Zanzibar, be redirected to KANU.[13]

In July 1962, Odinga and Okello again stopped in Prague, this time on their way to attend the World Congress for General Disarmament and Peace conference in Moscow. They again urged Prague to give KANU more financial assistance for the upcoming elections, which would decide the make-up of Kenya's first independent government. Odinga alleged that both the USA and United Kingdom were injecting large amounts of money into Kenya in an attempt to influence the elections, and declared that KANU had to rely on the Soviet Union and Czechoslovakia to offset Western attempts to 'buy' the election. He even went as far as to compare the situation in his country to that in the Congo, where he claimed that support from the socialist camp had come too late to save Patrice Lumumba's party. As a result, the ČSSR leadership gave Odinga additional small funding and a commitment that the Czechoslovak Press Agency (ČTK) would train six Kenyan editors to help KANU's campaign efforts and to form the nucleus of its Kenya News Agency (KNA).[14] While Czechoslovakia had minimal economic relations with Kenya throughout 1962 (exports to Kenya in 1960–2 totalled only Kčs 4.4 million), it hoped that its political contacts with Odinga and Okello would allow Prague to exert influence in Kenya after its independence.[15]

Czechoslovak Relations with Uganda Prior to Independence

In Uganda, Czechoslovak representatives established contact with both Milton Obote's Ugandan People's Congress (UPC) and Benedicto Kiwanuka's Democratic Party (DP) in the late 1950s. Both party leaders visited Czechoslovakia prior to independence (Kiwanuka in 1960 and

Obote in 1961) and were given small amounts of funding to assist their parties in preparing for elections.[16]

After serving in the prestigious King's African Rifles in World War II, where he rose to the rank of sergeant major, Benedicto Kiwanuka attended University College London from 1952 to 1956. He returned to practise law in Uganda between 1956 and 1959, and eventually became the leader of the Democratic Party in 1958. Although a member of the Buganda ethnic group (Uganda's largest and most powerful), Kiwanuka was both a commoner and Catholic and therefore was opposed by Buganda's kabaka (king), Sir Edward Mutesa, and most other Buganda who viewed him as a traitor for supporting the creation of a unified Uganda rather than a federal system which would protect Buganda's autonomy.[17]

Under Kiwanuka, the DP built its membership on the twin pillars of anti-communism and Catholic discontent over the fact that Protestants dominated colonial state appointments.[18] Kiwanuka further established his anti-communist credentials during three trips to the USA in 1959 and in both October and December 1961. Meeting with State Department officials, he took advantage of American paranoia over communism by claiming that his political rivals in Uganda had established contacts with the Soviet bloc and warning that his country was in danger of communist takeover. In order to attract American support, Kiwanuka marketed the DP as the bulwark against the spread of communism in Uganda.[19] US officials viewed Kiwanuka as 'staunchly anti-Communist, friendly towards the United States, and one of the few African leaders who has risen to power without stooping to the use of anti-Western invective to gain his ends'.[20] The State Department saw Kiwanuka as 'a man of unusual integrity', who, because of his Western education and support for constitutional law and unitary government, 'could play an important role [...] as a brake on any tendency [within East Africa] [...] to court friendship with the Communist Bloc'.[21]

During the pre-independence period, Kiwanuka's primary political rival was Apollo Milton Obote. Obote, who was the son of a chief of the Lango ethnic group, attended Makerere University in Kampala before moving to Kenya where he became involved in the anti-colonial independence movement. After returning to Uganda in 1956, Obote joined the Uganda National Congress (UNC) and was elected to the colonial Legislative Council in 1957. In 1959, the UNC split into two factions, with Obote leading one group into a merger with the Uganda

People's Union to form the Uganda People's Congress (UPC).[22] The UPC became a national coalition of those outside the Roman Catholic-dominated DP (Protestants, Muslims and other faiths), which transcended both ethnicity and regional loyalties in its leadership hierarchy and political orientation.[23] The State Department viewed Obote as someone who, although not openly hostile to the West, had socialist leanings and received funding from the Soviet bloc.[24] Like Kiwanuka before him, Obote was offered the chance to visit the USA on a Leader Grant, but turned down the opportunity.[25]

When the British announced that they would hold elections in Uganda for 'responsible government' (conceived as the penultimate step towards independence), Kabaka Mutesa boycotted the election in protest at the fact that the British had not promised post-independence autonomy to Buganda. Therefore, when the elections took place in March 1961, supporters of the DP were largely the only ones to vote within Buganda, giving the party 20 out of the region's 21 seats in the National Assembly from a jurisdiction in which only 2–3 per cent of eligible voters had participated as a result of the Kabaka's call for a boycott. The end result was that although the UPC garnered 495,000 popular votes to the DP's 416,000, the DP won 49 seats to 38 for the UPC.[26] This outcome allowed Kiwanuka to become chief minister of the Uganda Legislative Council, and after Uganda was granted internal self-government he became the country's first prime minister in March 1962.

However, with Uganda's date for full independence set for October 1962, new elections were scheduled for April to determine the make-up of the government that would lead the country to independence. Realizing the strategic mistake that having sat out the previous election had led to a commoner (Kiwanuka) becoming prime minister, supporters of the Kabaka formed a new party named Kabaka Yekka ('king only', KY) to contest the elections. In the run-up to the election, Obote's UPC formed an alliance with KY in order to defeat the incumbent Kiwanuka and his Democratic Party.

Although neither country appears to have intervened in the elections, both the USA and United Kingdom were wary of Obote, whom they viewed as a revolutionary socialist and potential disciple of Ghana's Kwame Nkrumah.[27] Washington and London both demurred on his requests to provide financial support for his party despite the fact that US diplomats in Kampala warned that Obote might turn to either the

Soviet bloc or Egypt if Western aid was not forthcoming.[28] With US diplomats in Kampala reporting that in Uganda '[t]here are yet no leaders in sight of the caliber of Tom Mboya', officials in Washington likewise also told Kiwanuka that the USA would not provide funding for the DP's electoral campaign.[29] The West therefore left an opportunity for Czechoslovakia to fill the void of foreign electoral funding in Uganda. With financial aid not forthcoming from the West, Obote sent a letter to Czechoslovak officials proclaiming his socialist credentials and requesting campaign funding for the upcoming elections. Obote was invited to Prague in October 1961, where the Czechoslovak leadership agreed to send financial assistance to the UPC earmarked for the election.[30] Prague's decision to support the UPC was in part a result of the fact that it viewed the DP 'as a protégé of Britain for the purposes of ensuring the continuance of [the] British economic and political grip on Uganda and as such a main enemy to socialist countries'.[31] Although probably not fully determinative of the outcome, Czechoslovak campaign funding was important to the UPC because it had limited financial resources and few wealthy individuals amongst its membership.[32] In the final results, the UPC–KY coalition successfully unseated Kiwanuka with the UPC winning 43 seats to 24 each for KY and DP.[33] Obote became prime minister and Kabaka Mutesa became the largely ceremonial president.

After the UPC won the April 1962 election, and prior to Uganda's formal independence, Obote visited the Czechoslovak Embassy in London to discuss the possibility of forming trade, economic, scientific and technical cooperation agreements with the ČSSR. The Ugandan prime minister-designate also proposed sending a group of print journalists, photo-journalists, and radio and television reporters to Prague for training.[34] Such requests made Czechoslovak officials optimistic that Uganda would seek close relations with the Soviet bloc after independence. This impression was given further legitimacy during Uganda's independence celebrations in September 1962, from which the head of the ČSSR delegation, Jozef Valo, reported that Obote gave him 'extraordinary attention' and granted Czechoslovak representatives precedence over all other government delegations at the ceremonies while stressing the role that Prague's support had played in the UPC's electoral victory.[35]

Originally, Czechoslovakia planned to wait until all three East African colonies had gained independence in order to send an ambassador accredited to Uganda, Kenya and Tanganyika, and it viewed Uganda as the least important of the three. But after Obote's blandishments on independence day and in response to his personal request for Prague to send an ambassador to Kampala as soon as possible, so that he could receive advice on developing his newly independent country, the Czechoslovak Ministry of Foreign Affairs advised sending an ambassador to Uganda immediately in order to not only strengthen relations with Obote's regime but also to expand interaction with the neighbouring states of Rwanda and Burundi, and to increase contact with Kenya's nationalist leaders.[36] However, the politburo demurred on this suggestion, most likely for a combination of reasons including the high cost of establishing embassies in each state in East Africa; Uganda's lack of geopolitical value to Czechoslovak foreign policy; and the fact that Uganda's former colonial power, the United Kingdom, continued to have paramount influence in the country – especially over the military. Instead it was decided that Prague's chargé d'affaires in Dar es Salaam, František Vomáčka, would also be accredited to Uganda. Nonetheless, Czechoslovak–Ugandan relations remained strong throughout the rest of the decade.[37]

Foreign Military Aid to Kenya and Uganda

Czechoslovakia had long been one of the world's leading exporters of weapons to the developing world. Through the sale of arms, the ČSSR was able to make a profit through the disposal of obsolete weapons, stimulate its industrial economy and form closer political relations with the states that purchased its arms. Arms exports and military training were a gateway to increased influence in Third World states because they created a technical dependence on Czechoslovakia for training, spare parts and ammunition. Military assistance was also often a precursor to enhanced trade relationships with recipient states. Therefore, Czechoslovak military aid played a significant role in the overall growth of the country's influence in both Kenya and Uganda in the mid-1960s.[38]

As part of its intensification of relations with sub-Saharan Africa from late 1958 through to 1962, Prague provided military aid to the radical states of Guinea, Mali and Ghana. In becoming an arms supplier to these radical states, Czechoslovakia was able to both prove itself a valuable ally of the Soviet Union in strengthening Soviet bloc influence in

West Africa and lay a foundation upon which greater economic relations between Prague and these states could be built. However, by 1963, in the midst of a severe economic recession and growing disenchantment over its relationships with the radical states, Czechoslovakia reoriented its approach in supplying military assistance to Africa. Prague drastically reduced the uneconomical practice of providing arms to friendly states as gifts or under arrangements for the recipient to pay in the future. Instead, it began looking for commercial partners who were willing (and, perhaps more importantly, able) to purchase Czechoslovak weapons up front, in cash, in order to provide Czechoslovakia with badly needed foreign exchange. As a result of this policy change, Prague's military ties with Guinea, Ghana and Mali were reduced while new relationships with Kenya, Uganda, Tanzania and Morocco were initiated.

Upon independence in December 1963, Kenyan President Jomo Kenyatta announced that his government wanted all British troops to depart the country by December 1964. Similarly, an agreement between Nairobi and Washington precluded the USA from posting a military or defence attaché in its Kenyan Embassy.[39] The Kenyans convinced their US counterparts that they should not accept military aid from the USA because if they did so they would feel obligated to accept similar aid from the Soviet Union.[40] In order to avoid dependence on either of the Cold War superpowers or its former colonizer, Kenya instead turned toward two mid-level powers – Canada and Czechoslovakia – for its military needs.

Building upon the relationship that Vice-President Oginga Odinga had formed with Czechoslovakia prior to independence, Prague was asked to assist in the task of reorientating the Kenyan Army, which KANU party leaders felt had been 'brainwashed' by previous British training. Shortly before independence, Kenyan authorities concluded an agreement for the Czechoslovak Government to train a new officer corps and security-apparatus personnel who would replace the British expatriates. Under the agreement, the ČSSR agreed to pay the transportation and tuition costs for Kenya to send 20 of its army officers to Czechoslovakia for a one-year course and 30 of its security personnel for six months of training.[41] In the end, 21 Kenyan Army officers studied in the ČSSR: nine received infantry training, six focused on tank combat, and the other six were enrolled on an artillery course. Even prior to this arrangement, an earlier agreement had been brokered by the

Egyptian Government the previous summer for six Kenyans from KANU's office in Cairo to receive military training for a year at the Antonín Zápotocký Military Academy of Technology in Brno.[42]

The Kenyan Government also requested from Czechoslovakia modern military armaments to outfit a 1,000-man army. The Kenyan defence minister, Njoroge Mungai, led a delegation to Prague to review a demonstration of Czechoslovak weapons, which included machine guns, aircraft, armoured personnel carriers, tanks and mortars. As a result of this visit, Czechoslovakia sold to Kenya 500 pistols with 50,000 rounds of ammunition and 500 submachine guns with 100,000 rounds of ammunition. Later in the year, Czechoslovakia sold the Kenyan security forces a fully equipped darkroom and surveillance cameras, and 50 pistols with ammunition, while 20 submachine guns were delivered to Odinga's personal security detail.[43]

However, the situation in East Africa would change dramatically in the final week of January 1964, when the armies of Tanganyika, Uganda and Kenya all mutinied over low pay and continued British control. Kenyatta, Obote and Julius Nyerere (the president of Tanganyika) each requested British intervention to put down the rebellions. British troops ended the mutinies without shots being fired, but the situation brought into perspective for the leaders of the newly independent East African states the fact that, like it or not, British influence over their militaries could not easily be eliminated.[44] While Czechoslovakia, Canada and other mid-level military powers may have been willing to provide arms and training, they did not have the logistical capability to intervene to suppress such mutinies in the way that the British could. As a result, a few months later Kenya changed course and signed a defence agreement with the United Kingdom.[45]

A similar situation occurred in neighbouring Uganda, where the Obote government was also seeking to reduce British influence within its military. At independence, virtually every army officer was a British national and, as a result, the British retained practical control over Uganda's military. Given the potential challenge from the ethnic Buganda who supported the Kabaka, Obote wanted to restructure the army into a strong and loyal supporter of his regime. Initially, he turned to Israel as an alternative source of military weapons and training in order to lessen Uganda's dependence on the United Kingdom and to begin the process of Africanizing Uganda's armed forces. The January

1964 mutiny accelerated Israel's opportunity to take a leading role in becoming Uganda's primary supplier of military and security assistance, and increased tensions and competition between British and Israeli representatives on the ground in Kampala.[46] Within six months of the mutiny, Obote had removed all British officers from his army and turned to Czechoslovakia as another source of military aid to supplement aid from Israel and the United Kingdom.[47]

The first Ugandan inquiry about the possibility of receiving Czechoslovak military training and weapons appears to have been in March 1964. Given the timing, one can presume that the mutiny a few weeks earlier played a significant role in Uganda's decision to approach Czechoslovakia for such aid. Prague responded favourably to the request, and within months the first ten Ugandan officers arrived in Czechoslovakia for a six-month training course.[48] Despite viewing Uganda as pro-Western, Prague would develop an extensive military relationship with Kampala on a commercial, rather than ideological, basis and eventually surpassed both the United Kingdom and Israel to become Uganda's main supplier of arms from 1966 to 1968.[49]

In April 1965, a Czechoslovak delegation went to Kampala to meet with Ugandan Defence Minister Felix Onama and, after a month of negotiations, concluded a contract in which Czechoslovakia would partner to help build Uganda's air force – the Ugandan People's Defence Force Air Wing. Under the terms of the deal, Uganda would send ten pilots and 18 aviation mechanics to Czechoslovakia to learn how to operate, maintain and repair the Czechoslovak-manufactured aircraft L-29 Delfín, while Prague would send 12 aviation experts to serve directly in Uganda. By the autumn of 1967, nine Ugandan pilots had successfully completed training in aerial navigation, aerial reconnaissance, aerial shooting, artillery fire and bombing, and Czechoslovakia delivered to Uganda three L-29s in exchange for about Kčs8.8 million in foreign exchange. Unfortunately, the potential financial profit from such transactions was hampered by the fact that the Soviet Union agreed to supply Uganda with Czechoslovak-made anti-aircraft systems and MiG fighter jets as gifts while constructing a military airport at Gulu through a long-term loan.[50] As expected, when possible the Ugandans preferred to build their aviation infrastructure through Soviet gifts as opposed to Czechoslovak commercial transactions. Historian David Dobrovda astutely notes that 'competition' between Moscow and Prague illustrates that Soviet and Czechoslovak aid to African states 'was, surprisingly, not as coordinated, collaborative and effective as it should have been'.[51]

Czechoslovakia also sold additional miscellaneous military equipment to Uganda, the most famous example of which was a consignment of 12 OT-64 SKOT amphibious armoured personnel carriers. In 1968, Uganda became the first country outside of the Soviet bloc to obtain OT-64s. They quickly became a favourite of Ugandan Army General Idi Amin, who was known to travel in them as often as possible. Interestingly, Uganda would partially pay for its 1968 order of OT-64s, missiles, ammunition and spare parts for the L-29s by preparing the largest transport of captured animals in the country's history. Czechoslovakia would use the exotic animals both for its zoos and in scientific research.[52]

Prague also played a leading role in the formation of Obote's intelligence apparatus, the General Service Unit (GSU). In March 1964, Czechoslovakia agreed to launch a course to train Ugandans in intelligence work. Instruction began a few months later in Czechoslovakia, where over 30 Ugandans would receive intelligence training in the following years. Upon returning to Uganda, graduates of these courses received high-ranking positions within the GSU – often replacing Israel-trained predecessors. One of the tasks that Obote assigned the GSU was monitoring contacts between the USA and several of the more Western-leaning members of his government, to ensure that they were not plotting against him.[53]

Unfulfilled Expectations

In the spring of 1964, Uganda looked like a promising potential ally for the ČSSR on both the economic and political fronts. In March, the Czechoslovak Ministry of Trade labelled Uganda as one of Africa's most promising trade markets for Czechoslovak goods.[54] That year, the turnover of trade between the two countries reached Kčs 6.4 million (with Czechoslovakia mostly exporting weapons to Uganda, and Uganda primarily sending coffee in return).[55] In the political realm, the Ugandan Government endeared itself to the Soviet bloc by providing refuge and support for the 'Simba Rebellion' across the border in eastern Congo while frequently criticizing the policies of the USA and its NATO allies for supporting Moise Tshombe's ascension to the office of prime minister of the Congo. US officials complained privately that, under Obote, Uganda's voting record in the United Nations 'coincided with the USSR 17 times, with the US 2, with both US and USSR and with neither US nor USSR 6 times', adding, 'What is perhaps more significant is the fact that out of all the African voting records, only Guinea and Ghana were worse than Uganda.'[56] The symbolic highpoint of Czechoslovak–Ugandan relations would come in July 1965, when Ugandan President Milton Obote made a state visit to Prague.

Czechoslovakia's attempt to build lasting relations with the African continent, which continually intensified during the years 1955–61, began to decline in 1962. Between 1964 and 1967, Prague viewed Uganda as one of the few bright spots in its African policy, where bilateral relations were on the upswing instead of in decline. But relations between Prague and Kampala could not survive the twin traumas of the Prague Spring (1968) and Idi Amin's coup d'état (1971) and by 1972 while Amin greatly increased his relations with the Soviet Union, relations with the ČSSR were minimal.

In Kenya, Prague's previous efforts to establish relations with prominent KANU politicians like Oginga Odinga initially seemed to pay dividends when the colony achieved its independence in December 1963. At that time, the Kenyan Government invited Czechoslovak economists to present to Nairobi an economic development plan as an alternative to the guidance that they were receiving from British and American advisors.[57] While the Kenyan Government kept its distance from the Soviet Union, it sought both economic and military assistance from Czechoslovakia, apparently calculating that this would draw less adverse reactions from the West. However, it soon became clear that the Kenyan Government was split into two factions led respectively by President Jomo Kenyatta, who favoured alignment with the West, and Vice-President Odinga, who preferred turning to the East.[58]

In his autobiography, Odinga says that he was not a communist and did not advocate for Kenya to be solely aligned with the communist bloc. Rather, he wished Kenya to pursue a truly non-aligned foreign policy. Since Kenyatta and Mboya leaned heavily towards the West, he felt the need to lobby for greater relations with the East in order to balance things out.[59] This led to Odinga making multiple visits to the communist bloc, beginning in 1960.[60] Nonetheless, the perception that Odinga was left-wing and Kenyatta right-wing added to the fact that the vice-president was ethnically Luo and the president Kikuyu to split the KANU party behind them along not only political but also ethnic lines. This political and ethnic divide led to a situation in which most of the Kenyans who went to the USA and United Kingdom for university or military training were Kikuyu, while most of those who received such training in the Eastern bloc were Luo.

Before long, the rivalry between Kenyatta and Odinga led to Prague entering into several agreements directly with Odinga that circumvented the Kenyan Government and, in effect, served to help finance a shadow government run by the Kenyan Vice-President. For example, Czechoslovakia armed Odinga's personal security detail and gave money to him to finance the revolutionary Stanleyville government's diplomatic outpost in Nairobi after Kenyatta refused to provide the Congolese with financial assistance.[61] In October 1964, a group of Kenyans returned from military training in Czechoslovakia with cases of weapons that were delivered directly to Odinga's office at the Home Affairs Ministry.[62] The following month rumours, fed by Western intelligence, began to circulate that Odinga had procured the Czechoslovak weapons with the intention of overthrowing Kenyatta.[63] Odinga denied these accusations, and later claimed that he and Kenyatta had jointly ordered the weapons from Prague in order to equip the Kenyan security forces independently of the United Kingdom.[64]

In December 1964, Odinga and other radicals within KANU, with direct funding from the Soviet Union and East Germany, created the Lumumba Institute to train party cadres, which served to further exacerbate tensions between the supporters of Kenyatta and Odinga.[65] Kenyatta increasingly saw Odinga as a potential political rival, and eventually became convinced that the vice-president was planning a coup against him. In order to mitigate this possibility, Kenyatta reappointed British nationals to head the army, air force, navy and police (in an effort to reduce the possibility of the military siding with Odinga) and ordered Mboya to draft a new constitution that weakened the power of the office of the vice-president and gave parliament the power to appoint his (Kenyatta's) successor in the event of his death (rather than allowing Odinga to automatically ascend to the presidency).[66] In an attempt to further tarnish Odinga's reputation, Daniel arap Moi (who succeeded Odinga as both minister of home affairs in 1964 and then as vice-president in 1967) publicly alleged that Odinga had personally received more than US$1 million of funding from communist sources.[67] This led to a gradual reduction in Odinga's influence throughout the early months of 1965; his removal as vice-president in May 1965; and his resignation from KANU to form an opposition party, the Kenya People's Union (KPU), in the spring of 1966.[68] This rift between Kenyatta and Odinga split KANU in two, alienated the Luo from Kenyatta's government and created tensions between the Luo and Kikuyu communities that continue to this day.[69]

Czechoslovakia's influence in Kenya deteriorated alongside Odinga's declining political fortunes. Prague continued to maintain relations with his opposition movement, but this ultimately greatly damaged its bilateral relations with Kenyatta's government when three Czechoslovak diplomats were expelled from the country in 1966 after making multiple trips to Odinga's Luo political stronghold in the Lake Victoria area. Thereafter the 30 members of the Kenyan security forces who had received training in Czechoslovakia were fired from their jobs and many of the Kenyan military officers who had received training at the Antonín Zápotocký Military Academy of Technology, derisively nicknamed 'Odinga's boys', also had their careers ruined.[70] In order to help ensure loyalty to his rule, Kenyatta moved to make Kenya's police and security forces Kikuyu dominated.[71] With Odinga's downfall, Kenya thus became a country with unfulfilled hopes of becoming an ally of Czechoslovakia.

Conclusion

Czechoslovakia initiated relations with British East Africa as early as 1937, when it opened a consulate in Mombasa. In the late 1950s, while Kenya and Uganda were still under British colonial rule, the ČSSR began developing contacts with the nationalist movements in both countries in an effort gain political capital in the soon-to-be independent states. After independence, political leaders in both African countries sought relations with Czechoslovakia as leverage both against domestic political rivals and against their Western allies.

In Uganda, both Milton Obote's Ugandan People's Congress and Benedicto Kiwanuka's Democratic Party courted relations with, and aid from, Prague in the course of their domestic political rivalry. In Kenya, Oginga Odinga, the vice-president of the ruling party – the Kenyan

African National Union – sought aid from Czechoslovakia in his clash with Kenyan President Jomo Kenyatta. Before long, the rivalry between Kenyatta and Odinga led to Prague entering into several agreements directly with Odinga that circumvented the Kenyan Government and, in effect, served to help finance a shadow government run by the Kenyan vice-president. Odinga's relationship with Czechoslovakia played a considerable role in his removal as vice-president in 1965 and his creation of an opposition party – the Kenya People's Union – in 1966.

Kenya and Uganda also both accepted military and intelligence training and weapons from Czechoslovakia as a means of reducing their dependency on Western military assistance. While Czechoslovak military assistance to Kenya was relatively minimal (and mostly went directly to Odinga's personal security force), Prague became Uganda's main provider of military assistance between the years 1964 and 1968, when it supplied nearly 60 per cent of the total arms imported into that country.[72] Czechoslovakia provided this aid as an attempt to create a loyal and effective security apparatus in support of their favoured politician's position within each respective country (Odinga and Obote) while simultaneously weakening the Western position in East Africa.

In pursuing its policy towards Kenya and Uganda, Prague was acting autonomously with little coordination or direction from Moscow. One should not take this to mean that Prague's foreign policy towards Africa in the 1960s was as independent as Cuba's was in the 1970s. I was unable to find a single instance in which Czechoslovakia directly opposed the Kremlin's wishes in conducting its relations with Africa. Moreover, Prague frequently consulted with Moscow prior to making major policy decisions or launching new initiatives on the continent. There were, however, also many occasions when the Czechoslovaks acted on their own and then informed Moscow of their actions after the fact. Far from being the puppet of the Kremlin, Czechoslovakia was given a fair amount of independence by Moscow in this endeavour, and in some instances Prague actually drove international communist policy in Africa.[73] The Kremlin seemingly approved of this arrangement because it was confident of Prague's loyalty to the Soviet bloc and was willing to defer to Czechoslovakia's expertise in African matters of lesser importance to Moscow. On issues of greater significance to the Soviet Union – such as relations with Egypt or Ghana, or in the case of the Congo Crisis – Moscow took a greater involvement and Prague followed its lead. However, in relations with countries such as Kenya and Uganda, which sought to distance themselves from the Soviet Union, Czechoslovakia often led Soviet bloc foreign policy in the mid-1960s. Although it was able to achieve moderate success in establishing influence in both Kenya and Uganda in the mid-1960s, in the long run Czechoslovakia overestimated the possibilities of building relations with the East African countries and by the end of the decade had little to show for its efforts in the region.

Notes

1. For a discussion of Czechoslovak policy towards the rest of Africa, see Philip E. Muehlenbeck, *Czechoslovakia in Africa, 1945–1968* (New York, 2015).
2. Petr Zidek, *Československo a francouzská Afrika 1948–1968* [Czechoslovakia and French Africa, 1948–1968] (Prague, 2006), p. 18.
3. History of Czechoslovak Diplomatic and Consular Presence in Rhodesia and Zimbabwe (1927–1992) on the website for the Embassy of the Czech Republic in Harare [online], rev. 7 February 2013. Available at http://www.mzv.cz/harare/en/bilateral_relations/historical_ties/index_1.html (accessed September 2017).
4. James P. Hubbard, *The United States and the End of British Colonial Rule in Africa, 1941–1968* (Jefferson, NC, 2010), p. 223.
5. Ibid. Also, see Edward Marks, oral history interview, 12 August 1996, *Frontline Diplomacy*, Manuscript Division, Library of Congress, Washington, DC (hereafter, *Frontline Diplomacy*) and Charles Hornsby, *Kenya: A History since Independence* (New York, 2012), pp. 52–3.
6. David Dobrovoda, 'Czechoslovakia and East Africa in the late colonial and early post-colonial period: The case studies of Kenya, Uganda, and Tanzania', PhD, University of London, 2016, p. 127.
7. Smith Hempstone, Jr., oral history interview, 6 May 1998, *Frontline Diplomacy*.
8. Ambassador E. Gregory Kryza, oral history interview, 14 June 1988, *Frontline Diplomacy*; William Attwood, *The Reds and the Blacks: A Personal Adventure* (New York, 1967), p. 237, and Hornsby, *Kenya*, p. 58.
9. Odhiambo Okello, oral history interview with historian David Dobrovoda. See Dobrovoda, 'Czechoslovakia and East Africa', pp. 119–20.
10. Dobrovoda, 'Czechoslovakia and East Africa', p. 120.
11. Ibid., pp. 128–9.
12. Resolution of the Political Bureau of the Central Committee of the KSČ (Communist Party of Czechoslovakia), 13 March 1962. National Archives of the Czech Republic, Records of the Communist Party of Czechoslovakia [hereafter, NA-UV KSC], f. 02/2, sv. 341, ar. j. 432, b. 7.

13. Petr Zídek and Karel Sieber, *Československo a subsaharská Afrika v letech 1948–1989* [Czechoslovakia and Sub-Saharan Africa, 1948–1989] (Prague, 2007), pp. 117–18.
14. Resolution of the Political Bureau of the Central Committee of the KSČ, July 24, 1962. NA-UV KSC, f. 02/2, sv. 358, ar. j. 448, b. 25; Hornsby. *Kenya*, p. 114.
15. Resolution of the Political Bureau of the Central Committee of the KSČ, November 12, 1963. NA-UV KSC, f. 02/1, sv. 40, ar. j. 45, b. 9.
16. Zídek and Sieber, *Československo a subsaharská Afrika*, pp. 212–13.
17. Moses Mulondo, 'Is Benedicto Kiwanuka Uganda's Greatest Hero?' *New Vision*, 12 January 2012.
18. Louise Pirouet, *Historical Dictionary of Uganda* (Metuchen, NJ, 1995), p. 91.
19. Albert Bade, *Benedicto Kiwanuka: The Man and His Politics* (Kampala, 1996), pp. 55–6.
20. Letter from Assistant Secretary of State for African Affairs G. Mennen Williams to Undersecretary of State Chester Bowles, 18 December 1961. General Records of the Department of State. Bureau of African Affairs, Office of Eastern and Southern African Affairs, Records Relating to Uganda, 1959–1964, Box 5, Folder, 'Uganda: Leader Grantee – Benedicto Kiwanuka', National Archives II, College Park, MD (hereafter, NARA).
21. Ibid.
22. Hubbard, *The United States and the End of British Colonial Rule in Africa*, p. 240; Yoga Adhola, 'The Roots, Emergence, and Growth of the Uganda Peoples Congress, 1600–1985', on the website for the Uganda People's Union. [Online], rev. 10 May 2016. Available at http://www.upcparty.net/upcparty/roots_adhola.htm (accessed September 2017).
23. Godfrey Mwakikagile, *Uganda: The Land and Its People* (Dar es Salaam, 2009), pp. 11–12.
24. Letter from Assistant Secretary of State for African Affairs G. Mennen Williams to Undersecretary of State Chester Bowles, 18 December 1961. General Records of the Department of State. Bureau of African Affairs, Office of Eastern and Southern African Affairs, Records Relating to Uganda, 1959–1964, Box 5, Folder, 'Uganda: Leader Grantee – Benedicto Kiwanuka', NARA.
25. See Ibid., In the fall of 1960, Hendrik van Oss, the US consul general to Uganda, voiced frustration over his attempts to get Obote to visit the USA, writing, 'I have rarely [sic] been so frustrated in my attempts to meet anyone. After unsuccessfully trying every ruse I could think of to get someone to introduce us, I went so far as to call him [Obote] up to invite him to lunch. His response to my invitation was so unenthusiastic, broaching on being downright rude, that I became disenchanted, and stopped trying. I certainly did not think it appropriate to chase him, hat in hand, trying to persuade him to accept our humble offer.' See Letter from US Consul General to Uganda Hendrik van Oss to Frederick Picard of the State Department's Office of Eastern and Southern African Affairs, 1 November 1960. General Records of the

Department of State. Bureau of African Affairs, Office of Eastern and Southern African Affairs, Records Relating to Uganda, 1959–1964, Box 5, Folder, 'Correspondence – Uganda', NARA.
26. Pirouet, *Historical Dictionary of Uganda*, p. 91; Mwakikagile, *Uganda*, pp. 11–12.
27. Ambassador Olcott H. Deming, oral history interview, 20 April 1988, *Frontline Diplomacy*; Circular Telegram from US Secretary of State Dean Rusk to US Embassies in Africa, 28 May 1963, in *Foreign Relations of the United States, 1961–1963, Volume XXI, Africa* (Washington, DC, 1996), p. 334.
28. Ambassador Stephen Low, oral history interview, 5 December 1997, *Frontline Diplomacy*; Hubbard, *The United States and the End of British Colonial Rule in Africa*, p. 242.
29. For the Mboya quote, see Letter from US Consul General to Uganda Hendrik van Oss to Frederick Picard of the State Department's Office of Eastern and Southern African Affairs, 24 January 1961. General Records of the Department of State. Bureau of African Affairs, Office of Eastern and Southern African Affairs, Records Relating to Uganda, 1959–1964, Box 5, Folder, 'Correspondence – Uganda', NARA. For information on the USA's decision not to fund Kiwanuka's Democratic Party, see Memorandum from William L. Wright, Jr. of the State Department's Office of Eastern and Southern African Affairs to Assistant Secretary of State for African Affairs G. Mennen Williams, 11 December 1961. General Records of the Department of State. Bureau of African Affairs, Office of Eastern and Southern African Affairs, Records Relating to Uganda, 1959–1964, Box 5, Folder, 'Uganda: Leader Grantee – Bendicto Kiwanuka', NARA.
30. Zídek and Sieber, *Československo a subsaharská Afrika*, pp. 212–13; Dobrovoda, 'Czechoslovakia and East Africa', p. 184.
31. Dobrovoda, 'Czechoslovakia and East Africa', pp. 185–6.
32. Ibid., p. 180.
33. For election results see Mwakikagile, *Uganda*, pp. 11–12. Kiwanuka remained the leader of Uganda's opposition party until Obote had him imprisoned in 1969. After his coup in 1971, Idi Amin freed many of the Obote-era political prisoners, including Kiwanuka who then became chief justice of the Ugandan Supreme Court under Amin, until his rulings fell foul of the mercurial dictator who eventually had him arrested, tortured and killed in 1972. See Bade, *Benedicto Kiwanuka*.
34. Zídek and Sieber, *Československo a subsaharská Afrika*, p. 213.
35. Resolution of the Political Bureau of the Central Committee of the KSČ, 13 November 1962. NA-UV KSC, f. 02/2, sv. 369, ar. j. 463, b. 14.
36. Ibid.
37. Zídek and Sieber, *Československo a subsaharská Afrika*, pp. 213–14.
38. For more on Czechoslovak arms exports, see Muehlenbeck, *Czechoslovakia in Africa*, Chapter 3 and Petr Zídek, 'Vývoz zbrani z Československa do zemí třetího světa v letech 1948–1962' [Export of arms from Czechoslovakia to

Third World countries in the years 1948–1962], *Historie a vojenství* 3 (2002), pp. 523–67.
39. Kryza, oral history interview, *Frontline Diplomacy*; Attwood, *The Reds and the Blacks*, p. 152.
40. Kryza, oral history interview, *Frontline Diplomacy*.
41. Resolution of the Political Bureau of the Central Committee of the KSČ, November 12, 1963. NA-UV KSC, f. 02/1, sv. 40, ar. j. 45, b. 9.
42. Zídek and Sieber, *Československo a subsaharská Afrika*, p. 120. According to William Attwood, the US ambassador to Kenya, supporters of Odinga also received military training in China and Bulgaria. See Attwood, *The Reds and the Blacks*, p. 241; Hornsby, *Kenya*, p. 88.
43. Zídek and Sieber, *Československo a subsaharská Afrika*, pp. 120–1.
44. For more information on the military mutinies in East Africa, see Timothy H. Parsons, *The 1964 Army Mutinies and the Making of Modern East Africa* (Westport, CT, 2003). Also see Zach Levey, *Israel in Africa: 1956–1976* (Dordrecht, 2012), pp. 117–18.
45. Hornsby, *Kenya*, pp. 98–9.
46. Levey, *Israel in Africa*, pp. 115–18.
47. Deming, oral history interview, *Frontline Diplomacy*.
48. Zídek and Sieber, *Československo a subsaharská Afrika*, pp. 214–15.
49. Stockholm International Peace Research Institute (SIPRI) Arms Transfer Database [online], rev. 17 May 2016. Available at http://www.sipri.org/databases/armstransfers (accessed September 2017). Interestingly, United States intelligence was apparently oblivious to the level of military aid that Czechoslovakia was providing to Uganda. A 1965 confidential State Department report titled 'Sino-Soviet Efforts in Uganda' mentions that Czechoslovakia had signed a scientific and technical cooperation agreement as well as a trade agreement with Uganda and that a Czech expert had been seconded to Uganda's governmental Economic Planning Division, but lists no military aid being given by Prague to Kampala. See General Records of the Department of State. Bureau of African Affairs, 1958–1966, LOT 57D34, Box 36, Folder, 'Communism – Uganda, 1965', NARA.
50. Zídek and Sieber, *Československo a subsaharská Afrika*, pp. 215–17.
51. Dobrovoda, 'Czechoslovakia and East Africa', p. 212.
52. Ministry of Foreign Affairs Report on Uganda, March 20, 1969. Archives of the Czech Ministry of Foreign Affairs [hereafter, AMZV], PZ, Kampala, 1969, e. 012/69, ej. 022. 149/69-SM.
53. Dobrovoda, 'Czechoslovakia and East Africa', pp. 198–201.
54. Report to the Political Bureau of the Central Committee of the KSČ, 17 March 1964. NA-A UV KSC, f. 02/1, sv. 56, ar. j. 60, b. 10.
55. Report to the Political Bureau of the Central Committee of the KSČ, 15 June 1965. NA-A UV KSC, f. 02/1, sv. 110, ar.j. 114, b. 11.
56. Letter from Uganda Desk Officer at the Office of Eastern and Southern African Affairs Beauveau B. Nalle to the Second Secretary of the US Embassy in

Kampala W. Kennedy Cromwell, 5 December 1963. General Records of the Department of State. Bureau of African Affairs, Office of Eastern and Southern African Affairs, Records Relating to Uganda, 1959–1964, Box 6, Folder, 'Political Affairs & Relations – Uganda (including Congo Operation)', NARA.

57. Report to the Political Bureau of the Central Committee of the KSČ, November 12, 1963. NA-UV KSC, f. 02/1, sv. 40, ar. j. 45, b. 9.
58. I would be remiss not to mention that in some ways labelling Kenyatta 'pro-West' and Odinga 'pro-East' is a simplification that lacks nuance. Both were pan-Africanists and Kenyan nationalists. Neither were puppets of the USA, the United Kingdom, the Soviet Union or Czechoslovakia. William Attwood astutely noted, 'There are several appropriate terms we can use to describe the protagonists: moderates vs. radicals, pragmatists vs. ideologists, modernizers vs. agitators, progressives vs. extremists. But we should try to avoid labeling them "pro-East" and "pro-West"'. See Attwood, *The Reds and the Blacks*, p. 239. Attwood's point is well taken, but I have chosen to oversimplify the characterization of Kenyatta and Odinga within the text of this chapter for the sake of brevity in order to emphasize the fact that although both leaders may have been intellectually non-aligned in the Cold War, Kenyatta most definitely leaned to the West, while Odinga leaned to the East.
59. Oginga Odinga, *Not Yet Uhuru* (New York, 1967), pp. 285–6 and 294.
60. Hornsby, *Kenya*, p. 58.
61. Report to the Political Bureau of the Central Committee of the KSČ, February 23, 1965. NA-UV KSC, f. 02/1, sv. 95, ar. j. 100, b. 10; Zídek and Sieber, *Československo a subsaharská Afrika*, pp. 120–1.
62. Hornsby, *Kenya*, pp. 146–7.
63. Odinga, *Not Yet Uhuru*, p. 278. Also see the London *Sunday Telegraph*, 29 November 1964 and Attwood, *The Reds and the Blacks*, p. 244.
64. Hornsby, *Kenya*, p. 147. Czechoslovak sources seem to corroborate Odinga's claim, as they mention Kenyatta discussing the arms delivery directly with Czechoslovak representatives in Nairobi.
65. Ibid., p. 146.
66. Attwood, *The Reds and the Blacks*, pp. 242–3.
67. Ibid., pp. 244 and 321.
68. Hornsby, *Kenya*, pp. 100–107.
69. Ibid., pp. 142 and 156.
70. Zídek and Sieber, *Československo a subsaharská Afrika*, p. 123; Odinga, *Not Yet Uhuru*, pp. 277–8. Besides the three expelled Czechoslovaks, eight other alleged intelligence agents from communist states were also expelled. See Attwood, *The Reds and the Blacks*, p. 329.
71. Hornsby, *Kenya*, pp. 100–101.
72. SIPRI Arms Transfer Database [Online], rev. 17 May 2016. Available at http://www.sipri.org/databases/armstransfers (accessed September 2017).
73. Muehlenbeck, *Czechoslovakia in Africa*.

CHAPTER 11

UNFULFILLED PROMISED LANDS: MISSED POTENTIALS IN RELATIONS BETWEEN HUNGARY AND THE COUNTRIES OF THE MIDDLE EAST, 1955-75

Csaba Békés and Dániel Vékony

This chapter focuses on Hungary's relations with the countries of the Middle East.[1] We chose to focus on this region, since it had the most intense diplomatic and commercial relations with Hungary compared with other countries of the 'Third World' in this era due to its geographical proximity and its historical links.

The 'Third World' in general, and the Middle East in particular, was never a region of strategic concern for Hungary, but its importance increased in the second half of the 1950s. There were a number of reasons for this. Firstly, the Middle East became important for Hungary – a member of the Soviet bloc – once the significance of the region for Moscow started to increase. Secondly, the diplomatic isolation of the country following the crushing of the 1956 Revolution meant that the Hungarian Government needed any possible political support to have the so-called 'Hungarian question' removed from the United Nations General Assembly's agenda. Thirdly, commercial relations with the countries in the Middle East meant potential sources of hard currency, which Hungary badly needed throughout the Cold War era. As Hungary needed trading partners to address its imbalance in trade and the resulting outflow of currency, these states were plausible trading candidates.[2]

In major works covering Hungary's history and foreign policy in the twentieth century, the Middle Eastern dimension has only marginal emphasis. Ignác Romsics mentions the Middle East as part of the Third World in connection with the country's diplomatic isolation during the post-1956 years.[3] Mihály Fülöp and Péter Sipos do not go into much more detail either; they also emphasize the Middle Eastern countries as potential partners, which could be used to put an end to the suspension of Hungary's UN membership after the revolution.[4] We found the same limited approach regarding Middle Eastern relations in the book edited by Ferenc Gazdag and J. László Kiss.[5] Academic works dealing with diplomatic relations between Hungary and the Middle East are very hard to come by. László J. Nagy's work is one of the few exceptions; building on archival research, Nagy highlights interesting diplomatic dynamics between Hungary, the Soviet bloc and the Middle East.[6] A Cold War International History Project (CWIHP) e-Dossier by Békés, Nagy and Vékony gives a somewhat broader insight to this topic.[7] A number of thematic works cover our topic from a certain point of view: Attila Mong mentions Middle Eastern relations with regard to Hungary's accumulation of international debt[8] and Pál Germuska focuses on military cooperation and exports,[9] whereas Gábor Búr analyses relations between Hungary and states of the Non-Aligned Movement.[10] We also relied on memoirs and books of former foreign ministers Endre Sík and Frigyes Puja. Besides the secondary literature, we also used primary-source documents from the Hungarian National Archives. These are mainly reports for the Hungarian Socialist Workers' Party (HSWP) Political Committee, and various documents from the Hungarian Ministry of Foreign Affairs.

Most Middle Eastern countries were former colonies, and as such were suspicious of Western governments. Some countries in the region aligned themselves with the Western alliance, such as the kingdoms of the Gulf, Israel and Iran before 1979. Others – such as Egypt, Syria, Libya and Iraq – leaned towards the Soviet bloc. These so-called 'friendly states' had closer relations with the Soviet bloc, and, as a result, with Hungary. However, these states guarded their hard-won independence passionately. Despite the fact that nationalist Arab regimes, and even the Israeli Government, adopted many measures that were part of socialist ideology – such as a centrally controlled judiciary and legislative bodies; the nationalization of key industries; and a state-interventionist attitude, increasing welfare services, etc. – they did not adopt a communist system and they never considered joining the Soviet bloc.[11] Besides, their disregard for human rights and social freedoms meant recurring conflicts with Western governments. According to Adeed Dawisha, Arab nationalists never intended to adopt the Western liberal democratic model either but rather one that suited their nationalist agenda and political survival.[12] This, paired with suspicion of former colonial powers and their Western allies, pushed a number of Arab regimes towards the Soviet bloc. Furthermore, even though these nationalist regimes did not adopt communism, most of the time they allowed the functioning of local communist parties.

As a Soviet bloc country small in size and population, Hungary was destined to play a secondary role in regional politics; however, it often played the role of a mediator whenever the Soviets could not or did not want to get involved in a primary capacity. These rare occasions increased the standing of Hungary within the Soviet bloc, and as such increased its government's room for manoeuvre. They also enabled Hungary to enhance its position in the Middle East, which was very helpful when commercial links needed to be managed and developed. After all, the countries of the region became trading partners with Budapest and in such a role they provided Hungary with much-needed hard currency, which was always in short supply during the Cold War. However, despite the fact that during the 1950s and 1960s prospects appeared very promising, political and commercial relations with Middle Eastern states could never occupy a vital position in Hungary's foreign-relations portfolio. The countries of the region lacked the level of financial and economic resources to become major strategic partners for Hungary. As Búr points out, although commercial relations played an increasingly important role between Hungary and Middle Eastern countries, they were dwarfed by the former's commercial ties within the Soviet bloc and to other European countries.[13] The only exception to this trend was trade in military hardware. Military exports to the region not only led to the blossoming of a marginalized industry in Hungary, but it also led

Diplomatic Relations Before the 1956 Revolution

Hungary's relations with the Middle Eastern region were not significant in the postwar years until Stalin's death in March 1953. After World War II, the short-lived Hungarian coalition government sent Viktor Csornoky as envoy to lead the legation in Cairo in 1947, only to be recalled to Budapest after the communists took power in Budapest the following year.[14] After the departure of Csornoky, diplomatic relations were lowered to the chargé level, but bilateral commercial ties with Egypt remained active. After 1948, in line with the Zhdanov Doctrine, according to which there was no possible third way between the West and the Soviet bloc, relations of the latter with Middle Eastern countries were negligible.[15] The region, where decolonization was gradually taking place but where in the late 1940s and early 1950s there was still considerable British and French influence, was regarded as part of the Western sphere of influence.[16] In those years, Hungary did not stand out from the rest of the Soviet bloc in its relations there.

Yet, in 1952, the Hungarian Government served as mediator between Egypt and the People's Republic of China (PRC). As is known, prior to its recognition of the PRC in 1954, Egypt had recognized the rival Kuomintang regime based in Taiwan. Since Cairo wanted to establish diplomatic and trade relations with Communist China, it asked for Hungarian assistance. To this effect, in 1952 an Egyptian delegation led by Gamel Salem, a member of the Revolutionary Committee in Egypt – a small executive group made up of the leading figures of the Free Officers Movement – visited Budapest. This meeting was the first step on the road to Egypt's recognition of the PRC, and thus trade between the two countries began to flourish in the following years. This example shows how even a smaller satellite of Moscow could play a mediating role in certain cases; as Hungary remained in the background in this case meetings between the two parties did not draw much attention. On a number of occasions, Hungary did not shy away from playing similar roles in order to improve its international standing.[17]

After Stalin's death, one of the main directions of the newly emerging dynamic in Soviet foreign policy was penetration into the Third Word states. Communist Party of the Soviet Union (CPSU) Central Committee (CC) First Secretary Nikita Khrushchev introduced the 'doctrine of active foreign policy', by which the other members of the Soviet bloc were encouraged by Moscow to play a more proactive role in international politics.[18] While this policy had been promoted by Moscow since as early as the spring of 1954, in early January 1956 – hardly a month before the Twentieth Congress of the CPSU, at the most important summit meeting of the Soviet bloc leaders since Stalin's death – Khrushchev presented his vision in a spectacular way. 'It is true that the Soviet Union is the great force of our camp', he declared, 'but if we organized our work in a more flexible way, the Soviet Union would not always have to be the first to take action. In certain situations one or another country of peoples' democracy could take action and then the Soviet Union would support that country. There are issues in which the countries of peoples' democracies could take action better [than the Soviet Union].'[19]

This strategy, and the doctrine of active foreign policy, became an effective model for cooperation amongst the states of the Soviet bloc in the field of foreign policy – especially from the mid-1960s up to the collapse of the communist regimes in East-Central Europe.[20] Thus, from the mid-1950s onwards, Moscow encouraged its allies to use their international reputations, with Soviet support, to the benefit of the Eastern bloc in the international area. The allies had to promote the success of Soviet goals in Europe, and even more so in the Third World – especially in Asia, the Arab states and Latin America.[21] While in Europe priority was given to the development of economic relations with the Western European states, in the Third World the main objective was to facilitate Soviet economic and political penetration, and thereby lasting influence.[22] This included assignments to build intensive political and economic links with the newly emerging independent countries of Africa and Asia. At Soviet initiative, Hungarian foreign policy in the region became somewhat more active after 1953, and the reorientation of the bloc's attitude towards the Middle East began to be especially visible from 1955 onwards. This new policy line towards the countries of the region was based on some of the shared values elaborated on above. As mentioned, nationalism was the main ideology of the region's regimes at that time. Soviet bloc leaders had high hopes for Arab nationalism, which had many left-leaning and internationalist dynamics. And the fact that communist parties had a legal status in most of these countries also helped to improve relations between the Soviet bloc and the 'friendly' states of the region.

The 1956 Revolution in the Mirror of Middle Eastern Relations

The crushing of the Hungarian Revolution, which coincided with the Suez Crisis in October–November 1956, isolated Hungary internationally. After the Soviet intervention on 4 November and the installment of the Kádár government, the Hungarian question was put on the agenda of the UN General Assembly (UNGA) and the country's UN membership was suspended. The UNGA discussed the situation in Hungary at its session every year until December 1962, and adopted resolutions condemning the Soviet intervention. Under the circumstances, the Hungarian question should have been on the agenda for a few months, maybe even a few years, but certainly not until the early 1960s. From the mid-1950s onwards, however, one of the main aims of US foreign policy was to arrest the development of Soviet influence in the Third World and to correspondingly increase the American presence there. For the USA, the Hungarian question represented low-hanging fruit that it did not want to waste. In the 1950s, it was still not clear that the communist system was not viable in the long term. Keeping the 1956 Revolution on the UN agenda for many years, Washington was able to use it as a propaganda tool against Moscow, repeatedly condemning the Kremlin's aggressive policies towards its own allies and its communist ideology as well. The UNGA, which now included a great number of newly independent Third World countries, provided an ideal arena for this propaganda campaign; therefore, the Americans kept the Hungarian question on the agenda as a device with this political objective up until 1962.[23]

The majority of the countries in the Middle East condemned both the Soviet intervention in Hungary and the Western military campaign against Egypt in 1956. The role of Egyptian leaders themselves regarding the revolution could be best described as ambivalent. Gamal Abdel Nasser, a capricious Soviet ally, took advantage of the Hungarian Revolution in his dealings with the Soviet leadership. According to Yevgeny Primakov, a Soviet Arabist (and a later Russian foreign and then prime minister) who had long worked as a Soviet journalist in the region, Nasser had ordered the redistribution of a US-made pamphlet written in Arabic, which described the Soviet intervention as a 'bloody action'.[24] It is highly likely that this was a demonstration of independence on the part of the Egyptian Government vis-á-vis Moscow. During a meeting with a high-level Hungarian delegation in August 1957, however, Nasser was very friendly and he promised support for the Kádár regime at the UN too. During this meeting, he mentioned the hypocrisy of Western powers who regularly intervened in the Middle East but yet condemned the Soviet intervention.[25]

This meeting was part of Budapest's diplomatic offensive to convince Third World nations to support the removal of the Hungarian question from the UNGA's agenda. This offensive had started earlier in 1957, when a goodwill mission led by a deputy foreign minister visited several non-aligned countries, including Egypt, Sudan and Syria.[26] Unable to convince the USA and its allies to abandon their agenda, Budapest wanted to convince individual member states to vote against keeping the Hungarian question on the agenda of the General Assembly. While Hungary managed to drum up support from some friendly countries, eventually it was Washington and Budapest that secretly agreed that the USA would request the removal of the Hungarian question in December 1962 in return for an amnesty granted to the political prisoners of the 1956 Revolution. As a result, as early as 1964, a memorandum by McGeorge Bundy, the national security advisor of US President Lyndon Johnson, was of the opinion that Hungary had achieved the greatest results amongst the Soviet bloc countries in de-Stalinizing the communist system.[27] Again, we can see that relations with Middle Eastern countries had some potential, but these were never actually put to the test.

Relations After the End of Diplomatic Isolation

Hungary's room for manoeuvre expanded considerably after the ending of its diplomatic isolation in 1963. Following the secret agreement with the USA, Hungary no longer needed the direct diplomatic support of the Third World countries in the UN, and as a result, the country's diplomacy could focus on other interests. Naturally, foreign relations needed to be aligned with the general policy of Moscow, but this did not mean that Hungarian foreign policy slavishly followed the Soviet line. By this time, the country clearly had its own set of interests – including a gradual opening to the West, especially in the economic field. On the other hand, Moscow, while regularly giving advice to bloc country officials as general guidance, from the early 1960s onwards the individual countries enjoyed considerable flexibility in forming their own foreign policies within this framework. Relations with the Soviet Union were maintained through a number of channels, and the diplomatic missions played an important role in bilateral communication. János Kádár and other leaders regularly met the Soviet ambassador in Budapest, who usually briefed them on international issues. The Hungarian Embassy in Moscow was also responsible for this communication.[28]

A good example for this is an embassy report from 1967 on the briefing that Soviet foreign ministry officials gave to diplomats of the Soviet bloc. According to the report, the Soviet Union was interested in Arab unity. Progressive or 'friendly' countries (Egypt, Syria, Iraq, Algeria, Yemen) should enjoy closer cooperation, but this should not interfere with the wider unity of the Arab countries. Thus, the Soviet Union was not interested in military cooperation between 'friendly' Arab states. The main reason for this was that Moscow regarded the Arab League as an essentially anti-imperialist bloc, even if some members were openly Western-leaning. According to the report, Moscow was also worried that China might choose to take a more active approach in the region. To prevent this from happening, Moscow deemed it necessary to strengthen political and economic ties with Middle Eastern nations. It realized that 'friendly' Arab countries might not want to adopt the Soviet development model, which focused on heavy industry. Soviet diplomats therefore indicated that allied countries, Hungary included, could play a role in helping 'friendly' Arab governments to design their own socialist-style development model. This was in line with the post-Stalinist approach that accepted the existence of 'various roads to Socialism'. It becomes clear from this report that by 1967, Moscow realized that the Soviet model was not universally applicable in every country.[29] By its stepping back and allowing allied countries to advise friendly Arab regimes, Hungary and other bloc members could play a more active role in promoting the communist model in a more flexible manner than before.

The main goal of the Kádár regime was building a special model of 'consumer' or 'goulash' socialism, and for this it needed to continually increase the standard of living of its subjects. A more comfortable life in return for forgetting about the two weeks of freedom during the revolution in 1956 – this was an unwritten deal between the regime and the Hungarian population, and it was also the basis of the legitimacy of communist rule in Hungary until 1989. As a result, the leadership actively looked for any trading partners outside the Soviet bloc who showed an interest in buying Hungarian export products for hard currency – and the Middle Eastern countries were amongst them. In this sense, Hungary had, by the early 1960s, already adopted a policy very similar to the one later devised under the leadership of CPSU General Secretary Leonid Brezhnev, which emphasized commercial relations based on economic rationality and on mutual benefits. Ideology played a secondary role in this sense. The Hungarian government did not hesitate to set up relations with states that were not openly friendly towards the Soviet bloc. In this respect, we can place the Middle Eastern countries in three main groups. Firstly, the group of 'friendly' or 'progressive' countries, mentioned earlier, contained states with close political, military and commercial ties to Moscow and other Eastern bloc governments. Secondly, there were countries such as Morocco or Lebanon that were not openly friendly; there was no closer political and military cooperation with them, but commercial relations were active. The third group consisted of states that were closely allied to the Western bloc, which allegiance restricted relations both politically and commercially. Naturally, these groups were permeable, as the case of Egypt during the 1960s and 1970s clearly demonstrates. We also need to point out that this grouping can be somewhat simplifying. For instance, even though diplomatic relations of the Soviet bloc states with Israel were cut off after the 1967 war,[30] this did not mean that some commercial ties did not remain in place. Bilateral commercial ties were, in fact, managed through the Israeli Communist Party even after the Six Day War.

Relations with Israel

Hungary's relations with Israel were somewhat different from those of other bloc countries. This was due to the fact that the Hungarian Jewish community survived the Holocaust in much greater numbers than in other countries of the region. Within the bloc, only the Soviet Union itself had a larger Jewish community. After the end of World War II, Jewish Holocaust survivors left Hungary in large numbers to Palestine and, later, to Israel. After the full communist takeover in 1948, this emigration was stopped. The government claimed that the Jewish community was not persecuted in Hungary; education at the prestigious rabbinical seminary in Budapest was maintained even during the most brutal Stalinist times. After 1956, during the Kádár era, the government again allowed a number of Jewish citizens to leave the country for Israel.[31] As a result, there was continuous pressure on the Hungarian Government to issue travel documents for those Jewish Hungarians who wanted to leave. Due to these facts, relations between the two states were already strained in the second part of the 1950s, but diplomatic relations were not yet cut. Budapest decided to use those Hungarian Jews who wanted to emigrate to Israel as bargaining chips in bilateral relations. Thus, until 1967, it was still possible for Hungarian Jews to legally make the *aliyah* – that is, to emigrate to Israel on religious grounds.

However, if Hungarian Jews wanted to perform the *aliyah*, they needed to leave behind most of their belongings, which, as a result, were vested to the Hungarian state. To solve this problem, the Israeli legation smuggled out jewellery and other precious belongings of emigrating Jews in diplomatic pouches. After the Hungarian Government found out about this practice, it stopped the process of allowing Jews to leave the country in September 1958.[32] Hungary held lengthy secret negotiations about this matter with Israel. The Hungarian Government demanded a compensation of US$3 million for the losses caused in exchange for restarting the issuing of permits for Jews to leave the country. Thanks to secret meetings between foreign ministers Golda Meir and Endre Sík, an agreement was negotiated according to which Israel paid US$1.5 million broken down into smaller instalments. In exchange, Hungary resumed the issuing of permits but only on a case-by-case basis, effectively creating a bottleneck in the process.[33]

Stalin's initial hope that Israel would become friendly towards the Soviet bloc did not materialize, as the Jewish state aligned itself increasingly with Western countries. Even in the 1950s, when the USA was still hesitant about giving it stronger support, the Israeli Government was already leaning towards the West. As far as Hungarian interests were concerned, the West-leaning Israeli Government supported the resolutions condemning the 1956 Hungarian question at the UN, which complicated bilateral relations.

During the 1960s, Hungary's relations with the Soviet Union were based on the principle of constructive loyalty. Therefore, Hungary cut off diplomatic relations with Israel after the Six Day War in 1967, in compliance with Moscow's general line.[34] Nevertheless, some commercial ties remained, which were managed in cooperation with the Israeli Communist Party (ICP) throughout the coming decades. This link to the ICP was so important after the Six Day War that an ICP shell-company, called Eximis, took over the management of bilateral commercial relations even though this meant some problems for trade due to the company's inexperience.[35] The ICP was put in a monopolistic position not only in the field of the trade in goods but of that in services as well. According to a Foreign Ministry proposal in 1981, all tourism-related business activities between the two countries had to be organized through the auspices of the ICP.[36] Thus, the Hungarian Government indirectly supported the ICP since in many instances the Party found itself in dire financial situations. To avoid bankruptcy, the ICP regularly reached out to communist parties in the Soviet bloc, and Hungary was no exception. At the end of the 1960s and the beginning of the 1970s, the Hungarian Government supported the ICP by providing it aid to a total value of US$13,000, given in financial assets and in kind. In 1971, Hungary offered a further US$5,000 to help the ICP.[37] The relationship with the ICP involved a mix of ideological and economic necessities. Hungary wanted to profit from trade with Israel, but it preferred to manage these relations through the institutions of the ICP even if this meant a bottleneck in trade and some lost deals in the process.

Hungary needed to play a delicate balancing act with regard to Israel. The government needed hard currency in order to modernize its economy and sustain the growth in living standards. Tourism from Israel and trade with Israeli companies meant a tangible source of foreign currency. The problem was that Budapest could not afford to lose the goodwill of other 'friendly' governments in the region. Throughout this period, Egypt, Syria and Iraq became increasingly important for Hungary. Trade with these countries grew, and the Hungarian Government could not afford to lose these trading partners. As a result, relations with Israel played only a minor role during these years; Hungary's Jewish community could not serve as a bridge between the two countries. The potential from trade and tourism could be only partly exploited, which could be blamed in large part on the frosty and eventually non-existent diplomatic relations after 1967. Hungary had to sacrifice close Israeli relations in order to remain in line with bloc policy on the one hand, and to secure lucrative trade deals with friendly Arab states on the other.

Since Hungary needed to maintain good relations with Middle Eastern countries, it did not hesitate to recognize the Palestine Liberation Organization (PLO). An organization led by Yasser Arafat, in 1975, the PLO opened an office in Budapest.[38] Hungary was sympathetic towards the PLO from an ideological aspect as well: the country regarded it as an anti-imperialist organization fighting the oppression of a Western-leaning Israeli Government.[39] After it established official relations with the PLO, Arafat visited Hungary several times during the 1970s and 1980s and relations were cordial.

In 1975, an aeroplane belonging to the Hungarian airline MALÉV was downed on its way to Beirut, Lebanon. To this day, it remains unclear who shot it down. There are speculations that MALÉV planes were used to deliver weapons to friendly regimes, and as a result Israel did so after a number of secret warnings to the Hungarian Government. Thus far, no archival evidence has been accessible that sheds light on the fate of this aircraft. Perhaps this could be an interesting subject for future research.

Economic Relations: When the East becomes 'West'

After the 1956 Revolution, the newly instated Kádár regime had to earn popular legitimacy. To gain public support, the government embarked on a strategy to gradually increase living standards. This required a reorientation of the economy, one that specifically focused more on the production of consumer goods – a task requiring a delicate balancing act. Full employment needed to be sustained in an economy dominated by state-owned enterprises, but new dimensions were also required as far as production was concerned. This problem was exacerbated by the challenge of balancing a budget with a trade deficit, reaching HUF20.083 million (Hungarian Forints) between 1955 and 1975.[40]

The main source of this deficit was Hungary's unbalanced commercial relations with Western countries, as the country required imports of advanced technologies that were not available in the Soviet bloc. This deficit needed to be balanced. On one hand, this led to the accumulation of foreign financial debt;[41] on the other hand, the government was continuously looking for new export markets outside the Soviet bloc. The countries of the Middle Eastern region were ideally positioned in this latter sense for a number of reasons: most of them were former colonies, and as such they had rather underdeveloped economies. Relative geographical proximity was also a positive factor. This meant opportunities for bloc countries, including Hungary.[42] As the socialist, planned economy of Hungary became increasingly uncompetitive compared to the free-market economies of Western Europe, manufactured products with a high degree of added value, such as machinery, could not be sold to those countries in high volumes. Since these products offered the highest profit, it was natural that Hungary was desperately looking for foreign customers who could pay for these export goods in the hard currency that it was chronically lacking.

The only problem was that the countries of the Middle East region had financial and economic difficulties themselves, especially before the first oil crisis of 1973. This is why creative solutions needed to be found to overcome this problem. One of the options was to strike barter agreements. However, such agreements led to further challenges. Firstly, they did not deliver the much-needed foreign currency for Hungary. In return for Hungarian goods, these countries 'paid' with what they could – mostly unprocessed agricultural products, such as cotton. In order to obtain some financial profit and the desired convertible currency, Hungary regularly re-exported these goods on the world market. This resulted in additional transportation costs, which led to a downward push on the prices. A number of bilateral relationships grew strained as a consequence, including the ones with Egypt and Morocco.[43] In order to avoid such situations, the Hungarian Government tried to set up bilateral clearing agreements with its trading partners. But due to the difficult financial situation of the newly independent countries, they often required pre-financing, which led to Hungary providing commercial credit to 'friendly' regimes in the region. This created a paradoxical outcome. According to one Foreign Ministry memorandum from 1965, the financial situation of some countries deteriorated to such a degree that the debt limit on these loans needed to be increased due to high demand.[44] This illustrates the main characteristics of these bilateral trade relationships. They were commercial contacts between countries with relatively weak finances. Therefore, they could not compare with the importance of the close commercial links that existed within the Soviet bloc, and, more crucially, they could never substitute for Hungary's trade relations with Western countries, the source of its chronic trade deficit. Hungary needed Western products to cover the demand for consumer goods on the one hand, and to access much needed modern technology for its own products on the other. The Middle Eastern countries could not offer any of these things, but only mainly raw materials and agricultural products. Commercial relations with the Middle East thus never became significant.

During the 1960s, when the Hungarian economy's weaknesses had not yet surfaced, providing loans for international trading partners seemed reasonable as this was common practice. Not providing commercial credit would have meant some missed deals on the one hand, as other bloc countries also provided similar arrangements for Middle Eastern customers. On the other hand, it would have also laid bare the weaknesses of the Hungarian economy, which was highly undesirable for the regime. If one looks at the trade balance in the 1960s, it becomes clear that while the economy performed reasonably well in that decade, its trade balance was positive only in 1961 and 1966. As such, Hungary was eager to increase trade not only with 'friendly' states but also with countries outside this group. Naturally, the bipolar setup and Hungary's position within the Soviet bloc limited trade with countries allied to Western nations, such as the monarchies of the Persian Gulf. Nevertheless, countries that were not openly 'friendly' also counted as potential commercial partners. A good example for this could be Morocco. Despite the fact that it was not a 'friendly' country during the Cold War, commercial relations were so active that it was one of the five most significant trading partners of Hungary in the region.[45] In 1963, goods with a total value of HUF85.8 million were traded, with a surplus of HUF6.4 million – crucially, in hard currency.[46] Although bilateral trade relations in ordinary products represented a tangible source of income, these were still not enough to address Hungary's overall long-term trade deficit. This is why the country needed export goods that were in high demand and that could have a high markup.[47] For Hungary, these were the so-called 'special goods': the code name for military products in Eastern bloc jargon, generally used even in top-secret documents.

'Special Goods'

For many countries in the Middle East, the second half of the twentieth century was marred by a number of military conflicts. This was the case especially with those in the vicinity of Israel. Successive regional wars with Israel meant that there was a constant demand for military hardware from Arab countries.

Egypt was the first country of the region to try and set up military cooperation with Hungary. In 1948, Egyptian Foreign Minister Ahmed Kashb conducted exploratory talks with Hungarian envoy Csornoky about possible weapons export to the country. In 1955, there was another round of negotiations between Egyptian and Hungarian officials in Egypt, but neither of these produced any tangible results.[48]

Arab defeat in the Six Day War of 1967 led to greater demand for military equipment from Arab governments, who wanted to match Israel. This was an opportunity for Hungary. During the first two decades of the postwar era, the military sector had played only a minor role in Hungarian industry. As János Kádár observed, exports of military equipment were mainly conducted by the Soviet Union and Czechoslovakia, with Hungary playing only a secondary role even in 1967.[49] Furthermore, most of the Hungarian weaponry and military equipment were obtained from the Soviet Union. Only a very marginal number of military products were developed domestically, as the majority of them were produced by using Soviet technology under licence agreements. However, as the Soviet Union could not fulfil the demand from 'friendly' Arab nations, Hungary and other allied countries had the opportunity to fill this gap with their own products.

The increase in Hungary's overall military exports between 1966 and 1970 was 60 per cent. During these four years, the country managed to sell military hardware to the United Arab Republic for £4.2 million, to Syria for £2.9 million and to Iraq for US$100,000.[50] And this was only the beginning. From 1970 onwards, its once-minor military industry became one of the engines of Hungary's exports to countries outside the Soviet bloc. Between 1971 and 1975, Iraq became the major destination for Hungarian military exports, with an overall value of US$57.6 million. This relationship meant an increase in exports from US$1.9 million in 1971 to US$25.6 million in 1975. Syria and Egypt were also important business partners, with overall receipts of

US$15 million and US$10.2 million respectively, but exports to these countries decreased significantly after 1972. Hungary also managed to export weaponry to the Arab Emirate of Dubai and to Lebanon through Bulgaria, with an overall value of US$3.6 million. These deals added up to more than 94 per cent of Hungary's military exports to non-Soviet bloc states in the first half of the 1970s.[51]

This military relationship between Hungary and the countries of the Middle East was not without its challenges. One of the main problems was that in many cases the countries of the Warsaw Pact offered military equipment that were substitutes for, rather than complements of, each other. As a result, Hungary and other bloc countries were acting as each others' rivals instead of being partners in dealing with Middle Eastern customers. Because of this rivalry, their Middle Eastern partners could negotiate individual deals via bilateral channels – and, in the process, they often managed to push prices down. Therefore, during a 1972 CMEA meeting, Hungarian politicians initiated a closer coordination within the Warsaw Pact in order to avoid such competition amongst the allies.[52]

Naturally, the Soviet Union was the best positioned in this rivalry, since it provided its allied states with military technology, in return for which these countries' companies needed to pay a licensing fee that increased the cost of production.[53] Besides, the Soviet Union usually offered a special 'political' price for non-Eastern bloc 'friendly' states that was usually 20–25 per cent lower than the official price. Other bloc countries found it very hard to compete under such conditions. As a result, the military products of Hungarian and other bloc country companies were at a competitive disadvantage. This was furthered when Moscow announced in 1972 that any military exports produced under Soviet licence agreements were to be subject to an additional 10 per cent licence fee. Naturally, this pushed export prices even higher, and eventually its allies managed to convince Moscow to postpone the collecting of these licence fees until 1 January 1976.[54] This disadvantage vis-á-vis the Soviet defence industry had a number of effects. Firstly, it meant an incentive for Hungary to specialize and come up with products developed domestically, since there was no need to pay the licensing fees in these cases. Secondly, when it came to heavy weaponry, Hungary sold products that did not represent the high end of Eastern bloc technology. Nevertheless, when the Soviet industry could not fulfil the increasing demand from Arab countries, allied states could profit from this. For example, when Moscow could not execute a delivery of locators to the Egyptian military, it gave permission to the Hungarians to develop production capacities in order to deliver these products.[55] As a result, Hungary not only secured additional investment in military communication engineering, but could also specialize in this field in the following years.

This initiative was presented during the aforementioned CMEA meeting, on 19 April 1972, held in Moscow. According to the proposition presented by Péter Vályi, Hungary's deputy prime minister, CMEA member states should create a platform that would enable multilateral coordination regarding deliveries of special goods to developing countries. The aim was to enable member states to better manage their inventories and to close the door on possible competition between themselves for customers, which could depress agreed prices. Although at first rejected, this initiative eventually also led to the specialization in research and development of military technologies within CMEA and the Warsaw Pact. Member states agreed to focus their military industries on certain areas. They also agreed to cooperate vis-á-vis third parties when selling military hardware. As a result, demand for weapons from Middle Eastern countries contributed to closer cooperation within CMEA.[56] In reality, however, the Warsaw Pact and CMEA member states could never fully develop an effective multilateral approach and coordination in this lucrative sector. As a result, commercial relations as far as military hardware was concerned remained mostly bilateral.

Satisfying the needs of some Arab governments, such as Egypt, often proved to be challenging for Hungary. As a member of CMEA and the Soviet bloc, its economy was coordinated by prearranged plans. However, demand from Middle Eastern trading partners changed dynamically – which is not surprising, given the tumultuous history of the region. This problem clearly showed the limits and challenges that planned economies faced in the world market, and Hungary was no exception. As produced quantities were predefined in plans, it was extremely hard to fulfil the ever-changing needs of foreign business partners. Another obstacle concerning military trade stemmed from obligations according to which the Warsaw Pact always enjoyed priority over world-market deals. The Hungarian Government approached these difficulties with reasonable creativity. One way of 'opening' this bottleneck was to dip into the reserves of the army and the people's militia. With this step, the government could kill two birds with one stone. It managed to react somewhat more flexibly to certain requests on the one hand, and it also enabled the military to refresh its strategic inventories on the other.[57]

But the Hungarian Government was not always in a position to deliver what 'friendly' Arab states requested. In his report to the Politburo of the HSWP in 1969, Minister of Defence Lajos Czinege reported that Hungary was not able to deliver many of the requested anti-aircraft guns and related radar equipment because the country either did not produce these or simply did not have enough of them available for export. Trade in military hardware also meant further financial burdens for the country in the short run, as these deals required similar commercial-credit arrangements as ordinary trade deals. Hungary and other bloc countries needed to pre-finance these deals, with clients fulfilling their obligations only at later dates. Nevertheless, Hungary did not have a choice: if it wanted to profit from the export of weapons, it needed to play according to the rules of this game. Arab trading partners, such as Egypt and Syria, did not hesitate to exploit their position, and they were aware of their favourable position vis-á-vis other members of the Soviet bloc. It seems that Hungary needed its Arab partners more than they needed Hungary. The assertive style of the Egyptian negotiators betrays this uneven interdependence in favour of Arab regimes and the limits of friendship between Hungary and Middle Eastern states in a report to the politburo by Defence Minister Czinege in 1969.[58] In the report, the staff of the Cairo Embassy described 'the exasperated and negative comments' made by leading Egyptian politicians to the embassy staff.[59] Egyptian negotiators did not try to hide their dissatisfaction, and made clear threats as well. They indicated that if the Hungarian leadership did not fulfil their requests, it would have consequences for the bilateral relations between the two countries. These remarks reveal the vulnerability of Hungary in this rather asymmetrically interdependent relationship.

Conclusion

Hungary, as part of the Soviet bloc, had limited relations with the Middle Eastern countries in the 1950s. After its revolution of 1956 and ensuing diplomatic isolation until 1963, the countries of that region gained special significance as the Hungarian Government wanted to convince those states to vote against keeping the Hungarian question on the United Nations' agenda. Nevertheless, in the end it was a secret deal with the USA, rather than the goodwill of Middle Eastern or other governments, that broke the international isolation. Thus, Middle Eastern countries never played a strategically significant role in Hungary's foreign policy.

After 1963, the country's room for manoeuvre increased significantly. The Soviet Union allowed its allied countries to devise their own foreign policy – even if those policies had to be very much in line with Moscow's general guidance, in the framework of the 'doctrine of active foreign policy'. Hungary used this expanded, but still limited, room for a semi-autonomous foreign policy to further the Kádár regime's legitimacy by increasing the living standards of its population. This system, which has become known as 'consumer' or 'goulash' socialism, required the introduction of consumer goods that relied on Western products and technology. This led to an increase in Hungary's trade deficit vis-à-vis Western economies, which left it in constant need of hard currency.

To address this problem, Hungary needed export markets for its goods, and countries of the Middle East were promising markets for them. According to Frigyes Puja, Hungarian foreign minister between 1973 and 1983, the Middle Eastern countries constituted the largest market for Hungarian machinery and industrial products outside of the Soviet bloc.[60] This, however, was still only a drop in the ocean. Although the Middle Eastern countries became significant trading partners for Hungary, their position was not comparable with that of its traditional regional trading partners. As a result, Hungarian foreign policy of the post-1963 era was based on a national interest rooted in the problematic legitimacy of the regime and its ensuing economic realities. As a result, Hungary often found itself competing with other Soviet bloc countries in finding markets for its export products. Even though Warsaw Pact countries were supposed to be allies, they often became each others' competitors. This development sheds light on the limits of cooperation between supposed allies and partners within the Soviet bloc, and further demonstrates the fact that this alliance was one of compulsion – even for the leaders of those regimes. Hungary's foreign policy towards countries of the Middle East could thus be characterized as the country pursuing its national interest based on domestic political and subsequent economic determinants within the limited framework defined by Moscow.

Nevertheless, commercial relations were active in the civilian sector, and in the military one too. This led to an increase in exports, in both ordinary and 'special' goods. By exporting arms to Arab regimes, the Hungarian Government managed to develop its own military industry, which became a strategic asset in its desperate attempts to narrow the trade deficit that the country had accumulated vis-a-vis Western states. Without additional demand from Middle Eastern states, the Hungarian military industry could never have flourished in the way that it did from the middle of the 1960s onwards.

Even though Arab-nationalist ideology had some common features with that of the Eastern European socialist countries, there was clearly a cleavage between the two. Many Middle Eastern countries were suspicious of the West due to its colonial influence, and this pushed several Arab states towards the Soviet bloc. However, the Arab regimes, having only recently become independent, were not willing to adopt the Soviet model. Therefore, while relations between the members of the Warsaw Pact and 'friendly' Middle Eastern states were indeed special in their character, in reality those countries were never ready to join the Soviet bloc. This was manifested by their occasional persecution of local communist parties if domestic politics necessitated it. These events were criticized in diplomatic, but rarely in official, circles. This asymmetry defined Hungary's attitude towards the countries of the Middle East, including Israel. As it had one of the most open economies in the Soviet bloc, it was extremely reliant on foreign trade and it was also in constant need of hard currency – it therefore badly needed trading partners.

Hungary tried to reap the benefits of this openness by promoting trade in both ordinary and 'special' (military) goods. But these relations had limited prospects. Middle Eastern countries were themselves in a dire financial situation, and, as a result, commercial relations with them could never really address the problem of Hungary's constant trade deficit. This led to the eventual entry of the country into the International Monetary Fund and the World Bank in 1982, to which the Soviet Union had previously objected on several occasions since 1967 but eventually had to accept. Nevertheless, the 20 years between 1955 and 1975 were characterized by increasingly active diplomatic and commercial relations between Hungary and the countries of the Middle

East, with military cooperation becoming steadily more important. On the margin of these relations, Hungary admitted a number of students to its universities, mostly from 'friendly' countries in the region. Many of these students chose to stay in Hungary after their studies, and now form a major part of the small but vibrant Muslim community in the country.[61]

Relations between Hungary and the Middle East started to develop in a promising manner in the 1950s, but due to the limited possibilities in trade and other complications in their relationship, the full potential of such relations was never actually realized. One testimony to the eventually decreasing importance of Middle Eastern Arab regimes is the fact that relations between Hungary and Israel started to thaw as the country's economic situation deteriorated during the 1970s and 1980s. The gradual rapprochement between Israel and Hungary between 1987 and 1989, culminating in the re-establishment of diplomatic relations in 1989, signalled a new era: in the midst of its political transition to democracy, Hungary now cared little about the feelings of governments of the unfulfilled 'promised lands' of the Arab world.

Appendix

Table A.1 Hungary's foreign trade with some Middle Eastern countries (million convertible Forints)

	Import				Export			
	1960	1965	1966	1967	1960	1965	1966	1967
Iraq	2.2	0.4	3.2	2.3	48.2	33.3	38.4	32.9
Iran	29.4	66.1	31.5	52.4	50.3	42.9	40.4	77.0
Israel	15.9	71.3	77.2	90.3	10.7	52.4	76.2	60.6
Jordan	-	-	-	-	5.0	11.1	12.2	7.1
Kuwait	-	-	-	-	1.0	12.8	16.5	50.2
Lebanon	1.0	1.1	1.0	3.1	13.7	43	60.1	81.7
Syria	7.6	54.8	54.7	86.0	13.2	36.2	61.8	55.8
Algeria	-	5.8	10.6	2.9	0.2	5.0	11.7	8.7
UAR Egypt	90.8	99.8	182.6	152.9	75.8	217.3	250.6	117.4
Morocco	2.5	107.4	93.4	37.2	8.9	103.4	21	8.1
Libya	-	-	0.2	0.1	2.7	24.8	30.8	62.4
Sudan	24.3	9.8	1.8	34.0	12.0	14.4	36.7	44.7
Tunisia	2.7	1.0	8.1	2.5	3.0	5.9	5.7	7.0
Total:	176.4	417.5	464.3	463.7	244.7	602.5	662.1	613.6

Source: 'Külkereskedelem' [Foreign trade], Volume 12, Issue 3 (1968), p. 112. Available at https://adtplus.arcanum.hu/hu/view/Kulkereskedelem_1968/?query=Egyiptom&pg=139&layout=s (accessed 2017.02.10).

Table A.2 Hungary's overall foreign trade (million convertible Forints)

Year	Import	Export	Balance
1955	6,506	7,055	549
1956	5,648	5,716	68
1957	8,011	5,728	−2,283
1958	7,407	8,024	617
1959	9,308	9,034	−274
1960	11,455	10,259	−1,196
1961	12,039	12,079	40
1962	13,485	12,905	−580
1963	15,326	14,155	−1,171
1964	17,546	15,870	−1,676

Continued

Table A.2 *Continued*

Year	Import	Export	Balance
1965	17,848	17,721	−127
1966	18,378	18,705	327
1967	20,841	19,971	−870
1968	21,162	21,004	−158
1969	22,631	24,462	1,831
1970	29,410	27,196	−2,214
1971	35,098	29,354	−5,744
1972	34,093	35,583	1,490
1973	37,299	42,038	4,739
1974	51,009	46,926	−4,083
1975	61,537	52,169	−9,368

Source: Tamás Csató, 'Külkereskedelem' [Foreign trade], in István Kollega Tarsoly, Babits Kiadó (eds), *Magyarország a XX. században* [Hungary in the 20th century] (Szekszárd, 1996–2000). Available at http://mek.oszk.hu/02100/02185/html/362.html (accessed October 2017).

Notes

1. In this chapter, we intend to use a wider interpretation of the Middle East. The approach we use covers a much larger area than normally envisaged – dealing with a region that stretches from Morocco to Iran. We are not, however, going to treat Turkey as part of the Middle East because that country was part of NATO and, as such, had insignificant relations with Hungary. Also, the group of countries that we are going to cover does not include Somalia or Mauritania. Thus, the states with which this chapter deals are those that the World Bank and other institutions call the 'MENA' region – that is, the Middle East and North Africa.
2. Hard currency meant any convertible foreign currency. Those of the Soviet bloc, including the Soviet Union itself, were not convertible to Western currencies.
3. Ignác Romsics, *Magyarország története a XX. században* [History of Hungary in the 20th century] (Budapest, 2010), pp. 512–13.
4. Mihály Fülöp and Péter Sipos, *Magyarország külpolitikája a XX. században* [The foreign policy of Hungary in the 20th century] (Budapest, 1998), pp. 429–35.
5. Ferenc Gazdag and J. László Kiss, *Magyar külpolitika a 20. században* [Hungarian foreign policy in the 20th century] (Budapest, 2004).
6. László J. Nagy, *Magyarország és az arab térség – Kapcsolatok, vélemények, álláspontos 1947–1975* [Hungary and the Arab World – Connections, opinions, standpoints 1947–1975] (Szeged, 2006).

7. Csaba Békés, László J. Nagy and Dániel Vékony, 'Bittersweet Friendships: Relations between Hungary and the Middle East, 1953–1988 Selected Documents', Cold War International History Project e-Dossier No. 67, 5 November 2015. Available at https://www.wilsoncenter.org/publication/bittersweet-friendships-relations-between-hungary-and-the-middle-east-1953-1988 (accessed October 2017).
8. Attila Mong, *Kádár hitele* [Kádár's debt] (Budapest, 2012).
9. Pál Germuska, 'A közel-keleti magyar haditechnikai export kezdetei' [The beginning of exports of military hardware to the Middle East], in M. János Rainer and Éva Standeisky (eds), *ÉVKÖNYV XI. 2003. Magyarország a jelenkorban* [Almanac XI. 2003. Hungary in the present day (Budapest, 2003), pp. 79–91; Pál Germuska, *Vörös Arzenál* [Red Arsenal] (Budapest, 2010).
10. Gábor Búr, 'Hungarian Diplomacy and the Non-Aligned Movement in the Cold War', in István Majoros, Zoltán Maruzsa and Oliver Rathkolb (eds), *Österreich und Ungarn im Kalten Krieg* [Austria and Hungary during the Cold War] (Vienna, Budapest, 2010), pp. 353–72.
11. Even though nationalist Arab governments conducted land reform, nationalized companies from key industries, and were not believers in the separation of powers, they never went as far as Soviet bloc countries did. They did not wish to exert total social control or to nationalize or directly coordinate the whole economy. For instance, private merchants in the souks were left to conduct their traditional business and non-strategic private enterprise was also able to compete on the market.
12. Adeed Dawisha, *The Second Arab Awakening* (New York, 2013), pp. 65–73.
13. Búr writes on non-aligned countries in general. According to him, trade from 1966 to 1970 between Hungary and non-aligned states represented no more than 1.5 per cent of all the Hungarian trade activities. Bearing in mind that most Middle Eastern countries were part of the Non-Aligned Movement, we can safely state that trade relations between Hungary and the Middle East could never cross a certain threshold. See Búr, 'Hungarian Diplomacy and the Non-Aligned Movement', p. 372.
14. Csornoky was the son-in-law of the president of the republic, Zoltán Tildy. He was executed in December 1948 after a Stalinist show trial on treason charges. His arrest was used to force Tildy to resign as president.
15. Andrei Zhdanov was the main ideologue of the Soviet Union who introduced this new theory about the existence of two camps, the peace-loving Eastern and the US-led imperialist one, at the founding conference of the Cominform in September 1947.
16. Nagy, *Magyarország és az arab térség*, pp. 23–4.
17. Ibid., pp. 32–4.
18. While the term 'active foreign policy' had been used in confidential as well as public documents since 1954, it was coined as a *doctrine* by Csaba Békés. See Csaba Békés: 'The Warsaw Pact and the Helsinki process, 1965–1970', in Wilfried

Loth and Georges-Henri Soutou (eds), *The Making of Détente: Eastern and Western Europe in the Cold War, 1965–75* (London–New York, 2007), p. 201.
19. Speech of N. S. Khrushchev at the meeting of the European socialist countries' leaders, Moscow, 4 January 1956, Magyar Nemzeti Levéltár – Országos Levéltár [Hungarian National Archives; hereafter, MNL-OL], M-KS-276. f.-62/84. ő.e., quoted in Csaba Békés, 'Cold War, Détente and the Soviet Bloc. The Evolution of intra-bloc Foreign Policy Coordination, 1953–1975', in Mark Kramer and Vit Smetana (eds), *Imposing, Maintaining and Tearing open the Iron Curtain: The Cold War and East-Central Europe, 1945–1989* (Lanham, MD, 2014), p. 251.
20. Csaba Békés, 'East Central Europe, 1953 1956', in Melvyn Leffler and Odd Arne Westad (eds), *The Cambridge History of the Cold War*, vol. 1 (Cambridge, 2010), p. 342.
21. For the text of a complex policy paper on the future role of the Soviet bloc in world policy, prepared by the Soviet Foreign Ministry for the summit meeting of European Communist leaders in Moscow in early January 1956, see Csaba Békés, Malcolm Byrne and János M. Rainer (eds), *The 1956 Hungarian Revolution. A history in documents* (Budapest–New York, 2002), pp. 106–13.
22. Békés, 'Cold War, Détente and the Soviet Bloc', p. 251.
23. Csaba Békés, *The 1956 Hungarian Revolution and World Politics*, Cold War International History Project Working Paper No. 16, Woodrow Wilson International Center for Scholars (Washington, DC, September 1996), p. 24.
24. Yevgeny Primakov, *Russia and the Arabs* (New York, 2009) p. 66.
25. MNL-OL, Küm, XIX-J-1-j, Egyiptom Tük, 1957. 5.d. 5/b–004399/1. Visit of a Hungarian government delegation to Egypt. Cairo, 26 September 1957. Report by the ambassador (excerpts). The visit took place between 5 and 28 September. Published in Hungarian in Nagy, *Magyarország és az arab térség*.
26. Búr, 'Hungarian Diplomacy and the Non-Aligned Movement', p. 369.
27. Memorandum from the President's Special Assistant for National Security (Bundy) to President Lyndon Johnson, 14 April 1964. *Foreign Relations of the United States, 1964–1968*, vol. XVII (Washington, DC, 1996), p. 301.
28. Meetings between communist parties were also significant channels of communication not just between Budapest and Moscow but also with other countries of the Soviet bloc and the Middle East, as we shall examine later.
29. MNL-OL, XIX-J-1-j-SZU-1001684/1967. Also see Alessandro Iandolo, 'The Rise and Fall of the "Soviet Model of Development" in West Africa, 1957–64', *Cold War History* 12 (4) (2012), pp. 683–704.
30. With the exception of Romania.
31. Josef Govrin, 'Egyszerre csak egy lépés: Izraeli–magyar kapcsolatok, 1967–1989' [One step at a time: Israeli-Hungarian relations, 1967–1989] *Nemzet és Biztonság* [Nation and Security] (2009).
32. MNL-OL, M-KS 288. f. 8/146. ő.e.
33. Endre Sík, *Bem rakparti évek* [Years in the Bem embankment] (Budapest, 1970), pp. 189–92.

34. On Hungarian foreign policy in the Kádár era, see Csaba Békés, 'Hungarian foreign policy in the Soviet alliance system, 1968–1989', *Foreign Policy Review* (Budapest), vol. 3, no. 1 (2004), pp. 87–127. Available at http://www.coldwar.hu/html/en/publications/foreign_policy.html (accessed October 2017).
35. MNL–OL, M-KS, 288. f. 5/434. ő.e.
36. MNL–OL, M-KS 288. f. 5/823. ő.e (1981.03.28.) 1R/67.
37. MNL-OL, M-KS 288. f. 5/563. ő.e. (1971.09.07.) 47R/79.
38. Magyar Köztársaság Külügyminisztériuma [Ministry of Foreign Affairs]. 2005. Palesztin Hatóság – Diplomáciai kapcsolatok [Palestinian Authority – Diplomatic relations]. Available at http://www.mfa.gov.hu/kum2005/Templates/OldTemplates/CikkSablonWord.aspx?NRMODE=Published&NRORIGINALURL=%2Fkum%2Fhu%2Fbal%2FKulpolitikank%2F_volt_ketoldalu_kapcsolatok%2FAzsia%2Fpalesztin_hatosag%2F&NRNODEGUID=%7B949930BA-FFB6-476D-BC02-C2BE252AA0F0%7D&NRCACHEHINT=NoModifyGuest&printable=true (accessed October 2017).
39. Foreign Ministry memorandum on the Palestine Liberation Movement in 1970 (Excerpts) (10 August 1970) Source: MNL–OL, Küm, XIX-J-1-j, Palesztina Tük 1971. 72. d. 001302/8. The state of the Palestine Liberation Organization (excerpts) Budapest 10 August 1970. Foreign Ministry analysis. Published in Hungarian in Nagy, *Magyarország és az arab térség*.
40. Tamás Csató, 'Külkereskedelem' [Foreign trade], in István Kollega Tarsoly,. Babits Kiadó (eds), *Magyarország a XX. században* [Hungary in the 20th century] (Szekszárd, 1996–2000). Available at http://mek.oszk.hu/02100/02185/html/362.html (accessed October 2017).
41. Mong, *Kádár hitele*.
42. The chapter by Przemysław Gasztold in this volume comes to a similar conclusion: Poland's African foreign policy was also motivated by economic profit.
43. MNL–OL, Küm, XIXJ-1-j, Arab országok Tük, 1965. 111. d. IV-14.
44. Ibid.
45. Imports from Morocco were mainly raw materials: unprocessed agricultural products such as phosphate, animal feed, rice and exotic fruits. In return, Hungary's main export goods were various types of machinery and components used in food processing, mining, electric infrastructure, etc. Besides, during the 1970s there was an increase in the export of textiles, chemical and pharmaceutical goods. Mátyás Domonkos, *A magyar-arab gazdasági kapcsolatok* [Hungarian-Arab Economic Relations] in *Külgazdaság*, Vol. 18, No. 2 (1974), pp. 95–101.
46. This figure can be broken down: out of this number, exports represented HUF46.1 million and imports numbered HUF39.7 million. For more information on bilateral trade relations and figures, see MNL–OL, Küm, XIX J-1-j, Arab országok, Tük, 1965. 111. d. IV-14. This document is also available in the e-Dossier by Békés, Nagy and Vékony: 'Bittersweet Friendships'.

47. A markup is the difference between the cost of production and the selling price. This is effectively the part of the price that will be pure profit. The higher the markup, the more profit one can realize. Manufactured goods usually have a higher markup than raw materials or unprocessed agricultural products.
48. J. Nagy, *Magyarország és az arab térség*, pp. 28–9.
49. MNL–OL M-KS 288. f. 5/430. ő.e. M-KS 288. f. 5/43.
50. Germuska 'A közel-keleti magyar haditechnikai export kezdetei', pp. 79–91.
51. Germuska, *Vörös Arzenál*, p. 168.
52. Ibid., pp. 148–50.
53. Ibid.
54. Ibid., p. 169.
55. MNL–OL, M-KS 288. f. 5/501 ő.e. (1969.10.21).
56. Germuska, *Vörös Arzenál*, pp. 148–50.
57. Ibid.
58. MNL–OL, M-KS 288. f. 5/501 ő-KS 288. F. 5/501. This document is also available in the e-Dossier by Békés, J. Nagy and Vékony: 'Bittersweet Friendships'.
59. Ibid.
60. Frigyes Puja, *Magyar külpolitika* [Hungarian foreign policy] (Budapest, 1980), p. 121.
61. For an in-depth assessment of the Hungarian Muslim community, see L. Csicsmann and Daniel Vékony, 'Muslims in Hungary: A Bridge Between East and West?' in J. Bures (ed.), *Muslims in Visegrad* (Prague, 2011), pp. 57–72.

CHAPTER 12

BULGARIAN MILITARY AND HUMANITARIAN AID TO THIRD WORLD COUNTRIES: 1955–75

Jordan Baev

Soviet bloc policy since the establishment of the Warsaw Treaty Organization in May 1955 was coordinated by the Kremlin on the principle of a 'distribution of tasks' amongst its smaller Eastern European allies. The primary aim of that 'coordinative framework' was focused towards the 'main adversary' – the USA and NATO – and towards Europe in general. Thus, Bulgarian foreign and security policy was oriented on the southern flank of the two military blocs – the Balkans and the eastern Mediterranean. Due to its geopolitical position and historical legacy within an Islamic empire, Bulgaria was also assigned the task of maintaining a more active policy in the Middle East. In the 1960s and the 1970s, Sofia became more involved with support for various leftist regimes and front organizations in Asia, Africa and Latin America. The global nature of the bipolar IR model during the Cold War era logically determined such long-distance involvements in military and political conflicts. At the height of the decolonization process, between 1955 and 1965, the countries of what was known as 'Black Africa' became a new significant target, and during the Indochina War, Vietnam and Laos also became recipients of large amounts of military, economic and humanitarian aid. Latin American countries (except Cuba) began to be a significant target for the Bulgarian leadership only after 1970.

While Warsaw Pact countries pursued fairly independent policy initiatives in the spheres of economic and cultural cooperation with the Third World, military and security policy was more 'sensitive' and was thus subject to confidential joint coordination in advance. The aim of this study is limited to the discussion of this highly sensitive area: the 'special' Bulgarian military and humanitarian aid and sales delivered to various governments and non-governmental actors in the Middle East, Asia, Africa and Latin America. The chapter is based on a huge variety of newly declassified Bulgarian political, governmental, diplomatic, military and intelligence records that have been the subject of this author's study over the previous two decades.[1] While the Third World military conflicts and political and economic bilateral relations with Third World countries have been discussed in various Bulgarian publications, the particular case of the delivery of military and humanitarian aid to those countries from Sofia has thus far been lacking, both in international and national Bulgarian historiography.

The first case of Bulgaria's involvement outside of Europe took the form of humanitarian support for North Korea during the 1950–3 Korean War. A small and undeveloped agrarian country, postwar Bulgaria could not contribute substantially with any concrete assistance; its support was required by Moscow rather as a symbolical moral gesture in favour of Stalin's and Mao Zedong's backing for North Korea. In 1952–6, Bulgaria sent two 'medical brigades' of about 60 physicians in total to North Korea under the flag of the Bulgarian Red Cross. In the 1952 campaign, for only four months, about 1,174,000 items of clothing and a large amount of food products worth BGN 52 million were collected in Bulgaria; they were transported by 60 freight wagons through Romania, the Soviet Union and China. In 1953–6, the Bulgarian Government also delivered free technical and economic aid for the postwar recovery of North Korea to the tune of about RUB80 million, including two factories. The communist regime in Bulgaria used the two public campaigns 'in support of the fighting Korean nation' in 1951 and 1952 for a wider psychological mobilization of its population 'against American imperialism'.[2]

With the exception of North Korea, Bulgaria's military and humanitarian assistance to Third World countries began at the height of the decolonization process in the late 1950s and early 1960s, reaching its peak in the mid-1970s.[3] A fundamental distinction should be drawn, however, between military aid to clandestine national-liberation movements and arms supply to independent governments through official bilateral agreements. Still, it is very difficult to give a universal definition and determine precisely the exact typology of terrorism since modern and contemporary history shows so many examples of illegal armed movements that formed future ruling elites, and whose leaders and commanders become respectful presidents or prime ministers of their newly established states. In the bipolar postwar world, the logic of Bulgaria's support sometimes followed a simple principle of 'the enemy of our enemy is our friend'. This logic became even more complicated in the mid-1960s as the split between the Soviet Union and the People's Republic of China added a third contender for influence in the Third World.

The Middle East

Until the 1950s, Soviet bloc countries did not pay any special attention to the Middle East. Until 1952, Bulgaria supported the 'struggle of the new Jewish state against British imperialism and reactionary Islamic empires' like other communist regimes in Eastern Europe. Soviet policy towards Israel and Arab reaction was reflected in the words of Abdullah I bin al-Hussein, the king of Transjordan, who in 1951 warned about 'the Russian-Jewish threat to the Arab world'.[4] Initial tensions in Israeli–Bulgarian relations appeared only in the summer of 1955, when a Bulgarian Air Forces pilot shot down an Israeli civilian aeroplane that had crossed from Yugoslavia into Bulgarian air space in error. The investigation that followed proved that the incident was not a premeditated action but a pilot error, caused mainly by the psychological confrontational atmosphere of a 'war of nerves' between the two blocs.[5] A radical change in policy came only after the Soviet Union and its allies backed Egypt following the coming to power of radical nationalist leader, Gamal Abdel Nasser in February 1954, followed by the Suez Crisis.

However, Bulgaria's first delivery of military aid to an Arab nation was for the National Liberation Front (FLN) who fought for the independence of Algeria from France during the 1958–62 Algerian War. On 19 August 1958, the Bulgarian Communist Party (BCP) Politburo adopted a Ministry of Defence proposal to send material aid to the FLN. In January 1959, material aid for the Algerian rebels was transported via Tunisia. The first arms delivery was transported by sea in July 1960. A second, secret, resolution for arms delivery to the FLN through Morocco was signed on 3 November 1960. On 19 November, the commercial ship *Bulgaria*, with 1,800 tonnes of weaponry and ammunition on board, ran a French naval blockade and reached the Moroccan port of Tangiers. In January of the next year, another arms delivery, worth BGN 700,000, was sent to the FLN along with three Bulgarian military instructors. The Algerian national-liberation army headquarters requested help to organize a secret base on Bulgarian territory for the delivery of armaments from the Warsaw Pact countries. After consultations with Moscow, the Bulgarian political leadership accepted the proposal. On 15 March 1961, BCP First Secretary Todor Zhivkov addressed confidential letters on the matter to his colleagues Gheorghe Gheorghiu-Dej in Romania, Walter Ulbricht in East Germany, János Kádár in Hungary, Władysław Gomułka in Poland and Antonín Novotný in Czechoslovakia because 'it was a common issue of the competence of all Warsaw Pact allies'. After about a month, positive responses were received from all these Eastern European leaders.[6] A few years later, Zhivkov explained in a confidential conversation with Raul Castro in Sofia that 'the [FLN] staff for providing the weaponry from the socialist countries for the Algerian insurgents was in Bulgaria'.[7] In 1962–3, the Bulgarian Government approved several other resolutions for the delivery of free military and material aid to the provisional Algerian government, and dispatched a large number of technical experts and a military medical brigade of 20 physicians.[8] In 1963–5, more than 400 young Algerian cadets received education or training at Bulgarian Air Force and Land Forces military schools.[9]

Soon after the Suez Crisis of 1956, contacts between Bulgaria and some Arab nationalist regimes became more intensive. The Middle East conflict was viewed by Soviet bloc experts as part of the global Cold War confrontation, and a direct result of the USA's attempt to dominate the region through the Eisenhower Doctrine. A mass anti-US campaign started in Eastern Europe after the landing of US and British marines and paratroopers in Lebanon and Jordan in the summer of 1958. During this campaign, both the Bulgarian Ministry of Defence and the Central Committee (CC) of the BCP received many requests from dismissed officers insisting to be sent as 'volunteers to support the struggle of the Arab people'.[10]

Bulgaria developed an ever-growing interest towards the Middle East crisis because of its proximity to the region. Despite the fact that the Bulgarian leadership was clearly suspicious about the true positions, intentions and goals of some Arab leaders like Nasser in Egypt or, later on, Hafiz al-Assad and Saddam Hussein in Syria and Iraq respectively, it provided military assistance and permitted the establishment of official contacts with the state-security services in those countries. Zhivkov's initial attitude towards Nasser was sceptical, as is clear from his statement at a CC BCP plenary session on 2 October 1958:

> Nasser is a nationalist, a military person, without necessary political and life experience, and with the ambitions of a dictator. He perhaps believes that life is something of a military barracks and that he can command and lead the people in whatever direction he wishes.[11]

Attitudes towards Nasser, however, changed slowly in Sofia over the next few years, influenced mostly by the Kremlin's closeness to the Egyptian leader.

The decision to begin arms deliveries to Middle East governments was made in 1959 with the signature of the first CC BCP Politburo resolution on the matter on 15 May 1959.[12] One of the reasons was that Bulgaria had a surplus of Soviet and Bulgarian-made small arms left from a radical reduction of the armed forces in 1956–9 and, according to a politburo discussion from May 1960, these arms should be sold to Third World countries like Iraq, the United Arab Republic (UAR), Indonesia and Ghana.[13] In January 1962, a Syrian military delegation visited Sofia. The head of the delegation raised the question of delivery of military equipment for strengthening the 'defence capacity of the Syrian armed forces against the hostile neighbouring countries Israel and Turkey'. The Syrian leadership formulated its request in four main points: to assist in the delivery of Soviet and Czech planes, tanks, missiles, artillery pieces, etc., which were not produced in Bulgaria; to deliver Bulgarian-made military equipment to Syria; to train pilots and paratroopers, assist in the establishment of an Air Forces school in Syria; and to participate in the build-up of Syrian military airfields, command posts, depots, repairs bases, etc. This request was immediately transferred to the Central Committee (CC) of the Communist Party of the Soviet Union (CPSU) Presidium, and very soon Moscow informed Sofia that 'the question had been resolved positively in principle'. On 25 January 1962, the CC BCP Politburo approved a special secret resolution on the matter. Over the following years, Bulgaria participated in the construction of Syrian airfields near Damascus, Dmer and Tifor, and of a naval base in Latakia.[14]

Despite some misunderstandings and mutual suspicions at the beginning, Bulgaria's relations with Arab countries grew in the 1960s. In 1963, a new agreement for the delivery of military equipment to the UAR was signed.[15] In June–July 1963, the CC BCP Secretariat and Council of Ministers approved additional resolutions for free arms delivery to the Yemen Arab Republic.[16] In February 1965, a Bulgarian ship delivered to the Yemeni port of Hodeyda weapons and military equipment worth approximately BGN 800,000 (about US$500,000). In November 1965, a Bulgarian official delegation, led by Prime Minister Todor Zhivkov, visited Cairo and discussed with Nasser, Field Marshal Amer and other Egyptian leaders the prospects for the enlargement of bilateral relations. A few months later, a Syrian delegation, led by Prime Minister Youssef Zuein, visited Sofia. Amongst the members of this delegation was General Hafiz al-Assad, then Syrian defence minister.

At the end of October 1966, a Bulgarian military delegation, headed by the defence minister General Dobri Dzhurov, paid a visit to the UAR. On 31 October, the two sides signed a long-term bilateral agreement on military equipment for the period 1967–71 in Cairo. However, ratification of the agreement was postponed until late May 1967, and thus the arms and ammunitions did not arrive in the UAR before the Six Day War in June.[17] In October 1966, Bulgaria and the UAR signed another protocol – this one for training Egyptian officers and exchanging observers during military exercises carried out in both countries.[18] Only the protocol was made public; the agreement for arms delivery was kept secret. Therefore, in a telegram from 2 November

1966, the US diplomatic representative in Sofia, John McSweeney, informed Washington that 'General Dzhurov visit to UAR was only return for UAR defense minister visit last March', and did not confirm the rumours of 'shipments of military equipment'.[19]

Bulgaria's commitment to Arab countries aggravated its official relations with Israel. The Bulgarian Government was seriously perturbed by a few preventative sanctions from the 'frontline' Arab countries against some Bulgarian foreign-trade companies such as its national airline, TABSO, and the Bulgarian merchant fleet because of their contacts with some Israeli companies. In a report to the CC BCP Politburo in May 1965, Bulgarian Foreign Minister Ivan Bashev suggested a 'clarification of the Bulgarian policy toward Israel in the light of Bulgarian-Arab relations'. The main conclusion in the report was: 'The political and economic interests of our country with the Arab world demand Bulgaria to determine its relations with Israel in frames that could not hamper its economic cooperation with the Arab countries.' On 6 July 1965, the Bulgarian leadership approved a resolution, which prescribed that trade with Israel be managed by a separate organization in order to avoid 'direct contacts with Israeli companies', and that cultural and sporting contacts be limited to a small number of individual visits.[20] From 1966 to early 1967, Bulgarian diplomatic missions in Damascus, Cairo and Tel Aviv sent a large number of reports and cipher telegrams regarding increasing tension in Israeli–Arab relations and border incidents.[21] Reports from Arab capitals increasingly discussed the indicators of total 'war psychosis' and the increase of everyday claims against Israeli 'border provocations'.[22]

During the Six Day War in June 1967, Bulgaria decisively backed the Arab countries. On 13 June, the Bulgarian Government adopted a secret decision for the immediate delivery of free military aid to Syria, and a week later the CC BCP Secretariat approved a proposal for providing humanitarian aid (medical goods, food, clothes, etc.) to the Arab nations worth more than BGN 1 million.[23] On 18 July 1967, the CC BCP Politburo discussed proposals made in a report by the ministers of foreign affairs and foreign trade, and approved a secret resolution for 'extending [...] contacts with the Arab countries'. Defence Minister Dzhurov was entrusted with the task of designing a new programme for 'increasing [...] collaboration with the Defense ministries in the UAR, Syria, and Algeria'. Amongst the measures recommended were increases in the size of arms deliveries and in the number of Arab officers admitted into Bulgarian military schools.[24] According to an additional proposal, the Bulgarian military and economic aid and loans that were to be delivered to the Arab states after the Six Day War exceeded the sum of BGN 22 million. On 27 September, the Council of Ministers approved a secret decision for additional arms sales to Syria, on credit, amounting to US$5 million for a period of eight years at 2.5 per cent interest per year.[25] On 28 June 1970, the governments of Bulgaria and Syria signed a new secret agreement for armaments delivery.[26]

The Six Day War radically changed the Soviet bloc position towards the Middle East conflict in favour of stronger and more categorical support of the Arab cause and a long-term break in bilateral relations with Israel. The main reasons for such a sharp turn were due to the domination of a general schematic communist vision of local conflicts throughout the world as outcomes of the global bipolar Cold War confrontation. The world arena was viewed in the light of only two, 'anti-imperialist' and 'pro-imperialist', alternatives. Unlike some other Eastern European nations (like Hungary in the early 1950s, Poland in the 1960s and Czechoslovakia after the 'Prague Spring'), however, there were no anti-Jewish official or public manifestations in communist Bulgaria. Amongst the reasons for this were the full integration of the Sephardic Jewish community within Bulgarian society since the Ottoman period, a relative tolerance towards religion and also the fact that some party functionaries and intellectuals of Jewish origin held influential positions amongst the communist elite. Therefore, state-sponsored propaganda and the ideological struggle against Zionism expressed by some joint Soviet bloc directives was expressed in Bulgaria not in ethnic or national terms but rather as a substantial part of the struggle against the 'Imperialist reactionary ideology'. However, Bulgaria's rupture in diplomatic relations with Israel on 10 June 1967 terminated any official contacts between the two states for about 20 years.

The governmental changes in Egypt after Nasser's death in 1970 were carefully observed in Sofia. The attitude towards the new Egyptian Government was reflected by Zhivkov in a special report on the international situation, delivered at a Communist Party plenary session in October 1971. The report pointed out the contradiction of Egyptian leaders speaking about war against Israel while experts underlined the unpreparedness of the armed forces of 'frontline' Arab countries. Zhivkov shared information on the state of the Egyptian Army: 'Soviet comrades, who are very well aware of the real situation, informed us that the Arabs have not yet overcome the fear of tanks and aircraft' and 'they could be defeated' in eventual hostilities in the near future. Therefore, the Soviet position was 'to withhold the Arabs from fighting'.[27] Very soon, however – in December 1971 – the Bulgarian Government approved a new agreement for arms delivery to Egypt.[28]

In July 1972, a few months after Zhivkov's visit to Syria and Egypt, the Bulgarian Government adopted a special programme for the development of relations with the Arab countries with a special emphasis on arms delivery. Its key elements included a pledge of 'strengthening and expanding the relations between the Ministry of People's Defense and the War Ministry of the Arab Republic of Egypt, seeking ways for influence and consolidation of the positions of the progressive forces in the Egyptian army'. The programme also outlined steps to expand relations with the Syrian Ministry of Defence by increasing the quantity of delivered 'special equipment', and measures to activate military cooperation with Algeria, Libya, Lebanon, Tunisia, Morocco and Sudan. Particular attention was paid to enhancing military relations with Iraq and PDR (the People's Democratic Republic of) Yemen:

> Taking into consideration the important role, played by the armies in Arab countries, the Ministry of People's Defense shall consolidate and expand their relations with their counterparts in Iraq, in order to strengthen the positions of progressive forces in the Iraqi army [...] The Ministry of People's Defense shall expand their relations with the Ministry of Defense of PDR Yemen and deliver support to strengthen their armed forces.[29]

Despite cautionary warnings from Soviet military advisors, on 6 October 1973 the armed forces of Syria and Egypt attacked Israel's positions in Arab territories that it had occupied in June 1967. The Iraqi Army became involved in the conflict with three divisions. Later, during a discussion with Zhivkov, Iraqi President Ahmed Hassan al Bakr claimed that it had been Egypt's President Anwar Sadat who had made the decision to commence hostilities, without giving them (the Iraqis) notice. According to some authors, Soviet leaders were aware of the preparation of an Egyptian–Syrian attack two days prior to the beginning of hostilities.[30] Bulgaria's involvement in the October 1973 war included the organization of an urgent sea and air lift to the Middle East with the code name 'Operation Danube'. From 11 to 30 October 1973, Bulgaria delivered to the Arab states 3,799 tonnes of armaments, ammunition and military equipment worth BGN 20 million. Of these, armaments, ammunition and equipment at a cost of BGN 5,145,860 were delivered to Syria by the Ministry of Defence. An additional 5,000 tonnes of armaments, ammunition and equipment were transferred via Bulgarian Black Sea ports on behalf of Poland.[31] A report of the Bulgarian Embassy in Cairo from December 1973 analysed some lessons learned from the October War and its impact on the status of the Egyptian armed forces. The document underlined:

> According to the experts, only officers ranking from brigadier and below possesses modern military thinking. This is due both to the work of Soviet military specialists and to the fact that along with Soviet weapons, the majority of the army adopted Soviet tactics. On the other hand, the senior command is old and unwilling to change. Specialization of general officers in various military schools has not brought positive results. The war in October proved that senior military leadership refused to adopt the Soviet military doctrine and is still a slave to the old ideas from the English schools during World War II. This was the reason for some gross errors of [a] strategic nature during the fighting in October. In this respect, Egyptian generals are far behind compared to the younger, more flexible and modern Israeli generals.[32]

The aggravation of Egypt's relations with Moscow and the Soviet bloc countries in the mid-1970s led logically to the reduction and eventual cessation of Bulgarian–Egyptian cooperation in the military field. The final agreement for arms delivery to Egypt was approved by the Bulgarian Government on 30 June 1975.[33] It was coincidental that on 30 June the Egyptian foreign minister, Ismail Fahmi, had a three-hour confidential talk with the Bulgarian ambassador to Cairo, Petar Vutov. Fahmi delivered a personal letter from Sadat to Zhivkov, and requested several times Bulgarian 'mediation' in deteriorating Soviet–Egyptian relations. Ambassador Vutov remarked on Fahmi's proposal in his report thus: 'I believe there is blackmailing and pressing the USSR, in order to receive military and economic support and increase Sadat's value while flirting with the Americans.'[34] Just three years later (soon after the 'Camp David deal'), a fabricated incident involving an attack by an Egyptian police team on the Bulgarian Embassy in Cairo led to a break in political and economic cooperation between Bulgaria and Egypt for several years. The provocative action of the Egyptian authorities led to the withdrawal of Bulgarian diplomatic personnel from Cairo, and was qualified in Sofia as the last straw in the process of 'de-Nasserisation' of the country.[35]

Military, political and economic contacts with Iraq became more intensive after General Hassan al Bakr came to power in 1968. Cables sent from the Bulgarian Embassy in Baghdad in 1969 for the first time informed Sofia about the increasing influence of Saddam Hussein, who gradually and quietly replaced the sick President al Bakr over the following years in order to concentrate absolute power in his hands ten years later.[36] While in 1967 Bulgaria sold military equipment to Iraq valued at only BGN 324,000, by 1968 its arms supply to Iraq had increased to BGN 2,562,000. An agreement for the sale of armaments to Iraq for the period 1969–75 was approved by the Bulgarian Government in April 1969. It was amended with a new long-term accord in December 1970, and with a widened agreement for 'special technical assistance and training' in December 1972.[37] During the implementation period of this agreement, Bulgaria received Iraqi officers for 'exchange of experience'. After Zhivkov's visit to Iraq in April 1974, the Bulgarian leadership approved a special Resolution No. 331, dated 25 July 1974, for 'joint participation with the USSR in the planning, construction and procurement of equipment for the defense industry in Iraq'. According to the resolution, Bulgaria was involved in the build-up of the Iraqi 'military-industrial complex' with arms and military equipment worth US$80 million.[38]

The first contacts between Warsaw Pact countries and Yasser Arafat's Palestine Liberation Organization (PLO) were established relatively late. The reason for this was a certain restraint regarding official connections until the end of the 1960s, caused by the PLO's strong extremist line with its objective to liquidate the state of Israel and its rejection of UN

Security Council Resolution No. 242 of 22 November 1967, which emphasized the 'termination of all claims or states of belligerency and respect for and acknowledgement of the sovereignty, territorial integrity and political independence of every State in the area'. This was probably what led the Bulgarian leadership to deny the PLO's request for arms in 1968.[39] At the same time, however, Moscow commented with concern on the intensification of Chinese activities in the Middle East through the extension of Beijing's contacts with the PLO, its provision of considerable military assistance and training of large groups of Palestinian fighters.

The 1970 'Black September' events in Jordan focused Soviet attention even more strongly on the PLO, which resulted in Arafat's secret visit to the USSR for the first time in 1971.[40] A CC BCP Politburo document of July 1972 underlined the changes from the previous Soviet bloc attitude towards the PLO: 'The ways to establish contacts with PLO are to be studied and our own approach to the Palestinian Liberation Movement elaborated.'[41] In February 1973, Arafat visited Bulgaria for the first time. After the visit of PLO Political Department Chairman Faruk Kadumi in 1974 to the country, an agreement was reached to open a PLO representation in Sofia. This change in the Bulgarian position was partially due to the change in the course of action of Arab countries and the states of the Non-Aligned Movement regarding the statute of the PLO.

In the early 1970s, the Bulgarian political leadership made infrequent decisions to grant small amounts of military aid to several leftist Arab paramilitary groups. For instance, in December 1970, the CC BCP Secretariat reacted positively to a joint request by the communist parties in Iraq, Syria, Jordan and Lebanon for free military and financial aid to the newly established 'guerrilla forces', intended to act against Israel from the territory of Jordan. The arms and military equipment were transported by a ship to the Syrian port of Latakia.[42] However, the idea of establishing a joint communist guerrilla force soon failed. Military aid from Bulgaria to some leftist and radical Palestinian armed groups increased after the war of 1973. In the second half of the 1970s, about 5,000 Arab students received their education in Bulgaria, some of them in army and air force military schools. However, the Bulgarian security services received information that amongst these young men were some devoted followers of extremist and terrorist organizations, such as the Muslim Brotherhood, Hezbollah and the Abu

Ayad group – which created a new security dilemma for Bulgaria in the final decade of the Cold War.[43]

Asia

The Soviet Union and Eastern European countries promised significant aid to North Vietnam for its postwar recovery after the 1946–54 Indochina War. When, in April 1955, the newly appointed Beijing-based Bulgarian Ambassador visited Hanoi and talked with North Vietnamese President Ho Chi Minh and other officials, he informed Sofia of a request for economic support from Bulgaria. On 15 June, the Bulgarian Government approved a proposal for the delivery of economic aid worth BGN 30 million and the dispatch of a medical team to North Vietnam. The first group of Bulgarian physicians arrived there in November of the same year. Following another decision in March 1956, Sofia dispatched a team of 32 physicians and material aid for the establishment of a hospital worth BGN 1.7 million to North Vietnam. When Ho Chi Minh visited Sofia in July 1957, both sides agreed on a new medical mission, and thus Bulgaria sent medical equipment and medicines totalling BGN 1.4 million; two more Bulgarian medical teams were dispatched over the following two years. Bulgarian aid contributed to the construction of two military hospitals – Nos. 108 and 303. By 1961, aid from the Warsaw Pact countries led to the elimination of malaria in North Vietnam, and an almost threefold reduction in the occurrence of other diseases like tuberculosis.[44]

Bulgaria's assistance to North Vietnam reached its height during the Vietnam War, also known as the 'Second Indochina War'. Between 1965 and 1973, the Bulgarian Government approved 21 secret resolutions for providing military, financial, economic and humanitarian aid to North Vietnam.[45] In the period 1966–72, the amount of Bulgarian military aid exceeded RUB 45 million. On 21 August 1971, North Vietnamese Prime Minister Pham Van Dong addressed a personal letter to his Bulgarian counterpart, Stanko Todorov, with a request for free economic aid in the amount of RUB 7.5 million, and additional military aid.[46] On the eve of Dong's planned visit to Sofia in July 1973, the CC BCP Politburo approved a secret resolution to provide free military aid to North Vietnam worth RUB7 million.[47] During the period 1973–5, Bulgarian arms deliveries to North Vietnam reached RUB20 million.[48]

Overall, Sofia delivered RUB 60 million worth of credits to North Vietnam between 1964 and 1975.

The Bulgarian political and state leadership established initial contacts with the South Vietnamese armed insurgents of the National Liberation Front ('Viet Cong') at the relatively late juncture of April 1967.[49] Most probably, this was the reason for the delivery of relatively small amounts of Bulgarian military and humanitarian aid to the Viet Cong at the end of the 1960s – under US$100,000 annually. In the early 1970s, however, Sofia approved several resolutions for the medical treatment of wounded Viet Cong soldiers in Bulgaria.[50]

Bulgaria also gave free medical military aid to Laos, via governmental decrees of 1 March 1961 and 25 July 1962.[51] In 1964–6, the Government of Laos received from Bulgaria about BGN 80,000–100,000 of material aid annually. With another government resolution of 22 May 1966, humanitarian and military assistance to Laos increased to BGN 2,151,000. Up to the end of 1970, Bulgarian military and humanitarian aid to Laos amounted to about BGN 8 million. On 2 March 1971, following the US air offensive against Laos, the political leadership in Sofia approved a new proposal for free arms delivery to Pathet Lao communist guerilla forces amounting to BGN 724,000.[52] In the period 1974–6, Bulgaria provided new military equipment to Laos worth about BGN 650,000.

Africa

Bulgaria also became involved in the Congo. Soon after the murder of the first prime minister of the Congo, Patrice Lumumba, the Bulgarian Government declared, on 17 February 1961, that it would 'give its full support and possible aid to the legal government of Congo'.[53] Actually, just a day before the announcement of that government declaration, a secret resolution was issued to send weaponry and military equipment to Lumumba's followers who had coalesced around Antoine Gizenga in Stanleyville. The weaponry included 2,000 Manlicher rifles, 30 Bren light machine guns and some ammunition, and was delivered to the Congolese office in Cairo.[54] After new confidential talks with one of Lumumba's ministers, Pierre Mulele, in Cairo in April 1961, another shipment of 200 tonnes of weaponry was transferred through Egypt, but subsequently disappeared somewhere on Sudanese territory. Four years later, during another round of the civil war known as the 'Simba Rebellion', a new, significant Bulgarian arms delivery was successfully transported through the territories of Egypt, Sudan and Tanzania to the National Liberation Council (CNL), which had been established by Lumumba's associates, Christophe Gbenye and Gaston Soumialot, in October 1963 in Congo-Brazzaville. Military aid for the Congolese National Liberation Army of General Nicholas Olenga and his 'Simba fighters' amounted to US$500,000, while at the same time about 100 Congolese men received military training in Bulgaria.[55]

In the early 1960s, Bulgaria established military contacts with some newly independent African states – Kenya, Zambia, Ghana, Tanzania, Mali, Nigeria and Guinea – as part of its policy of support for decolonization in Africa. The first contacts with the Kenya African National Congress (KANU) of Jomo Kenyatta came in 1960, when Bulgaria sent modest financial aid to that party. In 1964, shortly after Kenya become independent, the Bulgarian Government agreed to cover costs for the military training of more than 100 Kenyan cadets in Bulgarian military schools. Even before the announcement of Zambia's independence (formerly Northern Rhodesia), the government in Sofia delivered, in 1962, minor financial aid to the United National Independent Party (UNIP) of Kenneth Kaunda, who became the first president of the country in 1964.[56] Soon after a left-wing revolution in Zanzibar in January 1964, on 1 April that same year, the Bulgarian Government approved a proposal for delivery of arms and medical equipment delivery to that country.[57] In September 1967, an agreement was signed for an arms sale to the Sudanese armed forces. During the civil war in Nigeria, in 1968–9, Bulgaria delivered arms to for the federal government worth about US$12 million, while in October 1970 another long-term agreement for arms exports of US$15 million to Nigeria was approved for the period 1970–5.[58] On request by the Guinean president, Ahmed Sékou Touré, in December 1970, the Bulgarian Government approved a decision to send Guinea a free arms delivery worth BGN 100,000 and medical supplies of BGN 30,000.[59] Several hundred young African military officers received their training and education in Bulgarian military schools in the late 1960s and the early 1970s. From the early 1960s until the end of the 1970s, Bulgaria also provided some modest financial and military aid and training to several African national-liberation movements: the Popular Movement for the Liberation of Angola (MPLA), the Front for the Liberation of Mozambique (FRELIMO), the Party for the Independence of Guinea and Cape Verde (PAIGC), the Zimbabwe African National Union (ZANU), the African National Congress (ANC) and the South West Africa People's Organization (SWAPO).

Initial contact with the first president of the MPLA, Mario Pinto de Andrade, was established with the assistance of the leader of another Angolan national-liberation organization – UPA (since 1962, the FNLA: National Front for the Liberation of Angola) – Holden Roberto. When visiting the United Nations headquarters in New York in April 1961, he informed the Bulgarian Ambassador to the UN about the principal MPLA base in Conakry. During confidential talks between Mario de Andrade and Bulgarian representatives in Conakry in December 1961, it was agreed that Bulgaria would provide US$40,000 worth of free military aid to the MPLA.[60] In 1963, and again in 1964, the new MPLA president, Agostinho Neto, sent requests to the Bulgarian political leadership for further free military aid as well as military training of MPLA activists in Bulgarian military schools.[61] In 1964, ten MPLA functionaries received one year's military education, while in 1965 another 50 functionaries received military training in Bulgaria. In December 1966, another proposal for free military aid to the MPLA worth BGN 800,000 was approved.[62] In 1968, an additional BGN 722,000 worth of military and medical aid was also approved. Responding positively to a fresh request from Neto, in September 1971, a new delivery of arms and medical equipment worth BGN 548,000 was delivered to MPLA armed forces in Dar es Salaam.[63] Further military aid to the MPLA in Angola prior to the announcement of its independence was agreed in April 1973 (for BGN 595,000), September 1973 (BGN 944,000) and November 1975 (BGN 960,000).[64]

The first aid package to FRELIMO took place in 1965; it amounted to BGN 170,000.[65] In December 1966, a new proposal was approved totalling BGN 1,385,000.[66] After a visit by FRELIMO's leader, Samora Machel, to Bulgaria in March 1971, Bulgaria's military and humanitarian aid to that organization increased significantly. In 1971, it amounted to BGN 675,000; in 1973, BGN 788,000; and in 1974, BGN 100,000 (US$50,000).[67] In response to a request from Machel, in 1974, a Bulgarian military medical team was sent to Tanzania to organize a field hospital for medical treatment of FRELIMO's wounded soldiers.

The initial contact with PAIGC was established in September 1964 by the Bulgarian Embassy in Conakry. The following year, Bulgaria sent a small amount of material aid to that organization. When in February 1966, PAIGC leader Amilcar Cabral sent a request for medical treatment of wounded fighters, the Bulgarian Government reacted positively – and in the next few years, several groups of PAIGC functionaries were treated in Bulgarian military hospitals. Bulgarian military aid to PAIGC for 1966 amounted to BGN 316,000; BGN 300,000 for 1969; BGN 608,000 for 1971; and BGN 420,000 for 1973.[68]

Initial contacts with ZANU took place in 1964, when a representative of that organization raised the issue of free assistance in a message to the Bulgarian Embassy in Cairo.[69] However, over the following years, the ZANU leadership oriented its policy closer to Beijing than to Moscow, which was the main reason for the Warsaw Pact countries establishing closer relations with ZANU's main rival, the Zimbabwe African People's Union (ZAPU) led by Joshua Nkomo. In June 1968, a secret CC BCP resolution was issued for free military and humanitarian aid to ZAPU worth BGN 300,000 to be delivered to Dar es Salaam, and for military training of 30 ZAPU functionaries in Bulgaria.[70] In November 1964, initial information about SWAPO and its guerrilla bases in Tanzania and Zambia was also received in Sofia. A request for free military aid from Bulgaria for SWAPO was received in 1966 through that country's embassy in Dar es Salaam. In 1964, the Bulgarian political leadership approved another proposal for financial aid – this time to the ANC in support of some of its imprisoned leaders, such as Nelson Mandela. Soon after the visit of the ANC Secretary General Alfred Nzo to Sofia in 1972, free Bulgarian humanitarian aid for his organization was transported to Dar es Salaam.[71] Over the next few years, the ANC received military aid from Bulgaria totalling about BGN 500,000, and more than 100 ANC soldiers completed military training in Bulgarian military schools.

Latin America

The Cuban Revolution in January 1959 and the October Missile Crisis in 1962 induced a more serious Bulgarian public interest in political events in the western hemisphere. On its way back from Argentina and Mexico in late May–early June 1960, a Bulgarian governmental delegation visited Cuba and held talks with Raul Castro, Ernesto 'Che' Guevara and other Cuban officials. At the end of June, proposals for the establishment of diplomatic, commercial and cultural relations, and Bulgaria's rendering of economic and technical aid to Cuba, were coordinated between the two governments' representatives. At the 15th UN General Assembly session in September 1960, the first personal meeting between Todor Zhivkov and Fidel Castro was organized. Years later, Zhivkov related that their improvised unofficial meeting happened on 27 September 1960 in a small room at the Hotel Theresa in Harlem, where Castro also famously met Soviet Premier Nikita Khrushchev.[72] On 8 October 1960, Bulgarian Minister of Foreign Trade Luchezar Avramov and Che Guevara signed a bilateral commercial agreement in Havana. The same day, an official communiqué announced the establishment of diplomatic relations between Bulgaria and Cuba. A few months after the Playa Giron (Bay of Pigs) invasion in April 1961, the Bulgarian Government responded positively to a request for arms to Cuba. Bulgarian armaments deliveries and credits to Cuba in 1961 exceeded US$8 million in value.

The Bulgarian leadership had not been informed in advance about the Kremlin's decision to deploy Soviet missiles in Cuba. In his memoirs, Khrushchev wrote, 'While in Bulgaria, I could not even share these thoughts with Zhivkov, because I hadn't discussed them with my own comrades.'[73] Zhivkov confirmed in his own memoirs that there were no any bilateral or multilateral (within the Warsaw Pact) consultations on the issue. Nor was there direct consultation between Moscow and Sofia at the height of the Cuban Missile Crisis in October 1962. The Bulgarian leadership simply followed the official information from the available open sources, collected at the Foreign Ministry and the Foreign Policy and International Relations Department of the CC BCP.[74] At the height of the missile crisis, a few directives on raising the combat readiness of the Warsaw Pact joint armed forces and on intensification of military-intelligence activity against Turkey and Greece were received from the Pact's Joint Command. In its public declaration of 23 October 1962, the Bulgarian Government announced that an order had been issued for raising the combat readiness of its armed forces.[75] Similar actions were taken by other Warsaw Pact allies. Following the Missile Crisis, the CC BCP Politburo adopted another secret resolution for arms delivery to Cuba.[76] During a visit to Cuba in May 1966, Angel Solakov, the

Bulgarian state security chairman, discussed with Cuban Minister of the Interior Sergio Del Valle and Manuel Piñeiro, Cuban state security director, the possibility of organizing sabotage and counter-intelligence training for 30 Cuban officers in Bulgaria. On 8 June 1966, the CC BCP Secretariat adopted a secret decision for counter-intelligence training of 30 Cuban state-security servicemen. Zhivkov's handwritten resolution on the document stated, 'We have no conditions to train people in sabotage.'[77] In February 1967, a new protocol for arms exports to Cuba was signed in Havana.

In the 1960s, Bulgaria also gave some underground Latin American communist parties limited financial support. Following a request from Fidel Castro, on 2 November 1961, the CC BCP Secretariat approved a proposal for the delivery of 35,000 old German Mauser carbines to Cuba.[78] The guns were to be transferred by the Cubans to Latin American leftist guerrilla groups. At the same time, the Bulgarian leadership met with a degree of hostility – or, at least, with suspicion during the following years, over strategy for guerrilla warfare in the region – and all requests for military training of Latin American guerrillas in Bulgaria were declined. In March 1966, a report from the Bulgarian Embassy in Havana stated,

> We have recently sent several reports concerning the training of people in Cuba who are subsequently infiltrated back in other Latin American countries with the task to organize armed resistance [...] The guerrilla actions and their simultaneous opening in a wide range of countries – are considered as task number one. This strategy, its objective being to provoke imperialist occupation of the Latin American countries which will allegedly serve as an incentive for an anti-imperialist final victorious struggle, is very difficult to understand.[79]

The only known documentary evidence of Bulgarian military support for a Latin American armed group in those years refers to two special cases. In January 1967, the Bulgarian communist leadership approved a secret decision to meet the request of the Workers' Party of Guatemala (GPT) for arms delivery to the leftist FAR (Rebel Armed Forces) guerilla forces in that country. The proposed aid, which had to be transferred via Cuba, included five heavy machine guns, 50 sub-machine guns, 300 hand grenades and ammunition.[80] During his talks with Raul Castro in Sofia on 26 March 1965, Zhivkov surprisingly mentioned, 'Our partisan {guerilla} commanders are even in Venezuela.'[81] What Zhivkov had in mind became publicly known two years later when a former Venezuelan guerrilla commander, Teodoro Petkoff,[82] escaped sensationally along with two other communist party functionaries from the military prison San Carlos.[83] Teodoro's brother, Luben Petkoff (aka 'Sucre'), also a Venezuelan guerrilla commander, went illegally via Cuba to their father's homeland, Bulgaria, at the beginning of April 1967. On 15 April 1967, the CC BCP Secretariat reached a hitherto unprecedented decision to offer one month of military training to ten Venezuelan and three Guatemalan communist functionaries.[84]

On 5 October 1967, the CC BCP Politburo approved a series of measures to strengthen Bulgarian–Cuban relations.[85] However, the envisaged initial visit of Zhivkov to Cuba at the beginning of 1968 was postponed – mainly because in January 1968, Fidel Castro made a secret speech to a Cuban Communist Party plenary session with a sharp anti-Soviet critique. When Castro publicly approved the Warsaw Pact military invasion of Czechoslovakia in August 1968, it became possible to renew the preparation for Zhivkov's visit to Cuba, which was the subject of special discussions at the Bulgarian Foreign Ministry in March 1969. Todor Zhivkov's official visit in June 1970 – the first ever visit of an East European leader to Cuba – not only played a significant role in the development of bilateral relations but also gave impetus to the improvement of Soviet–Cuban relations soon afterwards. The first visit of a Soviet leader (Leonid Brezhnev) to Cuba took place at the end of January–early February 1974.

Analysis of postwar official relations between Bulgaria and Latin America shows that after the Cuban Revolution, in particular, those contacts were considerably intensified. During the first 15 postwar years, Bulgaria had official relations with only two countries in the region; in the course of the following decade, state relations (diplomatic and consular) were established with another six countries, and in 1970–1 with three more. Nevertheless, when compared with the other Eastern European countries' presence in Latin America, the foreign policy of the Bulgarian Government in the region does not seem to have been particularly active. At the end of the 1960s, Romania enjoyed diplomatic relations with nine Latin American countries, Yugoslavia with 13, Czechoslovakia with 15 and Poland with 18. In the same period, however, Bulgaria had only trade relations with 16 Latin American countries – and in nine of these, Bulgarian commercial representations were opened.

In the early 1960s, the smaller communist coalition partner, the Bulgarian Agrarian Union party (BANU), established contacts with certain farmers' unions, agricultural trade unions and other agrarian organizations – at first in Western Europe, and later on in the Third World. This was a trend with some echoes of the late 1950s, when the Bulgarian Communist Party increasingly began to utilize the activities of its smaller political partner. This tendency became a highly visible and important new element in the Bulgarian foreign-policy mechanism over the following three decades. At the same time, BANU regularly rendered support in the process of establishing new international contacts for its other East European partners, like the Agrarian parties in Poland and East Germany. In June 1971, one of the BANU leaders, Petar Tanchev, in his capacity as deputy prime minister, visited 12 Latin American countries, where besides signing a number of commercial and economic treaties he also held talks with leaders of various political parties. In the 1970s, BANU also strengthened its relations with influential centrist, radical, liberal, Christian-democratic and other parties, the greater number of which were members of government coalitions in their own countries. However, BANU's international activity was much more intensive that that of similar parties and organizations in other Eastern European countries, encompassing a wide range of activities. BANU was quite often used in the final two decades of the Cold War as a principal Eastern European non-communist organizer of representative international meetings and conferences for 'détente, peace and international dialogue'. A number of parties in Western Europe, Asia and the Americas found it more politically acceptable to maintain official relations with an agrarian, rather than with a communist, party in Eastern Europe.

On 10 June 1970, the CC BCP Politburo adopted an important resolution (No. 351) for intensifying relations between Bulgaria and Latin America countries.[86] It had been suggested three months earlier by the BCP's 'second in command', Boris Velchev, who in November 1969 had visited seven Latin American countries for talks with various political and government officials. The new 'policy, strategy and tactics related to the Latin-American continent' was predominantly motivated by the 'common struggle against [...] American imperialism' and the strategic intention 'to gradually win these countries and their peoples as our friends'. This new line of the Bulgarian communist leadership was not a surprising solo action. As early as December 1969, in a session of the Warsaw Pact Political Consultative Committee in Moscow, Zhivkov had suggested 'coordination' of the steps undertaken with regard to the Middle East and Latin American countries.[87] Soon after the approval of the June politburo resolution, at the end of July 1970, Velchev sent a letter to Boris Ponomarev, head of the CC CPSU International Department, in which he warned that 'the influence of the socialist countries [had] dropped behind the development of [...] progressive tendencies in that area'. Velchev underlined the necessity to follow a more coordinated policy towards Latin America, and proposed a coordinative CMEA session to be organized in the near future on the issue.[88]

The victory of the Unidad Popular leftist coalition in Chile in September 1970 was a significant political event, which gave a strong impetus for the development of Bulgarian–Chilean relations and was the Latin American political phenomenon most remarked upon in Bulgarian public opinion. On 3 April 1971, the CC BCP Politburo approved a special resolution for further development of bilateral relations with Chile, which was discussed during the first visit of Chilean Foreign Minister Clodomiro Almeyda to Bulgaria at the beginning of June. In January 1972, the Bulgarian Government approved a proposal for the delivery of long-term credit to the Government of Chile.[89] In October 1972 during a state visit in Chile, one of the BANU leaders and Vice-Chairman of the Bulgarian State Council, Georgi Andreev, was invited to dinner in the house of the Chilean president, Salvador Allende. Allende informed Andreev that the opposition had plans to destabilize the political situation in the country – an operation known as 'Plan September'.[90] To Lalyu Ganchev, another important personality within the Agrarian Party, who visited Chile around the same time, Allende allegedly addressed an 'appeal for help to the socialist countries in Europe'. As a result, a new loan of US$20 million was granted for the Allende government in January 1973.[91] On 11 September 1973, Commander-in-Chief General Augusto Pinochet launched a coup in Chile that led to Allende's death and mass repressions against the country's leftist, liberal and syndicalist functionaries, provoking a strong international protest campaign in Europe. Following the Soviet Union, on 22 September 1973 the Bulgarian Government broke off its relations with the Chilean military junta.

In the mid- and late 1970s, the BCP also maintained contacts with the leaders of the communist and socialist parties in Chile. When in February 1974, the leaders of the Chilean socialist and communist parties in Europe, Carlos Altamirano and Volodia Teitelboim, spoke with Todor Zhivkov in Sofia, it was agreed that financial aid amounting to US$30,000 would be given to the Chilean Communist Party, and another US$20,000 to the Chilean Socialist Party. In response to another request from Teitelboim, who presided over the emigration centre for Chilean communists in Moscow, on 14 October 1974 the CC BCP Secretariat approved a secret decision for the military training of 20 communist militants from Chile. However, during a meeting between Zhivkov and Altamirano in January 1976, a new agreement was reached for organizing six months of military training for 15 Socialist Party activists. With a number of top-secret resolutions in the 1970s, the Bulgarian Communist Party leadership also granted financial aid to several clandestine communist parties in Latin America, which were obliged to work under the military dictatorships in their countries.[92]

Conclusion

Moscow considered Bulgaria its most loyal ally because of many historic, cultural, geopolitical and other reasons. It is well known now that Todor Zhivkov's 'political prescription' for his long survival as a doyen of the Warsaw Pact leaders was 'political loyalty for economic benefits'. He even joked cynically in private talks with visiting US businessmen and members of the US Congress that the Soviet Union was a Bulgarian colony, because Bulgaria sold machinery and electronics and received cheap petroleum and raw materials from there in return.[93] In the field of foreign policy, Bulgarian leaders had a separate stance only regarding some key questions of national interest – for instance, on the so-called 'Macedonian question' with Yugoslavia and Greece or the question of the 'Bulgarian Islamic minority' with Turkey. While Warsaw Pact members enjoyed a relative amount of freedom in their bilateral relations with Third World countries in economic and cultural matters, the military sphere was subject to strict Soviet coordination – however unfashionable it might have been to remind them about former close ties, and even sometimes subordination, to Moscow.

Sometimes, however, Bulgarian actions went beyond the scope of coordinated Warsaw Pact policy. An indicative example was the maintenance of contacts with both Nkomo and Mugabe in Southern Rhodesia (Zimbabwe), while at the same time the Soviet Union promised support only to the Nkomo faction because of Mugabe's close relations with Maoist China. Another case was the development of Bulgarian–Cuban cooperation after the Cuban Missile Crisis, when Soviet–Cuban relations deteriorated visibly. Bulgarian Prime Minister Todor Zhivkov was the first Warsaw Pact leader to visit Cuba in the process of strengthening Havana's ties with Eastern Europe. Despite of the fact that Bulgaria focused its Third World policy mainly on the neighbouring Middle East and eastern Mediterranean areas, in some cases the political leadership in Sofia took independent initiatives towards more distant regions like Latin America, such as the example of the proposal to Moscow in July 1970.

Compared with relations between the developed European countries and Japan, this cooperation with underdeveloped Third World countries had no such significance for the Bulgarian economy. It was motivated mainly by reasons of political prestige in pursuing the 'internationalist' ideological imperatives of 'class solidarity' and of strictly following the common Warsaw Pact line towards regional and internal armed or social conflicts in the bipolar Cold War world. The generously granted 'military and humanitarian aid' to Third World leftist or nationalist regimes and insurgent organizations was the focal point of that policy. It continued with even higher level of engagement and intensity in the final 15 years of the Cold War.

Since the beginning of the transition period to pluralist democracy after the Cold War era, Bulgarian society has reassessed the ideological and political motivation of the economic and military support given to the Third World countries over the course of the previous decades. Now, new interpretations and questions arose in regard of that 'special assistance'. At what point did it go beyond the accepted international norms and to what degree did it turn from being a natural obligation under the spirit and according to the international community's principles into an unjustified 'burden' on the economy of small Bulgaria? The generous free aid extended to left-radical fronts and movements in many cases was undoubtedly dictated by political-propaganda motives and matters of prestige, and lay by no means within the limited resources and economic possibilities of Bulgaria. The enormous loans and credits delivered to several Third World countries, like Iraq, have never been refunded, and contributed in some way to the sharp financial crisis in Bulgaria in the post-Cold War years.

Notes

1. Yordan Baev, *Voennopoliticheskite konflikti sled Vtorata svetovna vojna I Bulgaria* [Military and Political Conflicts after World War II and Bulgaria] (Sofia, 1995); Yordan Baev, *Drugata studena vojna. Savetsko-Kitaiskiat konflikt I Iztochna Evropa* [The Other Cold War. Sino-Soviet Conflict and Eastern Europe] (Sofia, 2012); Jordan Baev (ed.), *Bulgaria and the Middle East Conflict in the Cold War years. Documents volume* (Sofia, 2006); Jordan Baev, 'Eastern Europe and the Six Day War: The Case of Bulgaria', in Yaakov Roi (ed.), *The Soviet Union and the Six Day War* (Stanford, CA, 2008); Jordan Baev, 'Bulgaria and the Cuban Missile Crisis', *CWIHP Bulletin*, vol. 17/18 (2012); Jordan Baev, 'Bulgaria and Latin America in the Cold War years: A Case Study for Soviet Bloc Political Relations with Latin American Countries', in Revista OPSIS, *Dossie Tematico: America Latina no Contexto da Guerra Fria* (Catalao, Brazil, 2014).
2. Jordan Baev and Soyoung Kim, 'Korea in the Bulgarian Archives, 1945–1995: An Introduction', *NKIDP Working Paper* No. 5, Woodrow Wilson International Center for Scholars (Washington, DC, September 2017), pp. 3–10.
3. For the period 1970–4, the expenses for free arms transfers from Bulgaria to Third World guerrilla movements were about BGN 7 million, which was an increase of 39 per cent in comparison with the late 1960s. Central State Archives (TsDA), Sofia, Fond 1-B, Opis 64 [CC BCP Politburo top-secret resolutions], A.E. 352, pp. 3–6.
4. TsDA, Fond 214-B, Opis 1, A.E. 709, p. 14. See also Laurent Rucker, *Moscow's Surprise: The Soviet – Israeli Alliance of 1947 – 1949*, CWIHP Working Paper No. 46 (Washington, DC, 2005).
5. The investigation results were summarized in a governmental report: TsDA, Fond 1-B, Opis 6, A.E. 2629, pp. 14–21; and two military ones: Central Military Archive (DVIA), Veliko Tarnovo, Fond 1, Opis 3, A.E. 6, pp. 166–70; and A.E. 7, pp. 380–5.
6. TsDA, Fond 1-B, Opis 6 [Politburo protocols], A.E. 3691, 3737, 3811; Opis 33 [CC BCP Foreign Policy & International Relations Department files], A.E. 11; Opis 64, A.E. 274, 282.
7. TSDA, Fond 378-B [Todor Zhivkov Personal Records], Opis 1, A.E. 140, p. 24.
8. TsDA, Fond 136 [Council of Ministers Records], Opis 86, A.E. 523, 572.
9. However, very soon some unpredictable problems appeared due to the 'lack of discipline' in the behaviour of many cadets.

10. TsDA, Fond 1-B, Opis 24 [CC BCP *Military* Department files], A.E. 239, pp. 1–7.
11. TsDA, Fond 1-B, Opis 5 [CC BCP Plenary protocols], A.E. 353, p. 8.
12. TsDA, Fond 1-B, Opis 64, A.E. 258, p. 1.
13. TsDA, Fond 1-B, Opis 64, A.E.268, pp. 2–4.
14. The list of Bulgarian-made weaponry included ammunitions for T-34 and T-54 tanks; parachutes; B-10 and B-11 heavy machine guns; land and ground mines; and 120 mm, 107 mm and 82 mm mortars. See TsDA, Fond 1-B, Opis 64, A.E. 294, pp. 10–13.
15. Approved with a Bulgarian Council of Ministers' Secret Protocol No. 354 / 16 May 1963: TsDA, Fond 136, Opis 86, A.E. 592.
16. TsDA, Fond 136, Opis 86, A.E.595, pp. 1–4.
17. Diplomatic Archive (DA), Sofia, Opis 23, A.E. 3104, pp. 5–13.
18. DA, Opis 22, A.E. 3653; TsDA, Fond 1-B, Opis 6, A.E. 6610; Fond 136, Opis 86, A.E. 674, 676.
19. National Archives & Record Administration (NARA), College Park, MD, Record Group 59, Central Files, 1964–1966, Box 1952, POL-BUL.
20. TsDA, Fond 1-B, Opis 6, A.E. 5896, pp. 2–3, 23–9.
21. DA, Opis 21, A.E. 1160; DA, Opis 22, A.E. 2053; DA, Opis 23, A.E. 1090; TsDA, Fond 1-B, Opis 51, A.E. 645, 649.
22. DA, Opis 5sh [Ciphercorrespondence], A.E. 151, 188, 254, 288, 348b, 380, 447, 483, 550, 585.
23. TsDA, Fond 1-B, Opis 8 [CC BCP Secretariat files], A.E. 7749, p. 2–3; TsDA, Fond 136, Opis 86, A.E. 703, pp. 1–3. The arms and ammunition totalled BGN 3.5 million.
24. TsDA, Fond 1-B, Opis 6, A.E. 6770, pp. 61–5.
25. TsDA, Fond 136, Opis 86, A.E. 690, pp. 1–5.
26. TsDA, Fond 136, Opis 86, A.E. 769, pp. 2–6.
27. TsDA, Fond 1-B, Opis 35 [CC BCP Politburo protocols], A.E. 2449, p. 46; TsDA, Fond 1-B, Opis 58 [CC BCP Plenaryprotocols], A.E. 60, p. 43.
28. TsDA, Fond 136, Opis 86, A.E. 797.
29. TsDA, Fond 1-B, Opis 35, A.E. 3304, pp. 7–72.
30. A Bulgarian Military Intelligence analysis of 1974, entitled 'Some conclusions from the Middle East war in October 1973' underlined that, '[a]ccording to our information, Syria and Egypt made the decision to attack Israel fourteen days prior to the beginning of battles'.
31. From report of General Dzhurov: TsDA, Fond 136, Opis 86, A.E. 817, pp. 6–24.
32. TsDA, Fond 1-B, Opis 81 [CC BCP Foreign Policy & International Relations Department files], unprocessed.
33. TsDA, Fond 136, Opis 84 [Secret government resolutions], A.E. 336.
34. DA, Opis 7sh, A.E. 107, pp. 129–32.
35. Baev, *Voennopoliticheskite konflikti sled Vtorata svetovna vojna I Bulgaria*, pp. 294–5.
36. DA, Opis. 5sh, A.E. 635, pp. 176, 204.

37. TsDA, Fond 136, Opis 86, A.E. 749, pp. 1–3; A.E. 777, pp. 3–5; A.E. 809, pp. 4–11.
38. TsDA, Fond 1-B, Opis 35, A.E. 4856, pp. 1, 12, 48–60.
39. TSDA, Fond 1-B, Opis 64, A.E. 378.
40. Ministry of Foreign Affairs' Sixth Department, *Palestinsko nacionalno-osvoboditelno dvizhenie* [Palestinian National Liberation Movement] (Sofia, 1973), pp. 41–6.
41. TSDA, Fond 1-B, Opis35, A.E. 3304, p. 67.
42. TSDA, Fond 1-B, Opis 64, A.E. 398.
43. See: Jordan Baev, 'Infiltration of Non-European Terrorist Groups in Europe and Antiterrorist Responses in Western and Eastern Europe (1969–1991)', in Siddik Ekici (ed.), *Counter Terrorism in Diverse Communities* (Amsterdam, 2011), pp. 58–74.
44. Krum Zlatkov, *Bulgarsko-vietnamski vzaimootnoshenia 1950–1989* [Bulgarian-Vietnamese relationship 1950–1989], PhD dissertation, Sofia University, 2016, pp. 108–12.
45. TsDA, Fond 136, Opis 84, A.E. 71, 75, 129, 152, 257; TsDA, Fond 136, Opis 86, A.E. 631, 633, 639, 648, 652, 662, 675, 689, 694, 716, 721, 755, 774, 775, 781, 801.
46. DA, Opis 22-P, A.E. 35.
47. TsDA, Fond 1-B, Opis 35, A.E. 4243, p. 7.
48. TsDA, Fond 136, Opis 84, A.E. 71, pp. 4–6.
49. DA, Opis 23, A.E. 750.
50. TsDA, Fond 1-B, Opis 36 [CC BCP Secretariat protocols], A.E. 2823, pp. 1–2; TsDA, Fond 1-B, Opis 36, A.E. 3717, pp. 1–3.
51. TsDA, Fond 136, Opis 86, A.E. 518, 568.
52. TsDA, Fond 1-B, Opis 64, A.E. 401.
53. *Vunshna politika na NR Bulgaria* [Foreign Policy of PR of Bulgaria], Documents, vol. 1, 1944–1962 (Sofia, 1970), pp. 558–9.
54. TsDA, Fond 1-B, Opis 64, A.E. 280.
55. TsDA, Fond 1-B, Opis 64, A.E. 326, 327.
56. TsDA, Fond 136, Opis 86, A.E. 571.
57. TsDA, Fond 136, Opis 86, A.E. 628.
58. TsDA, Fond 136, Opis 86, A.E. 705, 775.
59. TsDA, Fond 136, Opis 86, A.E. 786, pp. 2–4.
60. The request of de Andrade, of 6 December 1961, was discussed positively at the CC BCP Politburo session on 25 January 1962: TsDA, Fond 1-B, Opis 64, A.E. 294.
61. TsDA, Fond 1-B, Opis 51, A.E. 23. Parallel requests for military aid to the MPLA were also received from the Bulgarian embassies in Moscow and Algiers.
62. TsDA, Fond 136, Opis 86, A.E. 678.
63. TsDA, Fond 136, Opis 86, A.E. 409.
64. TsDA, Fond 1-B, Opis 64, A.E. 423, 459, 461.
65. TsDA, Fond 1-B, Opis 64, A.E. 332.

66. TsDA, Fond 136, Opis 86, A.E. 678.
67. TsDA, Fond 1-B, Opis 64, A.E. 405, 430, 447.
68. TsDA, Fond 1-B, Opis 64, A.E. 409, 428.
69. TsDA, Fond 1-B, Opis 51, A.E. 213.
70. TsDA, Fond 1-B, Opis 64, A.E. 375.
71. TsDA, Fond 1-B, Opis 64, A.E. 424.
72. *Dokumenti I materiali za sutrudnichestvoto mezhdu BCP I PCC 1960–1981* {Documents on the cooperation between BCP and PCC} (Sofia: Partizdat, 1982), pp. 17–22.
73. Nikita Khrushchev, *Memoirs*, vol. 3, *Statesman* (University Park, PA, 2007), pp. 324–6.
74. The folder on the Cuban Missile Crisis at the Diplomatic Archive in Sofia contains a collection of information from UPI, Reuters, France Press, Soviet agency TASS, and Bulgarian agency BTA: DA, Sofia, Documentacija, IV/39/1/X-1962.
75. *Vanshna politika na NRB* {Bulgarian Foreign Policy}, vol. 1, 1944–1962 (Sofia, 1963), pp. 613–15.
76. TsDA, Fond 1-B, Opis 64, A.E. 314.
77. TsDA, Fond 1-B, Opis 64, A.E. 352.
78. TsDA, Fond 1-B, Opis 64, A.E. 291.
79. TsDA, Fond 1-B, Opis 81 {CC BCP Foreign Policy & International Relations Department} – unprocessed.
80. TsDA, Fond 1-B, Opis 64, A.E. 360, pp. 1–3.
81. TsDA, Fond 378B {Todor Zhivkov Personal Records}, Opis1, A.E. 140, p. 24.
82. In 1968, Teodoro Petkoff left the Communist Party in protest against the Soviet bloc invasion of Czechoslovakia, and founded a new leftist organization: MAS (the Movement Towards Socialism). In the following two decades, he ran three times, unsuccessfully, for President of Venezuela.
83. See Guillermo Garcia Ponce, *El Tunel de San Carlos* (Caracas, 1968).
84. TsDA, Fond 1B, Opis 64, A.E. 362, p. 1.
85. TsDA, Fond 1B, Opis 6, A.E. 6879, p. 2; TsDA, Fond 1B, Opis 6, A.E. 6979, p. 1–2.
86. TsDA, Fond 1B, Opis 35, A.E. 1458, pp. 8–28.
87. TsDA, Fond 1B, Opis 35, A.E. 1044, p. 49.
88. TsDA, Fond 1-B, Opis 81 {CC BCP Foreign Policy & International Relations Department} – unprocessed.
89. TsDA, Fond 136, Opis 86, A.E. 41.
90. BANU International Relations Department Records, Information of G. Andreev, November 1972, pp. 1–6.
91. TsDA, Fond 1-B, Opis 36, A.E. 2507, pp. 1–4; Opis 60, A.E. 102, pp. 1–47. See also: Stoyan Tanev, 'Bulgaro-chilijskite otnoshenia, noemvri 1970-septemvri 1973', *Istoricheski pregled* No. 6 (1976), p. 11.
92. For instance, the Communist Party of Paraguay.
93. TsDA, Fond 1-B, Opis 60, A.E. 262, 323.

CONCLUSION

Philip E. Muehlenbeck and Natalia Telepneva

The Soviet Union was aware of the constraints on its ability to enact a fully active foreign policy into every corner of the globe, and was happy for the junior members of the Warsaw Pact to play significant roles in the Third World. As a result, by the mid- to late 1950s, the Non-Soviet Warsaw Pact (NSWP) countries enjoyed a certain degree of autonomy in their relations with the Third World. They were allowed to pursue policies only loosely coordinated with Moscow, and certainly not directed by the Kremlin, as long as those actions were not in direct opposition to the Soviet Union's own foreign-policy objectives. Such an arrangement allowed Central and Eastern European countries to pursue their own national interests as long their policies fell within the framework of what Békés, Nagy and Vékony have termed 'constructive loyalty'.[1] Moscow could not have, and in fact did not want, total control over the foreign policies of the other countries in the Warsaw Pact.

With both the most industrialized economy and the most extensive diplomatic network in the Soviet bloc, Czechoslovakia was the NSWP country most integrally involved with the Third World from the mid-1950s to the mid-1960s. As the chapters by Koura and Waters, Telepneva and Muehlenbeck demonstrate, Czechoslovakia had more experience and greater contacts in both Africa and Latin America than did the Soviet Union. Moscow understood this and frequently deferred to Prague's expertise in these regions of the world, entrusting its junior ally with spearheading the communist cause. Czechoslovakia was also one of the world's leading exporters of weapons to the developing world, and, as such, Czechoslovak military aid played a significant role in the overall growth of Soviet bloc influence in the Third World. Although the Czechoslovak arms trade operated under general guidelines agreed upon with the Soviet Union, Prague often sold or gave weapons to developing-world states and national-liberation movements in advance of, and without express consent from, the Soviet Union.[2] Between 1955 and 1962, Czechoslovakia's involvement in the developing world was massive in scale as compared to its small population and size of its national economy are taken into consideration. The Czechoslovak Ministry of the Interior also played a significant role in building up the security services of the newly independent states and liberation movements, and participating in joint intelligence operations with Soviet counterparts across the world. By 1963, however, Czechoslovakia's economy was in significant decline and it was forced to reduce its commitments to the Third World – a process that was further intensified by the events and aftermath of the Prague Spring.[3]

After the Prague Spring, the GDR would replace Czechoslovakia as the Soviet Union's most valuable Warsaw Pact ally in the Third World. In the 1950s and 1960s, the GDR's foreign policy was circumscribed by the Hallstein Doctrine, which meant that the search for diplomatic recognition, and thus relations with developing countries became a crucial national priority for East Berlin. As the chapters by De Vita, Roberts and Borowy show, the GDR's early involvement in the Third World was predicated on competition with West Germany in the 'German–German Cold War' in pursuit of elusive diplomatic recognition, and on its own economic considerations. In fact, East Berlin often pursued the kind of unsettling tactics that damaged rather than aided its cause to the extent that the Soviets at times had to curb Ulbricht's ambitions. By the 1970s, however, the GDR's aspirations made it well situated to replace Czechoslovakia as the most active NSWP country in the developing world.

Hungary was in a similar position to the GDR because it found itself in diplomatic isolation in the aftermath of 1956. However, the situation soon changed and Budapest initiated a role as a mediator in relation to the Third World.[4] Besides the diplomatic effort and transfers of economic relations, the Third World revolutions found resonance in Hungarian mass culture.[5] However, the one lasting consequence of 1956 and of the János Kádár regime was 'goulash communism' and its preoccupation with foreign exchange. In economic terms, Hungary's greatest involvement was with the Middle East, with the region accounting for 72.8 per cent of Hungarian exports and 31.4 per cent of its imports from the Third World.[6] As Békés and Vékony show, Arab countries were Hungary's largest market for accumulating foreign currency and thus became an economic necessity for the communist regime. As a result, relations between Hungary and the Middle East revolved around mutual economic interests with ideology playing a limited role. Although Kádár's regime was one of Moscow's most loyal allies, it still found itself competing against the Soviet Union (and other Warsaw Pact allies) in the lucrative Middle East arms market.

Of the six NSWP states, the relations that Bulgaria enjoyed with the Third World were seemingly the least autonomous from Moscow. However, this was probably not because of a lack of freedom granted by the Kremlin but rather due to a specific strategy that the Bulgarian leadership pursued in its relations with Moscow. Baev's chapter demonstrates that Bulgaria's relations with the developing world centred on its constituting an asset to the Soviet Union by supplying arms to Soviet allies in Africa, Asia and Latin America. Nonetheless, at times Sofia took the initiative to pursue policies in the Third World which were more activist than even those of the Soviet Union. The main difference between Bulgaria and the other NSWP countries seems to be that while the other states sought relations with the Third World for economic benefit, Sofia's policies towards the Global South were predicated more on demonstrating its loyalty to Moscow and its value within the Warsaw Pact so as to gain economic advantages directly from the Soviet Union itself.

If Bulgaria was the NSWP state with the least autonomy from Moscow, Romania was surely the most independent – something which was understood even by contemporary observers. Historians have labelled Cold War Romania a 'maverick' for its independent foreign policy.[7] As the chapters by Watts and Dragomir explain, Bucharest resisted Moscow by remaining neutral during the Sino–Soviet split, refusing to break off relations with Israel and (along with Poland) blocking Mongolia's membership in the Warsaw Pact, amongst other actions. By the late 1960s, the other members of the Warsaw Pact began to view Romania as a quasi-adversary. Its acknowledged independence from Moscow even allowed Bucharest to establish relations with several states such as Zaire, Ivory Coast and Costa Rica, all of which leaned heavily towards the West and refused relations with any other Warsaw Pact state.[8] Nonetheless, despite its 'maverick' foreign policy, Bucharest was always mindful of the limits of its deviation from the Soviet Union and carefully avoided any head-on collisions with Moscow.

Beginning in the mid-1950s, Poland became an active player in Asia by serving as a member in the international peace commissions in Korea and Indochina. Yet, of the six junior members of the Warsaw Pact featured in this volume, Poland's engagement with Africa, the Middle East and Latin America was probably the most limited. Following the events of 1956, Gomułka was keen to pursue diplomatic initiatives that strengthened Poland's leverage in its relationship with Moscow and benefited Polish national interests. Such independence caused Khrushchev to label the Gomułka regime a 'goat jumping in unpredictable directions'.[9] The Rapacki Plan was one of these ambitions initiatives, and Rutkowski's chapter highlights how Warsaw tried to enlist neutral states such as India in support of the plan. International diplomacy notwithstanding, Gasztold's chapter illustrates the fact that Warsaw's autonomy was also manifested in its ability to refuse disadvantageous commitments in Africa where Poland prioritized educational assistance as an inexpensive alternative to development assistance – with schools often run by members of the pre-war Polish elite who often did not subscribe to socialism. Warsaw thus based its policies on a pragmatic approach governed by economics, and not by ideology.

The degree of autonomy with which the NSWP countries were allowed to operate in the Third World generally represented a win–win situation for both the Soviet Union and the Central and Eastern European states. The NSWP states frequently enjoyed more favourable conditions in the developing world than did the Soviet Union, which was often suspected of having hegemonic intentions. For this reason, the NSWP countries were able to establish certain relationships in Africa, Asia and Latin America that Moscow could not, which at times became an asset for Soviet bloc foreign policy. On the other hand, membership of the Warsaw Pact and close relations with the Soviet superpower probably gave the NSWP states more influence in the developing world than they otherwise would have had in a unipolar or multipolar world.

The authors within this volume contribute to our understanding of the Warsaw Pact in several significant ways and raise questions for further research. The volume highlights the importance of 1956 as the crucial moment of change in the status of NSWP countries and their relationship with the Soviet Union. While events in Hungary showed the limits of a 'national road to socialism', Soviet allies in Eastern and Central Europe achieved a level of autonomy in foreign policy that was in fact encouraged under the Soviet 'active foreign policy' doctrine. The leadership of the communist parties responded to the shocks of 1956 with varied strategies, from Bulgaria choosing to follow the Soviets to the letter to Romania eventually asserting a high level of autonomy over foreign policy representing two opposite ends of the spectrum. Beyond the specific strategies, all NSWP states acted in their own 'national interests' – defined differently within each national context.

The volume thus emphasizes the fact that the Soviet bloc was not monolithic and highlights the agency of the NSWP countries, not only as substantial actors in the Warsaw Pact but also as key actors in Second–Third World exchange in the twentieth century. The authors in this volume also show that the Warsaw Pact and its structures served as not merely a vehicle of Soviet domination but also as one for the expression of 'socialist internationalism' and, increasingly, of economic self-interest. While mutually beneficial economic exchange was initially part of the attraction of the Third World for NSWP economies, the cases of Czechoslovakia, Hungary and Bulgaria show that it was mainly the trade in arms that proved to be fairly lucrative. This volume does not intend to provide a deterministic 'rise and decline' narrative of NSWP relations with the Third World, but it does stress that money should be a key factor in future research on the topic of 'Soviet bloc–Third World' interactions.

Finally, the volume highlights the roles of men and women whom we call 'meditators' – teachers, spies, journalists and medical professionals – who populated the schools, embassies, press agencies, hospitals and academic conferences where engagement between the Second and the Third World actually took place, often in transnational spaces that crossed national boundaries. Even a brief look at some of these people shows how crucial their roles were, notwithstanding the fact their backgrounds and beliefs – and their relationship with socialism – varied greatly. The investigation of these men and women in their national and institutional contexts provides a rich laboratory to investigate Second–Third World relations, and may also allow an avenue to break away from national and bureaucratic paradigms in order to write the history of Eastern and Central Europe into global and international developments.

Notes

1. Csaba Békés, László J. Nagy and Dániel Vékony, 'Bittersweet Friendships: Relations between Hungary and the Middle East, 1953–1988', Cold War International History Project', CWIHP e-Dossier No. 67 (November 2015).
2. See Philip E. Muehlenbeck, *Czechoslovakia in Africa, 1945–1968* (New York, 2016), especially Chapter 3.
3. For an overview of Czechoslovakia's foreign policy in the developing world, see ibid.
4. Zoltán Szóke, 'Delusion or Reality? Secret Hungarian Diplomacy during the Vietnam War', *Journal of Cold War Studies* 12 (4) (Fall 2010), pp. 119–80.
5. James Mark and Peter Apor, 'Socialism Goes Global: Decolonization and the Making of a New Culture of Internationalism in Socialist Hungary, 1956–1989', *Journal of Modern History* 87 (December 2015), pp. 852–91.
6. Scott Blau, 'Hungary and the Third World: An Analysis of East-South Trade', in Michael Radu (ed.), *Eastern Europe and the Third World: East vs. South* (New York, 1981), pp. 176–9.
7. See for example, Denis Deletant and Mihail Ionescu, 'Romania and the Warsaw Pact: 1955–1989', Cold War International History Project, Working Paper #43 (April 2004).
8. Michael Radu, 'Romania and the Third World: The Dilemmas of a "Free Rider"', in Michael Radu (ed.), *Eastern Europe and the Third World: East vs. South* (New York, 1981).
9. Khrushchev quoted in Margaret K. Gnoinska, 'Poland and the Cold War in East and Southeast Asia, 1949–1965', PhD dissertation, George Washington University, Washington, DC, 2010, p. 5.

SELECT BIBLIOGRAPHY

Archival Sources

Bulgaria
Central State Archives (Sofia, Bulgaria)

Canada
Library and Archives Canada (Ottawa, Canada)

Czech Republic
Archive of the Ministry of Foreign Affairs (Prague, Czech Republic)
The National Archives of the Czech Republic (Prague, Czech Republic)
Security Services Archive (Prague, Czech Republic)

France
Diplomatic Archives Centre (Nantes, France)

Germany
Federal Archives of Parties and Mass Organizations of the GDR (Berlin, Germany)
Political Archive of the Ministry of Foreign Affairs (Berlin, Germany)

Hungary
National Archives of Hungary (Budapest, Hungary)
Open Society Archives (Budapest, Hungary)

India
Nehru Memorial Museum and Library (New Delhi, India)

Poland
Archive of the Institute of National Remembrance (Warsaw, Poland)
Archive of New Records (Warsaw, Poland)
Archive of the Foreign Ministry (Warsaw, Poland)
Central Archive of Modern Records (Warsaw, Poland)

Romania
Ministry of Foreign Affairs Archive (Bucharest, Romania)
National Archives of Romania (Bucharest, Romania)

Russia
Archive of Foreign Policy of the Russian Federation (Moscow, Russia)
Russian State Archive for Contemporary History (Moscow, Russia)
State Archive of the Russian Federation (Moscow, Russia)

United Kingdom
The National Archives (Kew, United Kingdom)

United States
Library of Congress (Washington, DC, USA)
National Archives II (College Park, MD, USA)

Published Primary Source Document Collections

Dokumente zur Außenpolitik der DDR [Documents on the Foreign Policy of the GDR] (Berlin).

Kamitatu, Cléophas, *The Congo Crisis, 1960–1961: A Critical Oral History Conference* [transcript of conference], Woodrow Wilson International Center for Scholars, 23–24 September 2004.

Parallel History Project on Cooperative Security. Available at http://www.php.isn.ethz.ch/lory1.ethz.ch/collections/index.html (accessed September 2017).

Ruchniewicz, K. and T. Szumowski (eds), *Polskie Dokumenty Dyplomatyczne* [Documents on Polish Foreign Policy], Volume: 1957 (Warsaw, 2006).

Wilson Center Digital Archive. Available at http://digitalarchive.wilsoncenter.org/ (accessed September 2017).

Selected Published Sources

Anderson, Sheldon, *A Cold War in the Soviet Bloc: Polish-East German Relations, 1945–1962* (Boulder, CO, 2001).

Attwood, William, *The Reds and the Blacks: A Personal Adventure* (New York, 1967).

Baev, Jordan, *Voennopoliticheskite konflikti sled Vtorata svetovna vojna I Bulgaria* [Military and Political Conflicts after World War II and Bulgaria] (Sofia, 1995).

———, 'East-East Arms Trade: Bulgarian Arms Delivery to Third World Countries, 1950–1989', *Parallel History Project on Cooperative Security* (Zurich, 2006).

———, 'Eastern Europe and the Six Day War: The Case of Bulgaria', in Y. Roi and B. Morozov (eds), *The Soviet Union and the Six Day War* (Stanford, CA, 2008).

———, 'Bulgaria and the Cuban Missile Crisis', *Cold War International History Project Bulletin*, Vol. 17/18 (2012).

———, *Drugata studena vojna. Savetsko-Kitaiskiat konflikt I Iztochna Evropa* [The Other Cold War. Sino-Soviet Conflict and Eastern Europe] (Sofia, 2012).

———, 'Bulgaria and Latin America in the Cold War Years: A Case Study for Soviet Bloc Political Relations with Latin American Countries', in OPSIS, *Dossie Tematico: America Latina no Contexto da Guerra Fria* (Goias, 2014).

Baev, Jordan (ed.), *Bulgaria and the Middle East Conflict in the Cold War Years. Documents volume* (Sofia, 2006).

Békés, Csaba, *Eursaba, Eurraba. Magyarorsz a konfliktusok kereszttttsok k, 1945–1990.* [From Europe to Europe. Hungary in the Crossfire of Conflicts, 1945–1990] (Budapest, 2004).

———, 'Hungarian foreign policy in the Soviet alliance system, 1968–1989', *Foreign Policy Review* [Budapest], Vol. 3, No. 1 (2004), pp. 87–127. Available at www.coldwar.hu (accessed September 2017).

Békés, Csaba, László J. Nagy and Dániel Vékony, 'Bittersweet Friendships: Relations between Hungary and the Middle East, 1953–1988', Cold War International History Project, CWIHP e-Dossier No. 67 (November 2015). Available at https://www.wilsoncenter.org/publication/bittersweet-friendships-relations-between-hungary-and-the-middle-east-1953-1988 (accessed September 2017).

Búr, Gábor, 'Hungarian Diplomacy and the Non-Aligned Movement in the Cold War', in I. Majoros, Z. Maruzsa and O. Rathkolb (eds), *Österreich und Ungarn im Kalten Krieg* [Austria and Hungary in the Cold War] (Vienna and Budapest, 2010).

Crump, Laurien, *The Warsaw Pact Reconsidered. International Relations in Eastern Europe, 1955–1969* (London, 2015).

Cyrankiewicz, Jozef, 'Poland and Her Neighbours', *Foreign Affairs Reports*, Vol. VI, No. 4 (April 1957).

Devlin, Larry, *Chief of Station, Congo: A Memoir of 1960–67* (New York, 2007).

Dobrovoda, David, 'Czechoslovakia and East Africa in the late colonial and early post-colonial period: The case studies of Kenya, Uganda, and Tanzania', PhD dissertation, University of London, 2016.

Dragomir, Elena, 'The Formation of the Soviet Bloc's Council for Mutual Economic Assistance. Romania's Involvement', *Journal of Cold War Studies*, Vol. 14, No. 1 (Winter 2012).

———, 'The perceived threat of hegemonism in Romania during the second détente', *Cold War History*, Vol. 12, No. 1 (February 2012).

———, *Cold War Perceptions. Romania's Policy change towards the USSR, 1960–1964* (Newcastle upon Tyne, 2015).

Fursenko, Aleksandr and Timothy Naftali, *"One Hell of a Gamble": Khrushchev, Castro, and Kennedy, 1958–1964* (New York, 1997).

Gasztold-Seń, Przemysław, 'Wywiad PRL a problemy polityczno-gospodarcze Afryki Subsaharyjskiej w latach 80 XX wieku' [The Polish People's Republic

towards the Maghreb Countries, 1970–1989], *Olsztyńskie Studia Afrykanistyczne*, Vol. II (2011).
Germuska, Pál, 'A közel-keleti magyar haditechnikai export kezdetei' [The beginning of exports of military hardware to the Middle East], in M.J. Rainer and E. Standeisky (eds), *ÉVKÖNYV XI. 2003. Magyarország a jelenkorban* [Almanac XI. 2003. Hungary in present days] (Budapest, 2003).
———, *Vörös Arzenál* [Red Arsenal] (Budapest, 2010).
Gnoinska, Margaret K., 'Poland and the Cold War in East and Southeast Asia, 1949–1965', PhD dissertation, George Washington University, Washington, DC, 2009.
Govrin, Josef, 'Egyszerre csak egy lépés: Izraeli–magyar kapcsolatok, 1967–1989' [One step at a time: Israeli-Hungarian relations, 1967–1989], *Nemzet és Biztonság* [Nation and Security] (2009).
Gray, William Glenn, *Germany's Cold War: The Global Campaign to Isolate East Germany, 1949–1969* (Chapel Hill, NC, 2003).
Harrison, Hope, *Driving the Soviets Up the Wall: Soviet-East German Relations, 1953–1961* (Princeton, NJ, 2003).
Hong, Young-Sun, *Cold War Germany, the Third World, and the Global Humanitarian Regime* (Cambridge, 2015).
Hornsby, Charles, *Kenya: A History since Independence* (New York, 2012).
Hubbard, James P., *The United States and the End of British Colonial Rule in Africa, 1941–1968* (Jefferson, NC, 2010).
Kanet, Roger (ed.), *The Soviet Union, Eastern Europe, and the Third World* (New York, 1987).
Kilian, Werner, *Die Hallstein-Doktrin: der Diplomatische Krieg zwischen der BRD und der DDR, 1955–1973* [The Hallstein Doctrine: The Diplomatic War between the FRG and the GDR, 1955–1973] (Berlin, 2001).
Knopek, Jacek, *Stosunki polsko-zachodnioafrykańskie* [Polish–West African Relations] (Toruń, 2013).
Korbonski, Andrzej and Francis Fukuyama (eds), *The Soviet Union and the Third World: The Last Three Decades* (Ithaca, NY, 1987).
Koura, Jan and Robert Anthony Waters Jr, 'Cheddi Jagan and Guyanese Overtures to the East: Evidence from the Czech National Archives', Cold War International History Project. CWIHP e-Dossier No. 54 (October 2014). Available at https://www.wilsoncenter.org/publication/cheddi-jagan-and-guyanese-overtures-to-the-east-evidence-the-czech-national-archives (accessed September 2017).
Lopes, Rui, *West Germany and the Portuguese Dictatorship, 1968–1974: Between Cold War and Colonialism* (Basingstoke, 2014).
Lorenzini, Sara, 'Comecon and the South in the Years of Détente: A Study on East-South Economic Relations', *European Review of History: Revue Européenne d'Histoire* 21 (2) (2014), pp. 183–99.
Lühti, Lorentz M., 'The People's Republic of China and the Warsaw Pact Organization, 1955–63', *Cold War History*, Vol. 7, No. 4 (November 2007).
Mastny, Vojtech, 'The 1963 Nuclear Test Ban Treaty. A Missed Opportunity for Détente?' *Journal of Cold War Studies*, Vol. 10, No. 1 (Winter 2008).
Mastny, Vojetch and Malcolm Byrne (eds), *A Cardboard Castle?: An Inside History of the Warsaw Pact, 1955–1991* (Budapest, 2005).

Mazov, Sergey, *Kholodnaya Voyna v 'Serdze Afriki'. SSSR i Kongolezskiy Krizis, 1960–1964* [Cold War in the 'Heart of Africa'. The USSR and the Congo Crisis, 1960–1964] (Moscow, 2015).
Mong, Attila, *Kádár hitele* [Kádár's debt] (Budapest, 2012).
Muehlenbeck, Philip E., *Czechoslovakia in Africa, 1945–1968* (New York, 2015).
Munteanu, Mircea, 'Romania and the Sino-American Rapprochment, 1969–1971: New Evidence from the Bucharest Archives', *Cold War International History Bulletin*, Issue 16 (Fall 2007/Winter 2008).
Nagy, László J., *Magyarország és az arab térség – Kapcsolatok, vélemények, álláspontos 1947–1975* [Hungary and the Arab World – Connections, opinions, standpoints 1947–1975] (Szeged, 2006).
Namikas, Lise, *Battleground Africa: Cold War in the Congo, 1960–1965* (Stanford, CA, 2013).
Nazhestkin, Oleg, 'Gody kongolezskogo krizisa, 1960–1963. Zapiski Razvedchika' [The Years of the Congolese Crisis, 1960–1963. Notes of an Intelligence Officer] *Novaya i Noveishaia Istoria* (2003).
Odinga, Oginga, *Not Yet Uhuru* (New York, 1967).
Rabe, Stephen, *U.S. Intervention in British Guiana: A Cold War Story* (Chapel Hill, NC, 2005).
Radchenko, Sergey, *Two Suns in the Heavens. The Sino-Soviet Struggle for Supremacy, 1962–1967* (Washington, DC, 2009).
Radu, Michael (ed.), *Eastern Europe and the Third World: East vs. South* (New York, 1981).
Roberts, George, 'The assassination of Eduardo Mondlane: FRELIMO and the politics of exile in Dar es Salaam', *Cold War History* (November 2016).
———, 'Politics, decolonisation, and the Cold War in Dar es Salaam, c. 1965–1972', PhD dissertation, University of Warwick, 2016.
Skrzypek, Andrzej, *Mechanizmy Autonomii: Stosunki Polsko-Radzieckie 1956–1965* [The Mechanics of Autonomy: Polish-Soviet Relations 1956–1965] (Warsaw, 2005).
Smith, Tony, 'New Bottles for New Wine: A Pericentric Framework for the Study of the Cold War', *Diplomatic History* 24 (4) (2000), pp. 567–91.
Sturmer, Martin, *The Media History of Tanzania* (Mtwara, 1998).
Tebinka, Jacek, *Uzależnienie czy suwerenność? Odwilż październikowa w dyplomacji Polskiej Rzeczpospolitej Ludowej 1956–1961* [Dependence or Independence? The October Thaw in Diplomatic Relations of the Polish People's Republic, 1956–1961] (Warsaw, 2010).
Telepneva, Natalia, 'Our Sacred Duty: The Soviet Union, the Liberation Movements in the Portuguese Colonies, and the Cold War, 1961–1975', PhD dissertation, London School of Economics and Political Science, 2014.
Tismăneanu, Vladimir, *Stalinism for All Seasons. A Political History of Romanian Communism* (Berkeley, CA, 2003).
van der Heyden, Ulrich and Franziska Benger (eds), *Kalter Krieg in Ostafrika: Die Beziehungen der DDR zu Sansibar und Tansania* [Cold War in East Africa: The GDR's Relations with Zanzibar and Tanzania] (Berlin, 2009).
Waters, Robert Anthony Jr and Gordon O. Daniels, 'The World's Longest General Strike', *Diplomatic History*, Vol. 29 (2005).
———, 'Striking for Freedom? International intervention and the Guianese Sugar workers' strike of 1964', *Cold War History*, Vol. 10, No. 4 (November 2010).

Watts, Larry L., *With Friends Like These: The Soviet Bloc's Clandestine War Against Romania* (Bucharest, 2010).
———, 'The Soviet-Romanian Clash Over History, Identity and Dominion', Cold War International History Project. CWIHP e-Dossier No. 29 (January 2012). Available at https://www.wilsoncenter.org/publication/the-soviet-romanian-clash-over-history-identity-and-dominion (accessed September 2017).
———, 'Divided Loyalties: Romanian Objection to Informal Soviet Control, 1963–1964', Cold War International History Project. CWIHP e-Dossier No. 42 (October 2013). Available at https://www.wilsoncenter.org/publication/divided-loyalties-within-the-bloc-romanian-objection-to-soviet-informal-controls-1963 (accessed September 2017).
———, 'Mediating the Vietnam War: Romania and the First Trinh Signal 1965–1966', Cold War International History Project. CWIHP Working Paper #81 (July 2016). Available at https://www.wilsoncenter.org/sites/default/files/cwihp_wp_81_larry_watts_july_2016.pdf (accessed September 2017).
Westad, Odd Arne, *The Global Cold War: Third World Interventions and the Making of Our Times* (New York, 2013).
Winrow, Gareth M., *The Foreign Policy of the GDR in Africa* (Cambridge, 1990).
Zídek, Petr and Karl Sieber, *Československo a Subsaharská Afrika v Letech 1948–1989* [Czechoslovakia in Sub-Saharan Africa, 1948–1989] (Prague, 2007).

INDEX

Abu Ayad, 309–10
Accra University, 205
'active foreign policy doctrine' (of the Soviet
    Union), 6–7, 10, 17–18, 66, 275, 289,
    326, 330
Adenauer, Konrad, 25
Adoula, Cyrille, 137
Afghanistan, 113
African National Congress (ANC), 163,
    210, 313
African Party for the Independence of Guinea
    and Cape Verde (PAIGC), 164, 209–10,
    313–14
African Regroupment Party (CEREA),
    130, 138
African Solidarity Party (PSA), 129–30, 138
Afro-Asian People's Solidarity Organisation
    (AAPSO), 202, 207
Air India, 58
Albania, 1, 19n.6, 228–9, 237, 242
Algeria, 103, 141, 200–2, 210, 278, 292, 301,
    304, 306
Allende, Salvador, 319–20
Allgemeine Deutsche Nachrichtendienst
    (ADN), 12–13, 154–8, 161, 164
Alliance for Progress, 81, 86, 89
Alliance of Bakongo (ABAKO), 126, 129–30
Almeyda, Clodomiro, 319
Altamirano, Carlos, 320
Amathila, Libertina, 210
Amin, Idi, 261–2, 269n.33
Andreev, Georgi, 319
Angola, 112, 137–9, 153, 200, 202, 209–10,
    213, 313

Arafat, Yasser, 116n.29, 282, 308–9
Argentina, 76, 178, 314
arms sales
    Bulgaria and, 299–317, 321, 328
    Czechoslovakia and, 1, 9, 17, 29, 43, 79, 83,
        87, 129, 132–3, 135–6, 257–62, 285
    Hungary and, 17–18, 273–4, 284–8,
        290–1, 330
    Soviet Union and, 16–17, 203, 286, 302
Arusha Declaration, 158–9
al-Assad, Hafiz, 302–3
Aswan High Dam, 8, 28–9
Austria, 62, 109, 135, 186
Avramov, Luchezar, 315

Babu, Mohamed, 150, 156, 158–60
Baghdad Pact, 26, 43
al Bakr, Ahmed Hussan, 306, 308
Bandung Conference, 8, 27, 156
Barák, Rudolf, 125
Bashev, Ivan, 304
Batista, Fulgencio, 76
Baudouin, King, 126
Becker, Walter, 34
Békés, Csaba, 6, 17
Belgian Communist Party (BCP), 130
Belgium, 126, 130, 137
Ben-Gurion, David, 106
Benin, 200, 212
Berlin Wall, 3, 135, 152, 176–7
Bettelheim, Charles, 82–3
Bhagwan, Moses, 81, 92n.19
Bîrlădeanu, Alexandru, 236
Bodnăraş, Emil, 236–7, 242

INDEX 339

Bolz, Lothar, 41–2
Bomboko, Justin, 136–7
Borodziej, Włodzimierz, 53
Boyer, Paul, 149
Brazil, 13, 84, 182, 187–9
Brennan, James, 154
Brezezinski, Zbigniew, 2
Brezhnev, Leonid, 16, 103–4, 111, 134, 279, 317
British Communist Party, 77
British Guiana
  Cuba and, 81, 83, 85, 89
  German Democratic Republic (GDR) and, 84
  Hungary and, 84
  Poland and, 82–4
  Soviet Union and, 77–8, 82–4
  United Kingdom and, 74, 77–8, 82–8
  United States and, 82, 84, 87
Bulganin, Nikolai, 56
Bulgaria
  Abu Ayad and, 309–10
  Africa and, 18, 213, 298–9, 311–14, 328
  African National Congress (ANC) and, 313–14
  Algeria and, 103, 301, 304, 306
  Angola and, 313
  Arafat, Yasser and, 308–9
  Argentina and, 314
  arms exports from, 299–317, 321, 328
  Asia and, 298–9, 310–11, 328
  Benin and, 212
  Black September and, 309
  Cabral, Amilcar and, 314
  Castro, Fidel and, 315–17
  Chile and, 319–20
  China and, 299–300, 310
  Congo and, 311–12
  Council for Mutual Economic Assistance (CMEA) and, 319
  Cuba and, 299, 314–17, 321
  Cuban Missile Crisis and, 315, 321
  Czechoslovakia and, 302–3
  decolonization and, 300–1
  Egypt and, 103, 302–8, 311–12
  Front for the Liberation of Mozambique (FRELIMO) and, 312
  German Democratic Republic (GDR) and, 301, 318
  Ghana and, 302, 312
  Greece and, 315, 320
  Guatemala and, 316
  Guinea and, 312
  Hezbollah and, 309–10
  Ho Chi Minh and, 310
  Hungary and, 286, 301
  Indonesia and, 302
  Iraq and, 302, 306–9, 322
  Israel and, 300, 304–5
  Jordan and, 302, 309
  Kaunda, Kenneth and, 312
  Kaynyatta, Jomo and, 312
  Kenya and, 312
  Kenya African National Congress (KANU) and, 312
  Korean War and, 299
  Laos and, 298–9, 311
  Latin America and, 18, 298–9, 314–21, 328
  Lebanon and, 302, 306, 309
  Libya and, 306
  Machel, Samora and, 313
  Mali and, 312
  Mexico and, 314
  Middle East and, 18, 103, 298–310, 321
  Morocco and, 301
  Mozambique and, 313
  Muslim Brotherhood and, 309–10
  Namibia and, 313–14
  Nasser, Gamal Abdel and, 302–3, 305
  National Liberation Council (CNL) and, 312
  National Liberation Front (FLN) and, 301
  national-liberation movements and, 300–1, 308–9, 311–14
  Neto, Agostinho and, 313
  Nigeria and, 312
  North Korea and, 299–300
  North Vietnam and, 187, 298–9, 310–11
  Operation Danube and, 306
  Palestine Liberation Organization (PLO) and, 308–9
  Party for the Independence of Guinea and Cape Verde (PAIGC) and, 313–14
  Pathet Lao and, 311
  Poland and, 301, 307, 318
  Popular Movement for the Liberation of Angola (MPLA) and, 312–13
  propaganda of, 305, 322
  Roberto, Holden and, 313
  Romania and, 112, 299, 301
  Simba Rebellion and, 312
  Six Day War and, 303–5, 307
  South Africa and, 313–14

South West Africa People's Organization
 (SWAPO) and, 313–14
Soviet Union and, 2–3, 9, 18, 298–303,
 315, 320–1, 328
Sudan and, 306, 311–12
Syria and, 103, 302–7, 309
Tanzania and, 165, 312
Tunisia and, 306
Turkey and, 315, 320
United Kingdom and, 300
United National Independent Party (UNIP)
 and, 312
United Nations and, 313, 315
United States and, 299, 301–2, 320
Venezuela and, 317
Viet Cong and, 311
Vietnam War and, 298–9, 310–11
Warsaw Pact and, 1–2, 18, 298, 319–21,
 328
Workers' Party of Guatemala (GPT) and,
 316–17
Yemen and, 303, 306
Yugoslavia and, 320
Zambia and, 312
Zanzibar and, 312
Zimbabwe and, 313–14, 321
Zimbabwe African National Union (ZANU)
 and, 313–14, 321
Zimbabwe African People's Union (ZAPU)
 and, 314, 321
Bulgarian Agrarian Union party (BANU),
 318–19
Bundy, McGeorge, 277
Búr, Gábor, 272, 274
Burma, 55–8, 62, 66–7, 178, 185–6
Burnham, Forbes, 87–8
Burundi, 138, 257
Bušniak, Ján, 135

Cabral, Amílcar, 164, 209, 314
Cambodia, 58, 62, 66–7
Cameroon, 214
Canada, 84, 258–9
Cape Verde, 164, 209–10, 313–14
Castro, Fidel, 76, 79–81, 83, 85, 88–9, 112,
 315–17
Castro, Raúl, 79, 301, 315, 317
Ceaușescu, Nicolae, 98–101, 105–7, 109,
 111–12, 121n.101, 234
Černý, Zdeněk, 139, 141–2
Ćeteka, 12, 154
Chile, 76, 319–20

Chilu University, 185
China
 Bulgaria and, 299–300, 310
 Czechoslovakia and, 60
 Egypt and, 274
 German Democratic Republic (GDR) and,
  162, 180–1, 184–5
 Hungary and, 274
 Kenya and, 251
 Middle East and, 274, 278
 Mongolia and, 228
 Mugabe, Robert and, 321
 North Vietnam and, 101, 180–1, 229,
  232, 300
 Odinga, Oginga and, 251
 Palestine Liberation Organization (PLO)
  and, 309
 People's Republic of China (PRC), founding
  of, 7
 Poland and, 52–3, 55–7, 59–62, 68
 Romania and, 17, 100, 104, 225–7,
  230–3, 236–8, 240, 242
 Soviet Union and, 5–6, 45, 61, 226, 228,
  242, 300
 Tanzania and, 158–9, 161–2
 United States and, 101, 229
 Xinhua of, 154
 Zanzibar and, 150
 Zimbabwe and, 314, 321
 Zimbabwe African National Union (ZANU)
  and, 314
China and the Devil Slaves, 161–2
Chomętowski, Józef, 211
Colombia, 75, 189
Comintern, 6, 12, 140
Costa Rica, 76, 329
Council for Mutual Economic Assistance
 (CMEA), 2, 15, 36, 45, 97, 211, 224, 274
Congo
 Belgium and, 126–7, 130, 137
 civil in, 127
 Czechoslovakia and, 12–13, 126–39,
  141–2, 265–6
 Egypt and, 133–4
 German 'Cold War' and, 152
 Ghana and, 134
 Kenya and, 263
 Morocco and, 134
 Nasser, Gamal Abdel and, 133–4
 Poland and, 137
 Soviet Union and, 9, 12–13 127–37,
  139–43, 265–6

INDEX   341

Sudan and, 133–5
Uganda and, 261–2
United Nations and, 127, 130–40
United States and, 127–8, 131, 135–6, 139, 143
Congolese National Movement (MNC), 126–7, 129, 138–9
Crump, Laurien, 4, 226, 228
Csornoky, Viktor, 274, 285, 294n.14
Cuba
  Algeria and, 141
  Angola and, 112
  British Guiana and, 81, 83, 85, 89
  Bulgaria and, 299, 314–17, 321
  Cuban Revolution and, 8, 75, 80, 88
  Czechoslovakia and, 9, 75–6, 79–80, 83, 85, 89
  Ethiopia and, 112
  German Democratic Republic (GDR) and, 189
  journalists of, 12, 154
  Romania and, 112
  Soviet Union and, 3, 85, 88, 101–2, 265, 315–17, 321
  United Nations and, 315
Cuban Missile Crisis, 97, 100–1, 225, 231, 315–16, 321
Cyrankiewicz, Józef, 9, 51–2, 54, 57–62, 64–8, 204, 230
Czechoslovak intelligence, *see Státní bezpečnost* (StB)
Czechoslovak Press Agency, 253
Czechoslovakia
  Africa and, 80
  Algeria and, 141
  Angola and, 139
  arms exports from, 1, 9, 17, 29, 43, 79, 83, 87, 129, 132–3, 135–6, 257–62, 285
  British Guiana and, 9–10, 74–8, 81–8
  Bulgaria and, 302–3
  Burundi and, 138, 257
  Chile and, 76
  China and, 60
  Colombia and, 75
  Congo and, 12–13, 126–39, 141–2, 265–6
  Cuba and, 9, 75–6, 79–80, 83, 85, 89
  decolonization and, 249
  economy of, 75–6, 85, 87, 249, 257–8
  Egypt and, 1, 29, 43, 129, 250, 252, 258–9, 265–6

Ghana and, 257–8, 265
Guinea and, 257–8
Jagan, Cheddi and, 9–10, 75–8, 84, 86–7, 89
Jagan, Janet and, 75–6, 84
Kenya and, 17, 249–53, 257–9, 26–66
Latin America and, 9, 74–6, 79–89
Lumumba, Patrice and, 12–13
Mali and, 257–8
Mexico and, 76
Morocco and, 258
North Vietnam and, 187
Operation Manuel and, 85
People's Progressive Party of British Guiana and, 9–10, 81–2, 86–7, 89
Peru and, 76
Poland and, 54
Portugal and, 137
Rapacki Plan and, 54
Rhodesia and, 253
Rwanda and, 138, 257
Soviet Union and, 1, 9–10, 17, 74, 76–7, 79–80, 82, 84–5, 125–30, 132–3, 135–8, 142–3, 160, 257–8, 265–6
Státní bezpečnost (StB) of, 79–80, 83–4, 86, 88, 125–6, 128–9, 135–43
Tanzania and, 156, 165, 249, 253, 257–8
Uganda and, 17, 249, 253–54, 256–8, 260–2, 264–6
United Kingdom and, 249–50, 256
United Nations and, 138–9
United States and, 74–6, 81, 86, 89, 126, 128, 136, 139
Venezuela and, 75–6
Warsaw Pact and, 1–2
Warsaw Pact invasion of, 13, 17, 160
Zanzibar and, 253
Czinege, Lajos, 288

Dahlke, Dieter, 154–5
David, George, 86–7
David, Rudolf, 84, 86–7
Davidson, Bocheley, 140
Dawisha, Adeed, 273
Dayan, Moshe, 110
de Andrade, Mario Pinto, 313
de Coninck, Albert, 130
de Gaulle, Charles, 103–4
de Murville, Couve, 104
Del Valle, Sergio, 316

Democratic Party (DP), 253–6
Democratic People's Republic of Korea, *see* North Korea
Democratic Republic of Vietnam, *see* North Vietnam
Devlin, Larry, 131, 136, 140
Długołęcki, Piotr, 54
Dobrovda, David, 260–1
Dong, Pham Van, 310
Dresden Museum of Hygiene, 178, 180
Drewnowski, Jan, 205–6
Dubai, 286
Dubček, Alexander, 160
Dulles, John Foster, 27, 29
Dzhurov, Dobri, 303–4

East Germany, *see* German Democratic Republic
Eban, Abba, 109
Eggerath, Werner, 31
Egypt
 Bulgaria and, 103, 302–8, 311–12
 China and, 274
 Congo and, 133–4
 Czechoslovakia and, 1, 29, 43, 129, 250, 252, 258–9, 265–6
 decolonization and, 56
 Federal Republic of Germany (FRG) and, 29, 32–4, 37–8, 41
 German Democratic Republic (GDR) and, 8, 25–43, 178, 181, 183, 187
 Hungary and, 272–4, 276–7, 281, 283, 285–8, 292
 Israel and, 8, 16, 26–7, 29, 33, 38–41, 43, 100–11, 306–7
 Kenya and, 258–9
 Poland and, 56, 199–200
 Romania and, 100–2, 105–6, 108–11
 Six Day War and, 100–11
 Soviet Union and, 1, 28–9, 102–3, 105–8, 265–6, 272, 276–9, 287, 300, 302, 306–8
 Suez Crisis and, 8, 29, 38–42, 276–7, 300
 Uganda and, 255–6
 United States and, 1, 28–9, 38, 105, 107–8
Eisenhower Doctrine, 301–2
Eisenhower, Dwight D., 28, 301
Engerman, David, 56
England, *see* United Kingdom
Eshkol, Levi, 105
Ethiopia, 112, 200, 204, 211–12
Evening News, 156

Fahmi, Ismail, 307–8
Federal Republic of Germany (FRG)
 Afrikapolitik of, 162–5
 Aswan High Dam and, 29
 Egypt and, 29, 32–4, 37–8, 41
 founding of, 25
 German Democratic Republic (GDR) and, 4, 8, 13, 25–6, 29, 31, 33, 37–41, 43, 148, 150–6, 160, 162–6, 175–7, 180, 183, 189–90, 327
 Guinea and, 164–5
 Hallstein Doctrine and, 26, 29, 148, 150
 India and, 64–5
 Israel and, 8, 33, 38–41, 104
 Mozambique and, 163
 Poland and, 54, 64–5, 67, 201, 204
 Portugal and, 152–3, 162–6
 propaganda and, 29, 38–9, 41, 43, 152–3, 162, 164, 166, 188
 South Africa and, 160, 162–3, 166
 Soviet Union and, 8
 Suez Crisis and, 38–41
 Tanzania and, 150–1, 156–7, 159–60, 162–6
 Zanzibar and, 150
France, 7, 8, 29, 35, 39–43, 103–4, 151, 201, 274, 301
Frankfurter Allgemeine Zeitung, 34
Freie Deutsche Jugend (FDJ), 42
Frelek, Ryszard, 197–98
Fülöp, Mihály, 272

Ganchev, Lalyu, 319
Gazdag, Ferenc, 272
Gbenye, Christophe, 136, 137, 140–1, 312
GDR News, 164
German Democratic Republic (GDR)
 African liberation movements and, 152, 213
 Argentina and, 178
 Benin and, 212
 Brazil and, 13, 182, 187–9
 British Guiana and, 84
 Bulgaria and, 301, 318
 Burma and, 178, 185–6
 China and, 162, 180–1, 184–5
 Colombia and, 189
 Cuba and, 189
 Czechoslovakia and, 327
 economic relations with the Third World of, 30–3, 35–6, 41, 43, 182–9
 Egypt and, 8, 25–43, 178, 181, 183, 187

INDEX 343

Federal Republic of Germany (FRG) and, 4, 8, 13, 25–6, 29, 31, 33, 37–41, 43, 148, 150–6, 160, 162–6, 175–7, 180, 183, 189–90, 327
  founding of, 25–6
  Hallstein Doctrine and, 26, 29, 148–50, 327
  Hungary and, 154
  India and, 36–7, 54, 64
  Israel and, 39–41
  Kenya and, 263
  Korean War and, 175–6
  Lumumba Institute and, 263
  medical academics of, 8, 13–14, 173–91
  Middle East and, 36–45
  Mozambique and, 163
  North Vietnam and, 180–2, 185, 187
  Poland and, 36–7, 54, 180, 210
  population loss of, 176
  propaganda of, 13, 29–30, 34, 36, 38–9, 41, 43, 159–66, 176
  Rapacki Plan and, 54
  recognition of, 13, 25–7, 29–30, 32, 34–7, 39, 41, 43–4, 148–51, 161, 166–7, 175, 189, 213, 327
  Romania and, 98–9, 103–4, 110, 112, 176
  Six Day War and, 104
  Soviet Union and, 3, 6, 8–9, 26, 28, 31, 34–9, 42–5, 110, 148–9, 151, 166–7, 180, 183, 189–90, 327
  Stasi of, 12, 154
  Suez Crisis and, 8, 38–42
  Sweden and, 189
  Tanzania and, 13, 149–67
  United States and, 176
  Warsaw Pact and, 1–2, 148–9, 327
  Zanzibar and, 150–3, 166
Germuska, Pál, 272
Ghana, 14, 79, 134–5, 156, 203–6, 251, 255, 257–8, 262, 265, 302, 312
Gheorghiu-Dej, Gheorghe, 224, 230–1, 234–9, 241, 301
Gierek, Edward, 14, 198–9, 208, 210
Ginwala, Frene, 163–5
Gizenga, Antoine, 127–38, 142–3, 311
Goa, 65
Gomułka, Władysław, 7, 9, 14, 52–3, 61–2, 198–201, 203, 208, 213, 301, 329
Gorchakov, Ovidy, 78
Great Britain, *see* United Kingdom
Great Terror, 12

Grechko, Andrei, 110–11
Greece, 315, 320
Grela, Kwiryn, 208–9
Gromyko, Andrei, 207, 236–8, 240
Grotewohl, Otto, 26, 31–2, 39–40, 42–3
Guatemala, 316–17
Guevara, Che, 315
Guină, Nicolae, 236
Guinea, 79, 129–30, 134, 164–5, 203–4, 206, 257–8, 262, 312
Guinea-Bissau, 164, 209, 313

Habari Katika Czechoslovakia, 160
Hagen, Katrina, 152
Hallstein Doctrine, 26, 29–30, 148, 150, 327
Hammarskjöld, Dag, 130–1
Hanselka, Jiri, 11
Harrison, Hope, 3, 7
Hassan II, King, 134
Hassanein, Mohammed, 42
Helsinki Declaration, 5, 106
Hershberg, James, 5
Hezbollah, 309–10
Hitler, Adolph, 34
Ho Chi Minh, 310
Holocaust, 38, 279–80
Honecker, Erich, 110
Houphouet-Boigny, Félix, 207
Houska, Josef, 141
Humboldt University, 177, 185
Hungary
  Africa and, 7
  Algeria and, 292
  British Guiana and, 84
  Bulgaria and, 286, 301
  arms trade of, 17–18, 273–4, 284–8, 290–1, 330
  Asia and, 7
  China and, 274
  Council for Mutual Economic Assistance (CMEA) and, 274, 286–7
  Dubai and, 286
  economy of, 17–18, 271–3, 278–9, 281–93, 328
  Egypt and, 272–4, 276–7, 281, 283, 285–8, 292
  German Democratic Republic (GDR) and, 154
  International Monetary Fund (IMF) and, 290
  Iran and, 292
  Iraq and, 272–3, 281, 285, 292
  Israel and, 18, 273, 279–82, 290–2

Israeli Communist Party and, 281
Jordan and, 292
Kuwait and, 292
Latin America and, 7
Lebanon and, 286, 292
Libya and, 272–3, 292
Middle East and, 17–18, 271–7, 279–91, 328
Mongolia and, 241
Morocco and, 283–4, 292
Non-Aligned Movement and, 272
North Vietnam and, 187
Palestine Liberation Organization (PLO) and, 282
Poland and, 58, 65
Revolution of 1956 and, 7, 28, 43, 45, 53, 58, 65, 271, 276–7, 279, 282, 288–9, 327–28, 330
Romania and, 99
Six Day War and, 281
Soviet Union and, 2–3, 6–7, 17–18, 58, 65, 271, 273–8, 285–7, 289, 328
Sudan and, 277, 292
Syria and, 272–3, 277, 281, 285–6, 288, 292
Tunisia and, 292
United Nations and, 271–2, 276–7, 289
United States and, 276–7, 289
Warsaw Pact and, 1–2, 43, 286–9
World Bank and, 290
Hussein, Saddam, 302

Ileo, Joseph, 132, 136
India
    Federal Republic of Germany (FRG) and, 64–5
    German Democratic Republic (GDR) and, 36–7, 54, 64
    Poland and, 9, 51–2, 54–6, 58, 62–8, 207, 329
    Portugal and, 65
    Romania and, 233
    Soviet Union and, 56
    United Kingdom and, 65
    United Nations and, 67–8
Indonesia, 8, 27, 55–7, 178, 302
International Confederation of Free Trade Unions (ICFTU), 251
International Monetary Fund (IMF), 290
Iran, 26, 103, 112–13, 272, 292–3
Iraq, 26, 33, 42, 104–5, 155, 272, 278, 281, 285, 292, 302–3, 306–9, 322

Israel
    Amin, Idi and, 172n.85
    Bulgaria and, 300, 304–5
    Egypt and, 8, 16, 26–7, 29, 33, 38–41, 43, 100–11, 306–7
    Federal Republic of Germany (FRG) and, 8, 33, 38–41, 104
    German Democratic Republic (GDR) and, 39–41
    Hungary and, 18, 273, 279–82, 290–2
    Jordan and, 309
    Palestine and, 105, 308–9
    Romania and, 10, 104–9, 111, 328
    Six Day War and, 10, 104–5, 281, 285, 305
    socialism and, 273
    Soviet Union and, 100, 102, 108, 279–80, 300
    Sudan and, 164
    Syria and, 302
    Uganda and, 17, 172n.85, 259–61
    United States and, 38, 104, 107–8, 280–1
Israeli Communist Party (ICP), 279, 281
Ivory Coast, 207, 329
Izvestiya, 158

Jabłoński, Henryk, 210
Jagan, Cheddi, 9–10, 75–8, 81–4, 86–7, 89
Jagan, Janet, 9–10, 75–8, 81–4, 89
James, C. L. R., 250
Janouš, Josef, 132
Japan, 184, 230, 321
Jaruzelski, Wojciech, 199
Jenapharm, 184–6
Johnson, Lyndon B., 103, 105, 277
Jordan, 33, 110, 292, 302, 309

Kabaka Yekka (KY), 255–6
Kádár, János, 7, 17, 276–80, 285, 289, 301, 328
Kadumi, Faruk, 209
Kaisi, Nsa, 156–8
Kambona, Oscar, 156–7, 159
Kamitatu, Cléophas, 129
Kanet, Roger, 3
Kania, Stanisław, 197
Kapuściński, Ryszard, 54–5
Karume, Abeid, 150
Kasavubu, Joseph, 126, 132, 136, 140–1
Kashamura, Anicet, 130
Kashb, Ahmed, 285

INDEX

Kashmir, 65
Katz-Suchy, Juliusz, 67
Kaunda, Kenneth, 312
Kennedy, John F., 79, 81–2, 135
Kenya
  army mutiny in, 259
  Canada and, 258
  China and, 251
  Czechoslovakia and, 17, 249–53, 257–9, 26–66
  domestic politics of, 250–3, 262–5
  ethnic rivalries in, 264
  German Democratic Republic and, 154–5, 157
  Mau Mau and, 250
  Soviet Union and, 251, 253, 258
  United Kingdom and, 17, 249–53, 258–9, 262–4
  United States and, 251, 253, 258, 262–3
Kenya News Agency (KNA), 253
Kenya People's Union, 265
Kenyan African National Union (KANU), 250–3, 258–9, 262–4, 312
Kenyatta, Jomo, 250–2, 258–9, 262–5, 270n.58, 312
KGB, 12, 79–80, 84, 88, 125–6, 128–9, 131, 135–43
Khomeini, Ayatollah, 112–13
Khrushchev, Nikita, 5–7, 9–10, 15–17, 30, 44–5, 52–3, 56, 59–62, 66, 68, 75, 79, 125, 128–36, 226, 228–42, 275, 315, 329
Kirsch, Richard, 13–14, 185–8
Kiryluk, Stanisław, 60–1
Kiss, J. László, 272
Kissinger, Henry, 110
Kiwanuka, Benedicto, 253–6, 264, 268n.33
Klima, Karel, 132
Klinkmann, Horst, 189
Knöll, Hans, 13–14, 184–5
Knopek, Jacek, 214
Koch, Robert, 177–8
König, Johannes, 31–2
Korbonski, Andrzej, 3
Korean War, 175–6, 299
Kubitschek de Oliveira, Juscelino, 182
Kudryatstev, V. K., 158
Kułaga, Eugeniusz, 204–6
Kuryluk, Ewa, 62
Kuryluk, Karol, 62–6
Kuznetsov, Vasiliy, 134

Laos, 8, 181, 298–9, 311
Lebanon, 29, 33, 36, 279, 282, 286, 292, 302, 306, 309
Lenin, Vladimir, 111
Lessing, Gottfried, 153, 158–60, 162–3
Liberation Front in Algeria, 210
Liberia, 207
Libya, 36, 200, 272, 292, 306
Liu Shaoqi, 61
London School of Economics, 150
Lopes, Rui, 162
Lovanium Conference, 127, 128, 136, 139–40
Lübke, Heinrich, 153
Lumumba, Patrice, 12, 79, 126–34, 136, 138–9, 141–3, 253, 263, 311–12

MacDonald, Malcolm, 65
Madagascar, 207
Maji Maji rebellion, 152
Makerere University, 252, 254
MALÉV, 282
Mali, 79, 257–8, 312
Malik, Yakov, 133
Malinovskiy, Rodion, 134–5
Mandela, Nelson, 314
Mandungu, Antoine, 135
Manescu, Corneliu, 104
Mao Zedong, 45, 60, 299
Markham, James, 156–7
Markow, Walter, 161
Marxism, 98, 130, 148, 156, 198, 205, 211
Maurer, Ion Gheorghe, 103–7, 224–5, 232–7, 239
Mboya, Tom, 251–2, 256, 262–3
McMahon, Robert J., 56
McSweeney, John, 304
Meir, Golda, 105–6, 280
Mercl, Jaroslav, 84
Mexico, 76, 84, 112, 314
Mfanyakazi, 157, 161
Mgogo, Joel, 156–7
Mhando, Stephen, 156–7, 161–2
Milewski, Mirosław, 211
Mkapa, Benjamin, 157–8
Mobutu, Joseph-Désiré, 127, 132, 136–7, 141
Mondlane, Eduardo, 209
Mong, Attila, 272
Mongolia
  China and, 228
  Japan and, 230
  Poland and, 55, 59, 67, 230
  Romania and, 17, 223, 226–42

Soviet Union and, 228–37
United States and, 230
Warsaw Pact and, 17, 228–31, 328–9
Morocco, 110, 134, 200, 207, 258, 279, 283–4, 292, 301, 306
Mozambican Liberation Front (FRELIMO), 163, 209–10, 312
Mozambique, 153, 163, 200, 209, 313
Muehlenbeck, Philip, 127
Mugabe, Robert, 321
Mulele, Pierre, 129, 134–5, 311
Mungai, Njoroge, 259
Muslim Brotherhood, 309–310
Mutesa, Sir Edward (kbaka), 254–6, 260
Myakotnykh, Yury, 140–1

Nagy, Imre, 7
Nagy, László, 272, 326
Nasser, Gamal Abdel
　Aswan High Dam and, 28–9
　Bulgaria and, 302–3
　Congo Crisis and, 133–4
　Czechoslovakia and, 1, 29, 129
　death of, 305
　Free Officers Revolution and, 26, 37
　German Democratic Republic (GDR) and, 28, 30, 34, 37, 44
　Hungarian Revolution and, 276–7
　Israel and, 8, 26–7
　Non-Aligned Movement and, 26–7, 33
　Romania and, 101, 103, 105
　Six Day War and, 105
　Soviet Union and 102–3, 105, 276–7, 300
　Suez Crisis and, 8, 29, 32, 38–9, 41–3
　United Kingdom and, 28–9
　United States and, 28–9, 105
Naszkowski, Marian, 57–8, 66
National Liberation Council (CNL), 140, 312
National Liberation Front (FLN), 301
Nationalist, 150–1, 154–61, 163, 165
Nazhestkin, Oleg, 131, 136–7, 139–40
Ndele, Albert, 137
Nehru, Jawaharlal, 51–2, 58, 65
Nemchina, Sergei, 140
Nendaka, Victor, 137
Neto, Agostinho, 209, 313
Neto, António Alberto, 209
Neues Deutschland, 155
New York Times, 51–2
Nicaragua, 112
Nigeria, 200, 210–11, 214, 312

Nixon, Richard, 75
Nkomo, Joshua, 314, 321
Nkrumah, Kwame, 14, 134, 156, 204–6, 250–1, 255
Non-Aligned Movement, 27, 100, 272, 309
non-Soviet Warsaw Pact countries (NSWP), 2–19, 326–30
North Atlantic Treaty Organization (NATO), 67, 108, 152–3, 164, 200–1, 261, 298
North Korea, 3, 55, 59, 67, 103, 162, 228–9, 232, 237, 299–300
North Vietnam
　Bulgaria and, 187, 298–9, 310–11
　China and, 101, 180–1, 229, 232, 300
　Czechoslovakia and, 187
　German Democratic Republic (GDR) and, 180–2, 185, 187
　Hungary and, 187
　Poland and, 55–9, 66–7, 180, 201
　Romania and, 100–1, 187, 237
　Soviet Union and, 61, 101, 118, 180, 187, 310
　United States and, 100
　Warsaw Pact and, 228–9, 237, 310
Novosti Press Agency (APN), 12, 154
Novotný, Antonín, 9, 81–2, 125, 301
Nu, U, 76
Nujoma, Sam, 210
Nun May, Alan, 205
Nyerere, Julius, 150–3, 157–63, 166, 259
Nzo, Alfred, 314

Obote, Milton, 17, 253–62, 264–5, 267n.25
Odinga, Oginga, 17, 157, 250–3, 258–9, 262–5, 270n.58
Okello, Odhiambo, 252–3
Olenga, Nicholas, 312
Onama, Felix, 260
Organization of American States (OAS), 80
Organisation for Economic Co-Operation and Development (OECD), 2
Organization of Petroleum Exporting Countries (OPEC), 16
Outlook from the Pamirs, 159, 161

Padmore, George, 250–1
Pahlavi, Mohammad Reza Shah, 112
Pakistan, 26, 65
Palestine, 26, 100, 105, 110, 280, 282, 308–9

Palestine Liberation Organization (PLO), 282, 308–9
pan-Africanism, 156
Pathet Lao, 311
Pauker, Ana, 224
Peng Zhen, 61
People's Progressive Party (PPP), 9–10, 77–84, 86–9
People's Republic of China (PRC), *see* China
Petkoff, Luben, 317
Petkoff, Teodoro, 317
Pieck, Wilhelm, 25, 37
Pillai, N. R., 65
Piñeiro, Manuel, 316
Pinochet, Augusto, 319
Piper, Richard 'Peter', 83
Plavlíček, Vladimír, 86
Podgornov, Leonid, 131, 136–7
Poland
  Africa and, 14, 55–6, 198–9, 201–3, 206–14, 329
  African Party for the Independence of Guinea and Cape Verde (PAIGC) and, 209–11
  Algeria and, 200–2
  Angola and, 200, 202, 208–9, 213
  Asia and, 9, 52, 54–68, 201, 212, 329
  Benin and, 200, 212
  British Guiana and, 82–4
  Bulgaria and, 301, 307, 318
  Burma and, 55–8, 62, 66–7
  Cambodia and, 58, 62, 66–7
  Cameroon and, 214
  China and, 52–3, 55–7, 59–62, 68
  Congo and, 137
  Czechoslovakia and, 54
  economy of, 199–200, 203, 206–7, 210–13
  Egypt and, 56, 199–200
  Ethiopia and, 200, 204, 211–12
  Federal Republic of Germany (FRG) and, 54, 64–5, 67, 201, 204
  France and, 201
  Geneva Conference and, 55, 66
  German Democratic Republic (GDR) and, 36–7, 54, 64, 180, 210
  Ghana and, 14, 203–6
  Guinea and, 203–4, 206
  Hungary and, 58, 65
  India and, 9, 51–2, 54–6, 58, 62–8, 207, 329
  Indonesia and, 55–7
  Israel and, 328
  Ivory Coast and, 207
  Korean War and, 55
  Latin America and, 212, 317–18
  Liberia and, 207
  Libya and, 200
  Machel, Samora and, 313
  Madagascar and, 207
  Mongolia and, 55, 59, 67, 230
  Morocco and, 200, 207
  Mozambique and, 200, 208–9
  Mozambique Liberation Front (FRELIMO) and, 209–10
  national liberation movements and, 14, 55, 197–99, 201–2, 208–12
  Nigeria and, 200, 210–11, 214
  North Korea and, 55–6, 59, 67
  North Vietnam and, 55–9, 66–7, 180, 201
  Polisaro Front and, 200
  Polish October (1956) and, 7, 9, 27, 37, 45, 52–3, 57–60, 62, 65–8, 200, 213
  Popular Movement for the Liberation of Angola (MPLA) and, 209–10
  Portugal and, 66, 197–98, 208–9
  Rapacki Plan and, 9, 54, 62–8
  Romania and, 112
  Senegal and, 207
  South Africa and, 201, 206
  South West Africa People's Organization (SWAPO) and, 210
  Soviet Union and, 2–3, 7, 9, 52–6, 58–9, 61–2, 65–8, 200, 202, 207, 213, 329
  Sudan and, 200
  Tanzania and, 201, 210
  Thailand and, 55
  Togo and, 202
  Tunisia and, 200
  Uganda and, 201
  United Kingdom and, 201
  United Nations and, 55, 63, 68, 199, 202–3, 210, 213
  United States and, 63, 201
  Vietnam War and, 55
  Warsaw Pact and, 1–2, 43, 64, 198, 206, 208–10, 213–14
  Zambia and, 212
Polisario Front, 200
Polish–African Friendship Association, 202
Ponomarev, Boris, 319
Popular Movement for the Liberation of Angola (MPLA), 112, 138, 209–10, 312–13

Portugal
  Angola and, 137, 209
  Czechoslovakia and, 137
  decolonization and, 137, 152–3, 162–3
  Federal Republic of Germany (FRG) and, 152–3, 162–6
  Guinea and, 163
  India and, 65
  Poland and, 66, 197–8, 208–9
  Romania and, 122n.113
  Tanzania and, 163–6
Prażmowska, Anita, 53
Prensa Latina, 12, 154
Primakov, Yevgeny, 276–7
propaganda
  British Guiana and, 78, 87
  Bulgaria and, 305, 322
  China and, 159
  Czechoslovakia and, 78, 81, 87, 160
  Eastern bloc journalists and, 12–13
  Federal Republic of Germany (FRG) and, 29, 38–9, 41, 43, 152–3, 162, 164, 166, 188
  German Democratic Republic (GDR) and, 13, 29–30, 34, 36, 38–9, 41, 43, 159–66, 176
  Hungary and, 276
  India and, 66
  Israel and, 164
  Poland and, 61, 66, 198
  Portugal and, 162
  Soviet Union and, 34, 61, 160, 276
  Tanzania and, 159–66
  United States and, 29, 276
Puja, Frigyes, 272, 289
Pushkin, Georgy, 35–6, 44

Radchenko, Sergey, 229
Radio Free Europe, 52
Radio Tanzania, 155
Rapacki, Adam, 54, 63, 67
Rapacki Plan, 9, 54, 62–3, 65–8, 329
Rau, Heinrich, 33–6, 41–2, 44
Răutu, Leonte, 236
Red Cross, 179, 202, 299
Republic of Korea, see South Korea
Reuters, 154–5
Roberto, Holden, 313
Rokossovsky, Konstantin, 53
Romania
  Afghanistan and, 113
  Africa and, 10, 95–6, 112

Albania and, 228, 237
Algeria and, 301
Angola and, 112
Bulgaria and, 112, 299, 301
China and, 17, 100, 104, 225–7, 230–3, 236–8, 240, 242
Commission on Security and Cooperation in Europe and, 106
Costa Rica and, 329
Council for Mutual Economic Assistance (CMEA) and, 17, 97, 224–5, 227, 231–4, 236, 238–9, 242
Cuba and, 112
Cuban Missile Crisis and, 97, 100–1, 225, 231
Czechoslovakia and, 105
economy of, 95–6, 107
Egypt and, 100–2, 105–6, 108–11
German Democratic Republic (GDR) and, 98–9, 103–4, 110, 112, 176
Hungary and, 99
India and, 233
Iran and, 112–13
Israel and, 10, 100, 104–9, 111, 328
Ivory Coast and, 329
Jordan and, 110
Khomeini, Ayatollah and, 112–13
Korean War and, 226, 299
Latin America and, 10, 95–6, 112, 317–18
Mexico and, 112
Middle East and, 10, 95–6, 100–6, 108–11
Morocco and, 110
Mongolia and, 17, 223, 226–42
Nasser, Gamal Abdel and, 101–3, 105
NATO and, 108
Nicaragua and, 112
Non-Aligned Movement (NAM) and, 2, 10, 100
North Korea and, 233, 237
North Vietnam and, 100–1, 187, 237
Palestine and, 100, 110
Poland and, 112
Portugal and, 122n.113
Sino-Soviet dispute and, 100, 104, 225, 231, 233, 237–40, 328
Six Day War and, 10, 102–5
Soviet Union and, 2–3, 10, 16–17, 96–9, 100–2, 104–5, 107–13, 213, 223–43, 328–30
Sudan and, 110
Syria and, 108–10

United Nations and, 100, 104, 106, 108–9
United States and, 99–101, 104–5,
    108–9, 113
Vietnam War and, 100–1, 226
Warsaw Pact and, 1–2, 10, 16–17, 96–8,
    100, 102, 104, 107–10, 112–13,
    223–42, 328
Yugoslavia and, 233
Zaire and, 329
Romsics, Ignác, 272
Rostow, Walt, 15
Rudat, Klaus-Dietrich, 181
Russia, *see* Soviet Union
Rwanda, 138, 257

Sadat, Anwar, 100–1, 106–7, 111, 306–8
Sălăjan, Leontin, 236
Salem, Gamel, 274
Salisbury, Harrison E., 51–2
Sanchez-Sibony, Oscar, 4
Sauerbruch, Ferdinand, 178, 186, 194n.21
Savinov, Boris, 130
Schlegel, Horst, 155–7, 161–2
Schwab, Sepp, 31, 38–9
Selassie, Haile, 204
Semenov, Vladimir, 133–4
Senegal, 207
Shelepin, Alexander, 125, 136
Shepilov, Dmitry, 38–9
Sieber, Karl, 127
Sík, Endre, 272, 280
Silveira, José, 182
Simba Rebellion, 127, 140–1, 261, 312
Sino-Soviet split, 328
Sipos, Péter, 272
Škoda, 129
Słuczański, Edward, 56
Smith, Tony, 3
Solakov, Angel, 315–16
Soumialot, Gaston, 312
South Africa, 160, 162–3, 166, 201, 206
South African Communist Party, 165
South Korea, 56
Soviet Union
    'active foreign policy doctrine' and, 6–7, 10,
        17–18, 66, 275, 289, 326, 330
    Africa and, 6
    Albania and, 228, 242
    Angola and, 213
    Argentina and, 76
    arms sales of, 16–17, 203, 286, 302
    Asia and, 6, 55–6, 275

Aswan High Dam and, 29
British Guiana and, 77–8, 82–4
Bulgaria and, 2–3, 9, 18, 298–303, 315,
    320–1, 328
Chile and, 320
China and, 5–6, 45, 61, 226, 228, 242, 300
Congo and, 9, 12–13 127–37, 139–43,
    265–6
Council for Mutual Economic Assistance
    (CMEA) and, 15–17, 36, 225–36, 241
Cuba and, 3, 85, 88, 101–2, 265, 315–17,
    321
Czechoslovakia and, 1, 9–10, 17, 74, 76–7,
    79–80, 82, 84–5, 125–30, 132–3,
    135–8, 142–3, 160, 257–8,
    265–6
    economy of, 5
Egypt and, 1, 28–9, 102–3, 105–8,
    265–6, 272, 276–9, 287, 300, 302,
    306–8
Federal Republic of Germany (FRG) and, 8
German Democratic Republic (GDR) and,
    3, 6, 8–9, 26, 28, 31, 34–9, 42–5,
    110, 148–9, 151, 166–7, 180, 183,
    189–90, 327
Ghana and, 134, 205
Guinea and, 203
Hungary and, 2–3, 6–7, 17–18, 58, 65,
    271, 273–8, 285–7, 289, 328
industrialization in, 15–16
Ivory Coast and, 207
Kenya and, 251, 253, 258
'Khrushchev Thaw' and, 6–7, 75, 200
Latin America and, 6, 275
Liberia and, 207
India and, 56
Iran and, 112–13
Israel and, 100, 102, 108, 279–80, 300
journalists of, 12, 154, 158
Madagascar and, 207
Mexico and, 76
Middle East and, 29, 38–9
Mongolia and, 228–37
Morocco and, 207
Nasser, Gamal Abdel and, 102–3, 105,
    276–7, 300
North Vietnam and, 61, 101, 118, 180,
    187, 310
Palestine Liberation Organization (PLO)
    and, 309
Poland and, 2–3, 7, 9, 52–6, 58–9, 61–2,
    65–8, 200, 202, 207, 213, 329

propaganda and, 34, 61, 160, 276
Romania and, 2–3, 10, 16–17, 96–9, 100–2, 104–5, 107–13, 213, 223–43, 328–30
Senegal and, 207
Soviet 'model of development' and, 15–16, 278, 290
Sputnik I and, 51
Suez Crisis and, 38–9
Syria and, 102
Tanzania and, 151, 158, 160–1, 167
Uganda and, 260–2
United Kingdom and, 229
United Nations and, 131
United States and, 29, 101, 105, 109, 126, 136, 276, 301–2
Uruguay and, 76
Vietnam War and, 5, 61
Warsaw Pact and, 1–3, 4–6, 15–16, 29, 96–7, 102, 104, 107, 109–10, 113, 223–32, 238–41, 286, 320–1, 327, 330
Zimbabwe and, 321
Spacek, Peter, 155, 157
Spain, 35
Sputnik I, 51
Stalin, Joseph, 5–7, 11–12, 15, 25, 55–6, 67, 74–5, 78–9, 96, 201, 274–5, 280, 299
Stanciu, Cezar, 226
Standard, 160, 163–5
Státní bezpečnost (StB), 79–80, 83–4, 86, 88, 125–6, 128–9, 135–43
Steinbrück, Paul, 178
Steiner, Rudolf, 164
Stern, Carola, 34
Sudan, 29, 105, 110, 133–5, 164, 166, 200, 212, 277, 292, 306, 311–12
Suez Crisis, 8, 28–9, 32, 38–43, 106, 120n.187, 276, 300–1
Syria, 29, 33, 42, 102–03, 105, 109–10, 117n.41, 272, 277–78, 281, 285, 288, 292, 302–07, 309

TABSO, 304
Taiwan, 8, 274
Tanchev, Petar, 318
Tanzania
 army mutiny in, 259
 Bulgaria and, 165, 312
 China and, 158–9, 161–2
 Czechoslovakia and, 156, 165, 249, 253, 257–8

Federal Republic of Germany (FRG) and, 150–1, 156–7, 159–60, 162–6
German Democratic Republic (GDR) and, 13, 149–67
Guinea and, 164–5
liberation movements, support for, 152, 163, 210, 253, 312–14
non-alignment and, 157
Poland and, 210
Portugal and, 163–6
propaganda in, 159–66
Rhodesia and, 157
South West Africa People's Organization (SWAPO) and, 210, 314
Soviet Union and, 151, 158, 160–1, 167
ujamaa and, 158, 163
United Kingdom and, 150, 156–7, 249, 259
United States and, 156–7, 162
Vietnam and, 157
Warsaw Pact intervention in Czechoslovakia and, 160
Zanzibar Revolution and, 149–50
Tanzanian Party of the Revolution, 210
TASS, 12, 154, 162
Tatra 87, 11
Tebinka, Jacek, 52, 54
Teitelboim, Volodia, 320
Thailand, 55
Time, 1
Times of India, 64
Tito, Josef Broz, 104
Togo, 202
Touré, Ahmed Sékou, 120, 164–5, 203, 312
Tsedenbal, Yumjaagiyn, 230, 240–1
Tshombe, Moïse, 126, 132, 140–1, 261–2
Tunisia, 200, 292, 301, 306
Turkey, 26, 103, 293n.1, 302, 315, 320
Turnovsky, Stanislav, 139

Uganda
 army mutiny in, 259
 Czechoslovakia and, 17, 249, 253–4, 256–8, 260–2, 264–6
 domestic politics in, 253–6, 262, 264–5
 Egypt and, 255–6
 Israel and, 259–60
 Odinga, Oginga and, 252
 Soviet Union and, 260–2
 United Kingdom and, 17, 249, 255–60, 264
 United States and, 254–6, 261–2

INDEX   351

Ugandan People's Congress (UPC), 253–6
Uhuru, 155
Ukraine, 6
Ulbricht, Walter, 3, 8–9, 27–8, 30–7, 42–5, 301, 327
United Kingdom
  Aswan High Dam and, 29
  British Guiana and, 74, 77–8, 82–8
  Bulgaria and, 300
  Congo and, 126
  Czechoslovakia and, 249–50, 256
  decolonization and, 7, 250, 255, 274
  Egypt and, 28–9, 37–40
  Ghana and, 204–5
  India and, 65
  Jagan, Cheddi and, 77–8, 82
  Jagan, Janet and, 83
  Jordan and, 302
  Kambona, Oscar and, 156, 159
  Kenya and, 17, 249–53, 258–9, 262–4
  Kenyatta, Jomo and, 250–1, 258, 263
  Kiwanuka, Benedicto and, 254
  Lebanon and, 302
  Middle East and, 274, 300
  Obote, Milton and, 255–6, 259–60
  Odinga, Oginga and, 252–3
  Poland and, 201
  Soviet Union and, 229
  Suez Crisis and, 38–43
  Tanzania and, 150, 156–7, 249, 259
  Uganda and, 17, 249, 255–60, 264
  United States and, 229
  Zanzibar and, 149–50
United National Independent Party (UNIP), 312
United Nations
  Bulgaria and, 313, 315
  Congo and, 127, 130–40
  Cuba and, 315
  decolonization and, 7
  Egypt and, 108
  Hungary and, 271–2, 276–7, 289
  India and, 67–8
  Israel and, 108
  Namibia and, 210
  Poland and, 55, 63, 68, 199, 202–3, 210, 213
  Romania and, 100, 104, 106, 108–9
  Soviet Union and, 131
  Suez Crisis and, 40–1
  Uganda and, 262
  United States and, 276–7, 289

United States
  Aswan High Dam and, 29
  British Guiana and, 82, 84, 87
  Bulgaria and, 299, 301–2, 320
  Burma and, 186
  China and, 101, 229
  Congo and, 127–8, 131, 135–6, 139, 143
  Czechoslovakia and, 74–6, 81, 86, 89, 126, 128, 136, 139
  Egypt and, 1, 28–9, 38, 105, 107–8
  German Democratic Republic (GDR) and, 99, 110, 112, 176
  Guinea and, 203
  Hungary and, 276–7, 289
  India and, 272
  Israel and, 38, 104, 107–8, 280–1
  Jagan, Cheddi and, 82
  Japan and, 230
  Kenya and, 251, 253, 258, 262–3
  Kiwanuka, Benedicto and, 254, 256
  Latin America and, 76
  Mboya, Tom and, 251–2
  Nasser, Gamal Abdel and, 28–9, 105
  North Vietnam and, 100
  Obote, Milton and, 255, 261–2
  Poland and, 63, 201
  Romania and, 99–101, 104–5, 108–9, 113
  Six Day War and, 104–5
  Soviet Union and, 29, 101, 105, 109, 126, 136, 276, 301–2
  Tanzania and, 156–7, 162
  Uganda and, 254–6, 261–2
  United Kingdom and, 229
  United Nations and, 276–7, 289
  Zanzibar and, 150
University College London, 254
University of Jakarta, 178
University of Jena, 184
University of Rangoon, 178
Urafiki, 158, 164
Uruguay, 76
Urusi Leo, 160

Valo, Jozef, 256
Vályi, Péter, 287
Velchev, Boris, 318–19
Venezuela, 75–6, 317
Viet Cong, 311
Vietnam War, 4, 7, 55, 57, 100–1, 157, 201, 226, 298–9, 310–11, 329

Vigilance Africa, 156
Virius, Josef, 128–32, 142
Vomáča, František, 257
von Brentano, Heinrich, 65
von Hassel, Kai-Uwe, 159–60
Voronin, Boris, 140, 143
Voroshilov, Kliment, 61
Vutov, Petar, 307–8

Wandycz, Piotr, 54
Wang Bingnan, 60
Warsaw Pact
  Albania and, 1, 19n6.
  Bulgaria and, 1–2, 18, 298, 319–21, 328
  Cuban Missile Crisis and, 315
  Czechoslovakia and, 1–2
  Czechoslovakia intervention in by, 13, 17, 160, 317
  decolonization and, 5–6, 198, 206, 208–10, 213–14, 301
  economic competition amongst members of, 15–17, 96, 274, 286–9, 299, 328
  foundation of, 1–2
  German Democratic Republic (GDR) and, 1–2, 148–9, 327
  Hungary and, 1–2, 43, 286–9
  Mongolia and, 17, 228–31, 328–9
  North Vietnam and, 228–9, 237, 310
  Palestine Liberation Organization (PLO) and, 308–9
  Poland and, 1–2, 43, 64, 198, 206, 208–10, 213–14
  Romania and, 1–2, 10, 16–17, 96–8, 100, 102, 104, 107–10, 112–13, 223–42, 328–29
  Soviet Union and, 1–3, 4–6, 15–16, 29, 96–7, 102, 104, 107, 109–10, 113, 223–32, 238–41, 286, 320–1, 327, 330
  Zimbabwe African People's Union (ZAPU) and, 314

Warsaw School of Economics, 205
Warsaw University, 201, 204
Washington Post, 60
West Germany, *see* Federal Republic of Germany
Westad, Odd Arne, 3, 149, 167
Wieland, Deba, 154
Wolniewicz, Lucjan, 206–7
Workers' Party of Guatemala (GPT), 316–17
World Bank, 28–9, 290
World Federation of Trade Unions (WFTU), 251
World Youth Festival, 11
World War II, 6, 12, 52–4, 135, 184, 186, 200, 204–5, 224, 226, 233, 250, 254, 274, 280, 307

Xinhua, 154

Yakovlev, Mikhail, 131
Yemen, 33, 177, 278, 303, 306
Yugoslavia, 53, 61, 68, 104, 110, 204, 300, 316–17, 320

Zaire, 329
Zambia, 158, 212, 312
Zanzibar, 149–56, 166, 253, 312
Zanzibar Revolution, 149–50
Zawadzki, Aleksander, 204
Zhdanov Doctrine, 274
Zhegalin, Ivan Kuzmich, 230
Zhou Enlai, 57, 60
Zídek, Petr, 127
Ziegler, Kurt, 181
Zikmund, Miroslav, 11
Zimbabwe, 313–14, 321
Zimbabwe African National Union (ZANU), 313–14
Zimbabwe African People's Union (ZAPU), 314
Zorin, Valerian, 42, 44
Zuein, Youssef, 303

CPSIA information can be obtained
at www.ICGtesting.com
Printed in the USA
LVHW011607040221
678389LV00012B/1258